GETTING TO KNOW THE HIGHSCOPE CURRICULUM

Second Edition

Essentials
of Active Learning in Preschool

Getting to Know the HighScope Curriculum

Second Edition

Ann S. Epstein, PhD

Published by
HighScope® Press

A division of the
HighScope Educational Research Foundation
600 North River Street
Ypsilanti, Michigan 48198-2898
734.485.2000, FAX 734.485.0704

Orders: 800.40.PRESS; Fax: 800.442.4FAX; www.highscope.org
E-mail: press@highscope.org

Editor: Marcella Fecteau Weiner

Cover design, text design, production: Judy Seling, Seling Design LLC

Photography: All photos by Bob Foran, Ann Arbor, MI, with the following exceptions:

Gregory Fox — ix, 3, 5, 7, 27, 31, 37, 41, 45, 48, 52, 54, 55 (top left, middle, bottom), 57, 63, 64, 70, 74, 82, 96, 101, 108, 111, 114, 121, 132, 136, 144, 146, 148, 150, 153, 163, 164, 168, 171, 177, 179, 187, 188, 193, 194, 203, 204, 206, 208, 229

HighScope staff — 38, 55 (top right), 77, 80, 125, 129, 139, 155, 158, 198, 253

Nenov Brothers Images/Shutterstock.com — Front cover

Pat Thompson — 22

Library of Congress Cataloging-in-Publication Data
Epstein, Ann S.
Essentials of active learning in preschool: getting to know the highscope curriculum / Ann S. Epstein. -- Second edition.
pages cm
ISBN 978-1-57379-701-6 (soft cover : alk. paper) 1. Education, Preschool--Curricula. 2. Active learning. I. Title.
LB1140.4.E77 2014
372.21--dc23
2013040636

Printed in the United States of America
10 9 8 7 6 5 4 3 2

Contents

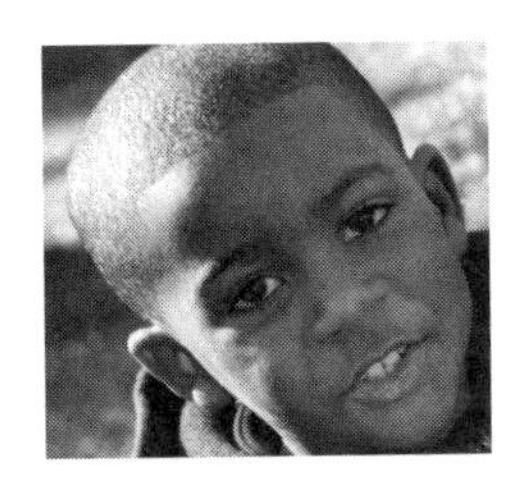

Preface

This book is written for several audiences — students in early childhood courses, program administrators, and teachers and caregivers — who want to learn about the HighScope Preschool Curriculum. For students new to the field, this book is an introduction to a well-researched and comprehensive early childhood curriculum model that is widely used in the United States and abroad. Administrators may be deciding on a curriculum for their program, or they may have already chosen HighScope but want to know more about it to support staff in its implementation. For these decision makers, the book explains what children in this research-based curriculum learn and how the HighScope assessment system can meet demands for accountability. For teachers and caregivers, whose agencies use or are about to begin using HighScope, this book describes all the basic parts of the curriculum — how to create an effective learning environment and daily routine, interact with children using effective instructional strategies, and provide the content at the heart of preschool teaching and learning. We hope the information presented here will help all our readers understand and begin to use the principles of HighScope in their work.

What Is HighScope?

For readers new to HighScope, some background on who we are and what we do may be helpful. The HighScope Educational Research Foundation is an independent nonprofit organization headquartered in Ypsilanti, Michigan. HighScope promotes child development worldwide and supports educators and families who nurture young children's growth. The HighScope Curriculum is a set of *teaching practices* for adults and *content* for children's learning in all areas of development. There is also an *assessment system* to measure program quality and evaluate what children learn and *professional development* to prepare teachers and caregivers to implement the HighScope Curriculum.

Mission and vision. To lift lives through education, HighScope engages in evaluative research, product and services development, publishing, and training. We envision a world in which all educational settings use active participatory learning so everyone has a chance to succeed in life and contribute to society.

History. HighScope was established in 1970 to carry on the work that Dr. David P. Weikart began with economically disadvantaged children in the Ypsilanti Public Schools in 1962. HighScope is best known for its early childhood curricula for infants, toddlers, and preschoolers and its studies of the lasting positive effects of high-quality early education. HighScope's curricula, staff development model, research, and publications have influenced educational programming and public policy for more than five decades.

Outreach. Today HighScope's curricula, staff development methods, assessments, and research findings are used in most every state in the United States and in nearly 20 countries abroad.

HighScope programs thrive in diverse settings that include Head Start, public school prekindergarten, center-based and family child care, corporate child care, university lab schools, and many other nonprofit and for-profit preschools and child care settings.

Because the HighScope Curriculum builds on children's interests and their communities' characteristics, it is appropriate for use with populations varying in culture and nationality, race and ethnicity, language, special needs, and geography. Through HighScope's professional development program and dissemination efforts, an estimated 125,000 teachers and caregivers worldwide have been trained in the HighScope Curriculum. These practitioners are supported by a corps of nearly 2,000 HighScope Certified Trainers and serve more than one million children and their families each year.

What Is in This Book?

This book is your introduction to the HighScope Preschool Curriculum. Each of the curriculum's four components — teaching practices, content for children's learning, an assessment system, and professional development — is discussed in its own section of the book.

Organization of this book. This book has five parts. **Part 1, Introduction and Overview,** has four chapters. Chapter 1 explains why educators should use a curriculum model; chapter 2 is an overview of the HighScope Preschool Curriculum itself; chapter 3 describes the theory underlying the curriculum; and chapter 4 presents the research evidence supporting the curriculum. The remaining four parts each deal with one curriculum component.

Part 2, HighScope Teaching Practices, describes the methods HighScope practitioners use to create an active participatory learning experience for young children. Chapters 5 through 9 cover, respectively, strategies for interacting with children, arranging and equipping indoor and outdoor learning environments, establishing a consistent daily routine that includes the plan-do-review process, working with families, and maintaining effective staff communication to plan for children and continuously improve program quality.

Part 3, HighScope Curriculum Content, describes HighScope's 58 key developmental indicators (KDIs) for preschool in eight areas that align readily with national and state early learning standards: Approaches to Learning (chapter 10); Social and Emotional Development (chapter 11); Physical Development and Health (chapter 12); Language, Literacy, and Communication (chapter 13); Mathematics (chapter 14); Creative Arts (chapter 15); Science and Technology (chapter 16); and Social Studies (chapter 17).

Part 4, HighScope Assessment, describes HighScope's validated assessment tools. Chapter 18 deals with child assessment and chapter 19, with program assessment. **Part 5, HighScope Professional Development,** describes the HighScope approach to training early childhood practitioners. Chapter 20 explains how we apply the principles of active participatory learning to working with adults, and Chapter 21 briefly describes HighScope's professional development options and certification procedures to maintain quality.

Each chapter begins with a story or thought (titled "Think About It") to help you connect the topic to experiences in your own life. Each chapter also includes a list of learning objectives and important terms used within the chapter to further assist the reader's learning and understanding. Terms appear in boldface upon first use within the chapter text. The suggested exercises or activities at the end of each chapter (titled "Try These Ideas Yourself") will help you apply the lessons learned to your particular situation as a student, teacher, or supervisor. These questions and activities will help you reflect on the chapter's main ideas as your thinking continues to develop.

Throughout the book you will also find many practical suggestions; illustrative examples; summary checklists; and observations from the diverse teachers, caregivers, and administrators who use the HighScope Curriculum.

Additional resources. Because this book can only serve as an introduction, we urge you to become more knowledgeable about the HighScope Curriculum as you begin to use its principles and methods. At the HighScope website (www.highscope.org), you can find additional resources to guide you toward further study and growth as an educator. HighScope professional development courses also provide additional information about the curriculum and how to implement it effectively in early childhood settings. It is our hope that learning about HighScope will help you grow as a practitioner and become an informed advocate for young children and their families.

*Because the HighScope Curriculum builds on children's interests, it is appropriate for use with **all** children.*

Acknowledgments

This second edition of *Essentials of Active Learning in Preschool* builds on over five decades of educational leadership by the HighScope Educational Research Foundation. Because contributors to HighScope's international role are too numerous to list individually, these acknowledgments focus on the major publications, services, and groups that collectively provided source material for this book. Foremost is HighScope's curriculum manual, *The HighScope Preschool Curriculum,* which details the active learning model, teaching strategies, and program content that engage young children. This book was a collaborative, multiyear effort of the HighScope early childhood staff, enriched by detailed feedback from thoughtful internal and external reviewers. Additional print and electronic resources used to write *Essentials* include step-by-step teacher idea books; assessment manuals; research-based policy papers; literally hundreds of articles in *ReSource* and *Extensions;* and in-depth publications on literacy, mathematics, science, social and emotional development (including conflict resolution), and the creative arts (including visual art as well as movement and music).

HighScope practitioners have gathered an impressive archive of objective anecdotes about children and families. Their qualitative observations, when used to supplement the findings of quantitative research, helped bring many ideas to life in this volume. The HighScope professional development model, created by its staff and implemented by an international team of dedicated field consultants, was the standard I aspired to in introducing HighScope to this book's readers.

HighScope leaders and staff members have contributed over the years to the development of the curriculum in general, and to the production of this book in particular. Past and current presidents and board members have been enthusiastic supporters of HighScope's vision in which active participatory learning is available to students of all ages, from birth through adulthood. Staff members, particularly in the early childhood and research divisions, have brought their collective expertise to creating a curriculum that builds on the latest research about early development, careful observations of young children, and reflective teaching practices. Individuals with expertise in editing, production, and marketing have further guaranteed that the words and images in these pages are inviting as well as informative to readers working in a variety of program settings.

A resounding thank-you goes to the teachers, children, and parents whose firsthand experience of the HighScope Curriculum continually informs our work and makes us better at fulfilling our mission — lifting lives through education. Finally, appreciation and encouragement are extended to you, the readers. My greatest hope and satisfaction rests with the potential for the words and images of *Essentials* to inspire active learning and active teaching on behalf of young children.

Part 1

Introduction and Overview

This part of the book provides an overview of the essential ingredients of the HighScope Preschool Curriculum and philosophy and discusses why the curriculum is effective.

Chapter 1 explains why educators should use a curriculum.

Chapter 2 provides an overview of the HighScope Curriculum.

Chapter 3 presents the child development theory behind the curriculum.

Chapter 4 describes the research on the effectiveness of the HighScope Curriculum.

Chapter 1

Why Should Early Childhood Programs Use a Curriculum?

Think About It

Many years ago, before there were good local bakeries in her town, Ann decided to bake her own bread. The ingredients looked simple enough (flour, yeast, water, sugar), and she'd been whipping up apple muffins and banana loaves for years. How hard could it be to bake bread?

She tried various recipes in cookbooks and magazines. Sometimes the dough didn't rise, either because the water was so hot it killed the yeast or it was so cold that the yeast never became "active." It was two months before Ann realized bread flour and cake flour were different. Arms aching after kneading, she was discouraged when the dough was as sticky as when she'd started. Every loaf smelled great coming out of the oven, but the results varied from inedible to incredible.

About a year later, books on bread-baking became popular — there were a lot to choose from. Some were so simple that Ann felt like an expert. Others were so complicated that she felt like a dunce. Finally she found one that worked for her. It began with simple recipes and advanced to more complex ones. Each step explained why *as well as* how. *Two weeks after buying the book, Ann had learned more than she had in a year of experimenting on her own. Now she could include homemade bread in her menu planning, confident of baking a reliably tasty loaf.*

Adults often learn by trial and error, but it's easier when learning follows a logical order. The same holds true for children. It helps when their self-discovery is guided by a knowledgeable teacher who knows where the children have been and where they're going. Teachers, in turn, rely on the guidance of experts who have spent years studying how children learn. They don't have to reinvent the wheel each time they plan an educational experience. A **curriculum** lets teachers build on the knowledge that already exists in the field, add in their own experience and observations, and then adjust what they do for the individuals and groups in their class. This chapter explores the benefits of just such a process.

The Benefits of Using a Proven Curriculum

> "While no single curriculum...can be identified as best, children who attend well-planned, high-quality early childhood programs in which curriculum aims are specified and integrated across domains tend to learn more and are better prepared to master the complex demands of formal schooling."
>
> — National Research Council (2001, p. 6)

Before you read about a particular curriculum — HighScope — you may be wondering "Why should I, or my program, use any published curriculum? Why can't teachers invent their own curriculum, using what they know about child development and appropriate teaching practices?"

Chapter Learning Objectives

By the end of this chapter, you will be able to

- Explain why using a curriculum helps teachers provide young children with a consistent learning experience.
- Describe why evidence of effectiveness is important in choosing a curriculum.
- Relate your own experiences as a learner and decision maker to choosing a proven curriculum model for young children.

To be a good teacher, you have to know how children grow and learn and how to help them feel secure and excited about being in school. But this basic knowledge and set of skills is not enough to create a curriculum. So much learning happens in the early years — from understanding how books work, to figuring out how two children can use one computer, to mastering the zipper on a jacket — that it would be very difficult for an individual or even the entire staff of one agency to invent a complete curriculum from scratch. Developing a curriculum takes years of work by a group of thoughtful practitioners and researchers who pool their knowledge and talents.

Most important, it is not enough to offer a curriculum in the *belief* that it is good. There must be *proof* that it works. To get funding these days, administrators must show their program is using a curriculum that has **research-based evidence** of effectiveness. The word **validated** also describes such a proven curriculum, meaning scientific studies have shown children in programs using the curriculum achieve certain educational goals. Further, the terms indicate that children achieve these goals more than children who are not attending any program or who are enrolled in a program that does not use an identified curriculum — or possibly even one that uses a different preschool curriculum.

Proof of effectiveness is important to policymakers who want to make sure taxpayer dollars are invested wisely. It is also important to educators who want to be sure that what they do in

For children to get the full benefits of preschool, use a validated curriculum model with proof of effectiveness.

the classroom truly benefits the young children in their care. Everyone concerned with early education therefore wants to make sure programs are of high enough quality to meet these objectives. (See "Components of High-Quality Early Childhood Programs" on p. 5). The research base for these components is elaborated in chapter 4.

Using a validated or proven curriculum model means you get all of the following ingredients and instructions: a set of appropriate teaching practices for adults, a list of learning objectives for children, research tools to measure whether the program is meeting its goals, and a staff training model to make sure teachers understand and use the curriculum correctly.

For these reasons, HighScope urges early childhood educators to use a single and established curriculum rather than something homegrown and untested. A program that borrows bits and pieces from various models (sometimes called an eclectic approach) will also be problematic. With a mixed bag of approaches, teachers lack a unifying set of principles to guide their practice. Different curricula may offer competing ideas, making it confusing for teachers to decide on the best course of action, which can result in contradictory messages being sent to young children about how and what to learn. For supplementary materials to work, it is preferable that they be spe-

Terms Used in This Chapter

• curriculum • research-based evidence • validated

Components of High-Quality Early Childhood Programs

High-quality early childhood programs have the following components:

- *Child development curriculum* with active participatory learning
- *Low-enrollment limits* so adults can give individualized attention to children
- *Staff trained in early childhood development* so they can observe, understand, and support children's learning in all areas
- *Supervisory support and inservice training* so staff can understand and carry out the curriculum
- *Involvement of parents as partners* because they are children's first and most lasting teachers
- *Sensitivity to the noneducational needs of children* because preschool is just one component of children's early experiences
- *Developmentally appropriate evaluation procedures* to accurately measure what children know and to plan effective ways to extend their learning

Source: Adapted from *A School Administrator's Guide to Early Childhood Programs* (Schweinhart, 2004, p. 15).

cifically designed for (or approved for use with) the program's unified curriculum model.

Using a single curriculum does not mean that education is rigid and inflexible. In fact, a good curriculum allows you to change it to fit the children and community you serve, much as you might follow a basic recipe but change the seasoning to meet your personal tastes. So, for example, you can use the curriculum approach to teach reading but choose books that reflect local language and customs. The HighScope Curriculum permits this flexibility while maintaining the standards and practices that guarantee the curriculum will achieve positive and lasting results. Ideally, this is the goal of the curriculum and the programs that choose to use it.

Try These Ideas Yourself

1. Think of a product or technique you tried because you heard (from a friend, advertisement, or article) that it "really works!" Did it? Describe this experience and what you learned from it. How might you relate what you learned to the process of choosing a classroom curriculum?

2. Think of things you learned to do as a child or an adult — riding a bike, doing long division, driving a car, or playing a musical instrument. Pick one where the learning went well and another that was difficult or frustrating. What accounts for the difference in your rate or ease of learning? Did you figure out what to do on your own? Did someone or something (a manual or instructional video) guide you? If you learned on your own, what helped or interfered with your discoveries? If you received guidance, did it make learning easier or harder? Why? (*Variation:* Think of a situation in which you taught something to another person where you considered yourself an "expert." Think of another situation in which you taught something where you knew more than the other person but did not consider yourself an expert. Describe and compare how effective your teaching style was with the learner in the two situations. Was one style more effective than the other, or were they equally effective in helping the learner?)

A good curriculum allows you to change it to fit the children and community you serve.

Chapter 2

What Is the HighScope Preschool Curriculum?

Think About It

"It's easy. Let me show you!"

You have just installed the Draw-A-Lot program on your computer. A coworker, who has used the program for a year, is eager to show you what it can do. Pulling up a chair beside you, she takes the mouse. "The templates to get you started are in this pull-down menu. I like the second and fifth ones," she explains. She opens and closes them so quickly you barely get a look. Then she continues, "But it's easy to design your own. Click this command, then scoot over to this column to pick a color and a line. Jigger the texture icon into place like this, then you can also rotate or flip the image and…" Your chair has gradually been shoved to the side as your colleague sits front and center at the monitor. When she's finished creating her "Still Life With Draw-A-Lot," you don't remember a thing she said. You thank her for the help, close the program, and click open Solitaire.

Early the next day, before anyone else gets to the office, you open Draw-A-Lot, click the "Get Started" tutorial, and go through it step by step. Then you play with the program on your own. At first, your designs and colors are limited. At one point you accidentally delete the entire image, and, another time, you flip it upside down. You laugh at yourself and start over. By the time your coworkers arrive, you've finished a simple but colorful poster advertising the agency's upcoming fundraiser. The colleague from yesterday stops by to admire your work. "I'm glad I was able to help you," she says.

We've all had an experience where someone has told or shown us how to do something. Usually their intent is to be helpful. Often, they know more about the subject than we do. Sometimes, in their eagerness to share, they overload us with information. But while they are active teachers, we are passive learners. As a result, we learn little or nothing. By contrast, when we have the time and materials to experiment independently, we can learn a great deal. As shown above, the best situation is when we have enough guidance to get started — whether it comes from a person or a manual — and then continue to explore on our own. Once we master the basics, we may turn back to the "expert" for advanced pointers or even share some of our own discoveries.

In the latter relationship, both the teacher and learner play an active role. And because the learner participates in the process, the lessons learned are meaningful and lasting. This shared approach to education is what HighScope is all about. In this chapter we will explore the active learning approach HighScope uses in its curriculum.

Components of the HighScope Curriculum

The HighScope Preschool Curriculum is a complete system of early childhood education, based on child development theory, research, and proven instructional practices. The curriculum has a set of *teaching practices* for adults, *curriculum content* in all areas with key developmental indicators

Chapter Learning Objectives

By the end of this chapter, you will be able to

- Define the ingredients of active participatory learning and use them to analyze children's educational experiences.
- Explain why active learning is effective for all age groups.
- Discuss how the content of the HighScope Preschool Curriculum addresses all areas of school readiness.
- Explain the important and diverse roles teachers play in early learning.
- Describe how assessment and professional development fit within the HighScope Curriculum.

The HighScope approach emphasizes active participatory learning, where teachers and students are partners in shaping the learning experience.

(KDIs) for children, *assessment tools* to measure teaching behaviors and children's progress, and *professional development* (also called training) to help adults use the curriculum. We will discuss each of these items further in this chapter.

The HighScope Philosophy

In the HighScope Preschool Curriculum, fully described in *The HighScope Preschool Curriculum* (Epstein & Hohmann, 2012) and the eight accompanying KDI volumes (Epstein, 2012a–h), young children build or *construct* their knowledge of the world. Learning is not a matter of adults giving information to children, but rather a process of *shared control* in which children make discoveries through direct experience with people, objects, events, and ideas. Using this curriculum, preschoolers also make plans and follow through on their interests and intentions as they build their knowledge and skills.

HighScope teachers are as active and involved as the children. They thoughtfully provide materials, plan activities, and talk with (not at) children in ways that both support and challenge what children are observing and thinking. Activities are both child initiated — built on children's natural curiosity — and developmentally appropriate (i.e., matched to children's current and emerging abilities). HighScope calls this approach **active participatory learning,** a process in which teachers and students are partners in shaping the learning experience.

This educational approach, in which children and adults share responsibility for learning, builds essential school-readiness skills. In addition to addressing traditional academic subjects, the HighScope Curriculum promotes independence, curiosity, decision making, cooperation, persistence, creativity, and problem solving in young children.

The principles that guide the HighScope Curriculum are illustrated in the "Wheel of Learning" on page 9. *Active learning* is at the center to highlight the importance of children's initiative and HighScope's comprehensive attention to educational content in its KDIs. The four quadrants represent teachers' responsibilities as they work with children: engaging in supportive *adult-child interactions,* creating a challenging *learning environment,* establishing a consistent *daily routine,* and doing ongoing *assessment* to make plans and meet children's educational needs. After reading

Terms Used in This Chapter

• active participatory learning • materials • manipulation • choice • child language and thought • adult scaffolding • curriculum content • key developmental indicators (KDIs) • plan-do-review process • comprehensive assessment tools • professional development

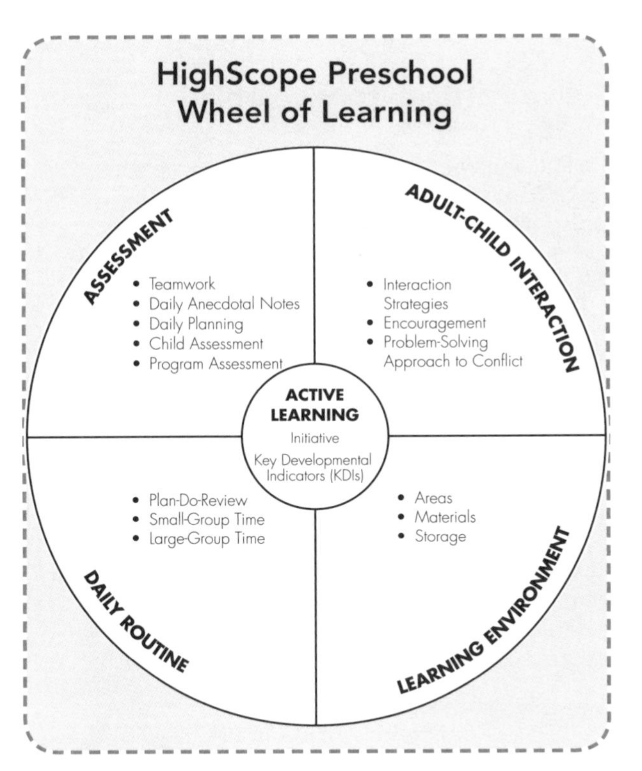

this book, you will have a complete picture of how these parts of the HighScope Curriculum fit together in a unified whole.

Active Participatory Learning

The National Education Goals Panel (NEGP; Kagan, Moore, & Bredekamp, 1995) says school readiness is enhanced when children are provided with play-oriented, exploratory activities that allow them to interact, make choices, and participate at their own developmental level. This vision is central to HighScope's ideal of active participatory learning, which has five ingredients:

1. Materials — Programs offer abundant supplies of diverse, age-appropriate materials. Materials appeal to all the senses and are open ended, that is, they lend themselves to being used in a variety of ways and help expand children's experiences and stimulate their thought.

2. Manipulation — Children handle, examine, combine, and transform materials and ideas. They make discoveries through direct hands-on and "minds-on" contact with these resources.

3. Choice — Children choose materials and play partners, change and build on their play ideas, and plan activities according to their interests and needs.

4. Child language and thought — Children describe what they are doing and understanding. They communicate verbally and nonverbally as they think about their actions and modify their thinking to take new learning into account.

5. Adult scaffolding — *Scaffolding* means adults support and gently extend children's current level of thinking and understanding. In this way, adults help children gain knowledge and develop creative problem-solving skills.

See "Applying the Five Ingredients of Active Participatory Learning" on page 10 for an example of how these ingredients helped a child learn how to write.

HighScope Curriculum Content

A comprehensive curriculum model, the HighScope Curriculum addresses all the content areas of children's learning and development. The **curriculum content** is organized into eight major divisions that are easily aligned and consistent with national and state early learning standards (Gronlund, 2006; National Association for the Education of Young Children & National Association of Early Childhood Specialists in State Departments of Education, 2002), the Common Core Standards (2012), and the Head Start Child Development and Early Learning Framework (Office of Head Start, 2012). HighScope's content areas are Approaches to Learning; Social and Emotional Development; Physical Development and Health; Language, Literacy, and Communication; Mathematics; Creative Arts; Science and Technology; and Social Studies. The NEGP (Kagan et al., 1995) emphasizes the interdependence of these areas and the need to address them all at every age and grade level.

HighScope teachers provide experiences that nurture all of these areas of learning in every child. They recognize that development varies widely across children — and within children — across areas. Therefore, adults scaffold early learning by supporting children at their current level and gently extending their knowledge and thinking as they progress along a developmental trajectory.

▲ Key Developmental Indicators

Within the eight preschool content areas, HighScope identifies 58 **key developmental indicators (KDIs)**. (See "HighScope Preschool Cur-

Applying the Five Ingredients of Active Participatory Learning

Below is an example of how the ingredients of active participatory learning helped Erin learn to write. Her teacher recorded the following anecdote (in *italics*), which happened at work time.

Materials. The classroom has a wide range of writing materials.

> *At work time in the art area, Erin brought a box of markers, a stack of plain white paper, and several sheets of yellow construction paper to the table.*

Manipulation. Children use writing materials in many ways, including making real letters and letterlike forms. They use, or pretend to use, writing in the same ways as adults.

> *Erin used a black marker to make lines, circles, and Xs on plain white paper. She wrote them in rows, like lines of print. Then she said, "I want to make invitations for my birthday party."*

Choice. Children are free to use materials however they want during child-initiated parts of the day (such as plan-do-review) and also during adult-initiated activities (such as small- and large-group time). The teacher asked how Erin was going to carry out her plan to make invitations.

> *I asked Erin, "How will you make the invitations?" Erin replied, "I'm going to use the yellow paper and a red marker." She selected these materials from the array she had set in front of her.*

Child language and thought. As children work, teachers talk naturally to them about what they are doing. Adults expand children's vocabulary without dominating the conversation.

> *Erin folded the paper in half and drew a pink flower with blue and green leaves on top. She said, "I have to decorate the cards first." I commented, "You're making a decoration on the outside before you write the invitation on the inside." Erin replied, "It's like the card my grandma gave me for Halloween. It has pictures and words."*

Adult scaffolding. Preschoolers learn to write letters and words in many different ways, for example, by tracing, copying, or writing letters as an adult spells out a word. Erin's teacher allowed her to use a combination of strategies, based on what Erin was ready for.

> *Erin said she needed help to write the words* birthday party. *I asked, "Do you want me to tell you the letters or write them for you to copy?" She asked me to write them. I wrote the word* birthday, *and Erin copied the letters on her invitation. Then she said, "Just tell me the letters for party because I can write them." I said them one at a time, and Erin wrote them down. Then she said, "I can spell my name all by myself" and wrote* ERIN.

riculum Content" on p. 12. For infant and toddler KDIs, see Post, Hohmann, & Epstein, 2011.) The KDIs are the building blocks of thinking and reasoning at each stage of a child's development and pave the way for school and adult success. They include both *knowledge* and the application of this knowledge in *thinking* (Marzano & Kendall, 2007). For example, preschoolers need to know color names (knowledge) to sort objects (thinking) by color.

HighScope chose the term *key developmental indicators* for several reasons. The word *key* refers to the fact that these are the most important and meaningful concepts and abilities in early education. Young learners need to master such a wide range of knowledge and skills that the list can seem endless in scope and detail. To avoid losing sight of the forest for the trees, the KDIs capture the major components that lay the foundation for further learning.

The second part of the term, *developmental,* emphasizes that learning is gradual and cumulative. Learning follows a sequence, generally moving from simple to more complex knowledge and skills. Moreover, *developmental* stresses that it is inappropriate, not to mention futile, to expect preschoolers to behave and learn like kindergarten or first-grade students. At each level, the curriculum must be consistent with what we know about human development at that age.

Finally, we chose *indicators* to emphasize that educators need evidence that children are developing the knowledge, skills, and understanding considered important for school and life readiness. To plan appropriately for students and to evaluate program effectiveness, we need observable indicators of our impact on children. Further, by defining these child outcomes in measurable terms, we can develop assessment tools that are consistent with the curriculum. In other words, the assessment system *indicates* whether the program is meeting its goals.

The continuity across content areas and KDIs allows for the fact that development occurs along a continuum and children of different ages and abilities cannot be pigeonholed into a single age-based category. This book focuses on the 58 KDIs that make up the HighScope Curriculum content for preschoolers (children aged three to five). However, children in this age-range may exhibit behaviors characteristic of older toddlers or early elementary students. Hence, the KDIs were developed with the entire early childhood spectrum, ages 0–8, in mind. Furthermore, children with special needs can fall at different points along the continuum, without regard to age, so a flexible system helps practitioners understand and plan for their development.

For children to learn the content contained in the KDIs, it is not enough for adults to simply pass along information. Children must experience the world firsthand. Adults can then scaffold (support and gently extend) children's thinking and understanding as they progress to each new level of insight and knowledge. Adults do this by being intentional in their teaching, that is, by understanding how young children develop and being knowledgeable about the content areas that are important in early learning (Epstein, 2007). Moreover, teachers understand that true learning takes time and repeated exposure. It is not a one-shot affair.

The HighScope KDIs are based on current child development research and decades of classroom practice. The KDIs are also written to be universal. Teachers and caregivers from different cultures in the United States and countries all over the world report that they see children engaging in these developmentally important experiences. Research confirms these commonalities among children of all backgrounds. For example, children everywhere sort objects into containers and take things apart and put them together. The exact materials used may vary from culture to culture, but the activity and the resulting learning about the nature of things is essentially the same.

Children engage with the KDIs — the building blocks of thinking and reasoning at each stage of development — as they interact with people, materials, events, and ideas.

Teachers use the KDIs to guide all aspects of their program. They set up the classroom, plan the day, observe children and extend their thinking, and measure children's progress based on the general principles of active learning and the specific content in the indicators. These HighScope teaching practices are described in the next section of this chapter. Part 3 of this book presents an in-depth look at the KDIs in all areas of children's learning and explains the thoughtful and practical strategies HighScope teachers use to promote them.

HighScope Teaching Practices

HighScope teachers arrange and label classroom interest areas and stock diverse materials to give children a broad range of experience and help them begin to understand how the world can be organized. To promote initiative and independence, teachers make sure the materials are easy for children to get and put away on their own.

HighScope Preschool Curriculum Content

Key Developmental Indicators

A. Approaches to Learning

1. **Initiative:** Children demonstrate initiative as they explore their world.
2. **Planning:** Children make plans and follow through on their intentions.
3. **Engagement:** Children focus on activities that interest them.
4. **Problem solving:** Children solve problems encountered in play.
5. **Use of resources:** Children gather information and formulate ideas about their world.
6. **Reflection:** Children reflect on their experiences.

B. Social and Emotional Development

7. **Self-identity:** Children have a positive self-identity.
8. **Sense of competence:** Children feel they are competent.
9. **Emotions:** Children recognize, label, and regulate their feelings.
10. **Empathy:** Children demonstrate empathy toward others.
11. **Community:** Children participate in the community of the classroom.
12. **Building relationships:** Children build relationships with other children and adults.
13. **Cooperative play:** Children engage in cooperative play.
14. **Moral development:** Children develop an internal sense of right and wrong.
15. **Conflict resolution:** Children resolve social conflicts.

C. Physical Development and Health

16. **Gross-motor skills:** Children demonstrate strength, flexibility, balance, and timing in using their large muscles.
17. **Fine-motor skills:** Children demonstrate dexterity and hand-eye coordination in using their small muscles.
18. **Body awareness:** Children know about their bodies and how to navigate them in space.
19. **Personal care:** Children carry out personal care routines on their own.
20. **Healthy behavior:** Children engage in healthy practices.

D. Language, Literacy, and Communication[1]

21. **Comprehension:** Children understand language.
22. **Speaking:** Children express themselves using language.
23. **Vocabulary:** Children understand and use a variety of words and phrases.
24. **Phonological awareness:** Children identify distinct sounds in spoken language.
25. **Alphabetic knowledge:** Children identify letter names and their sounds.
26. **Reading:** Children read for pleasure and information.
27. **Concepts about print:** Children demonstrate knowledge about environmental print.
28. **Book knowledge:** Children demonstrate knowledge about books.
29. **Writing:** Children write for many different purposes.
30. **English language learning:** (If applicable) Children use English and their home language(s) (including sign language).

E. Mathematics

31. **Number words and symbols:** Children recognize and use number words and symbols.
32. **Counting:** Children count things.
33. **Part-whole relationships:** Children combine and separate quantities of objects.
34. **Shapes:** Children identify, name, and describe shapes.
35. **Spatial awareness:** Children recognize spatial relationships among people and objects.
36. **Measuring:** Children measure to describe, compare, and order things.
37. **Unit:** Children understand and use the concept of unit.
38. **Patterns:** Children identify, describe, copy, complete, and create patterns.
39. **Data analysis:** Children use information about quantity to draw conclusions, make decisions, and solve problems.

F. Creative Arts

40. **Art:** Children express and represent what they observe, think, imagine, and feel through two- and three-dimensional art.
41. **Music:** Children express and represent what they observe, think, imagine, and feel through music.
42. **Movement:** Children express and represent what they observe, think, imagine, and feel through movement.
43. **Pretend play:** Children express and represent what they observe, think, imagine, and feel through pretend play.
44. **Appreciating the arts:** Children appreciate the creative arts.

G. Science and Technology

45. **Observing:** Children observe the materials and processes in their environment.
46. **Classifying:** Children classify materials, actions, people, and events.
47. **Experimenting:** Children experiment to test their ideas.
48. **Predicting:** Children predict what they expect will happen.
49. **Drawing conclusions:** Children draw conclusions based on their experiences and observations.
50. **Communicating ideas:** Children communicate their ideas about the characteristics of things and how they work.
51. **Natural and physical world:** Children gather knowledge about the natural and physical world.
52. **Tools and technology:** Children explore and use tools and technology.

H. Social Studies

53. **Diversity:** Children understand that people have diverse characteristics, interests, and abilities.
54. **Community roles:** Children recognize that people have different roles and functions in the community.
55. **Decision making:** Children participate in making classroom decisions.
56. **Geography:** Children recognize and interpret features and locations in their environment.
57. **History:** Children understand past, present, and future.
58. **Ecology:** Children understand the importance of taking care of their environment.

[1]Language, Literacy, and Communication KDIs 21–29 may be used for the child's home language(s) as well as English. KDI 30 refers specifically to English language learning.

Teachers also make sure materials reflect children's interests and their home culture so the children are both comfortable and excited about learning.

The daily routine provides a balanced variety of experiences. Children engage in both individual and social play, participate in small and large groups, assist with cleanup, socialize during meals, develop self-care skills, and exercise their small and large muscles. Some parts of the routine revolve around children's plans and choices: children are free to choose where to go in the classroom (or outdoor space) and what toys or materials to work with. Other parts of the routine are planned and set in motion by adults. Even in these adult-led activities, however, children contribute their own ideas and choose how to use the materials supplied by the teacher.

The heart of the HighScope daily routine is the **plan-do-review process** in which children make choices about what they will do, carry out their ideas, and reflect on their activities with adults and peers. We call these parts of the day *planning time, work time,* and *recall* (or *review*) *time*. By participating in the plan-do-review process, children gain confidence as thinkers, problem solvers, and decision makers. They act with intention and reflect on the consequences of their actions. These are abilities that will serve them well in school and throughout their lives.

HighScope Assessment Tools

Effective programs monitor how well teachers teach and how much children learn on an ongoing basis (Gilliam & Leiter, 2003). They use the results to continue what is working and improve what is not (e.g., to provide more teacher training or fill gaps in children's experiences).

HighScope has two **comprehensive assessment tools** — one for programs and one for children — to carry out this review and enhancement process. The Program Quality Assessment (PQA) evaluates whether teachers and agencies implement effective program practices. Observers rate classroom teaching and program operations to identify strengths and areas for improvement. The PQA is available in both preschool and infant-toddler versions. COR Advantage, the latest version of HighScope's Child Observation Record (COR), assesses children's learning in every content area from infancy through kindergarten. Each day, teachers and caregivers write brief anecdotes that objectively describe children's behavior. They use these notes to evaluate children's development and then plan activities to help individual children and the classroom as a whole progress.

Because both instruments reflect best practices in the classroom and basic child development principles and research, they are suitable for use in all developmentally based programs, not just those using the HighScope Curriculum.

HighScope Professional Development

A curriculum works only if it is used consistently and properly. We know from more than 50 years of research that HighScope offers significant benefits to young children. However, to get those benefits, children must receive the same program that was proven in the research. To guarantee these optimal conditions, HighScope has an extensive training program of **professional development** courses for supervisors, teachers, and caregivers.

To train adults, HighScope employs the same principles of active participatory learning that it uses with children. People in training do not just read theory and research; they practice using HighScope teaching strategies in the classroom. They reflect on what is and is not working and discuss their experiences with colleagues. HighScope Certified Trainers provide feedback and support as training participants learn about the curriculum and how to use it with children.

By using the suggestions at the end of each chapter in this book ("Try These Ideas Yourself"), you too can actively learn as you read about the HighScope Curriculum. Depending on your situation, practice the curriculum with children in your program, share your thoughts with other students and colleagues, mentor those you supervise, and even try some exercises with family and friends. Most important, apply the information to your personal and professional life and reflect on what you learn in the process. By exploring these ideas, and using them to build your own insights and practices, you will experience the HighScope way of teaching and learning.

Try These Ideas Yourself

1. Draw a line down the middle of a piece of paper to create two columns. Fold it in half so only one column shows. Pick an everyday object that you have readily available, such as an apple, book, or chair. Read a description of the object in the dictionary or encyclopedia, or ask someone you know to describe the object to you. In the first column, write down what you remember from reading or hearing about the object's description. Turn the paper over so the other column is showing. Now explore the same object for at least five minutes on your own, using all your senses. Write down what you learned about it in the second column. Open the paper and compare the two lists. Which method of learning produced more knowledge about the object? Why? Record your answer.

2. Observe a setting with at least one adult and one child where there is an opportunity for the child(ren) to learn something (e.g., a young child participating in an art activity, preschoolers playing with letters at group time, a parent and child cooking in the kitchen, or a parent and child grocery shopping). Next, review the five ingredients of active learning: materials, manipulation, choice, child language and thought, and adult scaffolding. Then answer these questions: Which ingredients of active learning are present in the situation you are observing? How does the adult set things up so these ingredients do (or do not) occur? What type of learning does (or does not) take place for the child(ren)? How would you change the situation to increase the amount of active learning?

3. Look at the diagram of the preschool "Wheel of Learning" on page 9. Observe children and staff in your own or another early childhood program. (It does not have to be a HighScope program.) Make a written note of each activity or situation you observe and where you think it fits on the wheel.

HighScope's daily routine gives children a balanced variety of experiences.

Chapter 3

What Is the Theory Behind the HighScope Curriculum?

Think About It

Have you ever passed a construction site and watched a tall building go up? The first thing the construction workers do is pour the foundation, accurate to a fraction of an inch, to make sure the building has a solid base that will support it under the most extreme conditions. Then they build the structure, one floor at a time. At each level, they construct a scaffold to stand on while they work on the floor above. Once the outer walls and roof walls are in place, they put in the "mechanicals," including the plumbing, electricity, and heating and cooling system. With these essentials completed, the structure can now be divided by adding floors, ceilings, and interior walls. This organization is followed by the installation of permanent fixtures in the bathrooms, kitchens, and so on. At last, the building is ready for the occupants to move in and add the details that personalize their space, such as window and floor treatments, paint or wallpaper, and furnishings. Over time, fixtures are occasionally updated as old ones wear out or improved models come on the market. Personal furnishings may be changed more often, as new tenants replace old ones or current tenants alter the use or appearance of their rooms.

Supporting children's development is a lot like constructing a building. Learning begins with a firm foundation based on a trusting relationship between the child and one or more adults. Growth then progresses one step at a time. For children to advance in their thinking, adults must provide a *scaffold* that is grounded at children's current level (the support) that allows them to climb one level up (a gentle extension). Bit by bit, through experience, children begin to fill in the structure with essential divisions, or concepts. Then they add more details, based on personal experience and preferences. Refinements and modifications continue as learning and life proceed.

The HighScope Curriculum is founded on theories that view learning as developmental and interactive. In this chapter we discuss the theory behind HighScope's philosophy and approach, particularly active participatory learning and the plan-do-review process.

The Theory Behind Active Learning

The HighScope Curriculum is grounded in child development theory and research. It originally drew extensively on the cognitive-developmental work pioneered by **Jean Piaget** (1950) and his colleagues and the progressive educational philosophy of **John Dewey** (1938/1963). Since then, we have updated the curriculum based on current cognitive-developmental research (Clements, 2004b; Gelman & Baillargeon, 1983; Gelman & Brenneman, 2004; Gelman & Gallistel, 1978/1986; Goswami, 2002; National Research Council, 2005; Newcombe, 2002; Smith, 2002) and brain research (Shore, 2003; Thompson & Nelson, 2001).

Chapter Learning Objectives

By the end of this chapter, you will be able to

- Describe the development of thinking (ways of knowing) from infancy through adulthood.
- Explain how the thinking of young children differs from that of adults.
- Relate the development of thinking to the use of *active participatory learning* in the HighScope Curriculum.
- Discuss the theory and developmental importance behind the HighScope plan-do-review process.

In order for children to actively learn something, they must see it and do it themselves, with adults present to encourage and challenge their thinking.

Our teaching practices, particularly the notion that child development occurs within sociocultural settings, were derived from the work of developmental psychologist and educator **Lev Vygotsky** (1934/1962) and elaborated to include the concept of **scaffolding** introduced by **Jerome Bruner** (1986). The educational practices in the HighScope teaching model continue to be updated, based on the theory and research of those who have followed their lead (Rowe & Wertsch, 2002).

Ways of knowing

To explain how children's thinking develops over time, Piaget described several general **ways of knowing:**

- From birth onward, children gain knowledge through **sensorimotor** exploration of the world, that is, by using their senses and their direct physical actions on objects.
- Later, children also gain knowledge through their ability to represent actions with symbols such as words and drawings. With the beginning of language, thought becomes possible. It is **preconceptual** and intuitive thought (also called **preoperational**) because the child is still tied to perceptual characteristics rather than underlying concepts.
- **Concrete operations** comes next as children begin to think more logically, draw conclusions, and solve problems based on the direct evidence of their observations. Since they are tied to the actual or concrete things they see and do, children at this point are unable to analyze the processes behind their observations. Thus, their conclusions about the world are sometimes "wrong" according to adult logic and understanding. Young children also tend see things from their own perspective and cannot "decenter" from themselves to understand the world from other points of view.
- Finally, knowledge built through **formal operations** allows older children and adults to consider all possibilities in a situation, form hypotheses and make observations or conduct experiments to test them, and use deductive logic to solve problems. These abilities are also referred to as abstract thinking. Formal operations are the basis of higher mathematics and controlled scientific experimentation.

Terms Used in This Chapter

• Jean Piaget • John Dewey • Lev Vygotsky • scaffolding • Jerome Bruner • ways of knowing • sensorimotor • preconceptual or preoperational • concrete operations • formal operations • cognitive-developmental • learning pathways/developmental trajectories • interaction • knowledge construction • developmental change • assimilation • accommodation • active participatory learning • zone of proximal development • plan-do-review • purposeful play

Although Piaget tied these ways of experiencing and interacting with the world to particular ages, we now know that he sometimes underestimated young children's understanding. For example, according to Gelman and Baillargeon (1983), "under certain conditions, preschoolers can and do use a principle of one-to-one correspondence to reason about number. And they do this with set sizes they cannot count accurately" (p. 215).

▲ Cognitive-developmental research

Today's **cognitive-developmental** researchers no longer focus on these broad age-related ways of knowing described by Piaget. Instead, they study **learning pathways** or **developmental trajectories** related to specific content and tasks (e.g., vocabulary and counting). These current perspectives are consistent with HighScope's observations of children's learning. They also guide HighScope's ongoing curriculum development work in all content areas. Goswami (2002) sums up current cognitive-developmental theory this way:

> "Children's cognitive development depends on a developing understanding of what makes something happen in the physical or social world, a developing understanding that derives from socially meaningful activity, that is representational from the outset, and that is shaped by language. Children, the universal novices, are apprenticed to the "expert" adults around them, and learn from them to operate with the physical, symbolic, and cognitive tools of their culture." (p. 514)

These ideas are also supported by current brain research, which shows that learning depends on **interaction.** By interaction, scientists mean encounters with people, objects, events or activities, and ideas: "Neuroscientists stress the fact that interaction with the environment is not simply an interesting feature of brain development; it is an absolute requirement…Early experiences have a decisive impact on the architecture of the brain, and on the nature and extent of adult capacities. They directly affect the way the brain is 'wired'" (Shore, 2003, pp. 15, 18). Put another way, without experiences, the brain has nothing to work with.

Some brain researchers suggest that the brain's initial overproduction of nerve cell connections captures the mass of early experiences and that these connections are later organized and pruned down through use. At the same time, researchers find that these connections are not rigidly locked in place after a certain point in development. There is evidence of the brain's continuing ability to change and form new connections (called *plasticity*) throughout the life span (Black, Jones, Nelson, & Greenough, 1998; Greenough & Black, 1992). Active engagement thus plays a critical role in learning from cradle to grave!

▲ Knowledge construction

Children attending HighScope preschools actively build their ideas about reality through their direct experiences with people, materials, events, and ideas. Vygotsky (1978) saw the social or cultural environment as being crucial in **knowledge construction**, particularly in how language and thinking develop. We see in adults, for example, that the character of a people is shaped by how those in their community express themselves and the values and beliefs they grow up with. With children, this idea is supported by the study of early vocabulary development in home settings (Hart & Risley, 1995, 1999) as well as by research on the role of gesture in early language development (Goodwyn, Acredolo, & Brown, 2000; Iverson & Goldin-Meadow, 2005; Namy, Acredolo, & Goodwyn, 2000).

In a cognitive-developmental model, learning is seen as a process of **developmental change** — a process in which we learn by relating and adding new information to what we already know and, if necessary, changing the way we thought before. For example, if we know how to care for a pet guinea pig — to give it certain kinds of food and clean water — then we have a knowledge base to care for other pets, such as a cat or dog. However, we will still have to learn new things as conscientious pet owners, such as whether what cats and dogs eat and drink differs from what guinea pigs eat and drink. This ongoing process, first identified by Piaget and upheld by current research, is called **assimilation** (using existing knowledge and behaviors to explore new things) and **accommodation** (changing mental models — ideas about how the world works — to take new and sometimes contradictory information into account). It often takes many experiences involving assimilation and accommodation before changes in thinking are fully formed and consistently applied in our actions.

▲ Active participatory learning

HighScope adopted the term **active participatory learning** to describe this interactive process between the learner and the environment. Learning that reflects a true change in thinking does not take place when children are simply told something. They must see and do it for themselves, with adults present to encourage and challenge their thinking.

Vygotsky (1934/1962) referred to the **zone of proximal development** as the area between what children can accomplish on their own and what they can do with the help of an adult or another child who is more developmentally advanced. HighScope teachers observe children carefully so they know when and how to enter this zone and thereby raise learning to the next level (otherwise known as *scaffolding*). Children must be secure and confident in what they already know before they are ready to move ahead. When HighScope says adults "support and gently extend" children's learning, it means that the adults first validate, or *support,* what children already know and then gently encourage them to *extend* their thinking and understanding to the next level.

Because they actively construct knowledge as they engage with the world, young children's thinking does not always make sense in terms of adult ways of thinking but has its own logic.

It's alive! Children distinguish (not always correctly) between living and nonliving things. In their minds, something that moves may be alive (e.g., a raindrop sliding down the windowpane). At the same time, three- and four-year-olds begin to use features such as animation to identify what is not real on television (Fitch, Huston, & Wright, 1993). Moreover, building on what they know about animals, toys, and objects, preschoolers can successfully distinguish between real animals that can cause themselves to move and change and nonreal animals that cannot because their feet are "not real" (i.e., not made of living matter) and, therefore, can only be moved by forces external to themselves (Subrahmanyam, Gelman, & Lafosse, 2002).

Literal definitions. Children interpret words quite literally. Thus, when four-year-old Becky was cautioned to be careful because "Big kids play rough," she asked her mother, "Do little kids play smooth?" At the same time, children learn new words directly connected to their experiences, even "big" words such as *observe, respiration,* and *nutrients* (Gelman & Brenneman, 2004).

Blending intuitive and scientific thought. Children's explanations for what they observe are framed in terms of what they know from past experience. For example, when there was a strong wind with clouds rushing by, Jason said, "The clouds are making it windy. The wind will stop when the clouds are gone." This shows early causal thinking: Rushing clouds create a wind, Jason reasons, just as a truck creates a wind when it speeds by. Eventually, children's thinking will be reshaped and reorganized; in Jason's case, by further experience with wind and air pressure.

One thing at a time. Young children tend to focus on one thing at a time and usually do not connect events or see multiple similarities. This means they may not apply or generalize a lesson to related objects or happenings or think in terms of cause and effect ("If X, then Y"). For example, Zack is pressing hard to glue Styrofoam bits to his picture. As he bears down and forward on the paper, it moves and the sequins he has piled up next to it are pushed to the floor. Zack picks them up and puts them in the same place. When it happens a second time, he yells, "Stop jumping to the floor!" He does not connect his pressing on the paper to the sequins falling.

Judging by appearances and counting. Young children tend to judge *how much* and *how many* by the way things look. For example, they judge that 15 candies spread out on the table are more than 15 candies bunched together because the row takes up more horizontal space than the pile. When working with small quantities, however, counting and matching often do carry more weight than appearances (Gelman & Gallistel, 1978/1986). So, for example, children can tell that three pretzels are more than two pretzels no matter how they are arranged.

In all these ways that children think, we see them actively using hands-on experiences to build or construct knowledge based on their own system of logic. From continued and direct encounters with the real world, children's thinking and understanding expands to take new observations and interpretations into account.

The Theory Behind Plan-Do-Review

In addition to active participatory learning, the other hallmark of the HighScope Curriculum is the **plan-do-review** process. Young children in HighScope programs express their intentions (make *plans* involving choices about materials, actions, and people), carry out their ideas (*do* things to achieve their goals), and reflect on the experience (*review* what they did and what they learned). The plan-do-review sequence is rooted in the work of several theorists and its importance in early development is supported by research conducted by HighScope and others.

▲ Making plans

Planning has both cognitive and social-emotional components. Cognitively, to make a plan, a child must have in mind a mental picture of what he or she wants to do. This ability to imagine or form mental images of something that has not yet happened develops along with a child's use of language. Developmental psychologists describe the mental tools children use to plan as *executive control structures* (Case, 1985) or *executive function* (Zelazo & Mueller, 2002), by which they mean the inner blueprints for framing a problem and using existing knowledge and skills to plan, try out, and evaluate a solution.

There is evidence that, over time, as children converse with adults and participate in everyday routines, their ability to talk about a plan develops along the following lines: at first they focus on the *here and now* ("Want block"); next they begin to focus on *now and not now,* with reference to past or future ("At work time, I'm going to play with Max"); then they relate two points in time ("I'm painting. It's wet now, but it's going to dry in a little bit"); and finally, they can coordinate several points in time and the sequence of events across time intervals ("I'll get scissors to cut the string. Then I'm going to tie the strings on the fence for the birds") (Benson, 1997; Weist, 1989).

From the perspective of social-emotional development, children's capacity to plan appears as they struggle with what psychoanalyst Erik Erikson (1950) called *initiative versus guilt.* Preschoolers have many ideas they want to try out. When they are successful in carrying out their intentions, they develop a sense of initiative. If they consistently meet with failure, or are made to feel bad in their attempts, they may feel guilty about taking the initiative. By encouraging children's initiative, exploration, and independent problem-solving, HighScope teachers give children the social-emotional support they need to become competent and confident planners.

▲ Carrying out plans

When children carry out their plans (the *do* part of plan-do-review), they are being purposeful as well as playful. In fact, what differentiates HighScope work time from the free-choice time found in other preschool programs is the sense of purpose that children bring to their play. Because they carry out plans they make for themselves, preschoolers approach play as a way to accomplish something important to them. Moreover, as adults play and converse with children based on the children's interests, the children's language learning increases (Tomasello & Farrar, 1986).

Many educators and psychologists recognize the value of **purposeful play** in young children's learning. Dewey (1938/1963), whose theories influenced decades of American education, saw playfulness and seriousness as the ideal combination for learning. Dietze and Kashin (2011) say that play is as vital in the early years as nutrition and human nurturing, enhancing a child's sense of wonderment and curiosity, which has lifelong implications for every aspect of social-emotional, cognitive, and physical development.

▲ Reviewing activities

Recall time is when children make sense of their purposeful play. It involves more than simply remembering what they planned or did. Recall is an opportunity for children to reflect on their actions and the lessons they learned while interacting with materials and people. During recall, children actually build, or construct, memory, forming a mental representation of their experience and interpreting it based on their current way of thinking. This process is similar to when adults tell a story about something that happened to them. The narrator selects which parts of the event to build the story around, chooses words to show how he or she reacted to what happened, and often gives a punch line to sum up what he or she gained from the experience.

When children talk with others about their actions, they are also engaging in the storytelling process: "Creating the story also creates the memory structure that will contain the gist of the story for the rest of our lives. Talking is remembering" (Schank, 1990, p. 115). Thus, the memories created when children review their activities helps to bring about permanent changes in their growing understanding of the world.

Further, memory itself involves several different thinking processes. Psychologists give each type of memory a distinct name. *Recall of facts* (What did you do?) engages the semantic memory; *recall of procedures* (How did you do that?) engages the procedural memory; *recall of events* (What did you do first?) engages the episodic memory; and *recall of path* or route (How did you get there?) engages spatial memory. Each type of memory is associated with a different brain structure (Bourtchouladze, 2004; Kagan & Kagan, 2003).

Dewey (1938/1963) and psychologist Sara Smilansky (1971) also commented on the importance of planning and reflection in learning and development. Dewey said education should be based on goal-directed activity and that children should actively participate in directing their own learning activities. Smilansky spent a great deal of time observing children's play and was a consultant to HighScope in the early 1960s. She urged the curriculum developers to add recall to planning and work time so children could reflect on their plans and actions and thereby gain more understanding of what they had learned in the process.

❖

The insights and application of developmental theory in the HighScope Curriculum have been borne out by decades of research showing that active learning develops initiative. Planning and reflection are the curriculum components most positively and significantly associated with child development. The key studies behind these conclusions are described in the next chapter.

Try These Ideas Yourself

1. Observe an infant, a toddler, and a preschooler each encountering something for the first time. How do they approach the object or experience? What does this tell you about differences in their development?

2. Share a new experience with a young child. Compare what you notice and how you react with what the child notices and how the child reacts. What does this tell you about differences in how adults and children think about and understand the world?

3. Remember when you moved into a new place. What essentials did you need first? What details did you add later? Are you someone who leaves things in place once they are set or do you like to rearrange them? Do you see any parallels between how you furnish your living space and how you take in new information? How might your reflections influence your work in the classroom?

4. Observe preschoolers at play in several different settings (e.g., a preschool classroom, an unsupervised playground or park, a family gathering, or a children's party). In each instance, decide whether or not the children's play is purposeful, that is, if it is (or is not) carried out with a goal in mind. Describe the differences between purposeful and nonpurposeful play. List the advantages and disadvantages of each type of play.

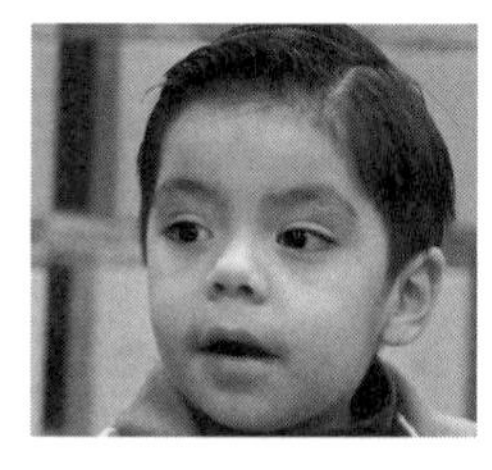

Chapter 4

What Is the Research-Based Evidence in Support of the HighScope Curriculum?

Think About It

Many doctors today warn patients that their weight and cholesterol levels are too high, putting them at risk for heart disease, diabetes, and other health problems. Some doctors recommend a program of diet and exercise. Others also prescribe medication. Because opinions differ on what works best for patients — and because not every patient is the same — medical researchers continue to study the effects of various treatments. New drugs regularly appear on the market.

If you are being treated for these problems, you want to know if what you are doing is working. For example, if you are taking medications that cost a lot of money and have side effects, you may be especially eager to know whether the benefits outweigh the drawbacks. Stepping on the scale answers the question of whether you are losing weight. However, since cholesterol levels can't be seen, your doctor will order a blood test. If the results are good, you and your doctor know the treatment is worthwhile. If the results are not good, or not good enough, the doctor may suggest changes in the medication or how you are taking it, as well as changes in diet or exercise.

Just like doctors and scientists, early childhood educators wonder whether their practices are effective. The push for accountability is an example of people asking whether the investment in preschool makes a difference in the outcomes for children and their families. HighScope has asked itself this question right from the start, beginning with its first preschool program in 1962. HighScope accepts the need to prove the curriculum works — and that it works with different populations under different program conditions. Moreover, since tests tell only part of the story, HighScope measures outcomes in different ways, including what happens in the "real world" as children engage with people and materials in their daily lives. Finally, since, like diets, effects can show up and then disappear, HighScope wants to make sure the improvements are lasting.

A Commitment to Research

Since its beginnings in the early 1960s, HighScope has conducted research and evaluation on the educational programs it develops. The first objective was to see if the programs were generally effective in achieving their goals. Overwhelmingly, they were. The second was to find out which specific components were — or were not — working, so improvements could be made. This commitment to research has allowed HighScope to maintain its basic, proven curriculum while continually adding features that address the changing educational policies and the needs of today's children.

Evidence for the effectiveness of HighScope's curriculum and training model comes from three major studies carried out by HighScope, which have been confirmed by independent investigations in the United States and abroad. These studies are discussed in the remainder of this chapter.

Chapter Learning Objectives

By the end of this chapter, you will be able to

- Describe the major research studies conducted by HighScope on its curriculum and training model.
- Describe research conducted by independent investigators that confirms the findings of the HighScope research.
- Explain how the components of high-quality preschool programs are derived from research.

▲ Research conducted by HighScope

The HighScope Perry Preschool Study. This study, reported in *Lifetime Effects* (Schweinhart et al., 2005), examines the long-lasting influences of the HighScope Preschool Curriculum on children born into poverty. The study is based on **random assignment** (arrangement of participants under different conditions, based on chance) of 123 children to either a program group (participating in a high-quality preschool program) or a no-program group (not participating in a high-quality preschool program). To date, the research has found that the curriculum had positive effects through age 40 on school achievement and literacy, high school graduation, adult earnings, home ownership, and lifetime arrest rates. A **cost-benefit analysis** (comparison of the costs of a particular investment with the advantages it is likely to offer) shows society saves more than 16 dollars[1] for every dollar invested in a high-quality early childhood program. In his invited comments on these results, Nobel Prize–winning University of Chicago economist James J. Heckman said, "This report substantially bolsters the case for early interventions in disadvantaged populations. More than 35 years after they received an enriched preschool program, the Perry Preschool participants achieve much greater success in social and economic life than their counterparts who are randomly denied treatment." (Schweinhart et al., 2005, p. 229).

Research has shown that the more teachers provided opportunities for young children to plan and review activities of their own choice, the higher they scored on measures of the skills needed for later school success.

The HighScope Preschool Curriculum Comparison Study. This study, reported in *Lasting Differences* (Schweinhart & Weikart, 1997), also examines the long-term effects of preschool on children from low-income families. It compares 68 preschoolers randomly assigned to one of three different curriculum models. Some attended HighScope, a comprehensive program in which children and teachers share responsibility for the learning experience (Epstein & Hohmann, 2012). A second group went to a program with a traditional nursery school curriculum, where the major focus is on social development and children determine the nature and content of their own learning (Sears & Dowley, 1963). The third group attended a program that used a direct instruction model, in which learning is confined to academic subjects and is directed by adults (Bereiter & Engelmann, 1966). The data, analyzed through age 23, finds

[1]Based on constant 2000 dollars, discounted at 3 percent.

Terms Used in This Chapter

• HighScope Perry Preschool Study • random assignment • cost-benefit analysis • HighScope Preschool Curriculum Comparison Study • HighScope National Training of Trainers Evaluation • inservice training • Head Start Family and Child Experiences Survey (FACES) • child-initiated learning activity • developmentally appropriate • open ended

no significant and lasting group differences on language, literacy, or school achievement. However, adults who attended the direct instruction program as children have had consistently higher rates of criminal activity compared to the other two groups.

The HighScope National Training of Trainers Evaluation. This study, reported in *Training for Quality* (Epstein, 1993), surveyed 203 HighScope trainers, interviewed and observed 366 teachers in HighScope and non-HighScope early childhood settings, and assessed 200 preschool children in HighScope and comparison classrooms. It found positive results demonstrating the effectiveness of systematic **inservice training** at all levels — for supervisors, teachers, and children. HighScope training resulted in significantly better supervisory and teaching practices than other training programs.

Children in HighScope programs, compared to those in non-HighScope programs, were rated significantly higher on measures of development. Most notably, the findings showcased the importance of the plan-do-review process. The more teachers provided opportunities for children to *plan and review activities of their own choice* — a hallmark of the HighScope Curriculum — the higher children scored on measures of the academic and social skills needed for school success.

▲ Research performed by independent investigators

Independent studies confirm that preschool children attending well-run HighScope programs do better than those in other program settings. Studies in the United Kingdom (Sylva, 1992) and the Netherlands (Veen, Roeleveld, & Leseman, 2000) found that when children plan, carry out, and review their own learning activities, they play with more purpose and perform better on measures of language and intellectual development. The **Head Start Family and Child Experiences Survey (FACES)** (Zill, Resnick, Kim, O'Donnell, & Sorongon, 2003), conducted with 2,800 Head Start children around the country, found those in HighScope programs improved significantly more from fall to spring on measures of literacy and social development than did children attending classrooms using the Creative Curriculum® or other curriculum models.

Lessons Learned From Research

The sidebar on page 5 lists the seven elements of high-quality preschool programs. Based on research conducted by HighScope and other investigators, we can elaborate these components as follows (Schweinhart, 2004):

Child development curriculum. Of all the ingredients in a high-quality program, an educational model that recognizes the value of child-initiated active learning is the most important. Research that has tested child development theory, and verified it in practice, identifies these principles:

- **"Child-initiated learning activity** acknowledges both the developmental limits of young children and their potential for learning" (Schweinhart, 2004, p. 18). In a balanced approach, young children are neither pushed to do things more suitable for older children, nor seen as uninterested in or incapable of engaging with meaningful content.
- "The best early childhood learning activities are child initiated, **developmentally appropriate,** and **open ended"** (p. 19). This means activities build on children's natural curiosity, are matched to children's current and emerging abilities, and allow for exploration and variation rather than having to be performed a single "right way."
- "Open communication between teacher and child and among children broadens children's perspectives as they learn to share ideas" (p. 19). Research on teaching and childrearing shows the benefits of shared control over either authoritarian or permissive extremes. A democratic style allows children to see things from different perspectives, which is an important social as well as cognitive skill.

Low enrollment limits. Studies have found that the fewer children per adult, the better the adult-child interaction. In addition to favorable staff-child ratios, the total group size should be limited based on standards recommended by the National Association for the Education of Young Children for the ages of the children served (Copple & Bredekamp, 2009).

Staff trained in early childhood development. Adults who provide care and education for young children need specialized training in child development and early childhood education. Research also shows that the higher the level of teachers' formal education, the more developmentally appropriate their teaching practices (National Research Council, 2001). Current efforts within the field to raise teachers' educational levels and credentials stem from these research findings.

Supervisory support and inservice training. In addition to hiring well-qualified staff, program administrators determine their ongoing inservice training. Training should occur at least once a month and help teachers implement the program's child development curriculum.

Involvement of families as partners. Family involvement is essential to good education throughout their children's school years. Although there may be obstacles to such involvement (e.g., working-parent schedules and multiple demands on the family), high-quality programs are creative in overcoming these barriers. They offer many options for inviting family participation. For ideas on how HighScope programs involve families, see chapter 8.

Sensitivity to the noneducational needs of children and their families. Today's families cope with many demands and stresses. In addition to being concerned about the education of their children, many parents also contend with financial, medical, social, or legal issues. Early childhood programs cannot meet all these needs directly. However, as part of a community network, high-quality programs are aware of the services available and help families obtain the assistance they need. The smoother the family's functioning, the better the child's adjustment.

Developmentally appropriate evaluation procedures. The main objectives of evaluation are to assess program quality and children's development. Administrators use program evaluation to make decisions about agency policies and staff development. Teachers use child evaluation to plan appropriate educational activities for individual children and the class as a whole. For evaluation results to be accurate and useful, they should be based on objective and observable behavior. Moreover, they should examine the elements of curriculum implementation and child development that are consistent with the program's philosophy and goals.

❖

To achieve the lifetime effects demonstrated in the Perry Preschool Study and other research, preschools must provide the same type and quality of educational services offered by the programs evaluated. First and foremost, this means adopting a child development curriculum that fosters active learning. It also means hiring and supporting qualified staff, involving families, and conducting ongoing and authentic assessment of teaching practices and children.

Try These Ideas Yourself

1. Look at the list of the seven elements of high-quality preschool programs shown on page 5 and then answer the following questions: What does it mean to include each of these elements in an early childhood setting? Think of your own program or one you have observed. What would you change to improve its quality? (*Variation:* You and a colleague observe the same program and compare the extent to which you think it has each of the seven elements of quality.)

2. Practice writing a grant proposal to get funding for your early childhood program. (If you don't have a program, think of one you would like to start in your community.) What information about your program do you think will persuade a funding agency that your program is worth investing in? Cover the following areas: the need or problem your program addresses, the number and characteristics of the clients it serves, the range of services it provides, the features that distinguish it from other programs, and the outcomes or benefits it provides clients. Do you have this information collected and tabulated? How can you best present it? If you do not have the information, how could you get it and organize it for your proposal? Can you use the HighScope research findings to support your program? If you feel you can, on what basis can you claim that the proven benefits of HighScope will also apply to your early childhood program?

Part 2

HighScope Teaching Practices

This part of the book discusses how the program's supportive interaction strategies, learning environment, and daily schedule promote active learning.

Chapter 5 looks at adult-child interaction and how to create a supportive climate for children.

Chapter 6 deals with setting up a physical learning environment that is comfortable and well organized to engage children in active learning.

Chapter 7 discusses how to set up a consistent daily routine that provides diverse learning opportunities.

Chapter 8 describes how to work with families so they can better understand and promote their child's education.

Chapter 9 looks at how teaching teams work together to observe children and plan appropriate learning experiences.

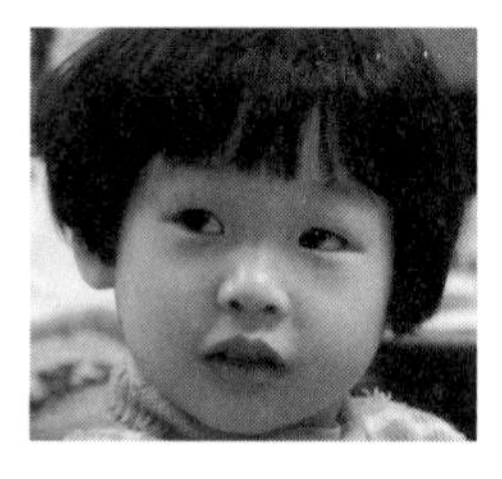

Chapter 5

What Does Adult-Child Interaction Look Like in a HighScope Program?

Think About It

Remember a time as a child when an adult asked your opinion or let you help make an important decision. For example, your parents might have called a "family council" to solve the problem of undone household chores or to decide where to go on vacation. Perhaps you recall a teacher who let students choose their own seats or who asked the class to help create rules for playing safely on the playground. HighScope teachers call this sharing control.

Thinking back, how did it feel to be a partner with adults? Did you worry that grown-ups didn't have the answers and think, "How should I know? I'm just a kid?" Or did it make you feel more grown-up to be asked for your ideas? Did you see an opportunity to suggest something that might be considered out of bounds? Or did you think seriously about something that you'd be responsible for helping to carry out?

Now reverse roles and remember a time when you shared control with children. Maybe you let a child decide what to order at a restaurant, mix her own paints, or suggest a way to rotate passing out snacks. How did you feel as an adult in these situations? Were you afraid children would test the limits? Did you offer real choices, or did you restrict the options to two or three that you felt comfortable with? Were the ideas predictable, or were you surprised (maybe even impressed) by their thoughtfulness and creativity? Did you carry out children's suggestions (with reasonable modifications, if necessary) or revert to what you really wanted to do?

Sharing control can be both scary and exciting, for children and adults alike. Most programs put teachers firmly in charge of solving problems and making decisions or else give limited choice or responsibility to children. In the HighScope Curriculum, however, **shared control** is central to how adults and children interact. The curriculum offers realistic strategies for accomplishing this goal so adults are not afraid of losing control and children don't feel insecure because they have too much freedom. Both sides know what to expect and what their respective roles are. Children rise to the occasion and meet the learning challenge. And adults are often amazed by what they learn from and about young children's capacity to think. This chapter looks at what a supportive climate for learning means for the adults and children who share an early childhood HighScope classroom.

A Supportive Climate for Learning

Early childhood programs are sometimes described according to two extremes — the **laissez-faire climate** and the **directive climate.** In a laissez-faire (permissive) climate, children are in control. There is little structure to the classroom or daily routine. Teachers keep children safe and take care of their basic needs, but otherwise they leave children free to play as they wish.

Chapter Learning Objectives

By the end of this chapter, you will be able to

- Explain the difference between supportive and restrictive learning environments and how each affects children's behavior.
- Participate as a real partner in children's play and conversations.
- Recognize and plan learning experiences that build on children's interests and strengths.
- Explain how to support children's development by using encouragement rather than praise.
- Treat young children's social conflicts as learning opportunities.

At the other end, a directive or adult-controlled climate is one where teachers take charge. They tell children what to do and when to do it, often using scripted lessons to teach specific academic skills and concepts. Some programs combine both approaches: part of the day is devoted to lessons (e.g., reading, mathematics) and the rest of the day children are permitted to play with very little adult supervision or involvement.

A third type of program, which HighScope provides, is a **supportive climate,** where adults and children share control of the learning process. Adults balance the freedom children need to explore with the limits children need to feel secure. They also provide materials and experiences that build on children's interests and promote learning. In a supportive climate, children initiate many of their own learning experiences. Even when teachers plan an activity, as for a small- or large-group time, they consider the objects, actions, and ideas children are interested in.

In a supportive learning environment, adults and children are partners throughout the day. Learning is its own reward, and children know adults are there to encourage their initiative. When conflicts arise, adults understand that children are not deliberately acting "bad" or "naughty." Rather, the adults know that children need to learn how to handle their feelings appropriately. Therefore, social conflicts are seen as another opportunity for social and cognitive learning.

Active participatory learning thrives in supportive settings like these, where children are comfortable with themselves and with others, have the freedom to explore materials, and interact with people from a place of security. In the opposite approach, children are limited in their exploration or even punished for expressing feelings and trying out ideas. These restrictive conditions can turn education into a negative experience.

A major goal of the HighScope Curriculum, therefore, is to create an environment where children can work and play free of fear, anxiety, and boredom. In HighScope settings, adults value and appreciate children and work to create a supportive climate in which children are given the intellectual challenges they need to grow, and learning is a positive, exciting, and natural experience.

▲ The effects of a supportive climate

The partnership that children and adults share in a supportive environment brings intellectual and social benefits to both. (See "Effects of Different Types of Classroom Environments" on p. 29.)

Children and adults are free to learn. Children are encouraged to pursue subjects and ideas that interest them. While carefully observing what children say and do, teachers develop an understanding of how the children think and the further learning experiences they need.

Children form positive relationships. When teachers model patient and respectful behavior, children learn to act this way with others and develop a positive attitude toward schooling.

Adults see children's behavior in terms of development. Understanding that children act based on their knowledge and development, adults can teach rather than judge them.

Children become trusting and independent. Children trust adults to take care of their

Terms Used in This Chapter

• shared control • laissez-faire climate • directive climate • supportive climate • authentic relationships • closed-ended question • open-ended question • exploratory play • constructive play • dramatic play • games with rules • encouragement rather than praise • problem-solving approach to conflict

Effects of Different Types of Classroom Environments

Positive Effects of a Supportive Climate

- Allows children to pursue their own interests and ideas and to learn from them
- Helps children develop independence and initiative
- Increases children's confidence in their own abilities
- Teaches children to trust others
- Develops children's sense of empathy and caring behavior
- Teaches children to solve social problems by talking and trying solutions
- Continually increases adults' understanding of children's development
- Encourages adults to interpret children's behavior positively in terms of development, not as stubborn, naughty, mean, or otherwise negatively motivated

Negative Effects of a Restrictive or Punitive Climate

- Increases children's dependence on adults
- Addresses adults' short-term need for authority, rather than children's long-term need for self-control
- Promotes compliance and conformity
- Promotes fear, aggression, and resentment
- Encourages mindless obedience rather than a desire to act constructively
- Teaches a desire to avoid being caught
- Inhibits children's ability to express strong emotions appropriately
- Models physical punishment as an acceptable way of expressing anger; demonstrates that if you are bigger, you are allowed to hurt others
- Decreases initiative by making children *other directed* rather than *inner directed*
- Increases guilt by focusing on children's "badness" rather than the problem or action

needs while gaining confidence in their own abilities to help themselves and others.

The Elements of Supportive Interactions

To establish a positive climate for early learning, HighScope identifies six elements of supportive adult-child interactions. Strategies to create these conditions in your classroom are listed here.

▲ 1. Sharing control between adults and children

Sharing control in a supportive climate means children and adults take turns being the leader and the follower, the speaker and the listener, the teacher and the learner. Everyone gets a chance to be heard and to try things. To share control with children, try the following strategies:

Participate with children on their terms. In play and conversation, take cues from the children. Share in children's interests, take pleasure in the things that capture their imagination, and appreciate children's creative ideas and actions. When entering children's play, take on the roles children assign to you and follow their directions:

Shirley, the teacher, walks to the house area where several children are playing. Janey says to her, "I'm the doctor and everyone has the flu. You better get a shot too." Shirley says, "I don't feel well, doctor. What should I do?" Janey replies, "Lie on this mat and roll up your sleeve." Shirley gets on the mat and Janey gives her a "shot" using a capped marker as a needle.

Learn from children. Rather than viewing yourself as an all-knowing authority figure, see yourself as a learner too — sometimes young children have skills to teach us. For example, they may be more comfortable using technology than we are. At other times, they can tell us things about their needs and feelings that we could not have figured out on our own. See "Learning From Children" on page 30.

Consciously give control to children. Plan ways and times to put children in charge so they can feel the power of their own ideas (e.g., ask children how to move down the hall to the gym).

▲ 2. Focusing on children's strengths

Learning occurs best when children are motivated by their own goals and interests. HighScope differs from "deficit models" in which adults focus on what children *can't do* and try to correct those weaknesses. The more pressure children feel, the more anxious they become, which can actually interfere with learning. By instead beginning with what children *can do* and what they are interested in, the motivation to learn is built in. To focus on children's strengths, you can:

Pay close attention to children's interests. Children are more willing to try something new if it builds on what they know. Sometimes we think children repeat the same thing, but if we look closely, we discover they are varying or adding to the activity. Providing them with related materials or information allows additional learning to occur.

See situations from children's point of view. Think of a child learning to get dressed. Clothing may be mismatched, buttoned the wrong way, and perhaps put on backwards! Getting dressed takes longer at times when you may be feeling rushed. However, the ability to dress him- or herself is very satisfying for the child. By openly acknowledging this, you can encourage the child to make further attempts at independence.

Share children's interests with families and staff. When talking with family members or coworkers, focus on children's strengths. For example, instead of reporting that "Tommy hardly played with the other children today," comment on his progress: "Tommy enjoyed playing with the trucks today. He gave one to Mark to push down the ramp he built." If problems arise, share what the child actually did and work together with other adults to find a solution all can agree on.

Plan around children's strengths and interests. Because each child is unique, focusing on children's strengths lets you *individualize* the program. HighScope teachers take anecdotal notes each day on what children do and use these observations in their daily planning. Teachers consciously think about how to support every child's learning, and each child is therefore assured of finding things of interest every day.

Learning From Children

Mrs. Walters, a volunteer parent, had a very loud laugh and played boisterously with the children. They all seemed to gather around her whenever she visited the classroom. One day she called to Jimmy, a new child, to ask if he wanted a turn with the swinging game they were playing. Jimmy shook his head and went to the other side of the yard, where he dug in the dirt. Later, Mrs. Walters went over to him and said in a booming voice, "What's the matter, Jimmy? Don't you like to swing?" "Too loud," said Jimmy. Puzzled, Mrs. Walters asked, "What's too loud?" Jimmy said, "You." Mrs. Walters said in a quieter voice, "Is it better if I talk like this?" Jimmy smiled and nodded his head. From then on, whenever Mrs. Walters approached Jimmy, she lowered the volume of her voice. She also found he preferred to do things with her one-on-one instead of with the whole group.

▲ 3. Forming authentic relationships with children

Authenticity means being genuine in your relationships with children. Learning is often a social activity, so children must trust adults to be honest and open with them. Because adults, like children, are unique, each adult must find his or her own way to act authentically in two-way communications. The following are strategies you can use to create meaningful interactions and develop **authentic relationships** with children.

Share your own interests with children. Joelle, a preschool teacher, loved to play the guitar and sing. She made singing a regular feature of greeting time, which made transitioning into the program day easy and fun. The children in her class taught the songs they learned to their parents and often brought in new songs to share.

Respond attentively to children's interests. Give your full attention to what children do and say. Children can sense when teachers have their minds elsewhere. By contrast, when an adult is eager to share in a child's excitement, it communicates that the activity and learning are important.

Give children specific feedback. General statements imply an adult is not paying attention or does not attach importance to what the child is doing. Specific comments, by contrast, show you are focused on the child and value his or her work. For example, if a child shows you a painting, instead of commenting that it's colorful, describe it (e.g., "You made a wide red stripe on the top and two skinny green ones at the bottom").

Ask and respond to questions honestly. An honest question is one in which the asker does not know the answer. Too often, teachers ask **closed-ended questions** — those for which they seek the "right" answer. By contrast, an **open-ended question** can have many possible answers. And just as adults should only ask questions when they are honestly interested in learning the answer, so too should they answer children's questions with thoughtfulness.

Here are two honest (open-ended) questions that reflect the teacher's genuine curiosity about the child's answer: "Jeremy, how did you get this block to balance on top of the pile?" and "Salima, what materials will you use to make your rocket ship?" Here is an honest answer to a child's question about whether she had to wear boots to the pumpkin farm: "We won't know until we hear the weather report tonight, so bring them just in case."

Limit questioning. In addition to considering the *type* of question you ask, limit the *amount* of questioning you do (Sawyer, 2004; Wood, McMahon, & Cranstoun, 1980). When adults ask so many questions that children feel they are being quizzed, children may simply stop talking. It is better to make comments when conversing with a child, the same as when talking to another adult. A HighScope teacher modeled this behavior for a parent, with a happy result:

> *When Mrs. M. picks up her son Jonathan at the end of each day, she peppers him with questions about what he did in school. Because she is genuinely interested in hearing how he spent his time, she is frustrated that he clams up after answering the first question. Jonathan's teacher stands by them one day and when Mrs. M. asks, "What did you do today" and he answers, "Made a tower," his teacher joins in with a comment: "I saw you building that tower with Veronica." Jonathan elaborates: "I used the blue blocks, and she added red ones." Mrs. M. listens as his teacher makes more comments and Jonathan offers more details. While Jonathan gets his coat, his mother asks the teacher, "How come he talks to you so much? He never does that with me." The teacher answers, "Sometimes I find that if I just comment on what they say, children open up more than if I ask a lot of questions." Over the next few days, Jonathan's teacher notices Mrs. M. making a conscious attempt to limit her questioning and talk to her son in a more conversational way. Jonathan becomes increasingly eager to share his day with his mother, and two weeks later, Mrs. M. says to the teacher, "Thanks for the tip. I'm using it with my older son too — at the dinner table — and it's amazing how much both boys share with us now!"*

By responding attentively to children's interests, adults create meaningful interactions and develop authentic relationships with them.

▲ 4. Supporting children's play

HighScope is a strong proponent of the idea that play is a child's work. Children play because it is pleasurable and rewarding. Play is an activity in which they are free to make choices and discover new things. The play may be noisy or quiet, messy or orderly, silly or serious, and effortful or easy. Whatever form it takes, play is a time when a great deal of learning takes place. Use the following strategies to make sure that play encourages children's initiative and learning:

Observe and understand children's play. Young children engage in many types of play. In **exploratory play,** they use materials to learn about them, not to make something with them (e.g., squeezing and pounding on play dough). **Constructive play** involves building things, such as a block house, while **dramatic play** is pretending and acting out roles. Older children play **games with rules,** although at the beginning of this stage, the rules may keep changing. Observing children's play helps us understand their intentions.

Be playful with children. Join enthusiastically in children's play. Get down on the floor, lap up "milk" with the other "kitties," and climb to the top of the slide. Let yourself be "locked up in jail" or get "shots" from the doctor. While play comes naturally to children, most adults must make a conscious choice to be playful. Once they do, they experience great satisfaction. Adults can also gain insight into children's thoughts and needs by becoming part of the action.

▲ 5. Using encouragement instead of praise

Many adults use praise because they think it helps children feel good about themselves and their work. They may also use praise as a behavior management tool, to help children "act like good boys and girls." However, research shows that praise can be damaging (Henderlong & Lepper, 2002; Kohn, 1999). When adults use praise, children learn to depend on adults to figure out what is right or wrong, instead of developing this ability themselves. Use of praise can also invite children to perform for external rewards rather than to embrace learning because it is self-rewarding. Children may be afraid to try something new for fear they will not be complimented, or worse, that they will be criticized. Just the absence of praise may be seen by some children as criticism.

HighScope, therefore, trains teachers to use **encouragement rather than praise.** By encouraging children, adults acknowledge their efforts and accomplishments. The focus is on children's actions and what they are learning, not on whether the children have pleased the adult. Try using the following strategies to encourage (rather than praise) the children in your program.

Participate in children's play. Work side by side with children using the same materials in similar fashion. Become a partner with the children by taking turns with them during play, matching the level of complexity of their play and generally following their lead. Consider this example:

Becki, a teacher, notices that Allison, Graham, and Chelsea are making "pizzas" in the block area. As a way of entering their play, Becky goes to the house area and calls the pizza store on a phone, asking if she could have a pizza delivered to her. This leads to many other children calling the pizza store and asking for pizza. Becki soon finds herself in the pizza store pretending to take orders and help make pizzas while some of the other children deliver them. The next day the teachers build on the children's interest in pizza by having the children make mini-pizzas out of English muffins, cheese, and different toppings at snacktime.

Another teacher might have responded to this situation with praise, for example, commenting on how nice or tasty the pizza was. Instead, Becki told the children *by her actions* that what they were doing was valued and accepted. She responded directly to their interests. Her active involvement conveyed a more meaningful message than statements of praise. Moreover, by becoming a partner, Becki encouraged the children to expand on their pretend play. She used the opportunity to scaffold (support and gently extend) children's learning in early literacy (building language skills as children communicated with her and one another) and mathematics (using numerals to record orders and counting the number of toppings on their pizzas).

Encourage children to describe their efforts, ideas, and products. The goal is for children, not adults, to evaluate their own work. This allows children to develop a healthy sense of self-esteem by feeling good about their actions and ideas. Instead of telling children they have done a "good job" or made something "beautiful," encourage them to talk about what they are doing, how they are doing it, and anything else that is important to them. Focus on actions, not results. For example, rather than saying "That's a lovely painting," ask "What can you tell me about your picture?" "How did you layer all the colors?" or "I see you mixed more colors. What will you paint next?" Such statements show that you are interested and encourage the child to reflect on and describe what he or she did. It also leads to a natural conversation about the activity and helps you to build an authentic relationship with the child.

Acknowledge children's work and ideas by making *specific* comments. In addition to encouraging children to talk about their work, adults can also comment directly on what the children are doing. These comments can be part of an ongoing conversation and are a useful alternative to praise when the child seems to be asking for recognition. Instead of making subjective comments (e.g., "Nice work"), make a specific and concrete observation (e.g., "You put blue stripes on the top of your paper and red stripes on the bottom") or offer an acknowledgment (e.g., "You worked on your block tower for a long time"). Such comments open the door for the child to add his or her own observations. A statement of praise, by contrast, can signal that the teacher sees the child's work is done and the conversation is over.

▲ 6. Adopting a problem-solving approach to conflict

Conflicts are an inevitable part of children's play. Some common examples: two children want to be the daddy in a pretend-play scenario, four children want to use three swings, and an entire small group wants to sit next to the teacher while she reads them a story. In a supportive climate, teachers see such conflicts as learning opportunities and approach them in a matter-of-fact manner. They know that disagreements arise from children's normal development and desires, not because they are being "bad" or "stubborn." The children are not the problem and should not be punished. Rather, the problem is the behavior, and it is a problem that can be solved. Children need to learn social skills just as they need to learn to read and write. Part of this learning is identifying that there is a problem and understanding that people can solve such problems together.

When children practice resolving social conflicts from an early age, they develop the skills and confidence to interact effectively with others throughout their lives. Adults in HighScope settings use a six-step problem-solving approach to help young children learn to resolve social conflicts in the classroom. This approach is summarized below with brief examples, illustrating the different steps. See chapter 11 for a more detailed description of the **problem-solving approach to conflict** as a component of the Social and Emotional Development content area.

Approach social conflicts calmly (step 1), and acknowledge children's feelings (step 2). Adults calmly stop hurtful behavior and acknowledge children's feelings so children can let go of their emotions and regain control, which allows them to identify and solve the problem.

Adult: *(Kneels between Lyle and Hank with an arm around each one.)* You look angry, Lyle, and you seem really upset, Hank. *(The boys nod in agreement.)*

Gather information (step 3), and restate the problem (step 4). It is important for adults to hear both sides of the dispute without taking sides so each child's position is heard and acknowledged.

Adult: What's the problem?

Lyle: I want to be the dad. I said so first.

Hank: You're always the dad. I want to be big.

Lyle: I'm the biggest, so huh! You can't be the dad. You're too little.

Adult: So the problem is, Lyle, you want to be the dad, and Hank, you want to be the dad. *(Both boys nod in agreement.)*

Ask for solutions to try, choose one together (step 5), and be prepared to give follow-up support (step 6). This puts children in control: "THEY agree on the situation, THEY figure out what to do about it, and THEY choose what happens next. Mastery and autonomy are developed here!" (Curry & Johnson, 1990, p. 117).

Adult: What can we do to solve this problem? *(The boys look at her, thinking.)*

Lyle: I could be the dad today, and then you can be the dad the next day.

Hank: Well, I could be the dad today!

Adult: It sounds like you both want to be the dad today.

Lyle: We don't need two dads...Hank, you could be the ladder guy and wear the tool belt!

Hank: And the gloves!

Lyle: Okay, the gloves. *(Both boys look pleased.)*

Adult: So, Lyle, you're going to be the dad and Hank, you're going to be the ladder guy who wears the tool belt and the gloves. *(The boys nod yes. The adult watches them get started and checks in with them as ladder guy and dad build a "swamp boat.")*

HighScope teachers use a problem-solving approach to help children resolve conflicts.

Finding alternatives to hurtful behavior, naming their feelings, and thinking of solutions are not easy to do, especially for young children who live in the present and often see things from their own point of view. Given repeated opportunities to practice working through social conflict in a supportive climate, however, children learn to trust themselves as problem solvers, to trust adults to assist them when they need it, to be empathic and helpful to others, and to have faith in their individual and collective capacities to make relationships work. See also "Preventing Classroom Conflicts" on this page for other ways the HighScope Curriculum helps prevent problems from happening.

Preventing Classroom Conflicts

The following characteristics of the HighScope Curriculum help prevent problems and conflicts from happening in the classroom:

- Spacious work areas with enough materials for all children
- Predictable daily routine
- Children carrying out their own plans during work time
- Children having choices during group times and transitions
- Group activities being planned around children's interests
- Little or no waiting before getting started on activities
- Adults helping children identify and express their feelings
- Adults making daily observations and anecdotal notes about children

Try These Ideas Yourself

1. Describe an interaction you recently had with a child (in your class, at home, or elsewhere). What interaction strategies did you use? How did the child respond?

2. Read the following scenarios from a preschool classroom. Using the six elements of adult support discussed in this chapter, describe how you would handle each situation.

At cleanup time, Sasha runs from one area of the room to another.

Roger and Jack are sitting on the couch, looking at a tool catalog. Bella sits down next to Jack and asks, "Can I see too?" "No girls allowed," says Roger, and Jack pushes her off.

After greeting circle, the children go to their small-group tables for planning time. Emily walks directly to the art area and begins to paint. Frank, who is in Emily's group, says, "She can't do that! She has to make a plan first." Emily drops the paintbrush on the floor and walks to the block area, where she proceeds to build a tower.

3. Divide a piece of paper into two columns. At the top of one column write "Praise," and at the top of the other write "Encouragement." In the first column, write down the things you say or do to praise children (or adults). For each one, in the second column, make a list of alternative things you could say and do to provide encouragement.

4. Children can say hurtful or untrue things when they are angry or frustrated. Below are some typical statements made by preschoolers. How would you, as the adult mediator, restate their comments to acknowledge their feelings but help them communicate more effectively?

I can too get on the swing if I want to. I hate you, you big dummy!

Tim and John can come to my birthday party, but not Sam.

If I can't play with the ball, I'm not coming back. I'll tell my mommy this school stinks!

How come Sarah always gets to sit in your lap? You like her better than me.

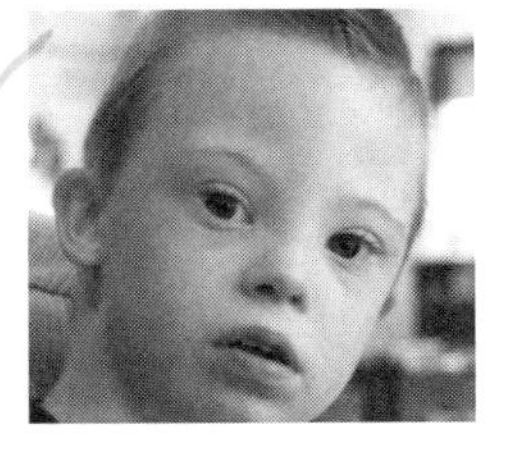

Chapter 6

What Does the Learning Environment Look Like in a HighScope Program?

Think About It

Think about your favorite supermarket. What makes it appealing? Perhaps it is not so big that you feel lost, yet not so small that your choices are limited. It is well stocked. Aisles are wide enough so shoppers' carts do not bump into one another. The produce isn't prepackaged, so you can check if it's fresh and buy only as much as you need. The signs over each aisle are large and easy to see, and good lighting lets you read prices and labels. You can reach everything, even the top shelf. In addition, the store offers weekly specials, the cashiers are friendly, and the service department answers your questions and invites your suggestions.

The environments where we carry out our activities affect what we do and how we feel. If a place is attractive, comfortable, well organized, and interesting, we are more likely to spend time there. We may visit the place on our own; go with others; or do both, mixing solitary and social times. The more we get to know the setting and the people in it, the safer we feel about taking risks and exploring.

In many ways, an early **learning environment** is like the settings in which grown-ups work or perform the daily chores of living. Children, like adults, must have their basic needs for health, safety, and comfort met. Beyond that, they too need a balance of organization and variety, the chance to do things on their own and with others, and opportunities to practice existing skills while mastering new ones. An optimal environment stirs a child's sense of adventure while providing the security of knowing help is there when needed. In this chapter, we will look at how the indoor and outdoor spaces in HighScope programs take all these needs into account while creating active learning environments for young children and the adults who care for them.

Why the Learning Environment Is Important

Most young children spend a significant part of their day in a preschool classroom or child care center. We want children to feel comfortable and secure in that place. All types of learning occur in the preschool or child care setting, from recognizing letter sounds to painting pictures to solving social conflicts. Therefore, when you create a well-organized environment full of interesting materials, you make it possible for active participatory learning to occur in every area of development.

Intellectual development. When space is logically divided into interest areas, each with its associated equipment and materials, children develop ideas about how the world as a whole is organized. For example, they find printed materials (such as books and magazines) and writing supplies in the reading area and paint and brushes in the art area. Further, having areas based on children's interests lets them know their ideas and discoveries are important. This message sets the

Chapter Learning Objectives

By the end of this chapter, you will be able to

- Explain how a well-designed learning environment contributes to children's growth in all areas of development.
- Organize and label a learning environment that accommodates a wide range of activities and types of play, is inviting to children, and is easy for children and adults to navigate.
- Choose appropriate equipment and materials for all the indoor and outdoor learning areas of a preschool program.

stage for them to eagerly anticipate formal learning when they enter the elementary grades.

Emotional development. Having a consistent play space, with things always stored in the same location, gives children a sense of security and control over the environment. This can be especially important for children whose home lives do not provide such predictability. Labels for each area and the materials in it allow children to find and use the materials they need to carry out their plans and then return the materials to their storage spaces. When children know where to find materials, they do not have to wait or depend on teachers to achieve their goals. The materials they enjoy using are available every day, rather than being set out only on certain days. A constant and regular arrangement of materials and equipment promotes self-confidence and independent problem solving.

Social development. Space arrangements can also foster social interactions by encouraging children to gather in pairs and groups. Because HighScope does not limit the number of children who can play in each area, the children are free to socialize in small and large groups. Program settings also provide intimate or cozy places where children can curl up with a teacher or one or two classmates to read, tell stories, pretend, or just talk and be together.

An optimal learning environment stirs a child's sense of curiosity while providing the security of knowing help is there when needed.

Physical development. A classroom and a spacious outdoor area that are easy to get around in are important for children's physical development. In such settings, children can move freely without fear of falling, bumping into things, or colliding with others. The predictable layout of the classroom and playground also helps young children build *cognitive maps* in their minds. Being able to create this internal picture of the shape, size, and relative position of things is important to the development of later mathematical skills, such as geometry.

Artistic development. HighScope classrooms and outdoor spaces intentionally provide an array of colors, textures, natural materials, types of lighting, and sounds. Varied and attractive design, lighting, and furnishings all help young children develop aesthetic principles and encourage their independent creative pursuits.

The classroom is also the early educator's primary workspace, so it is essential that teachers feel comfortable there too. The environment should allow them to perform their jobs; that is, to serve children and families in ways that are compatible with their philosophy and curriculum training.

Terms Used in This Chapter

• learning environment • interest areas or learning centers • label, labeling • open-ended materials • find-use-return cycle

Organizing the Learning Space

It is easy to recognize a HighScope classroom as soon as you walk into it. The room is clearly divided into **interest areas** or **learning centers.** Each area has a simple name such as the house area or art area, and these names are indicated with a **label** made of words and pictures or objects representative of that area. Classroom equipment and materials, also labeled, are logically organized and grouped by function or type within these areas. (See pp. 42–44 for a checklist of areas and materials often found in HighScope settings.)

The following principles can help guide you in arranging the indoor play space. Later sections in this chapter provide guidelines for choosing materials and equipment and for setting up the outdoor play space.

▲ 1. The space is divided into interest areas

Young children enjoy many types of play, including exploring with all their senses, building and creating things, pretending and role playing, reading and writing, drawing and sculpting, solving simple puzzles, and playing simple games. HighScope settings are divided into areas to support these activities. Areas have simple names that make sense to children (e.g., toy area rather than manipulatives).

The areas are chosen to reflect young children's natural interests. Typical areas in HighScope classrooms include the block area, house area, art area, toy area, reading and writing area, sand and water area, woodworking area, movement and music area, and outdoor area. (Because mathematics and science exploration occur with materials from all areas, HighScope classrooms do not have a specific mathematics or science area.) If certain types of materials or activities are of common interest to children in a particular culture or community, these can also be reflected in a HighScope program. For example, in a northern community, children renamed the water table the snow area during the winter months and brought in a fresh supply of snow at the beginning of each day. In another preschool, after visiting the studio of a local artist, the children set up a special bead area next to the art area to explore their interest in this activity.

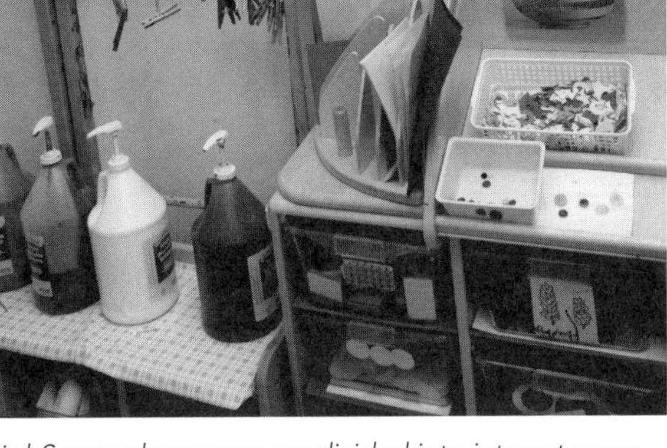

HighScope classrooms are divided into interest areas — such as the art area — with simple names and clear labels that children can understand.

The areas are *defined* by low boundaries and the materials that are logically stored in them. Each area is *labeled* with a large sign that may display an actual object found there, a picture of the materials or activities typical of the area (represented with a printout, drawing, tracing, photo, or catalog picture), and the written name of the area. For example, children might see a real paintbrush or a large drawing of a crayon and the words *Art Area* on a sign **labeling** that part of the room. This system allows children at various stages of literacy to comprehend the labels and practice literacy skills. Labels are covered on both sides with clear contact paper or clear tape, which makes them easy to attach to shelves or containers (e.g., with loops of masking tape) and easy to move when it is time to make room for new materials. Although materials are arranged by area, children are free to carry materials from one area to another to support their play.

There are no hard and fast rules for the number of areas to have in your program. Generally, it is better to have fewer areas, each stocked with diverse materials that can be used in many ways, rather than many areas supplied with a limited number of items. Too many areas can overwhelm young children, and arbitrarily assigning materials to an area does not allow them to discover why they are grouped together or to explore them in creative ways.

If your program is in a small space it will likely have fewer areas, but you can compensate by changing the areas now and then, as long as such changes are made infrequently. For example, you may have permanent house, art, block, sand and water, and toy areas but add a sixth area that rotates, such as woodworking or something that captures children's current interests (such as a pet area). Some programs begin with fewer areas to make it easier for children to learn them. Once these become familiar, the teachers add one or two areas. The children can then work with the teachers to decide which materials should be moved from the existing areas to the new ones.

Softness, pleasing colors and textures, natural building materials and light, and coziness are design elements that make spaces inviting to children.

Where you decide to locate areas also depends on your program's facilities and how each area is used. For example, putting the art area near a sink or other water supply enables children to mix paints and clean up easily. You might put the book area near a window to make use of natural light for reading. Or you can make the book area part of the house area, with the bookcase next to a comfortable couch or beanbag chairs and a table with the computer nearby. If the room is sectioned or divided, put the block area in the biggest space so children can carry materials and build large structures. Since children often use materials from the block area to pretend play in the house area, and vice versa, locate these two areas next to or near one another.

Each area should have enough space for materials and however many children want to play there. Avoid limiting the number of children who can use an area — doing so restricts their freedom to make choices, pursue their interests, and learn to resolve conflicts over space and materials.

Most important, to ensure adequate space for children's play, locate non-play equipment, supplies, and functions elsewhere. This means situating teachers' desks, custodial supplies, adult meeting areas, and so forth outside the classroom. The classroom is for children and the activities adults share with them.

▲ 2. The space is inviting to children

The hours children spend in preschool or child care are an important, and sometimes a large, part of their day. They should therefore anticipate and enjoy their time in this setting. The following characteristics make a play space comfortable and welcoming to children:

Softness. Just as in a home, softness in the classroom creates a sense of warmth and safety. Carpets and throw rugs, stuffed chairs and beanbag chairs, cushions and pillows, mattresses and futons, and curtains and fabric wall hangings all add softness to a setting. They also help to absorb sound, which is important in a room full of active, noisy children.

Pleasing colors and textures. Bright colors and soft pastel shades can all appeal to children. Harsh and garish hues can be off-putting, however, just as they are with adults. Too many colors jumbled together can also be overwhelming and make it difficult for children to focus and concentrate. The same principle holds true for patterns and textures. Some variety is important, but, in general, avoid glaring extremes that can lead to sensory overload.

Natural building materials and light. Natural building materials, such as wood and stone, provide variety and a contrast to our society's overuse of plastic and other artificial materials. While all programs depend on artificial light, it is also good to use natural light whenever possible. Sources of natural light include windows, skylights, and Plexiglas panes in doors.

Coziness. Even the most active and social children occasionally need a quiet place to be alone or to curl up with one or two other people. HighScope classrooms always include one or more cozy spots, such as an easy chair, a couch, a pile of pillows, a loft, a window seat, or a nook. These spaces are especially inviting for reading and are often part of the book area.

▲ 3. The space accommodates activities and storage needs

Because the HighScope daily routine includes activities that can be done alone, in pairs, in small groups, and in large groups, all these possibilities must be accommodated in the same setting. Many programs also include a snack or meal, and full-day programs may include naptime. Be sure to take these activities into account when arranging the classroom or center.

In a large space, it is helpful to locate interest areas around the outer edges (perimeter) of the room. This keeps the central space open for group activities and easy movement from one area to another. If the overall space is small, has odd angles, or is divided into several rooms (such as in a family child care home), one area may serve multiple purposes. For example, a spacious block area can also be used for large-group times, and snacks and meals can be eaten at the same tables where children make plans and do small-group activities.

Individual storage space is also important because each child needs an area to call his or her own. The space might be a locker, cubby, shelf, tub, box, or basket — any surface area or container where children can put their things. Its location should be easy for children to reach so they can store and retrieve things on their own. Individual storage spaces allow children to keep track of personal belongings, such as clothing or a painting they want to take home. Each storage space in a HighScope classroom is also labeled with the *letter-linked* picture and name of the child who uses the space. (For more on letter links, see chapter 13.) Since the first letters children learn are often those in their own name, the label on a personal storage site is important for literacy learning as well as developing a sense of ownership and responsibility for one's things.

▲ 4. The space is open and accessible

Children should be able to see all the areas from different parts of the room. This allows them to consider all the possibilities available to them when they plan and to see what's happening around the room as they play. To permit children to see everywhere, define and separate areas by using low boundary separators. These might include low shelves, carpeting, floor lanes (spaces or aisles), and tape on the floor. In multiroom settings — such as family child care homes — open doors, interior windows, and mirrors can help children see from one part of the space into another.

Ease of movement between areas is also important, for several reasons. One is safety. Boundaries between areas should not pose any danger to children, such as sharp edges or something that could cause them to trip and fall. This consideration is especially important for children with special needs who use mobility devices (e.g., wheelchairs, walkers) or have visual or other sensory limitations that should be accommodated throughout the setting. Second, children's play should not be interrupted by classmates going through one space to reach another. If children do have to pass through an area, they should be able to do so quickly and easily so as to minimize disruption to others. Third, ease of movement from one area of the room to another encourages children to explore and expand their play. They feel free to elaborate on their ideas when they are able to carry materials between areas. Finally, free movement between areas promotes social interaction. Individuals and groups of children can readily join one another when something in a nearby area catches their attention. This fluidity often results in more complex play across curriculum content areas, especially among older preschoolers, as illustrated in the following anecdote:

Janelle and Frieda are playing in the house area. Their baby dolls are sick, and they bring them to the doctor for shots. Frieda goes to the nearby block area to get a dowel to use as a hypodermic needle. Mario, Orin, and Alex are in the block area. Mario says, "You need an ambulance to get to the hospital." Mario and Orin use some large hollow blocks to make an ambulance and then build a road from the block area to the house area with long, flat blocks.

Janelle and Frieda bring their dolls to the block area and put them in the ambulance. As they are getting ready to "drive" back to the house area, Alex says, "Wait! There's going to be an accident. We better get the cops." He goes to the art area to make a badge, which he cuts out of yellow construction paper and attaches to his shirt pocket with a clothespin. Alex also makes a stop sign by writing the letters "STP" on a piece of cardboard. Liza, who just finished a painting in the art area, brings a large paintbrush to the block area and announces, "This is the flashlight to direct the traffic." Alex and Liza direct traffic, Mario and Orin drive the ambulance to the house area, and Janelle gives the babies their shots while Frieda rocks and soothes them by saying, "There, there, baby. Don't cry."

Being able to see and move easily between all the areas is also important so adults can keep tabs on what is happening throughout the room. This lets you monitor children's safety and be alert to conflicts you may need to help mediate. Seeing and hearing everything that is going on also allows you to take advantage of opportunities to join children's play and scaffold their learning.

Choosing Equipment and Materials

The "raw materials" of learning are the physical objects, activities, and social interactions we provide young children. Therefore, a great deal of thought must go into the equipment and materials we select for these experiences. Choosing them involves making decisions about the type and amount of each, as well as where and how to organize and store them.

Children need to be able to use materials wherever they choose and in whatever way they need to carry out their plans and solve the problems they encounter in play. However, it is equally important that where and how the materials are stored be consistent. When you add new materials to the classroom, or when you occasionally must move something, do so with thought and, as often as possible, with input from the children. (*Consistency with flexibility* is also a hallmark of the daily routine, which is covered in the next chapter.)

As you make important decisions about equipment and materials, keep in mind the following guidelines used by teachers in HighScope programs.

▲ 1. Materials are varied, open ended, and plentiful

Because their interests are varied, children need a wide range of materials to support their play and learning. It is important, therefore, to have many different types of equipment and materials available in each classroom area and outdoors. (See pp. 42–44 for a list of material types and specific examples for each area.) Stock **open-ended materials,** that is, items that can be used in many different ways. In addition to items made specifically for preschoolers (e.g., toys, puzzles, climbing equipment), it is important to include actual, everyday items such as phones, hammers, uniforms, order pads, measuring tapes, and so on. Children enjoy imitating adults by using such real items in their play. They also investigate and learn about these objects as they incorporate them in pretend play, building, problem solving, and other activities.

Also be sure to stock the classroom and outdoor play space with natural, found, and recycled items. Materials of this type are often available at a low cost or free. For example, on neighborhood walks children can collect natural and found objects such as shells, twigs, rocks, and fallen leaves. Materials gathered in this way provide a useful contrast in texture and color to purchased items, which tend to be made of plastic or a limited range of other materials. Children need opportunities to explore and discover the properties of wood, stone, fiber, shells, leaves, and other natural materials. Discovering and contrasting the properties of such items is an important foundation for mathematics, science, art, and other areas of learning.

Families can also contribute many items to your classroom, including recyclable paper and containers, old clothes, small appliances that no longer work, and tools and equipment for the house and yard. Donations brought in by family members offer several advantages. One is financial, since the items are free. Second is the opportunity to involve families in your program. Even parents whose work schedules may not permit them to volunteer in the classroom feel they can play an important role by donating play items. Finally, it is important for classroom materials to reflect children's home lives. Familiar objects help children feel comfortable in the classroom. Using such objects in the classroom also validates children's family and cultural experiences.

Having plentiful materials means there are enough in each area for several children to play there at the same time. For example, if several children want to paint, it is useful to have a couple of easels, enough table or floor space, multiple paint containers, several brushes in different widths, and a number of smocks. Having enough materials means that each child can carry out his or her plans without having to wait, as waiting is difficult for young children. It also means children can make many choices in terms of the materials they can use and combine these materials to achieve their goals, as demonstrated in these two anecdotes:

Six children in Miss Peggy's small group decide to send her get-well cards. Since there are four complete sets of markers, each child is able to find the colors he or she needs to draw or write a message.

◆

After completing a puzzle, Bing announces his next plan is to paint. He wants to work at one of the two easels, but Cheryl and Yvonne are already there. Marcus, Bing's teacher, wonders what he could do instead. Bing gets a piece of paper and asks Marcus to hold it against the wall by the table while he uses masking tape to attach it. Yvonne says Bing should put newspaper under it in case he drips, and she brings him a piece. Bing pumps red, blue, and white paint into an ice cube tray. He sets the tray on the table and begins to paint.

Include everyday items (such as real teapots and bowls) among classroom materials so that children can incorporate them in their pretend play.

Having ample materials also helps minimize the number of conflicts children have over who gets to use what and when. While a certain number of conflicts are inevitable — and provide young children with valuable learning experiences — constant fighting over materials cuts into the time available for other types of play and exploration.

Finally, children need materials that support a wide range of play experiences to increase their knowledge and abilities in each area of development. Provide equipment and materials for sensory exploration, building, making things, pretending, and playing simple games. When children are free to use even simple materials that support their interests, they often combine them in unique and complex ways.

▲ 2. Materials reflect children's family lives

The materials in the classroom send children a message about what adults think is important. To show that you value children's home and family life, include many items found in homes, such as books, magazines, photos, dolls, clothing, music, and food containers that accurately reflect the

Sample Materials List for a HighScope Classroom	
Art Area Materials	
Materials for mixing and painting	Tempera paint, liquid starch for finger paint, soap flakes, watercolor paints, easels, plastic squeeze bottles, jars with lids for storing paints, paintbrushes of different sizes, muffin tins, cleaned frozen-food aluminum tins, saucers for painting and printing, sponges, paper towels, smocks or paint shirts, toothbrushes, screening
Materials for holding things together and taking them apart	Scissors, yarn, shoestrings, string, rubber bands, paperclips, cellophane tape, masking tape, white glue, paste, paper punch, staplers
Materials for two-dimensional representation	Pencils, colored pencils, crayons, chalk and chalkboard, markers, ink pads and stamps, magazines and catalogs, paper of different sizes and colors and textures, newsprint, aluminum foil, wax paper, tissue paper, cotton balls, paper scraps, paper plates, shoe boxes, wallpaper samples, cardboard pieces
Materials for three-dimensional representation	Clay, play dough and accessories, buttons, straws, ice cream tubs, empty thread spools, pipe cleaners, clothespins, bits of wood, sequins, cardboard tubes, paper bags, scraps (cloth, felt, rug, vinyl), feathers, Styrofoam bits
House Area Materials	
Materials children see at home	Old cell and telephones (with cords removed), old clocks, step stool, tool box, child-sized iron and ironing board, soft chair, small vacuum cleaner, broom and dustpan, nonworking toaster, nonworking microwave, luggage, cooler, desk, blankets, old computer equipment (e.g., keyboard, mouse)
Materials for pretend play	Props for pretend play (e.g., pretend barbershop, farm, fire station, doctor's office, restaurant, gas station), dolls, stuffed animals, doll beds, baby equipment (rattles, bibs, bottles), clothes and hats, mirror, sleeping bag
Kitchen equipment	Pots and pans, cooking utensils, large and small spoons, large and small spatulas, egg beater, child-sized appliances (stove, refrigerator, sink), timer, teapot, coffee maker, ladle, ice cube trays, hamburger press, cake and pie tins, mixing bowls, measuring cups and spoons, canister set, sifter, potholders, plastic dishes (plates, cups, bowls), cleanup equipment (sponges, dish clothes, towels), table linens (napkins, placemats), plastic fruits and vegetables, small items to use as pretend food items (e.g., poker chips, bottle caps, Styrofoam bits, acorns), empty food boxes and plastic containers, jars, produce and trash bags
Block Area Materials	
Materials for building	Large hollow blocks, unit blocks, small blocks, cardboard blocks, blocks made from shoeboxes, milk cartons, carpet pieces, fabric (bedspreads, old sheets, blankets), large and small boxes, wood scraps, tubes, string, rope
Materials for representing	Steering wheel, small trucks, small cars and people, Tinkertoys, interlocking boards, wooden train set and track, barn and farm animals

Sample Materials List for a HighScope Classroom (cont.)

Toy Area Materials	
Materials for sorting	Marble games, nesting and stacking toys (cups, boxes, blocks, rings, cans), Cuisenaire rods, beads and strings, attribute blocks, natural materials (shells, stones, pine cones, seed pods), buttons
Materials for taking apart and putting together	Legos, washers, nuts and bolts, pegs and pegboards, magnets, interlocking blocks
Materials for pretend play	Puppets, counting bears, miniature animals, small people, wooden village (city, farm)
Games	Puzzles, marbles, picture dominoes, simple card games (Go Fish, Snap, Old Maid), simple board games

Mathematics and Science Materials (distributed among other areas)	
Materials for identifying and comparing attributes (making collections, matching and sorting)	Blocks of different sizes and shapes and colors, boxes, lids, plates, shape sorters, carpet squares, wallpaper samples, rings, dominoes, attribute blocks, Cuisenaire rods, shaving cream, foil, paper with different textures (sandpaper, crepe paper, tissue paper), natural items (leaves, pebbles, shells), magnets, containers for collecting and sorting (boxes, bags, buckets, plastic containers)
Materials for making series and patterns	Nesting blocks, stacking rings, measuring cups and spoons, pegs and pegboards, beads and string, cardboard and felt pieces in different colors and graduated sizes
Materials for making ordered sets	Three or four sizes of flower pots and saucers, plastic containers and cans with lids, cups and saucers, squeeze bottles and tops, cards and envelopes, nuts and bolts, boxes and covers
Materials for counting, measuring, and comparing quantities	Beads, blocks, toy vehicles, toy animals, buttons, rocks, shells, leaves, acorns, bottle caps, materials with numerals (adding machine, old cell phone, old keyboard, calculator, playing cards, play money, number stamps, number stickers), board games and dice, devices for conventional and unconventional measuring (rulers, tape measures, balance scales and weights, lengths of string)
Materials for exploring space (filling and emptying, putting together and taking apart, shaping and arranging)	Continuous materials to pour (sand, water, salt, flour, birdseed), discrete materials (small plastic animals, beads, poker chips, nuts, shells, pea gravel, buttons), inch cubes (plastic cubes that can be snapped together), bottle caps, various scoops and containers, toys and blocks with interlocking parts, beads and string, keys and key rings, paper and cloth, clay and dough, yarn and ribbon, pipe cleaners
Materials for observing things from different perspectives	Print materials depicting various viewpoints (picture and photo books, magazines, art prints), stools, steps, ramps, outdoor equipment with different levels and viewpoints (climber, ladder, trampoline, seesaw), natural variations in elevation (hills and tree stumps, holes and pits in the ground), magnifying glasses
Materials for exploring time (stopping and starting, setting in motion)	Timers (egg, sand, water, kitchen), wind-up clocks, musical instruments, objects with wheels, objects that move in different ways (rock, roll, spin, and drip)

Sample Materials List for a HighScope Classroom (cont.)	
Reading and Writing Area Materials	
Materials for writing	Pencils, crayons, erasers, old keyboard, markers, typewriter, rubber stamps and ink pads, paperclips, tape, rulers, different kinds of paper (with and without lines), envelopes, stamps or stickers, computer with appropriate (open-ended, interactive) writing software
Materials for reading	Assorted published books (picture books, wordless books, predictable format books, poetry books, alphabet books, information books, folktale books), homemade and child-made books, photo books (including pictures of children, their families, the classroom, field trips, special events), recorded stories and equipment for listening, beanbag chair, pillows
Sand and Water Area Materials	
Materials for a water table	Plastic cars and trucks, kitchenware (pans, dishes, silverware), plastic tubing, squeeze bottles, siphon and pump, funnels, measuring cups and spoons, smocks, snow, ice cubes, shaving cream
Materials for a sand table	Shovels, spoons, sifters and strainers, Styrofoam packing peanuts, sawdust, wood shavings, pine needles, birdseed, materials also found in water table
Movement and Music Area Materials	
Equipment	Music players, music representing a variety of musical styles and cultures, microphone, earphones
Instruments	Percussion instruments (e.g., drums, tambourines, triangles, maracas, sandpaper blocks, cymbals, bells, xylophones), wind instruments (e.g., whistles, slide whistles, kazoos, harmonicas)
Props for dancing	Scarves, ribbons, hoops, sticks
Woodworking Area Materials	
Tools	Claw hammers, saws, hand drills, screwdrivers, pliers, vises, C-clamps, sandpaper, safety goggles
Fasteners	Nails, golf tees, screws, nuts, bolts, washers, wire, wood glue
Wood and building materials	Wood pieces and scraps, Styrofoam pieces, bottle caps and jar lids (for wheels), dowel-rod pieces
Outdoor Area Materials	
Stationary structures	Climbers, raised areas (platforms, hills, boulders, tree stumps, snow and dirt piles), swings, slides, balances (balance beam, railroad ties, rows of bricks in different patterns)
Wheeled toys	Tricycles, scooters, wagons, wheelbarrow, push vehicles with steering wheels, strollers, carriages
Loose materials	Jumping equipment (inner tubes, leaf piles, ropes to jump over), throwing and kicking equipment (balls, beanbags, low basketball hoop and net, pails, bull's eye or other targets), building materials (boards, cardboard boxes, twine, old sheets and blankets, small sawhorses, tires and inner tubes, workbench and tools), sand materials (sand pit or table), water materials (water table, spigot, hose, flexible tubing), gardening equipment, role-play props, musical instruments, art materials (*Note:* Many materials for the art, house, sand and water, and movement and music areas can be used outdoors)

cultural and linguistic diversity of the children in your program. Equipment and materials can also portray such realities as disabilities and differences in a family's makeup. So, for example, there might be weaving supplies, folk or traditional music popular in the local community, stuffed or plastic "house pets," books in different languages, crutches, eyeglasses with the lenses removed, and work clothes from jobs held by the children's parents. See "Family Diversity Classroom Checklist" on page 46.

▲ 3. Storage and labeling promote the find-use-return cycle

A central principle of the HighScope learning environment is that children should be able to find, use, and return the materials they need on their own (called the **find-use-return cycle**). Labeled interest areas, organized by function, help children figure out where materials are likely to be located. Labels on areas and materials further help children find what they need and return things when they are done using them.

This basic feature of all HighScope classrooms lets children take the initiative and act with independence in carrying out their plans. Organized and labeled materials also help children develop concepts about how things can be grouped by appearance, function, and other features. To help children in these ways, use the following guidelines to store and label materials:

Store similar items together. Storing things that go together in the same area helps children find and return the things they need in their play. For example, store painting, drawing, and sculpting supplies in the art area. When similar materials are located near one another (e.g., markers, tape, and string kept on adjacent shelves), children can think about different alternatives for carrying out their ideas or solving problems.

Use containers children can see into and handle. Containers with open tops or see-through sides make it easy for children to find what they need. Choose containers of a size and shape that small hands can manage. Place containers on low shelves or on the floor so children can reach them easily. Some materials, such as blocks, can be stacked or stored directly on floors or shelves.

Label containers in ways that make sense to children. As with classroom areas, label materials with simple names that are easy for children to understand. Also, as with areas, label materials and their containers in a variety of ways that reflect different stages of children's literacy development. For example, include words, drawings, tracings, photos, and examples of the actual objects. Young children enjoy deciding where new materials should go and making labels for them. Involving children in making labels for new materials encourages the children to focus on the features of the materials as they draw, trace, or represent them in other ways. Invite children who are writing words to make the labels that use words. See "Labeling Areas and Materials" on page 47.

Labeled materials help children find, use, and return the materials they need on their own.

The Outdoor Learning Environment

Young children like and need to be outdoors, where they are freer to move and make noise than indoors. In addition to helping them develop large-motor skills such as climbing and running, being outdoors gives children opportunities to design and build things on a larger scale than in

Family Diversity Classroom Checklist

To evaluate how well a classroom reflects the diversity of children's home cultures, HighScope teachers use the following checklist to examine the different areas of the classroom.

Art Area

___ Paint, crayons, and paper mirror the skin colors of people in the school and community.

___ Other art materials reflect the arts and crafts found in the community.

Block Area

___ Toy people are multiracial and without sex-role stereotyping.

___ Animal figures represent house pets and farm animals found in the local area.

___ Toy vehicles represent real vehicles found in the community.

Reading and Writing Area

___ Books include writing in children's home language(s).

___ Books depict a variety of racial, ethnic, and cultural groups.

___ Books avoid negative racial, ethnic, cultural, and gender stereotypes.

___ Books represent a variety of family situations.

___ Books show children and adults with special needs, portrayed as real people who happen to have disabilities, not as objects of pity.

House Area

___ Multiracial boy and girl dolls have appropriate skin color, hair, and facial features.

___ House area mirrors the style and content of homes in the community.

___ Kitchen utensils and food containers reflect family's food preparation and eating habits.

___ Dress-up clothing reflects local styles and the occupations of children's families.

___ Equipment used by people with special needs, preferably child sized, is available for role play.

Movement and Music Area

___ Music and instruments reflect children's cultures.

___ Movement games and dance steps reflect children's cultures.

Toy Area

___ Puzzles depict familiar community settings and activities.

___ Puzzles represent the occupations of children's family members and other community members.

___ Toy figures and puzzles depict multiracial people and avoid sex-role stereotypes.

the classroom. The outdoor environment is also a place for children to appreciate nature; experience variations in light, temperature, and wind; and enjoy different sights, sounds, smells, and textures. Children with one or more sensory disabilities may especially benefit from the heightened experience outdoors.

Outdoor play spaces are best located on open land or in a yard next to the school building. This allows children to go in and out quickly and safely and to move appropriate materials from one location to another. If your program is located in a city, you may not have this option, in which case a nearby park or open field will do. A rooftop area may be suitable for an outdoor space, provided it has high walls and smooth surfaces that make it safe for young children to play.

If your setting shares outdoor space with older children, designate separate areas for each age group. Choose equipment and materials that can be easily moved. Schedule each age group to use the space at different times so all children can move about safely and freely.

Your program's outdoor space, just like its indoor space, should have separate areas for different types of play. There should be areas for vigorous activities such as running, riding wheeled toys, climbing, and sliding. There should also be places for quieter, focused play, such as digging, building things, drawing with chalk or water on

Labeling Areas and Materials

Labels or signs help children find what they need to carry out their plans, solve the problems they encounter in play, and return things when they are done using them. When children can take care of these needs themselves, it frees teachers to spend their time in more meaningful interactions with their students. Below are some pointers for making labels (or signs) for areas and materials.

- Use names and labels that make sense to young children (e.g., *toys* rather than *manipulatives*).
- Create labels that children can understand, such as using the material itself (e.g., a paintbrush taped to a piece of cardboard), tracings, drawings, catalog pictures, photos, and photocopies.
- Involve children in making labels for new materials. This encourages them to focus on their properties. Children who are writing can make a word label for an area or material.
- Write words in large, clear letters.
- Cover labels on both sides with clear contact paper or clear tape. This makes them easy to attach to shelves or containers (e.g., with loops of masking tape). They can also be moved easily when it is time to make room for new materials.

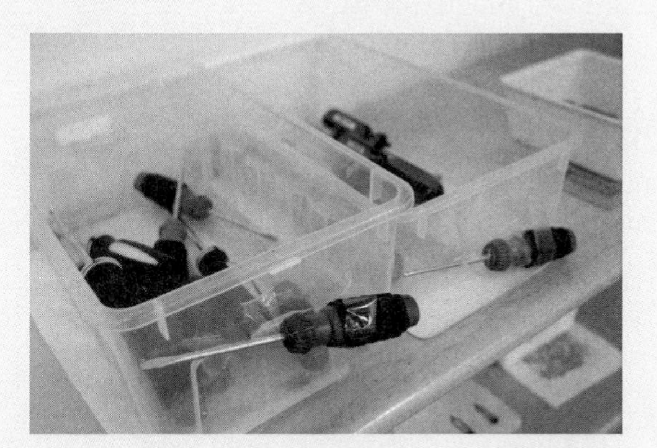

One way to create a label that children will understand is to use the actual material itself, for example, a screwdriver taped to the container that holds this tool.

pavement, or telling or acting out stories. There are several ways that you can mark and separate these areas using low barriers or different surface materials. For example, the area for wheeled toys needs a hard surface, while pea gravel or wood chips work well under swings and slides. You can also use naturally occurring boundaries, such as trees, shrubs, flower beds, or low stone walls, to differentiate outdoor spaces.

Outdoor materials also need storage space. A locked outdoor shed is preferable for wheeled toys. You can store smaller materials in portable containers with handles, such as plastic tubs or baskets, that children can carry back and forth from the classroom to the outdoor play space.

Finally, safety is always an important consideration in outdoor play spaces. HighScope identifies four key factors in keeping children safe when they play outdoors: adult supervision; equipment that is age- and size-appropriate (and accommodates children with special needs); impact-absorbing surfaces; and well-maintained equipment. Check local licensing requirements and the US Product Safety Commission for current safety guidelines.

Try These Ideas Yourself

1. Observe your own or another early childhood classroom. If possible, take photos. How would you rearrange the room to better promote active learning? Draw a diagram of the modified room arrangement, and briefly describe how or why it improves on the original setup.

2. Visit an early childhood classroom when the children are not there. Spend an hour playing with the toys and materials. (Remember to clean up afterward!) Think about what you did and did not enjoy playing with and why. (*Variation:* Do this activity with one or more friends. Compare the materials you each enjoyed playing with. Which materials lent themselves to solitary, parallel, or cooperative play? What were the benefits of each type of play?)

3. Pretend you just received a $15,000 grant to design and furnish a new preschool classroom

and outdoor space. Draw a diagram of the new room and the outdoor play space. List the materials you will use to furnish each area, including open-ended, found, and real-life materials. Identify which items you will buy (look at school supply catalogs but don't forget garage sales and thrift shops) and those you can build, collect, or recycle from existing supplies and donations.

4. Visit a neighborhood playground and observe the play of children aged three to five. What equipment and activities are they most engaged with? What are they doing? What makes that particular equipment or activity appealing to them? What are they learning as they play?

Children develop their gross-motor skills, such as running and climbing, in the outdoor learning environment.

Chapter 7

What Is the HighScope Daily Routine?

Think About It

Your early morning weekday routine is to get up at 6:00 a.m., take a 45-minute walk, shower at 7:00 a.m. and get dressed, eat breakfast at 7:20 a.m., pack lunch at 7:50 a.m., and leave for work at 8:00 a.m. when you can catch your favorite news show on the car radio.

A houseguest arrives on Sunday evening to spend the week. Monday morning when you return from your walk, your guest is in the shower. You discover the yogurt you were planning to have for breakfast has been eaten, as has the fruit you were going to pack for lunch. When you finally leave the house half an hour behind schedule, you discover your guest's car is blocking yours in the driveway. Although you are looking forward to a planned change in routine tonight — the appreciative guest is taking you out to dinner — right now you feel totally discombobulated.

Routines allow us to be organized and efficient and give us a sense of control. When we follow a routine, we are less likely to forget things or make careless errors. Routines are also comforting. We know what to expect and worry less about unwanted "surprises." Children need routines for the same reasons adults do, especially since so many daily events are beyond their control. When children can predict the order and content of their day, they feel both reassured and empowered.

Of course children, like adults, can also be overscheduled. Their days may be crammed with too many events so there isn't enough time to extend enjoyable or complex activities, while tedious ones cannot be skipped or shortened. Thus, schedules and routines require careful planning and must take into account the full range of our physical, intellectual, personal, and interpersonal needs.

Daily routines in HighScope programs are designed to provide consistency and predictability with enough flexibility so that children feel neither rushed nor slowed down in carrying out their activities. Most important, children make choices — within reasonable limits — during each part of the day. Because activities build on their interests and abilities, and because they know they have a say in the learning experience, children in HighScope programs feel that the daily routine belongs to them. They enjoy learning it and following it. In fact, when visitors or new children come to the classroom, children who are "old hands" and eager to show them the ropes often begin by leading them through each part of the day's schedule.

Overview of the HighScope Daily Routine

The HighScope **daily routine** is the order of the day's events, each with a specified amount of time. This schedule is the same every day, which is what makes it *routine,* although time periods are occasionally altered to accommodate children's interests and there are exceptions for field trips, celebrations, or other special activities.

Chapter Learning Objectives

By the end of this chapter, you will be able to

- Explain the importance of routine in the lives of children as well as adults.
- Identify the basic components of the HighScope daily routine.
- Support young children as they plan, carry out, and review their activities (use the plan-do-review cycle).
- Act as a partner in different types of children's play.
- Define and plan for different types of small- and large-group experiences in the classroom, based on children's interests.
- Implement strategies that can make outside time an effective learning experience for young children.
- Turn transitions into positive learning experiences for children.

The daily routine provides consistency and predictability with enough flexibility so that children feel neither rushed nor slowed down in carrying out their activities.

Just as the HighScope learning environment organizes space, the daily routine organizes time. In addition to giving children a sense of control and allowing them to act independently, the regular organization of the day's events helps them develop important concepts about sequence (the order of events) and duration (how long something lasts). These concepts play a central role in early mathematics and scientific thinking. See "HighScope Preschool Daily Routine Components" on page 51.

The largest part of the HighScope day, generally over an hour in total, is devoted to a sequence of **planning time, work time,** and **recall time,** called **plan-do-review.** Meeting in a small group, each child decides what to do during work time — what area to play in, what materials to use, and who else will be involved — and shares this plan with an adult and possibly other children in his or her group. Work time is when children carry out their plans, alone and/or with others, and then clean up. At recall time, they meet with the same adult and small group of children with whom they planned to share and discuss what they did and learned during work time.

A HighScope program day also includes **large-group times** — those times when the entire class does something together. These occur not only during large-group time itself but also during other daily routine segments such as greeting time (including message board), outdoor time, and transitions. **Small-group times** (in addition to planning and recall) that take place outside small-group time include meals or snacks. Small-group activities involve the whole class but are carried out in smaller groups. Children meet with

Terms Used in This Chapter

• daily routine • plan-do-review (planning time, work time, recall time) • large-group times • small-group times • transitions • exploratory play • constructive play • pretend play • games

HighScope Preschool Daily Routine* Components

Greeting time/message board (5–10 minutes)
Planning time (10–15 minutes)
Work time (45–60 minutes)
Cleanup time (10 minutes)
Recall time (10–15 minutes)
Large-group time (10–15 minutes)
Small-group time (15–20 minutes)
Outside time (30–40 minutes)
Transition times, including arrival and departure (variable)
Eating and resting times (variable)

*The order of components may vary, depending on the hours and structure of the program. However, planning time, work time, cleanup time, and recall time always occur in that order. In half-day programs, each component typically happens once. In full-day programs, one or more components may be repeated.

the same adult and set of classmates for all small-group activities. This arrangement provides continuity and security for children and also allows the adult to develop a thorough knowledge of each child in his or her group over time.

In part-day programs, each segment of the daily routine typically happens once, except for **transitions,** which happen between segments. Full-day programs may repeat one or more segments and include additional meals and naptime. (See p. 52 for sample daily routines for part- and full-day programs.) The remainder of this chapter describes each of these program components and how to support children's initiative and learning during them.

The Importance of the Daily Routine

A predictable sequence of events, with room to make choices within that routine, offers the following benefits to children and adults in HighScope programs:

Creates a sense of security and control. A consistent routine means children know what to expect each day. Since child care or preschool is generally a young child's first separation from family and home, predictability provides comfort during this physical and emotional transition. Children are confident they won't face unwelcome surprises or arbitrary demands. If there are occasional changes in the routine, children know they will be told ahead of time what they are and why they are taking place, so they can prepare for these exceptions to the rule.

Consistency is especially important for children whose home lives may not be stable or organized. A Seattle teacher put it this way: "The child who comes from a chaotic home environment may have very little understanding of routine. The low self-esteem that comes from this kind of powerlessness is exactly the reason why elements of HighScope, such as giving choices and planning one's own activities, are so important for our children. Gradually the child will discover in himself the ability to make a plan and will begin to get satisfaction from the things he can accomplish through his own planning and exploration."

Supports initiative. Although a routine defines the type of activity in each segment of the day, it does not dictate or limit what children can do during that time. Within this set framework, children know they will have choices. These options are most obvious during plan-do-review, when children carry out their intentions. However, even during adult-planned group times, children have choices and follow their individual interests at their own developmental level.

Provides a social community. When people do the same thing at the same time, it creates a bond between them. Even though children pursue the same activity in individual ways, they are still sharing a common experience. As an example, think of eating at a restaurant with family and friends. People often order different dishes from the menu, but they may sample one another's choices and discover something new they like. Conversations sometimes involve the whole group, and at other times, pairs and small groups. While each person's dining experience is somewhat different, everyone shares the sense of adventure and togetherness.

Provides a framework for adults to observe and plan. A consistent routine helps adults understand and meet children's needs. Teachers can observe and think about children's needs and interests during each part of the day, every day.

Sample Daily Routine

Arrival & Departure Pattern	Half-Day Program	Full-Day Program
Children arrive and depart at the same time 	◆ Greeting time, message board ◆ Planning, work, cleanup, recall ◆ Snack ◆ Large-group time ◆ Small-group time ◆ Outside time ◆ Departure	◆ Greeting time, breakfast, message board ◆ Large-group time ◆ Planning, work, cleanup, recall ◆ Small-group time ◆ Outside time ◆ Lunch ◆ Books and rest ◆ Snack ◆ Outside time and departure
Children arrive and/or depart at different times 	◆ Small-group time for early arrivers ◆ Greeting time, message board ◆ Planning, work, cleanup, recall ◆ Snack ◆ Outside time ◆ Large-group time ◆ Small-group time for late departers	◆ Breakfast/free play/outside time at arrival ◆ Greeting time, message board ◆ Planning, work, cleanup, recall ◆ Outside time and snack ◆ Small-group time ◆ Large-group time ◆ Lunch ◆ Singing, rest ◆ Outside time and snack ◆ Planning, work, cleanup, recall with parents
Variations 	◆ Small-group time for early arrivers ◆ Greeting time, message board ◆ Ballet/outside time ◆ Snack and planning ◆ Planning, work, cleanup, recall ◆ Large-group time ◆ Small-group time for late departures	◆ Breakfast/free play/outside time at arrival ◆ Greeting time, message board ◆ Planning, work, cleanup, recall ◆ Outside time and snack ◆ Visiting artists ◆ Large-group time ◆ Lunch ◆ Singing and rest ◆ Outside time and snack ◆ Planning, work, cleanup, recall with parents

> "The plan-do-review routine creates more interdependent relationships between adults and children in our setting, compared to last year. Plan-do-review sets up a required child-adult interaction that establishes patterns of reflection, critical to long-term successful learning and living. Merely selecting and playing without recall lacks a vital element for growth and development."
>
> — Teacher, Dayton, Ohio

Since each segment is unique — with its own content, tempo, and social patterns — adults can plan for many types of learning to occur.

Plan-Do-Review

The plan-do-review process is both a critical and unique part of the HighScope Preschool Curriculum. It involves all the elements of active participatory learning.

The abilities children develop as they take initiative, solve problems independently, work with others, and build knowledge and skills carry over into their subsequent schooling and even their lifetime patterns of thought and action.

▲ Planning time

Planning time, which takes about 10–15 minutes, begins the plan-do-review sequence. When young children plan, they begin with an intention or purpose. Depending on their age and ability to communicate, they express their plan in actions (e.g., picking up a paintbrush), gestures (e.g., pointing to the art area), or words (e.g., "I'm going to make a painting of my house").

In order to plan, children must be able to hold in their minds a picture of something that is not actually present or that has not yet happened. Planning is different from simply making a choice, because it involves children in developing specific ideas about what they want to do and how they will do it. In other words, planning involves more purpose and intentionality than choosing. Infants and young toddlers *make choices,* while older toddlers and preschools begin to *plan*.

Young children can quickly change their plans, and often do as they carry out their ideas or get interested in what someone else is doing. This is similar to adults who alter their plans depending on how a sequence of events unfolds. Therefore, children are not required to stick to their initial plans or criticized for not completing them. Instead, adults follow up with children at work time and help them express a new plan. Children may also complete their initial plan and then, with adult encouragement, come up with a next plan to continue their work-time activity.

HighScope was the first comprehensive curriculum model to include planning by children as a major component. Today, planning is recognized as an important activity in the Head Start Program Performance Standards and the best practices advocated by the National Association for the Education of Young Children and other professional organizations. Planning provides the following developmental benefits to young children:

Encourages children to communicate their ideas, choices, and decisions. Because adults value their plans, children are eager and motivated to share them.

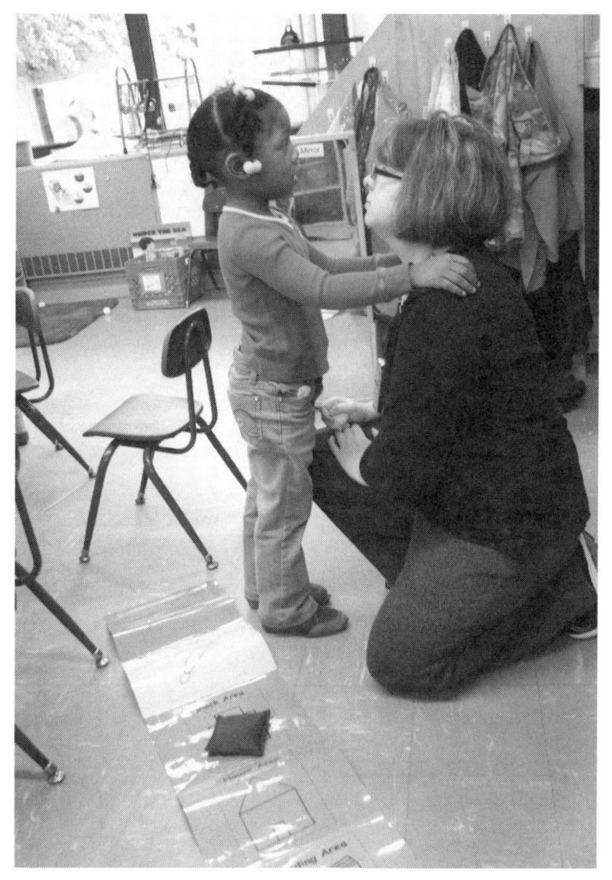

At planning time, children express their intentions about the materials, actions, people, and ideas they want to include in their work-time activities.

The HighScope Daily Routine

Greeting Time

Plan ⇨ Do ⇨ Review

Planning Time

Work Time

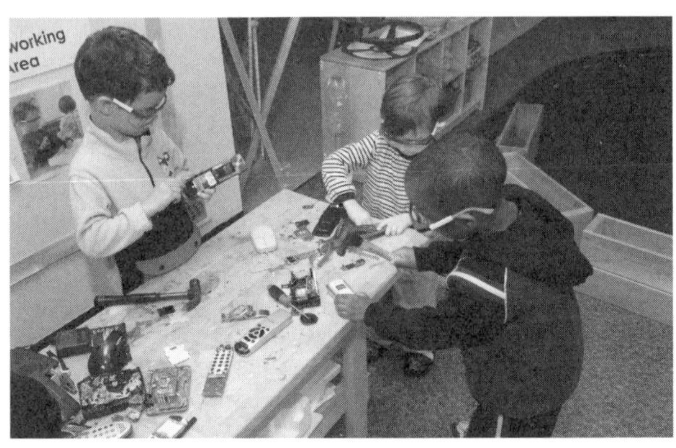

Cleanup Time

Recall Time

Large-Group Time

Small-Group Time

Outside Time

Snacks and Meals

Transitions

Supporting Children at Planning Time

Consider This...
Think about your own ideas about child planning.
Many adults are enthusiastic about child planning because they know children learn best by carrying out their own ideas. Others are skeptical, fearing they will lose control of the classroom or children will repeat the same simple activities without learning school-readiness basics. Research shows these fears are not justified (Sylva, Smith, & Moore, 1986). Children who plan become more purposeful in their play and responsible for the consequences of their actions. Further, hearing others plan exposes children to a wider range of experiences than more controlled settings.

You can use these strategies to help support planning:

Plan with children in an intimate setting. Planning can occur at a table, on the floor, on the couch — wherever children feel comfortable sharing their ideas with an adult. It helps children focus if planning occurs in the same place every day, although an occasional variation (e.g., planning outside) keeps the activity fresh. The smaller the number of children in the group (typically one adult with 5–10 children, although 6–8 children is ideal), the more detailed children's plans tend to be. To make the process relaxed, be patient and plan where people and materials are easily visible

Provide materials and experiences to maintain children's interest in planning time. Use props, partners, playfulness, and novelty so planning does not become mechanical and boring. Let children introduce their own games or variations. Children can also begin to plan with each other (and may make more detailed plans with another child than they do with an adult).

Converse with individual children about their plans. Give each child an opportunity to express a plan. Put equal time and effort into eliciting each child's ideas, whether these are communicated verbally or nonverbally. First, ask "what" questions that are simple and open ended (e.g., "What would you like to do today?"). If children are reluctant to express plans, gently figure out why (e.g., a child may want to play with another but is afraid of not being accepted). By not pushing, an adult can often get the child to open up so together they can problem-solve ways to overcome any barriers to planning. Second, listen attentively as the child's plan emerges. Although some children respond directly to questions or games, others plan indirectly. For example, at planning time, Janice told her teacher about her new brother. By listening to Janice talk about the hospital, the baby, and her daddy making breakfast, the teacher helped Janice make a plan to bathe dolls in the house area, cook sand pancakes, and put the dolls to bed. Finally, offer alternatives when children do not respond, based on their interests. For example, to a child who often worked in the art area, you might say, "Yesterday, you made a painting." If the child nods, you might ask, "Would you like to work in the art area again today or in a different area?" The child might nod again or point to a different area. You would then comment, "So your plan is to work in the art area" or "Today you're going to the book area."

Special Planning Games and Experiences
Ideas for planning time might include

- Taking a tour around the room or making a "train" that goes from one interest area to another, allowing children to make plans when they arrive at an area where they want to play.
- Rolling a ball from child to child as each one plans.
- Making up rhymes with children's names to indicate who plans next.
- Using props such as phones or puppets to initiate planning.
- Taking dictation from children.
- Having children draw pictures, or write down letters and words involved with their plans.

Whatever the idea, be sure all children can understand and perform it in a way consistent with their development. Never use these planning experiences as a "test" of children's knowledge.

Promotes children's self-confidence and sense of control. Children come to rely on their own capacity to make decisions, solve problems, and turn their ideas into reality.

Leads to involvement in and concentration on play. People are more committed to things they choose to do than things imposed on them by others. Researchers Carla Berry and Kathy Sylva (1987), studying HighScope programs in Great Britain, found that children who planned played more purposefully and concentrated for longer periods of time than those who did not plan.

Supports the development of increasingly complex play. Planned play is unlike ordinary play, which tends to be repetitive, random, and aimless. When children carry out their plans, they play with "more imagination, concentration, and intellectual complexity" than when they engage in ordinary, unplanned play (Berry & Sylva, 1987, p. 34). Children are also more likely to set goals and learn new knowledge and skills when they plan and engage in complex play.

It's important to remember that children's planning will change over time. Although each child handles the planning process differently, it is useful to keep in mind these basic principles:

Children's plans become more complex and detailed as children develop. Younger children and new planners may simply point to an area or express a plan in one or two words. Older children and experienced planners can create very elaborate plans.

Planning is an adult-child partnership. The child supplies ideas and intentions, and the adult encourages the child to think about how he or she will carry them out. Through give-and-take communication, the adult helps the child express plans in gestures and words, depending on the child's capabilities. Thus, planning is a shared process that involves cooperation.

Planning is just the beginning. A child's plan is a starting point. Once he or she expresses a set of intentions, the next step is to carry them out during work time with adult support and encouragement. See "Supporting Children at Planning Time" on page 56 for more ideas.

▲ Work time

Work time — the *do* of plan-do-review — is when children carry out their plans. This part of the daily routine generally lasts 45–60 minutes. The expression "play is a child's work" is consistent with the HighScope Curriculum, and calling this segment *work time* captures this philosophy. Many early childhood programs have a similar period they call free-choice time. However, work time is often more purposeful because children have thought about and described their intentions beforehand. They encounter interesting challenges and solve problems in the course of their play. Based on their developmental level and interests, preschoolers typically engage in four types of play: **exploratory play, constructive play, pretend play,** and **games.** Exploratory play usually develops first, followed by constructive and pretend play, and finally games (Bergen, 1988a,1988b). However, any child at any point may be involved in one or more types of play.

Work time provides the following benefits to young children:

Allows children to carry out intentions and play with purpose. Work time is when children put their ideas into action. They see themselves as *doers,* capable of following through on a plan and achieving their goals.

Enables children to participate in a social setting. As they work, children naturally come together in pairs and groups of different sizes. Even children who choose to work alone are aware of the presence and activities of those around them.

Provides many opportunities to solve problems. Because children are engaged in ac-

At work time, children carry out their plans with interest and a sense of purpose. They learn through hands-on experience and by solving problems with people and materials that arise during their play.

tivities they have defined for themselves, they are likely to meet up with unexpected problems — for example, a piece of paper may be too big to fit in the envelope or two children may want the same truck. As children develop solutions, either alone or with assistance from adults and playmates, they come to see themselves as competent problem solvers.

Enables children to construct their own knowledge and build new skills. As children carry out their plans and solve problems, they develop a new understanding of the world of things and people; they expand their knowledge and skills in literacy, math, science, art, music, and so on (see the HighScope key developmental indicators listed on p. 12 and discussed in chapters 10–17).

Allows adults to observe, learn from, and support children's play. By observing, supporting, and entering children's play, adults gain insight into each child's development.

See "Supporting Children at Work Time" on pages 59–60 for additional strategies.

▲ Recall time

HighScope programs have a designated *recall time,* which lasts 10–15 minutes, and immediately follows the work- and cleanup-time sequence. During recall time, adults encourage children to reflect on their actions and what they have learned throughout the day. For preschoolers, it is easiest to remember when recall happens close to the actual event. Younger preschoolers often recall the last thing they did, since it is freshest in their minds. As children become able to hold images and ideas in their minds for longer periods and in greater detail, they are more apt to recall the sequence of what they did at work time and may even recall their original plans.

We noted previously that planning time differs from ordinary free choice because planning involves purpose and intention. Similarly, recall is different from simple remembering because children take time to think not only about what they did but also about what they learned. Further, they share these observations with the teacher and group of children with whom they planned, which supports the development of thinking and language. If children draw or write down what they did, they are also representing their activities in ways that help develop literacy skills. Finally, as the last step in the plan-do-review process, recall makes it more likely that the lessons children learn will last and be applied to future actions and interactions. To summarize, recall time provides the following benefits:

Exercises children's capacities to form and talk about mental images. Recall encourages children to mentally picture and express their ideas about past events.

Consolidates children's understanding of experiences and events. Recall helps children examine their choices and actions and the effects these had on objects and people (themselves and others).

Extends children's consciousness beyond the present. Preschoolers live in the present. By helping them think about past events and how they were affected by them, we enable them to build on what they've already learned and apply it to new experiences and subject matter.

Makes children's experiences public. Recall is a form of social interaction. During recall, children are narrators, telling a "story" about what happened to them at work time (which means they are also the stars). As preschoolers mature, they become more open to other children adding details to their recollections and enhance the "stories" told by others as well. In these ways, recall becomes a shared undertaking that helps children develop a sense of trust.

For more suggestions, see "Supporting Children at Recall Time" on page 61.

Group Times

Although plan-do-review is a major part of the HighScope daily routine, children also benefit from a variety of other regular group experiences. These scheduled parts of the day include *small-group time, large-group time, outside time,* and *transition times.*

Small- and large-group times for preschoolers each generally last about 15 minutes. During these times, adults introduce children to new materials, ideas, and activities, which the children can then continue to explore at work time. Group experiences also offer many opportunities for social interaction. At outside time, which runs at least 30 minutes, children work with equipment and enjoy a range of physical activity not possible indoors.

Supporting Children at Work Time

Consider This...

Think about your own ideas about how children learn.

In HighScope programs, the learning that happens during work time depends on participants' being active; that is, teachers neither direct the learning with children passively taking in the information *nor* do teachers withdraw and let children take all the responsibility for their own education. Instead, children pursue self-initiated interests and plans while adults become involved in their play and scaffold their learning using adult-child interaction strategies.

To ensure work time is a satisfying educational experience, use the following support strategies:

Provide work places and materials based on children's interests. Because work time generally occurs in the program's interest areas, make sure these areas are easily accessible and contain a wide range of age-appropriate materials.

Offer children comfort and contact as needed. Sometimes children need adult reassurance about their feelings or ideas. Be alert to children's signs indicating that they need immediate attention before they can proceed with their plans. A child may express anxiety through gestures (e.g., shaking the head "no"), actions (e.g., withdrawing to a corner), or words (e.g., "No one wants to play with me"). In these instances, you might offer reassuring physical contact by sitting next to the child, rocking or stroking, and so on.

Acknowledge children's actions and accomplishments. Sometimes children need adults to simply take notice of what they did. You might offer a simple acknowledgment by looking at something a child has done, imitating a child's actions (e.g., moving in the same way to a song), or repeating a child's comment (e.g., "Yes, I see you made a tall tower with those blocks").

Participate in children's play. Joining in children's play lets them know that you think their interests and intentions are important. However, adults need to participate without taking over. When participating as a partner in children's play:

- *Look for natural play openings.* Explore materials alongside the child, take on a role assigned by a child in pretend play, or take a turn in a child-directed or -invented game.
- *Play as a partner with children.* Being a partner means acting as a follower and equal, not as a director. Therefore, adjust your speech and actions to the ideas and pace of the play, take directions from children, and follow the rules set by the group of players.
- *Join play on the children's level.* By seeing things from children's perspective, adults are less likely to take over the play situation. If, for example, you are playing with children who are mixing Legos in a bowl to make "soup," you might begin by getting another spoon and stirring the pot, rather than adding new ingredients to the mixture.
- *Play in parallel.* Playing in parallel means playing near a child and using the same materials in the same or a similar manner (e.g., rolling out play dough or filling and emptying containers with sand).
- *Suggest ideas within the play situation.* While being careful not to raise the level of complexity of children's play, you may offer suggestions to extend it. To avoid crossing that fine line between extending and directing play, try offering suggestions within the theme of the play rather than introduce a new theme (Smilanksy, 1971). For example, an adult could join the other "mothers" bringing babies to the doctor for a checkup rather than pretend there is a medical emergency.

Converse with children. Conversations help children express their ideas, build vocabulary, and develop other language skills that are important in early literacy development. The strategies for talking naturally with children are similar to those for entering into their play. Adults need to take their cues from children and be sensitive to times when conversation is welcome (e.g., when a child eagerly talks about a painting he or she is making). At other times, talking may interfere with a child's activities (e.g., if the child is concentrating on adding specific details to the picture).

To help children develop their thinking and language skills without inhibiting their actions, look for natural opportunities for conversation, talk at the children's physical level, give children a chance to begin conversations, converse in a give-and-take manner, and limit questions.

Supporting Children at Work Time (cont.)

Encourage children's problem solving. Sometimes adults mistakenly believe that children should exist in a problem-free environment. Solving problems, however, is one of the most important experiences children can have during work time. In fact, children enjoy posing and solving problems. You can help children encounter these developmentally important experiences by waiting patiently for children to do things for themselves, referring children to one another for help, and seeing yourself as a partner rather than as a manager.

Observe and record what children do. Adults in HighScope programs make plans to support and extend learning based on what children do and say. With so much going on at work time, it is often difficult to remember everything that went on for each child. Therefore, as you work and play with children, jot down notes to help you recall details later during team planning.

Bring work time to an end with cleanup time. Teachers sometimes dread cleanup time. If they see it as an unpleasant chore, however, children are likely to pick up a negative and resistant attitude. But if you approach cleanup time as an opportunity to solve problems ("I wonder where we can hang this to dry?"), learn something (such as how materials are organized and arranged), and even have fun (inventing put-away games, using mops and sponges, reciting rhymes and chants), then children learn that this last part of work time is a natural step in carrying out one's plans.

Adults can also make cleanup time easier on everyone if their expectations for children are realistic. Children can do things to the best of their ability, but that is not the same as meeting adult standards for health and equipment maintenance. Teachers, janitorial staff, and/or other staff will need to finish the process between program sessions. Rather than emphasizing perfection, help children complete cleanup quickly so they can immediately proceed to reviewing and evaluating their work-time activities.

Transitions are the times in between the other activities. In HighScope programs, transitions are not seen as incidental but as planned opportunities for children to make choices, move in different ways, and learn important concepts.

During all these other parts of the day, the principles of active participatory learning continue to apply. So, even though adults plan large- and small-group times around specific content, they base them on children's wide-ranging interests, encourage children to make choices about how they use the materials, and talk with children about what they are doing and learning. Group times also offer all children the chance to interact with others. This can be especially important for those who choose to work alone during the plan-do-review sequence. HighScope group times are unpressured, so even shy or solitary children can participate in ways that feel comfortable to them.

HighScope teachers put thought and effort into planning group times. Their daily observations help them see what children are interested in and how to further exploration in these areas. Group times are also the parts of the day when learning that needs to be systematic and sequenced — such as skills and concepts in literacy or mathematics — can be guaranteed for all children. To make sure group times provide the maximum intellectual, social, and physical benefit to children, teachers complete a Group-Time Planning Sheet with the information shown on page 62.

▲ Small-group time

During small-group time, the same group of children — typically 5 to 10 individuals, ideally 6 to 8 — meets each day for 15–20 minutes with the same adult. This is also the same grouping that meets for planning and recall time. These stable groups help teachers get to know each child and help the children feel comfortable with one another. (*Note:* In many programs, children also eat with the members of their small group. Snack- or mealtime is discussed briefly at the end of this chapter.)

After the teacher briefly introduces the activity, children are generally given their own set of materials to work with. Teachers also have a set of materials for themselves. Sometimes there are additional materials or tools in large enough quantity for everyone to share. For example, each person

Supporting Children at Recall Time

Consider This…

Think about your own ideas about children recalling.

Recall is successful when children tell their own stories in their own words, gestures, and drawings. The experience can be fun and social and can take many creative forms. If, however, teachers see recall as another time of day to be "gotten through," it can become rote and mechanical. Or, if they mistakenly think recall is a time when children should be held accountable for their plans, it can take on a punitive tone.

The adult's role at recall time is similar to his or her role at planning time. It grows out of observations of, and interactions with, children, based on the children's interests and the principles of active participatory learning. During recall time, use the following strategies to help young children think about and learn from their work-time activities.

Recall with children in a calm, cozy setting. As with child planning, recalling with the same familiar group of people in a consistent place creates a comfortable and trusting situation. The fewer distractions around, the more that children will be able to focus on recalling.

Provide materials and experiences to maintain children's interest in recall. As with planning, props and games keep recall interesting and help children wait their turn. For example, you might "tour" the room to the areas where children played, ask each child to bring an item he or she played with to the recall table, or use digital photos taken at work time to spark conversations about what children did. The materials or activity should be kept simple. Otherwise, children may become so interested in the prop or game (e.g., spinning the hula hoop or calling the next child on the old cell phone), that the purpose of recall is lost.

Converse with children about their work-time experiences. Again, the process of talking to children during recall is similar to that used in planning. Be patient, pay careful attention, and let the ideas unfold naturally from each child. A simple opening question may help, but avoid making the child dependent on adult prompting. Instead, you can make comments and observations to keep the conversation going. For example:

Child: I played in the house area.

Teacher: I saw you with the dolls.

Child: They were taking a bath. I filled the tub with water.

Teacher: You brought water from the sink to the house area.

Child: I took a bucket and filled it up and then I carried it to the bathtub.

Teacher: It looked like you carried lots of water.

Child: About ten-hundred-eight buckets of water. And I didn't spill any!

Teacher: You didn't spill any water. How did you keep from doing that?

Child: I only filled it up to here *(gestures)* so it wouldn't go over the top.

With development and experience, children become more skillful at recall. As you implement various strategies to support children at recall time, remember to stay flexible and observant. As you will also notice at planning time, children will gradually include more detail during recall, tell longer stories, listen to and contribute to the recall of others, and make plans for subsequent days based on what happened that day. The recall process helps them bring closure to their experiences.

may get a pegboard and a basket of pegs, with a large tub of additional pegs in the center of the table for everyone in the group to use as needed. If the activity is something like reading a book or introducing a new piece of computer software, the teacher places or uses the one shared copy where all the children can see, hear, touch, talk about their discoveries, and so on.

As they work with the materials, children make choices about how to use them. They talk with one another and the adult about what they are doing and seeing. The adult works alongside them, observes and comments on the children's actions and thoughts, refers them to one another for ideas and help, acknowledges and encourages each child's efforts, promotes independent

Supporting Children at Small-Group Time

Consider This...

Think about your own ideas about how children learn at small-group time.

Some non-HighScope programs use small-group time to drill children in skills and concepts such as writing letters of the alphabet or learning color names. Adult-directed activities, worksheets, or children copying a craft project from an adult-made example are not part of the HighScope approach. While HighScope adults take the lead planning the small-group activity and providing materials, they realize that each child will respond to the experience differently.

The role of the adult is to support and extend each child's learning, based on the child's developmental level and individual interests. Unlike many other programs, HighScope small-group times do NOT mean that all children do the same thing with the same set of materials. In fact, to verify that a small-group experience is appropriate for every child, HighScope teachers make sure that all the ingredients of active participatory learning are present.

As with other parts of the daily routine, it is important to use a variety of support strategies to make sure children enjoy and learn from small-group experiences. Here are some you can try:

Plan small-group experiences ahead of time. Successful small-group times appeal to children's interests, allow them to engage with materials and ideas at their own developmental level, and promote learning. The following sources will give you a wealth of small-group-time ideas.

- *Children's interests.* Many inspirations come from observing children at work time. For example, if children working in the art area become fascinated with mixing paints, you might plan a small-group time in which each child is given two cups of paint (*one* primary color — red, yellow, or blue — and white), paper, and a brush. Additional cups could be set out so children could pump a second primary color or more white from big plastic jars. You could also set out extra paper and other painting tools (e.g., sticks, sponges, kitchen utensils) to explore.
- *Curriculum content.* Perhaps the members of your teaching team look back through their anecdotal notes and realize children are rarely engaging in certain curriculum content areas. Or you and your coteachers may decide to ensure that every child receives planned and equal opportunities for learning in each area. In either case, you can use small-group time to engage children with materials and activities related to that content area. For example, to focus attention on patterns (an important area of early mathematics), you could provide each child with a cardboard grid and set out piles of small squares in different colors. After demonstrating a pattern on your board, you might say, "I wonder what patterns you can make with these pieces."
- *New, unexplored, underused, or favorite materials.* Small-group time lets you introduce new materials (such as interactive media) or call children's attention to existing materials that are being overlooked (e.g., puzzles in the toy area). It is also a chance to encourage children to approach familiar or favorite materials in new ways (e.g., using toy truck tires to make impressions in play dough).
- *Local traditions and community events.* Children often bring ideas and experiences from outside the classroom into the program. These may originate in their families or the wider community and are a rich source of small-group-time ideas. For example, if several children were to talk about going to the farmer's market with their parents, you might plan a small-group activity to explore the color, shape, smell, texture, taste, and other properties of locally grown fruits and vegetables.
- *Teacher idea books and other curriculum materials.* To get started with small-group activities, some teachers turn to plans that have been designed and tested by experienced HighScope teachers. See, for example, the teacher idea books and related curriculum resources at www.highscope.org.

Supporting Children at Small-Group Time (cont.)

Prepare for small-group time before children arrive. With a plan clearly in mind, HighScope teachers get ready for small-group activities ahead of time, often in the morning before children arrive. This way, children do not have to wait to get started and can make good use of every minute. Getting ready means (1) gathering the necessary materials, often one set for each child and for the teacher, and (2) storing materials in a place where the adult can get them easily and quickly as soon as small-group time begins. This is particularly important since groups generally meet in an area that is also used for other activities.

What to do during each part of small-group time. Use the following steps to guide children through small-group time.

- *Beginning.* Engage children as soon as they arrive at the gathering place. Make a brief introductory statement or offer a simple challenge. For example, you might say, "Today we have boxes in different sizes and some small, medium, and large bears. I wonder what we can do with them" or "Let's see what we can find out about this book by looking at the picture on the cover."
- *Middle.* Once children have begun to work with the materials, the teacher's role is to pay attention to their actions and ideas, scaffold (support and gently extend) further learning, and encourage them to interact with and learn from one another. You can do this by closely attending to each child, physically getting down on his or her level, watching and listening to the child, imitating and building on his or her actions, conversing with the child while following his or her leads, asking questions sparingly, and encouraging the child to solve problems both individually and with assistance from other children.

  Teachers also support children's highly individual use of materials and their observations about what they are doing and learning. In fact, one indication of an effective small-group time is the sheer variety of ideas the children come up with. For example, in the small-group time one teacher planned with dinosaurs and carpet squares, children used the materials in the following ways: sorting dinosaurs and squares by size and/or color; making "dinosaur houses" with the carpet squares; grouping the dinosaurs into families; piling the carpet squares into towers; finding carpet squares big enough to hide different-sized dinosaurs under; making patterns with the carpet squares; and lining up dinosaurs — and then themselves — by size.
- *End.* Letting children know when small-group time is about to end (a two- or three-minute warning) gives them control over how to bring the session to closure. Some may be ready to stop, and others may want to store their projects and materials to continue at work time the following day. Also, although small-group time has a set length, children will nevertheless finish at different times. On any given day, some will finish with the materials and activity quickly, while others will want to linger. Teachers, therefore, schedule the day so children can move to the next segment as they are ready (e.g., getting ready for snack or outside time).

During small-group time, the same group of children meets each day with the same adult. After the adult introduces the activity, children work with their own set of materials in ways they determine themselves.

problem-solving, and assists children as needed in carrying out their intentions. Children often work with the materials or extend their ideas during work time on subsequent days.

Small groups gather at a consistent, designated place each day. By establishing a consistent place, children then know where to go on their own when this part of the daily routine begins. Small-group gathering places might be a table (perhaps the same one used for planning, recall, or snack), the floor in one area of the room, or the couch and chairs in the reading area. If the activity is happening elsewhere that day (e.g., outdoors), the adult and children then move as a group to that location. See "Supporting Children at Small-Group Time" for additional strategies on pages 62–63.

▲ Large-group time

Large-group time is when all children and adults participate in an activity together. There are several whole-class activities throughout the day. In this section, we specifically discuss the segment called *large-group time.* Greeting time, including using the message board, is also conducted with the entire class and is covered briefly at the end of the chapter.

Large-group time, which lasts 10–15 minutes, contributes to the sense of community in the classroom. It is a time when everyone comes together to participate in music and movement activities, storytelling, or other shared physical activities. Like every other part of the HighScope day, the five ingredients of active participatory learning are present at large-group time. There are *materials* for children to *manipulate* (such as props for storytelling, scarves for dancing, their bodies for jumping, or their voices for singing); *children make choices* about how to use the materials or move their bodies; *children talk and think* about their ideas and actions; and *adults scaffold learning* by building on children's interests and knowledge as illustrated in this large-group time:

> *Ursula, a teacher, begins to tell a story about a raft journey and then pauses to invite children to board this imaginary raft with her. Some children decide to gather materials they want to bring with them — cooking utensils from*

Group-Time Planning Sheet

(Use this sheet for small- or large-group time.)

Originating idea: ______________________________

____

(Note the concept, local event, particular material, and/or what you observed children say or do that led to the idea.)

Materials: ______________________________

____

(List the materials you will need, including what and how many.)

Curriculum content: ______________________________

____

(List the main key developmental indicators [KDIs] the activity focuses on and any others that might occur.)

Beginning: ______________________________

____

(Describe how you will introduce the activity to the children, including your opening statement and/or action.)

Middle: ______________________________

____

(Describe what children might do during the activity and how you will support them.)

End: ______________________________

____

(Describe how you will bring the activity to a close.)

Follow-up: ______________________________

____

(Describe the materials and activities you can provide on subsequent days to build on the children's experience with this activity.)

the house area to prepare meals, boards from the block area to build a rain shelter, books to read at bedtime, and stationery and markers to write letters home to their parents.

When everyone is "on board," Ursula opens her bag of spyglasses (empty paper towel tubes). As they "drift out to sea," the rafters call out the sights they "spy." Some are literal ("I see an easel"), while others are imaginative ("There's a whale!"). Ursula acknowledges and supports each child's observations. After escaping some "hungry sharks" and weathering a "bad storm," Ursula says, "I see land. We're almost home." They "dock" the raft and return the items they brought aboard to their appropriate areas. Ursula then says, "That was a long trip; I'm hungry," and children move in different ways to their snack tables.

Large-group meetings require a space that can handle vigorous activity without children hurting themselves or bumping into one another. Programs with enough space may have a permanent gathering area, such as a rug in the middle of the room. In smaller facilities, they may have to move equipment aside to create this space. In warm climates or seasons, the class may gather outside under a tree or on a patio.

The formation of the group depends on the experience planned for that day. In fact, one way teachers can provide enough variety in the large-group experiences they plan is to make sure that they don't all start from the same position. For example, certain games take place in a circle; a movement activity may involve children going from one carpet square to another in different ways; and the use of various props, such as hula hoops, may require that children be spread out widely so they don't bump into one another.

As with small-group activities, large-group time is planned and initiated by adults, but children have many choices. For example, children decide how to move their bodies as they listen to music of different moods and tempos. They can make various motions for others to imitate or suggest a favorite song or rhyme for everyone to sing or recite. Large-group time provides many opportunities for children who want to take turns being the leader. For example, if the group is singing "The Hokey Pokey," a child can choose which body part everyone will put in and take out. Children are never forced to be leaders, but most are eager to have everyone's attention. In fact, children who are otherwise shy or withdrawn may welcome a situation where others naturally listen to them because it is their turn to lead. See "Supporting Children at Large-Group Time" on pages 66–67.

▲ Outside time

During outside time, which lasts 30–40 minutes, children can enjoy physical, noisy, and vigorous play. Rather than standing to the side and just observing, HighScope teachers join children in their outdoor exertions. Being outside also lets children and adults alike connect to the school campus and/or neighborhood community and use all their senses to appreciate nature.

The outdoors is a place where young children can run, jump, throw, kick, swing, climb, dig, and ride. Their pretend play ranges over a wider area than is possible indoors and can incorporate props not found inside (e.g., a tree, the flower bed, a climber, a slide). Outdoor surfaces also provide larger areas for artwork; for example, children can make chalk drawings or water paintings on the pavement and weave yarn and twigs through the lattice of a fence. Additionally, outdoor equipment promotes social play. For example, children face one another through the openings in the climber, and they dig beside one another in the sandbox. Discoveries are also eagerly shared ("Look at the shiny green bug I found!").

In most cases, outside time takes place in a play area on the grounds of the building where the program is located. This space is specifically designed for use by young children, with size and safety taken into account. When programs do not have their own playgrounds, they may use a neighborhood park. If possible, the teachers and children bring loose or free-standing equipment (balls, scarves, bikes, or wagons) to add to the fixtures that are there. Occasionally, especially in inner cities, there may not be a nearby park or one that can be reached safely. In such cases, a rooftop or similar area made safe for young children may suffice. If no outdoor area is available, or the weather is extreme, a gym or other large indoor space can substitute. See "Supporting Children at Outside Time" on page 68 for more ideas.

Supporting Children at Large-Group Time

Consider This...

Think about your own ideas about how children learn at large-group time.

In HighScope programs, large-group time is a segment of the day when adults and children share an experience as partners. It is not a time for the teacher to lecture children, for example, about the weather, the calendar, or the "letter of the week." Preschoolers will generally not sit still for such instruction, and such abstract methods are not appropriate for them. Some teachers may see large-group time as a chance to be the "star," leading the children in a song or entertaining them with a story. However, HighScope's active learning approach recognizes that children need to move and sing and talk, not listen passively to someone else perform these activities. Children and adults both play important and equal roles in large-group time.

The adult's role at large-group time is similar to his or her role at small-group time. Adults provide ideas and/or materials to get things started and then support children's explorations and encourage their ideas. Use the following strategies to help children learn from their activities:

Plan large-group experiences ahead of time. The following sources of ideas will help you plan:

- *Children's interests.* Children will be enthusiastic about large-group time if they are already interested in its focus. Use your observations of what children do at other times of the day to come up with ideas for large-group activities. For example, when the Olympic Games are being broadcast, perhaps you notice at outside time that several children are using the railroad ties in the yard as balance beams. You and your coteacher might then plan a large-group time in which several objects — a long block, a rubber mat, a strip of masking tape on the floor, and a row of carpet squares — can serve as balance beams for the children to walk across.
- *Curriculum content in Physical Development and Health and Creative Arts content areas.* The KDIs in Physical Development and Health and Creative Arts, especially movement, music, and pretend play, are fruitful sources of ideas.

  For example, you might plan a movement activity in which children move their bodies in different ways using scarves, batons, sheets of newspaper, or other portable items. A music-inspired activity could involve children playing various percussion instruments while listening to different types of music. Using props to act out the story in a favorite book is an example of pretend play.
- *Cooperative play and projects.* Whole-group storytelling, dancing, and singing are all good ways to get the classroom community involved. To keep all the children focused, however, make sure that each child has an active role to play. You can encourage this level of involvement by giving everyone an object to manipulate, an individual space in which to move, words to sing, and so on. For example, in making up a group story about a dog and a cat, one teacher gave children two different color socks to put over their hands. Whenever they wanted the dog in the story to say or do something, they would move their red sock, while the cat was represented by the blue sock. Children moved their sock-covered hands in all kinds of ways, inventing roles for the two characters in the story.
- *Events currently meaningful to the children.* Large-group activities built around holidays or other topical events will only work if the children find them meaningful. If they are based on what adults find current (e.g., Groundhog Day or summer vacation), children may not relate to them. Therefore, it is important to first observe what engages children before planning large-group time.

  For example, in one classroom, children were not caught up in Christmas gifts or decorations. However, twins who spent time with their grandmother were interested in her seasonal baking and got other children involved in role playing in the house area. On a field trip, the class visited a bakery where children saw these activities on a large scale and tried them out with their own pieces of dough. Then the teachers planned a large-group time in which children sang a bakery song while they rolled, kneaded, folded, and made other baking-related motions with their bodies.

Supporting Children at Large-Group Time (cont.)

- *Teacher idea books and other curriculum materials.* Teachers sometimes try proven large-group activities and adapt them for use with the children in their own classroom. (For HighScope teacher idea books and related curriculum resources, visit www.highscope.org.) This strategy is useful for new teachers developing confidence in their planning skills, as well as experienced teachers seeking new ideas.

Prepare for large-group time before children arrive. As with small groups, it is important for large-group activities to begin right away. Prepare materials beforehand to avoid having children wait. If you plan to use songs or stories, practice them in advance — both for a smoother performance and also so children aren't distracted by false starts or mistakes that make them lose interest. Check all equipment for proper functioning ahead of time.

What to do during each part of large-group time. Use the following steps to guide children through large-group time.

- *Opener.* Draw the group together with a "starter" activity that children can join as soon as they come to the gathering area; for example, singing the "run-around-the-circle song" and running around the circle or singing a familiar song and doing the hand motions that go with it. Once everyone is assembled, the rest of the planned activity can begin.
- *Activity.* Briefly explain the activity (e.g., "Today let's see how we can move in and out of the tires"). Give props and materials (in this case, inflatable inner tubes) to children immediately and show interest in what they do with them. Encourage children to come up with ideas, ask children who would like a turn as leader, and repeat and follow up on children's suggestions. For example, you might say, "Tim says we should curl up inside our tires, then pop out like space ships" (then everyone tries this action).
- *Transition.* Most of the time you will end large-group time with a transition to the next activity. If the session has been quite physically active, something quieter can help children settle down. The transition can also build on the learning that took place during the large-group time. For example, after children have figured out ways to move in and out of hoops, you might ask them move to their tables for planning time with just one part of their body inside the hoop.

Supporting Children at Outside Time

Consider This...

Think about your own ideas about how children learn at outside time.

To guarantee that children learn actively outside as well as inside, HighScope teachers act as partners in the outdoor setting. Children take the initiative, and adults follow their lead with enthusiasm and energy. Adults don't see this part of the day as their time to relax and chat with one another nor do they direct children in sports or rule-bound games that are inappropriate for young children.

Outside time presents many opportunities for learning, not only in the area of physical growth, but in all the other domains of development as well. There are signs in and around the playground to read, leaves and rocks to arrange by color or size, insects and clouds to study, and social conflicts to resolve about who has the next turn on the slide. To support development in each of the areas, use the following strategies at outside time:

Help children get the materials they need. Playgrounds have permanent structures, and other materials can be stored in an adjacent shed or brought outside from the classroom. With the other members of your teaching team, think of ways to store and easily transport materials (e.g., milk crates, buckets, plastic baskets with handles), to involve children (and sometimes parents) in gathering materials at the end of the day, and to ensure children can get the things they need independently or with minimal assistance.

Use work-time support strategies. The same interaction strategies adults use to support children's indoor play (see pp. 59–60) apply to their outdoor play. Teachers participate as partners, talk to children, and encourage them to solve problems.

Observe nature with children. The outdoors presents children with a whole new environment to explore. Share their discoveries enthusiastically and call their attention to such natural features as the wind, clouds, changing light, air temperature, mud and dirt, snow and ice, different smells and textures, and the wide diversity of plant and animal life. Keep in mind that walks in the neighborhood, field trips to farms and ranches, and strolls along city streets with houses and businesses also increase children's experiences with the outdoors.

Bring outside time to a close. As with other activities, give children a warning when outside time is almost over so they can bring their play to an end. For example, you might announce, "In three minutes, parents will begin to arrive and we'll have to put away the bikes and other toys." Encourage children to help with cleanup, storing portable equipment in the shed or bringing items such as scarves and chalk back into the classroom. When outside time is at the end of the day, parents may assist with cleanup too. If children are reluctant to end their play, you can help them make a plan to continue it the next day.

▲ Transitions

Although transitions happen between other activities, they are important enough to treat as activities in themselves. Transitions include arrivals and departures (discussed on p. 69), and the intervals between each of the daily routine components described previously. In addition to involving a change in activity, transitions may also include a shift in location (e.g., from the greeting circle to a work-time area), materials (from crackers at snacktime to pipe cleaners at small-group time), clothing (adding or removing outerwear), caregiver (if there is a shift change), or playmates (when groupings change between small-group time and large-group time).

Some children take transitions in stride, while others find them stressful. Transitions are often most difficult when children are first getting used to the routine — a child may cry and cling to a parent when beginning school, or he or she may not want work time to end, not yet realizing the same play materials will be available the next day. Generally, once children experience the sense of comfort and inner control that develops from following a consistent routine, transitions are no longer stressful. However, for any child at any time, a transition may be hard. This could be due to fatigue, an ongoing home situation (divorce, a new sibling), or something that happened in school that day (such as a conflict with a peer). (See "Supporting Children During Transitions" on p. 70).

▲ Other group times

The HighScope daily routine also includes other group times, discussed here.

Meal and snacktimes. In most part-day programs, children and adults share a snack, while full-day programs have both meal- and snacktimes. Eating together is generally done in small groups, preferably with the same children who gather together for planning, recall, and small-group time.

The emphasis during snacks and meals is on social interaction. It is important for adults to eat with children, as a natural opportunity to share relaxed conversation and support children's ideas. Teachers should not have a hidden agenda to teach academic skills during mealtimes, although opportunities for teaching and learning often occur naturally. For example, a list indicating whose turn it is to set out the plates and cups can help children develop literacy skills, and children taking a turn will be involved in one-to-one matching of utensils and people who will be eating, which helps develop mathematics skills. Snack- and mealtime are also occasions when children enjoy practicing self-help skills such as pouring their own juice, cutting things into portions (with plastic child-safety knives), folding napkins, wiping up spills, and so on.

Greeting and departure times. Elements of both individual and group activities characterize greeting and departure times. These periods are also transitions, and you can use the transition strategies described previously to help children make the shift from home to school and back again. For arrivals, it is important that each child be welcomed every day by a teacher. When an adult brings a child to school (as opposed to arrivals by van or bus), that adult should also receive a personal hello from a staff member. The same holds true for saying good-bye on a daily basis.

If arrival and departure times are staggered, the teacher helps each child enter into or finish up whatever part of the routine is underway. For example, you may plan with a child so he or she can begin working, or you may help a child put things away and get dressed shortly before a parent is due to pick up the child. If children arrive at the same time, greeting takes on more of the character of a group event; however, it also may happen in various pairings and small groups. For example, children, along with parents who can stay a while, may look at books until the rest of the children arrive. When most of the children depart from the program at the same time, departure is still likely to be more individualized since parents rarely come at the same moment. Nevertheless, since a child is leaving the group as well as the current activity, teachers help the child bring his or her day to a close with a sense of completion.

During message board, children and adults share important information about the day ahead, such as new materials for outside time and the art area.

Message board. Gathering at the message board is a whole-group activity that generally takes place once everyone has arrived. This is a time to share announcements and let children

Supporting Children During Transitions

Consider This...

Think about your own ideas about how children learn during transitions.

Teachers often dread transitions, those times between activities. At best, they are seen as periods to get through quickly so the class can begin the next "real" activity in the daily routine. At worst, transitions become power struggles between children resisting a shift and adults eager to move them along without losing momentum or throwing off the day's schedule. In HighScope programs, by contrast, transitions are seen as real and meaningful activities in themselves. When viewed as educational opportunities — for example, how to solve the problem of storing a work in progress so a child can continue with it the next day — transitions incorporate all the aspects of active participatory learning. Approached with this positive attitude, transitions not only go more smoothly but also allow children and adults to enter into the next activity calmly and eagerly.

To ensure that transitions go as smoothly as possible, and to also make them positive learning experiences, use the following strategies:

Adjust transition times to suit children's developmental needs. As a general rule, the fewer the number of transitions, the better. Preschoolers can more easily remember a daily routine that has fewer components. They can quickly derive comfort and control from its predictability. It also helps to keep changes in location to a minimum. For example, if children begin the day with breakfast, they might then plan at the same table. Within this consistent framework, use your creativity to make transitions fun (e.g., with varied movements, songs, rhymes, and chants). Children can act as leaders at these times. Finally, keep the amount of waiting between activities to a minimum (e.g., by having materials ready for small- and large-group times). This helps children transition smoothly.

Plan for transitions with individual children in mind. While the previous strategies work well for the group as a whole, there may be individual children who still find any change, or perhaps certain times of the day, difficult. In these cases, giving ample warning, maximizing choices, and providing extra support can help. For example, if a child has trouble with cleanup, you might say, "Work time is almost over. You played in the house and block areas today. Which area would you like to clean up first?" If transitions are a time when a child might hide or act aggressively toward a classmate, adults can position themselves nearby at that point. For example, Timmy hid under the table whenever the lights were flicked for cleanup time. Rachel, his teacher, joined his activity near the end of work time and was able to engage him in cleaning up.

Plan for cleanup time, the longest transition. Cleanup time is the longest and often the most stressful transition of the day. Adults know it must be done before moving on to the next activity, but a child's natural inclination is to continue playing. To help cleanup time go more smoothly, teachers first need to realize that children are not being bad or resistant (negative) when they want to keep playing but, rather, that they are motivated and engaged in purposeful activity (positive). Adults also need to keep their expectations realistic and view cleanup time as another learning opportunity. Children will not clean up as thoroughly as adults, nor should they (program staff can do this at the end of the day).

It can also help to clean up as work time goes along, provided it does not interrupt purposeful play. (Think of cleaning up the kitchen as you cook, instead of leaving all the pots and pans until after dinner.) Finally, use children's individual and group interests to make cleanup time fun. For example, if children were "writing" grocery lists at work time, they might write down, in order, the areas or materials they will clean up.

know about things happening that day or coming up soon. For example, visitors may be expected (e.g., a local artist, a prospective student), perhaps new equipment introduced at small-group time the day before can now be found in a specific area of the room, or perhaps a field trip is planned for the next day. You can also use this time to discuss a problem that affects the whole class. For example, if running through the classroom is a safety hazard, children can brainstorm possible solutions and choose one or two to try out. A few days later, during message board time, they may review the situation and decide whether the problem is solved or they need to try a different approach.

Teachers write these messages — on a dry-erase board, easel pad, chalkboard, or similar surface — using pictures and words. Writing messages in various ways allows children of all literacy levels to "read" them, know what to expect, and participate in the discussion. It is also an opportunity for children to recognize letters and words (especially their own and others' names) and for adults to introduce language and literacy games, such as rhyming and alliteration. Finally, the message board creates a sense of community as adults and children begin their day.

❖

Throughout the daily routine, HighScope teachers are continually aware of what children are experiencing and learning. To guide their planning and interactions with children, teachers keep in mind the KDIs that are important in the early years. These essential indicators — in all content domains of learning — are described in the next part of this book.

Try These Ideas Yourself

1. On Friday, make a plan for the weekend. Write down what you will do, the materials or information you will need, who else is involved, how long each activity will take, and so on. On Sunday evening, review your plan. Think about what happened as planned and what got changed. What did you learn about planning similar activities in the future? How does reflecting on this plan-do-review process help you think about the importance of plan-do-review for children?

2. Think about a young child from a chaotic, disorganized household. Think about a child from a rigid, overly scheduled household. How might each react to a consistent daily routine at school?

3. How would you help a child who does not speak English learn the daily routine?

4. Think about the daily routine in your classroom (or observe someone else's). Write down the parts of the day in order and how much time is spent on each. Note whether the day has an appropriate number of segments and transitions, or whether parts need to be added, omitted, or combined. Next to each part of the day, note whether its place in the order makes sense. Is it too short, too long, or just right? Based on your comments, revise the daily routine. How will you introduce children to the new routine? Will you change it all at once or gradually? Why?

5. List five strategies you can use to encourage children to plan. List five different strategies you can use to encourage children to recall. Remember to identify strategies that can be used with children of different ages and ability levels (e.g., from nontalkers to highly verbal children). Try out your ideas (or ask a teacher you know to try them out while you observe). Write down what happened and reflect on what did (or did not) work. How would you modify your original ideas based on your observations? (*Note:* The same strategies can often be used for both planning and recall, so think of different ones for each to end up with a total of 10 ideas.)

6. Divide a piece of paper into two columns, one headed "Child-Initiated" and the other, "Adult-Initiated." Observe a small-group activity in an early childhood program. Whenever children make a comment, contribute an idea, or use materials in their own way, make a check mark in the child-initiated column. When adults introduce materials, model behavior, or ask questions, make a check mark in the adult-initiated column. At the end, add up the number of check marks in each column. What is the balance of child- and adult-initiated activity? If it is predominantly adult initiated, what would encourage more child initiation? If it is mostly child initiated, did adults miss opportunities to scaffold (support and gently extend) children's learning?

7. Plan a small-group activity for eight preschool children based on something you observed them to be interested in. Include each of the features listed in the group-time planning sheet on page 64.

8. Plan a large-group activity for 16 preschool children based on something you observed them to be interested in. Include each of the features listed in the group-time planning sheet on page 64.

9. Think of a problematic transition in your classroom or one you have observed (e.g., the children take so long to clean up after snack that they only have 10 minutes left to play outside). Make a plan for this transition based on one or more KDIs, incorporating the five ingredients of active learning. Try out the plan. Did the transition go more smoothly? Did you feel it was valuable time instead of wasted time? Why (or why not)? If necessary, what else could you do to make this transition a positive learning experience for the children?

During pickup time, this teacher shares with the child's father what his son did during work time.

Chapter **8**

How Do HighScope Programs Work With Families?

Think About It

How was your family involved in your education? For example, did your parents or other family members help you with your homework? Send treats for you to share with classmates on your birthday or holidays? Encourage you to practice certain skills? Attend school performances and sporting events? Volunteer to help out in the class or chaperone field trips? Attend conferences, open-school nights, or similar events? Call or e-mail your teachers? Go to PTA or school board meetings or serve as an officer? Discuss your report card or grades with you? Get involved in other ways? How did you feel about each of the ways in which your parent(s) or other family members did — or did not — participate in your education?

The term **family involvement** (or **parent involvement**) means many things. As the list above shows, it can include participating in activities at school or encouraging a child at home. Parents can communicate with various adults including teachers, principals, and the family members of other children at the school. They can work directly with their own child or help the child's classmates. Family contributions can also take many forms, including time (such as volunteering in the classroom or on a school committee), resources (e.g., providing food and supplies, sharing skills), and ideas (e.g., helping to shape school policies).

HighScope programs provide varied and meaningful opportunities for families to participate in the life of the program. Staff are sensitive to other demands that might limit family members' availability, and because staff also understand that not everyone is comfortable participating in the same way, they offer choice and options. HighScope acknowledges that families are a child's first and most important source of learning and that teachers can learn from them as well as vice versa. In this chapter, we'll look at how families in HighScope programs can contribute to the education of their own child, their child's classmates, the staff, and even to the program in ways that may have an effect beyond the time their child is enrolled in the program.

Benefits of Family Involvement

The importance of the **home-school connection** is shown by its prominence in virtually all state program quality standards (Barnett et al., 2010) and accreditation guidelines (National Association for the Education of Young Children, 2005). Research shows family involvement is critical to a child's success in school. For example, the Head Start Family and Child Experiences Survey (Zill et al., 2003) found that parent involvement in Head Start was associated with a number of positive outcomes for children. Academically, children whose parents read to them more frequently had higher scores on early literacy assessments. Socially, the more parents participated in activities with their children, the fewer behavioral problems children had in school. Importantly, parents' involvement

Chapter Learning Objectives

By the end of this chapter, you will be able to

- Explain how family involvement provides benefits to children, parents, teachers, and the program as a whole.
- Promote family involvement using diverse strategies that both respect differences and build bridges between home and school.
- List effective ways to share information with families about their child's development, how the program promotes it, and what families can do to further their child's learning at home.

Talking to family members who drop off and pick up their children each day is one way teachers can foster supportive relationships between the program and home.

in Head Start moderated the negative effects of violence, depression, and other risk factors on children's school readiness and emotional well-being.

Supportive relationships between early childhood programs and families benefit children, parents, staff, and the program as a whole. Educators can foster these relationships in many ways, for example, by talking to family members who drop off and pick up their children each day, inviting families to volunteer their time, conducting home visits, and becoming involved in the community themselves. HighScope advocates family involvement in its programs for these reasons:

To build bridges between home and school. Child care or preschool is often a young child's first extended experience outside the family. From that point forward, the child needs to function in at least two worlds — home and school. It can be quite a challenge for toddlers and preschoolers to navigate different places, each with its own expectations and experiences. The more teachers can connect these two important places for young children, the easier it will be for children to make the twice-daily transition between them. To help children feel comfortable, teachers can incorporate familiar materials and activities from home into the classroom and help children understand what to expect and how to adapt their behavior in the two settings.

Establishing continuity between school and home also eases the transition from preschool to kindergarten. It allows parents and other family members to continue their involvement from one setting to the other because they have come to think of themselves as an important part of the school experience. And children will have established the routine of sharing educational activities with their families.

To enhance teachers' understanding of children. The more staff members learn about children's home life and culture, the better they can support children's development in school. An awareness of the materials, activities, and values at home lets teachers plan meaningful experiences that build on the children's knowledge, interests, and skills. For example, a teacher may learn that a child is interested in insects or knows a repertoire of gospel songs. Knowledge of home and family life can also help make staff aware of any circumstances that may affect a child's ability to concen-

Terms Used in This Chapter

• family involvement, parent involvement • home-school connection • personal filter • home visits

trate, learn, or socialize. Staff can then provide the child and family with assistance, through services offered directly by the program or community referrals for medical, social, financial, or legal aid.

To enhance families' understanding of children. Staff have many opportunities to share information with families about how young children develop. They can also help them become better observers of their own children. This information can be exchanged formally, for example, during parent-teacher conferences or family education workshops. It can also be shared informally — for instance, while talking about what a child did and learned at school that day when the parent or other family member arrives to pick up the child.

Many adults form ideas about education based on their own school experiences, which may not reflect current research and practices. Or they may have seen products advertised to make their children "smarter" and wonder if the program uses similar techniques. As a result, teachers often find that parents or other family members do not realize the importance of play in young children's learning. By drawing attention to play-based learning experiences, such as math concepts involved in block building, educators can help families understand and support their child's development in appropriate ways.

In addition to enhancing childrearing knowledge and skills, involvement in their child's HighScope program can also empower parents. By becoming more effective in their parenting role, they may increase their feelings of competence as individuals and as community members as well. For example, agencies that use the HighScope Curriculum with children (such as Head Start programs) may also provide adult family members with opportunities to serve on policy councils and planning committees, continue their own education, or enroll in job training programs.

To promote child development at home. Parents are a child's first teacher, and children spend more time at home than in school. Teachers play a critical role "translating" the curriculum for parents and other family members and suggesting ways to apply active learning principles to everyday family situations. For example, identifying letters while grocery shopping is a literacy experience, sorting clothes by size is mathematics, and both activities provide opportunities for parent-child conversations. A parent involvement coordinator in Sacramento, California, noted that "parents realize they are already providing learning experiences for their children during the normal course of the day — for example, setting the table or sorting the laundry. They are allowing their children greater independence in self-care, and some have provided child-manageable storage containers in their bedrooms. Parents are more accepting of letting children explore and are not so concerned about 'mess.'"

> "Parents have seen how HighScope deals with many conceptual skills that are prerequisite to academics. The comment 'All they do is play' is becoming a thing of the past as parents gain insights into the developmental appropriateness of HighScope."
>
> — Teacher, Houghton, Michigan

To enrich the program. Families can contribute to programs in many concrete ways, such as volunteering in the classroom, assisting on field trips, and serving on committees. Parents who cannot volunteer on a regular basis may have interests and talents to share during occasional visits or may be able to invite children to visit their workplace or studio. Even busy adults can donate materials, such as old clothes for the dress-up area, empty food containers and cooking utensils for the house area, and other items that would otherwise be recycled or discarded.

When parents and other family members do volunteer their time, it is important for them to be given meaningful roles in the classroom. Assigning them custodial chores, such as mixing paints, may help teachers, but it doesn't allow parents to interact directly with children and learn about their development. With appropriate orientation and ongoing support from staff, families can play an active role in children's learning in the classroom. Moreover, when families understand the goals and methods of the program, they can become its strongest advocates. See "The HighScope Approach to Working With Family Members" on page 76 for more information.

Strategies to Promote Family Involvement

HighScope promotes diverse strategies to encourage family involvement in children's programs.

The HighScope Approach to Working With Family Members

The HighScope approach

- *Focuses on the family.* Teachers learn about the family's background and culture, discover their strengths, and identify what they can contribute to their child's education and the program as a whole. They support and encourage family initiative. Staff are also sensitive to issues that affect child and family well-being and assist families in obtaining the assistance they need.
- *Promotes partnerships.* Information is shared in both directions. Parents and other family members educate teachers about their children. Teachers offer families insights into child development and how the curriculum supports their child's learning. The relationship is characterized by mutual respect.
- *Is guided by the plan-do-review process.* Teachers and family members discuss their goals for a child and how active learning both at home and school can help the child achieve them. As they carry out their respective roles, teachers and families periodically review the child's progress and make adjustments if needed.
- *Shares child observations.* Teachers share anecdotal information from COR Advantage, HighScope's child assessment tool, with parents and other family members to help them understand and support their child's development. Adults are encouraged to record and share observations about what the child does and says at home.
- *Incorporates home-based materials and activities.* Teachers include real and familiar objects from the home in the classroom. They plan activities that reflect the home and community environment. Families are encouraged to share materials, experiences, interests, and skills with all the children in the program.
- *Emphasizes adult-child interaction.* Staff help parents and other family members become better observers of their children so adults can scaffold learning at home. Adult volunteers are also given meaningful roles in the classroom so they can interact with children and become partners in the active learning process.

Many of these ideas are not unique to HighScope and are recommended as part of general best practices. However, as you carry out these strategies, continually review their effectiveness from the perspective of the curriculum's *five ingredients of active participatory learning*. Emphasize the use of familiar *materials* from home that children can *manipulate* as they investigate ideas, acquire knowledge, and practice skills. Give children *choices* that reflect family life, and explain to parents how they can offer children many choices in their daily activities at home. Encourage *language and thought from children* in many ways, such as welcoming children's talk about their home experiences; hiring staff who speak the children's home languages; and, if you do not speak these languages, taking the time to learn important words and phrases so children (and family members) feel comfortable communicating with you. Finally, *scaffold children's learning* by building on the experiences the children bring from home and by helping parents support and gently extend education from the classroom to the family environment.

Four Elements of Family Involvement

Below are the four main elements of involving families in HighScope programs, along with suggestions for carrying them out. The sidebar on page 78 lists 50 strategies for connecting with families, generated by teachers and family engagement specialists attending HighScope training sessions.

▲ 1. Examine your own family roots, beliefs, and attitudes

To understand the beliefs and practices of the children and families you serve, first reflect on how your own background influences your perception of others. The following strategies can help you better understand yourself so you do not unintentionally judge or misinterpret others.

List your family origins and living arrangements. You may be surprised by the diversity within your own family, going back two or three generations. For instance, family members may have moved from one part of the country to another and found creative ways of adapting their language, clothing, food, home furnishings, and so on to their local environment.

Living situations also change in a society or family over time. For example, multigenerational families living under one roof are more or less common in certain cultures or periods of history. Similarly, children may be raised by people other than their parents — not just today, but in past times of economic hardship or migration. Discovering this type of diversity in your own family tree can help you realize that there is not one right way to do things.

Examine your "whats, hows, and whys." Examine what is important to you and what makes you feel comfortable and "at home" — such as certain types of food, art, music, or humor; particular topics of conversation; or different levels of affection or reserve. Think about your behavior as a parent, family member, friend, and colleague. Reflect on how and why you behave in certain ways and what it says about your beliefs and attitudes. When you and your coworkers share these things about yourselves, it can help the staff to become more open to — and respectful of — individual differences.

Be aware of personal filters. A **personal filter** is that combination of beliefs, attitudes, and lifetime experiences that affect our impressions of people and events. Once you see the roots of your own beliefs and practices, you can separate your views from those of the families in your program. It is then easier for you to say, "I may not do it that way, but I can appreciate why this family does."

▲ 2. Learn from children and families about their traditions

Knowing ourselves is the first step; learning about others comes next. The following can help you learn about children and their families.

Conduct home visits. Home visits are occasions when teachers go to families, instead of families coming to the program. At a minimum, HighScope teachers visit each child's family before the children begin the program. A visit later in the year or at the end of the program (for sites that close over the summer) also wraps up and personalizes the home-school relationship. When you visit families, especially when children are entering the program, you see and hear firsthand what children are like on their own turf, surrounded by familiar people, sights, and sounds. Children are often eager to show teachers where they sleep, eat, keep their toys, or engage in favorite activities. Making an effort to visit with family members in their own home also shows parents that you are genuine in your invitation to have them partner with you in educating their child. Moreover, by keeping the focus of the visit on a shared interest in the child, parents are reassured that teachers are not there to judge them or their living situation.

> "Parents play a real part in the choice of materials. Very often they will not only send them in with their children, but will make an effort to bring in the materials themselves. Parents feel appreciated when the children react and choose what area to put the materials in."
>
> — Teacher, Battle Creek, Michigan

Participate in community life. This strategy is especially important if you do not live in or near the community in which you teach. Joining local events and visiting neighborhood places demonstrates to families that you are eager to connect with them as citizens and community members. It is also one of the ways you can understand the experiences and expectations children bring to school. Examples of community participation include shopping at local markets, attending street

Home visits offer teachers insights into children's interests and the materials and activities they enjoy.

50 Ways of Connecting With Families

1. Newsletters (printed or online)
2. Family meetings and workshops
3. School and/or classroom website and blogs
4. Personal notes
5. Phone calls
6. E-mail and text messages
7. Activity calendars (may be posted on web page)
8. Home visits
9. Family networks
10. Field trips
11. Orientation visits
12. Family handbooks
13. Classroom volunteer opportunities
14. Family bulletin board (may be posted on web page)
15. Family library
16. Toy-lending library
17. Family room
18. Family support groups
19. Continuing education (such as GED)[1]
20. Family literacy program[1]
21. Job training[1]
22. CDA training[1]
23. Links with agencies of interest to families
24. Invitations to professional meetings
25. Visits to other early childhood programs
26. Child activity logs for each part of the daily routine
27. Family-teacher conferences
28. Child, family, and classroom photos posted in the classroom
29. Donations of materials from home
30. Advisory board or policy committee
31. Book study group
32. Family night
33. Potluck dinners and picnics
34. Suggestion box
35. Discount coupons for family activities

You can also connect with families by involving them in the following:

36. Classroom setup
37. Fundraising
38. Creating content for the school or classroom website
39. Building the playground
40. Repairing classroom equipment
41. Helping children transition to kindergarten
42. Preparing special snacks
43. Sharing a talent
44. Making furniture or materials
45. Getting books from the library
46. Sharing observations of children
47. Completing child assessment together
48. Conducting playground assessment
49. Completing program assessment
50. Sharing their photos or videos of the classroom

[1]Provided directly by the program or by referring family members to relevant community agencies

fairs, and getting to know community leaders (e.g., elected officials, corporate donors) and services (e.g., clinics that provide health care to the families in your program).

Observe children every day. Home visits and community events, while important, are infrequent occurrences. On the other hand, staff observe children on a daily basis. The conversations and activities initiated by children provide a window into their interests, thoughts, and experiences outside of school. So, for example, when a teacher in one program saw a child "weaving" strips of paper in a collage, she learned that the child's mother had a small loom at home. The teacher invited this parent to demonstrate weaving to the children. After the demonstration, children wove with simple frame looms made of wooden canvas stretchers using a variety of materials. During outside time, later that day, several laced yarn and twigs through the fence.

Reach out to families. You and your co-workers can welcome families into your program in many ways (see p. 78.)

▲ 3. Share information about child development with families

When families understand how children learn and how the curriculum supports active learning, they are better able to be partners in the educational process. Teachers in HighScope programs share information with families using several proven strategies (Brand, 1996; DiNatale, 2002) as described here:

Family orientation. Recruitment and enrollment offer many opportunities to present family members with information about the HighScope Curriculum and the types of experiences their child will have in the program. Encourage family members to visit during program hours so they can see the curriculum in action and allow their child to start becoming familiar with the setting and the people in it. Once family members have signed up, provide them with a family handbook that lists program policies and procedures and includes a brief description of the curriculum.

Family workshops. Many HighScope teachers conduct monthly family workshops about the curriculum and how to use its key elements at home. Encourage families to suggest workshop topics of interest to them (e.g., how to choose appropriate books for preschoolers, what to do when siblings fight). To carry out effective workshops, apply the same principles of active participatory learning you use with children to working with adults. (For family workshop resources, visit the HighScope website at www.highscope.org.)

Newsletters. Each HighScope program is encouraged to periodically produce a newsletter sent by mail or e-mail or posted on a program's website. Newsletters provide general information about the program's policies and procedures and upcoming events. Your program's newsletter might introduce a new staff member, report on a field trip, describe an activity the children enjoy, highlight an upcoming family potluck, or include frequently asked questions. Encourage families to contribute articles and photos too. Each issue might also highlight an aspect of the curriculum. For example, an article on early literacy might describe the classroom's new lending library and include pointers on how to read with children at home every day.

Formal conferences. Regular parent-teacher conferences, ideally held at least twice a year, are another opportunity to share information with families about the program and individual children. HighScope teachers share the anecdotes and portfolio entries they use to complete COR Advantage, HighScope's child assessment tool (see chapter 18). Additionally, parents are invited to ask questions, share information about the child and family, express concerns, and offer ideas for the program as a whole.

Informal contact. Dropoff and pickup times provide natural opportunities for teachers to chat briefly with family members about what their child did at school that day as well as about anything noteworthy happening at home. Sending work home also creates a context for talking about the child's activities and development (e.g., about how the child made a painting or dictated a story and what he or she learned in the process). You can also write notes, make phone calls, send e-mails or texts, and/or post updates to your program's website, strategies especially important when children are transported to and from school by a bus or van or if daily face-to-face meetings with adults are rushed. It is important to use these informal contacts to share the "good" things children do and learn, not just as a means to discuss problems.

▲ 4. Join families in expecting excellence from each child

Families have high expectations for their children and want them to do well in school. They also want teachers to recognize what is special about their child and give them the individual attention they need to succeed. Because HighScope teachers are attuned to child development, they also know each child is capable of succeeding on his or her own terms. To convey this belief and confidence to parents, use the following strategies:

Avoid labeling or stereotyping children and families. Labels set limits on who a person is and what he or she can become. Terms such as *immature, shy, disadvantaged,* or *bully* are subjective. They often say more about what the labeler sees as "weakness" than they do about the child

When families join in activities in the classroom, they also learn how to extend their children's learning opportunities at home.

or family being described. In HighScope programs, people are instead identified by their strengths — for example, "Ramon draws detailed pictures" or "Madison's dad asks many questions about where to find low-cost educational materials." Learning how to observe and record objective anecdotal notes (see chapters 9 and 18) can help you focus on actual behavior, not judgmental labels. Then, if there is a problem, you can use your observations to examine when and how the behavior occurs and devise appropriate strategies to deal with it (e.g., to help a child who bites express and channel feelings in safer ways).

Assume each child will succeed. When you regard all children as competent learners, you subscribe to the idea that they can and will do well in a supportive setting. Sometimes teachers and parents of children with special needs question whether such children can succeed in a HighScope program (Dowling & Mitchell, 2007). By focusing on the disability, they overlook a child's potential to plan, explore the world with all available senses, and solve problems. Because HighScope builds on strengths, every child has a chance to learn and succeed.

Try These Ideas Yourself

1. Think about how the person you are today was influenced by your family (e.g., your values, beliefs about education, choice of career, attitudes toward money, feelings about marriage and parenthood, hobbies, friendships, favorite foods, political positions). In what ways are you the same or different from other members of your family? In what ways might these insights about yourself help you appreciate the diversity in a classroom of children?

2. Divide a piece of paper into three columns. In the first column, labeled A, list all the ways families can become involved in their child's preschool program. In the second column, labeled B, list all the barriers that might prevent their involvement. In the third column, labeled C, list what you as an administrator or teacher could do to help eliminate each barrier. For example, the first row in your chart might read like this: A. Coming to a family workshop, B. No transportation, C. Arranging a car pool.

3. A teacher writes the following:

I teach in a center-based preschool program with a home-visit component. Some parents make it clear they expect the home visitor to teach the child letters, numbers, colors, and shapes using very directive methods. This is not our view of education. I don't know how to respond.

What suggestions do you have for this teacher?

Chapter 9

How Do Staff in HighScope Programs Work Together?

Think About It

Imagine you are a member of a group working on a new playground for your local community center. You first meet to discuss your ideas about how the playground should look and how children and families in the neighborhood will use it. You invite people from the area to share their hopes and concerns. Through negotiation and compromise, you develop an overall plan everyone can live with and that has at least one feature each person is really excited about.

Some committee members research different playground designs and costs. They invite a local architect who specializes in play spaces to talk to the group. Other members look into paying for the playground through grants and charitable contributions. A few people on the committee, as well as parents in the neighborhood, are skilled carpenters who donate time to build and to supervise volunteer work crews. The project takes two years, from discussion of the original idea to the completion of the playground. There is a big party to celebrate the opening, and the city council votes to give the community center money each year to maintain the playground.

What makes a **team** experience like this one successful? How does it differ from groups where members think meetings are a waste of time and have little confidence in the outcome? What does it say about people listening to different viewpoints, handling disagreements, and learning to trust one another? Think about the importance of gathering information before making decisions, sharing the work according to each person's abilities, and continually taking stock of what's been accomplished and what still needs to be done. You might call it plan-do-review at the team or group level. The process is just as necessary for adults' work as it is for children's work.

Based on research and practice, HighScope has created a system to apply these principles to early childhood teams. **Team members** include supervisors and teachers as well as support staff such as bus drivers, janitors, and cooks. (We discussed ways to include families as part of the team in chapter 8.) Why is **teamwork** important? For staff to serve children and families well, they must be able to work well among themselves. They must share goals for clients and have guidelines they can depend on to resolve differences. In HighScope programs, this guidance comes from the curriculum, which gives team members a common understanding of human development and practical information about how to accomplish shared goals.

Early childhood team members must maintain two important sets of relationships. One is with the children and families they serve. The other is with their coworkers. In this chapter, we'll explore how HighScope team members work together on a daily basis to observe and learn about children and plan experiences that meet their developmental needs. We'll also look at how the HighScope

Chapter Learning Objectives

By the end of this chapter, you will be able to

- Describe the characteristics and processes that create an effective working team.
- Record objective anecdotal notes about children.
- State why and describe how daily team planning is essential to operating an effective early childhood program.
- Describe what is unique about HighScope's approach to providing staff support and supervision through observation/feedback (O/F) and the Preschool Program Quality Assessment (Preschool PQA).

During team planning, teachers share objective anecdotes about children to plan supportive educational experiences for individuals and the group as a whole.

model of supervision helps staff meet their own needs to continue growing as professionals. (For more on the principles of adult learning and teacher training, see chapter 20.)

Forming the Team

A team in a HighScope program consists primarily of the staff members responsible for taking care of children and communicating with families. This would typically include the teachers or caregivers who work with children every day and others who may also have regular contact with children or families such staff as the center director, bus driver, cook, and family involvement coordinator. Those who support the work of the direct service providers (e.g., administrative assistants, curriculum specialists, or evaluators) can also be considered members of the team.

While all team members must communicate with and trust one another, it is especially important that the teaching or caregiving team observe children and participate in lesson planning regularly and consistently, preferably on a daily basis. It is also essential that teachers and supervisors have a system for observing and evaluating what is happening in the classroom or center so they can work together to guarantee a high-quality program for the children and their families.

▲ Characteristics of effective teams

Effective teams establish a trusting and supportive climate for working together. You and your co-workers can create this atmosphere using the following strategies.

Communicate openly. Simple and honest communication is at the heart of good working relationships. Psychologist Virginia Satir (1988) calls such direct communication **leveling.** In everyday language, we may call it "being straight" with one another.

Leveling is a straightforward statement of how one sees a problem, how one feels about it, and the solutions proposed to address it. If, for example, the members of your teaching team disagree on the value of a bubble-blowing activity at small-group time, a teacher might say, "I'm sure the children will enjoy blowing through the straws to make bubbles. But how can we make sure all the ingredients of active learning are included in

Terms Used in This Chapter

• team, team members, teamwork • leveling • key developmental indicators (KDIs) • anecdotal notes • objective anecdote • subjective anecdote • team planning • observation/feedback (O/F) • Preschool Program Quality Assessment (Preschool PQA) • professional development

the activity?" This statement can then lead to a team discussion of what other materials to provide and how children might use them, things children might be expected to do and say, how the activity relates to the **key developmental indicators (KDIs),** ways adults can support and build on children's explorations, and how teachers can document what happens to plan appropriate follow-up activities.

Leveling is not easy. It is human nature to feel afraid of rejection, loss of power or control, embarrassment, or any of the other emotions that make us act protectively. However, leveling allows all team members to be heard, to listen to others, to make mistakes without fear of punishment or humiliation, to arrive at a solution together, and to review the agreed-upon solution later to see if it worked or whether it needs to be revised. This open communication system not only helps staff members work together well but also maximizes the chances that the solution they arrive at will be in the best interests of the children.

Respect individual differences. Team members will naturally differ in ideas, preferences, and personalities. In the HighScope model of teamwork, these differences are seen as a source of creativity and variation rather than a cause for anger or failure to reach agreement. Looking at things from more than one perspective can help teachers understand and plan for all the ways children might respond to a situation. Tapping both personal and role differences to brainstorm alternatives can increase the choices and learning opportunities the team provides.

Have patience with the teamwork process. As staff members get used to working in teams, and as new members are added, it is common for staff to feel frustrated or impatient with the teamwork process. Often, team members are getting to know the curriculum and one another at the same time. Support staff, such as cooks or bus drivers, often have less access to training and may be more narrowly focused on their specific tasks (such as feeding or transporting children). Despite these occasional frustrations, teamwork does get easier with practice.

As staff in all positions become familiar with the curriculum, it guides them in understanding and supporting children's development. As you and your coworkers get to know each other and the different roles each team member is called on to perform, you will appreciate one another's strengths, accept one another's limitations, feel secure taking risks in front of the team, and trust that the group process will result in a good educational experience for children. For more information on the characteristics, see "Characteristics of an Effective Team" on this page.

Characteristics of an Effective Team

1. **Climate:** There is a positive climate of mutual sharing and trust. Staff and administrators know what is expected of them.
2. **Goal setting:** Staff work together to set goals. The goals then drive the team.
3. **Expectations:** Expectations are clear and are based on a shared philosophy and set of goals.
4. **Decision making:** Whenever possible, staff make decisions by consensus. They discuss many alternatives. Once a decision is made, everyone commits to carrying it out.
5. **Handling conflict:** Problems are viewed as a normal part of working together. Staff use conflict-resolution strategies to solve problems effectively.
6. **Regular evaluation of teamwork:** All members work together to achieve team goals. Program evaluation is based on whether the team as a whole has achieved the group's goals.

Gathering Information About Children: Anecdotal Notes

A critical input to team planning is individual teachers' **anecdotal notes** — written observations about what children do and say. These notes, which teachers learn to record objectively, are not only used in daily lesson planning but also to complete and score COR Advantage, an assessment tool for monitoring children's developmental progress (see chapter 18). Anecdotal notes are also used to share meaningful information with families.

▲ Recording anecdotal notes

Teachers take several anecdotes a week on each child and make sure, over a period of several months, that all developmental areas are covered for individual children and for the class as a whole. To record **objective anecdotes** (i.e., notes that are factual and neutral):

Observe children throughout the day. Watch and listen to children as you support and interact with them during all parts of the daily routine. Pay attention to the ingredients of active participatory learning, noting what materials children choose, how they manipulate them, and what they say and do in their interactions with adults and other children. Use the HighScope KDIs to describe the problems children encounter in play, how children solve the problems, and the kinds of knowledge and skills the children demonstrate. Your observations can also guide on-the-spot interactions with children. During planning, refer to team members' observations to plan individual and group experiences that will further children's learning.

Briefly note observations. So much happens each day that teachers cannot depend on their memory to recall what each child or group of children did and said. Therefore, it is important to try to write brief but complete anecdotes on the spot, or jot down a few key words you can refer to later for writing more detailed anecdotes. You have many options for recording events as they happen. See "Anecdotal Notes: A Summary" on page 85 for an overview of anecdotal note taking.

Teachers take several anecdotes a week on each child and make sure, over the course of the program, that all developmental areas are covered for individuals and for the class as a whole. (See chapter 18 for guidelines on how often to take notes on each child and how to cover all categories of the KDIs.)

Suspend judgment. Anecdotal notes are meant to record what happens, not to guess what a child intends or to state whether the teacher thinks the child is acting "good" or "bad." For example, an objective anecdote might say, "At work time in the art area, John made three paintings — one with wide red and thin blue stripes, another with wide green and yellow stripes, and then a third with all four colors. He hung them up to dry." A **subjective** (or judgmental) **anecdote** might state, "John painted three pictures using just a few lines. He left most of each page blank. Wasted lots of paper." Objective anecdotes help teachers both value what each child does and plan according to children's needs, interests, and developmental and ability levels.

▲ Using your anecdotal notes

Anecdotal notes offer you and your coworkers many benefits. Recording and reviewing them helps you *learn and think about how young children develop.* Because observations are organized by KDIs, note taking also helps you *become more knowledgeable about the learning content of the HighScope Curriculum.*

As you review the notes with the rest of your planning team, you may find that you have little information about particular children or few examples of learning in a particular content area or KDI. This alerts the team to the fact that teachers need to pay more attention to certain class members, plan individual and group experiences to fill in the gaps, and/or add materials that promote a particular area of development. The team may decide to set up an inservice training session to learn more about early development in that domain. Finally, although note taking adds some time to each day's tasks, it is less burdensome and the information is more reliable and valid than compiling several months' worth of data at the end of each assessment period.

Recording and reviewing anecdotal notes helps teachers learn and think about how young children develop. Because observations are organized by the KDIs, note taking also helps teachers become more knowledgeable about the HighScope Curriculum.

Anecdotal Notes: A Summary

How to Use Anecdotes

Use anecdotes to

- Learn about and plan for individual children.
- Learn about and plan for groups of children.
- Share information about children with family members.
- Complete and score COR Advantage.

How to Write Objective Anecdotes

When writing anecdotes,

- Focus on what the child did and said.
- Be factual.
- Be specific.
- Be brief.

Format for Anecdotes

Each anecdote should include the following:

- Date the anecdote happened.
- *Beginning:* Identify when a behavior or activity took place, where it took place, and who was involved.
- *Middle:* Describe what a child did and said; use quotes to document the child's language.
- *End:* When applicable, state the outcome.

Tips for Taking Anecdotes

- Use abbreviations (e.g., the child's initials, HA for house area, SGT for small-group time). Record just enough information to jog your memory, and then elaborate on the anecdote later.
- In each area, keep a supply of note-taking materials, such as sticky notes, index cards, mailing labels, clipboards, digital camera, or a notepad attached to the wall with string. Other options include wearing a necklace pen or a shop-type apron with several pockets. You can also use your smartphone or tablet to take pictures and record brief anecdotes.
- Set a realistic goal for the number of anecdotes to record each day. Begin with four or five and gradually increase the number as the process becomes routine.

Example

A teacher jotted the following information on a sticky note: Maddy, WT, HA, dressed up, asked Mike "marry, not same," "older, red hair." Later that day, she wrote this anecdote and shared it with her team member:

> *12/07/13 At work time, in the house area, Madeline put on a dress, hat, and beads, and then asked Michael if he would marry her because "You are not the same." When I asked what was different, she said, "He is older and has red hair."*

In Madeline's file, the teacher entered this anecdote under Creative Arts as an example of KDI 43. Pretend play and copied it under Science and Technology as an example of KDI 46. Classifying.

Team Planning

Once team members have gathered information about children, their next step is deciding what it means and how to act on it. Teachers use the KDIs to reflect on the significance of an event or activity for a child or a group of children. The teachers then generate ideas for building on individual and group interests and for scaffolding (supporting and gently extending) children's development. Team members decide on one or more strategies, try them out, and review them the next day to see what did or did not work. Use the following strategies to make planning an effective and rewarding experience for your teaching team.

Plan together at a consistent, mutually acceptable time. While daily **team planning** is recommended, it is not always possible. Planning every other day or twice a week can work, but planning should happen not less than once a week. If scheduling is an issue in your program, think creatively about when the team can plan. If you have a half-day program, the team might plan each day right after the children leave and before the adults do a final cleanup. If you have a full-day program, the team might plan quietly in the nap area while children are resting, close enough to keep watch but far enough not to disturb children or be overheard discussing them. Occasion-

A Successful Team Planning Session

Margaret told her coteacher Becky that at work time several children were moving and making noises like their pets — cats, dogs, and a parrot. Based on this observation, they decided to do a large-group time in which children would pretend to be animals and imitate animal sounds. This would let them focus on the Creative Arts KDIs 41. Music, 42. Movement, and 43. Pretend play.

To begin, the teachers decided they would sing a favorite song ("Old MacDonald Had a Farm"), encourage the children to name an animal, and then stop singing in order to imitate the animal's actions and sounds.

The teachers agreed Becky would introduce the activity by saying something like "Yesterday, I heard some of you barking like dogs and chirping like birds. I thought today we'd sing 'Old MacDonald' and pretend to be different animals on his farm." She would begin singing the song, stopping after the words "And on his farm he had a _______." Once a child named an animal and everyone pretended to be and make a noise like that animal, Margaret would begin the song again and then stop to call on children who volunteered animal names.

Finally, the teachers decided that Becky would bring large-group time to a close by suggesting children move and make noises like an animal of their choice on their way to the snack tables (the next part of the daily routine).

ally, other onsite staff or parent volunteers might help watch children at naptime while the teachers plan. When team members are used to the planning process, team planning time does not take long — teachers can go over the day's notes and make plans for individual children and the group as a whole in about half an hour.

Review and reflect on the day to plan for the next day. During planning time, turn the strengths and problems of one day into the plans and strategies for the next day. The team can do this systematically, by reviewing what happened, developing a new work plan, deciding how to carry it out, and establishing criteria for evaluating its success. As you plan, do the following together with your team members:

Evaluate what did and did not work in the previous day's plan.

Pool the day's anecdotal observations; add to what each team member was able to observe children doing and saying.

Discuss what each anecdote reveals about the observed child's development and make plans about how to act on that knowledge the next day. Strive for consensus on plans.

Plan group activities based on observations, children's interests and developmental levels, and the curriculum's learning content.

Plan for individual children based on observations, children's interests and developmental levels, and the curriculum's learning content.

Set responsibilities for each team member, and make sure everyone holds the same expectations for carrying out the next day's plan.

Set long-range goals for individual children based on their particular interests and development, and plan strategies for engaging children in activities and interactions to help them accomplish these goals.

Discuss and resolve any group or individual problems; for example, agreeing on when and where children can run, hop, and jump in the classroom or how to respond to a parent's concern about the food served at snacktime. Strive for consensus on solutions to problems. If team members cannot agree on one idea, decide to try out alternative solutions and then review them later to see what did and did not work.

Occasionally, review the team planning process itself to identify both strengths and areas for improvement. It is useful for team members to ask themselves three questions as they plan: (1) What do you know (what happened today)? (2) What does it mean (what do you understand about children's interests, development, and learning)? and (3) What actions will you take tomorrow (what will you do to support children)?

Remain focused and organized during the planning session. To keep planning manageable, break each task into smaller parts. For example, as a source of ideas when planning a large-group time, each team member might first share what he

The Elements of Team Planning

- Plan regularly and consistently, preferably daily.
- Plan as a team.
- Keep planning forms simple, based on the program's daily routine.
- Use anecdotes to assess children's interests and abilities.
- Plan by incorporating
  - Children's interests
  - Children's developmental abilities
  - Curriculum content (KDIs and COR Advantage items)
  - Classroom materials
  - Adult ideas

or she observed children doing that day, suggest an idea for the next day's large-group time, and talk about the KDIs that could happen during the activity. Next, the team might go over the materials needed for the activity and decide who will be responsible for preparing which materials. After making sure they are clear about these expectations, team members might discuss who will introduce the activity and in what way, who will do what in the middle of the activity, and which team member will use which strategy to bring the large-group time to a close. See "A Successful Team Planning Session" on page 86 for an example of how one group of teachers conducted a planning session.

Decide together on the form for planning and recording decisions. A standard form serves several purposes. It highlights what needs to be reviewed and decided. It helps team members organize and focus their discussion. Finally, when information and decisions are written down for all to see, confusion or disagreements become obvious and can be resolved.

The most convenient forms are those which follow the order of the daily routine. For activities the class does as a whole, use one row. For those in which the class is divided into small groups, divide the row into however many groups there are. Another useful tool is to use the numbers of the KDIs and COR Advantage items to indicate the area(s) of focus for each part of the day. As a reminder, you can also briefly note what children at earlier, middle, and later stages of development might do and say so you can scaffold their learning. (See *Key Developmental Indicator [KDI] Scaffolding Charts* [HighScope Educational Research Foundation, 2013] for examples of children's behavior and adult scaffolding strategies for each KDI.) Your program might also include state standards, Head Start Child Outcomes, or other important categories in a legend on the form and indicate when these are being addressed in the daily plan.

Whatever form your program develops, it should be simple, convenient, and reflect the daily schedule and composition of your setting. See page 88 for a sample daily planning form.

Rotate tasks. Take turns carrying out different parts of the plan. Dividing the labor keeps each team member attuned to each part of the day. It also makes it less likely anyone will feel he or she is regularly stuck with a difficult or less desirable task. Rotation also allows team members to grow as professionals. Even if someone is unsure of his or her ability to do something, such as leading the children in a song, colleagues can provide the support and encouragement to take a risk and try something new. When teams establish trust, anything is possible!

Take advantage of each team member's strengths. Every adult brings unique interests and talents to the team. Just as teachers acknowledge children's efforts and accomplishments, HighScope recognizes team members need to know their contributions are valued. Likewise, teachers use encouragement rather than praise with one another. For example, adults feel acknowledged when the other adults they work with ask them to contribute to a classroom activity, observe what they do to learn from them, comment on how children reacted to the experience, and suggest ways for continuing and building on the activity in the future. See the sidebar on this page for a summary of the elements of team planning.

Staff Support and Supervision

Just as observation is essential to teachers' learning about and supporting children, it also helps adults learn about and improve their teaching practices. In addition to being observation based,

Sample Daily Planning Form

Adults: Shannon and Dora **Date:** 10-4-2013

Greeting Time KDI/COR Advantage: KDIs 11, 24, 25, 26, 27/COR Advantage items E, F, N, O, P, Q
Door: Shannon **Books:** Dora
Child Messages:
1. Joey's turn to choose song in song book
2. New Legos in the toy area
3. Matthew's birthday, 4 years old

Transition: By children's ages

Planning Time KDI/COR: KDIs 1, 2, 56/COR item A (Shannon) Have children drive Lego car on a map of the classroom (using area signs)	**Planning Time KDI/COR:** KDIs 1, 2, 35/COR item A (Dora) Have children wrap a toy they want to play with in a scarf and bring it back to the table

Work Time
Support the new Legos; spend time with Anna in the art area

Cleanup
5-more-minute song, ring bell and play soft music

Recall Time KDI/COR: KDIs 6, 21, 22/COR item L (Shannon) Have children talk to each other on play phones	**Recall Time KDI/COR:** KDIs 6, 21, 22, 25, 29, 39/COR items O, R (Dora) Have children write their letter under the area where they played in an area chart

Snack: Milk, water, carrots, and dip **KDI/COR:** KDIs 19, 20, 21, 22, 26/COR items E, F, L, Q

Large-Group Time: Easy to join: Sing "I dropped my head on the floor" and ask children what other parts of the body they can drop
Activity: Song book: Joey
Activity: Give each child a scarf; play fast and slow music
Large-Group Time KDI/COR: KDIs 16, 41, 42/COR items Y, Z
Transition: Ask children to put away scarves as we say the color of the scarves and then move to small-group time

Small-Group Time Shannon **Materials:** Blue and yellow paint, paper **Small-Group Time KDI/COR:** KDIs 40, 48/COR items A, BB	**Small-Group Time** Dora **Materials:** Pegs and pegboards **Small-Group Time KDI/COR:** KDIs 31, 32/COR item S

Earlier	Middle	Later	Earlier	Middle	Later
Children will paint with hands, saying it changed color	Children will paint with hands, saying it changed to green, then explain how they got green	Children will predict what will happen before they try it, then test their predictions	Children will say random numbers	Children will point and count 1–5	Children will point and count more than 5, using the last number to say the total

Outside Time KDI/COR: KDI 16/COR items I, J
Bikes, balls, sand toys, bubbles

To Remember
Parent meeting tonight

Content -----> Interests -----> Planning Ideas -----> Developmental Range ----> Support Strategies

In programs that use HighScope, supervisors and teachers use observation-based tools, such as the Preschool PQA, to identify goals for individual staff members or teaching teams.

supervision in HighScope programs is also mutual and interactive. Unlike styles of supervision that go in one direction (top-down), supervisory relationships in HighScope settings are joint problem-solving endeavors. All the players are motivated to serve the best interests of children and families. Put another way, supervisors and teachers act as a team to promote professional development in the same way that teachers work together to promote child development.

HighScope uses two techniques, both based on observation and supervisor-teacher interaction, to support curriculum implementation and solve problems in the classroom. One form of support is called **observation/feedback (O/F).** This process may be initiated by the supervisor or teaching team and occurs in response to a specific question or concern about curriculum implementation. The supervisor writes an extensive narrative based on the focus of the observation (e.g., the learning environment), makes the relevant curriculum notes (e.g., how well the setup of the environment encourages children to elaborate on their play and interact with others), and then discusses these in a mutual feedback process with the teachers.

The other system for supporting and supervising teachers uses the **Preschool Program Quality Assessment (Preschool PQA),** a tool for evaluating specific aspects of program implementation (see chapter 19 for additional information on this tool). The supervisor conducts a classroom observation using one or more PQA sections (such as the learning environment or daily routine) and shares the results with the teachers. Together they set goals for program improvement. In addition to identifying goals for individuals or teaching teams, the PQA can serve as an agency-wide needs assessment. The results can then be used to design a tailor-made **professional development** program, in which staff members can enhance existing skills and develop new ones.

Each of these observation-based procedures for providing staff support are described briefly below. To carry them out effectively, staff in supervisory positions receive extensive training and practice in the techniques during the HighScope training of trainers course (described in chapter 21).

▲ Observation/feedback (O/F)

In O/F, supervisors observe children in the classroom and how teachers interact with them. Supervisors then provide feedback on teachers' strengths and areas for improvement (also referred to as *modifiable issues*). Teachers and supervisors together decide on the focus for the observation session. They agree on a time of day, the child or children to observe, and the part of the curriculum that will be the focus of the observation (e.g., active learning, small-group time, adult support during work time). The observation itself lasts approximately 15–20 minutes. The observer uses a two-column narrative/notes form to record a detailed narrative of what happens and notes about its relevance to the curriculum issue(s) in question. The supervisor and teaching team then discuss the observation, list strengths and modifiable issues, generate solutions to problems together, and make a plan for improvement that includes follow-up support.

O/F is effective for several reasons:

Supervisors and teachers share a commitment to understanding children. Because they are interested in providing the best program possible, supervisors and teachers are able to look objectively at what is working well and what is working less well in terms of outcomes for children, rather than viewing the session as a personal critique of the teacher.

Observation and Feedback

Two teachers asked their supervisor to observe a large-group time. The planned activity was for children to move their bodies in different ways to slow and fast music. After the observation, the team talked about where the teachers got the idea for the activity, the KDIs featured, the elements of active learning that were present or missing, the extent to which children were engaged, and what the teachers would continue or do differently the next time they planned a similar activity.

Supervisor (sharing her observations): Eleven of the 16 children — Jeremy, Dahlia, Noah, Patsy, Bing, Jacob, Dewan, Juan, Tiffany, Pilar, and Sasha — were engaged the whole time. That's two-thirds of the children! During the slow music, Karl and Bella went to the house area and brought back scarves to move with.

Teacher A: We planned the activity to focus on KDIs 41. Music and 42. Movement.

Teacher B: Several children called out what they were doing. I cracked up when Jeremy wiggled his bottom and said, "Look at me shake that thing!" Dahlia and Jacob used words like *bend* and *turn*.

Supervisor: Yes, and I heard Bing say, "Twist, twisting my arms!" I also noticed Jackson, Kate, and Bethany stopped moving to the music and went to the toy area about three minutes after you began the slow piece. You called them back to the group but they continued building with the Legos.

Teacher B: They weren't disrupting things, but it bothered me that they weren't engaged with the rest of the group.

Teacher A: I was frustrated, because then I had to go over and bring them back to the group, and I feel like that disrupted the group, especially after it happened several times.

Teacher B: Yes, the fast section of the song was next and then more kids left the group. It was like a chase game to them.

Teacher A: *(to Supervisor)* Do you know how long large-group time had been going on at that point?

Supervisor: My observation says it was about 17 minutes to when those three children left during the slow music.

Teacher A: Really? I had no idea it was that long!

Teacher B: Neither did I. No wonder they left, they were probably bored!

Supervisor: Children often communicate with actions as well as words, don't they.

Teacher A: Now I feel bad for feeling frustrated with them.

Supervisor: I wonder what you could do if something like this happens in the future?

Teacher B: Well, I think we need to rethink our plans. We did an easy-to-join activity, sang three songs, and then did the movements to the fast and slow music.

Supervisor: That does seem like a lot.

Teacher A: I think we got into this habit because last year's children really loved large-group time. I have to remind myself that it's still early in the school year, and this is a different group of children.

Teacher B: We've talked about this before in other areas, haven't we? Maybe for now, we either sing songs OR do a movement activity.

Teacher A: Maybe we could also keep an eye on the clock ourselves.

Teacher B: I like that idea. What if you keep track of time when I'm leading the large group, and I'll keep track of time when it's your turn to lead?

Supervisor: These ideas sound like they would really help, but I don't want you to feel you have to exactly stick to a time frame.

Teacher A: We know, but we both enjoy this time of day so much, it's easy to get carried away.

Teacher B: We also need to remember to look to the children for cues about when they've had enough.

Supervisor: So the strategies for now are that after the easy-to-join activity, either sing songs or do a movement activity, but don't try to fit in both. The person who isn't leading large-group time will keep an eye on the clock, and you'll both watch the children to see when they've had enough.

Teacher A: Sounds like a plan!

Teacher B: I'm anxious to try it out tomorrow!

Supervisor: Let me know how it goes.

Children are the focus of the observation. By focusing on the children, supervisors actually learn more about the quality of the program's teaching and learning than when their focus is on the adult's behavior. Supervisors can identify which elements of the curriculum are being implemented well and where the gaps might be. The process is also less anxiety-provoking for teachers since the spotlight is on the children, not on them.

The curriculum guides observation and team discussion. By reviewing the ingredients of active learning, the elements of adult support, and other distinctive features of the curriculum, the team can see what is working and, when necessary, develop strategies for improving teaching practices.

Conversation about the observation is reciprocal. In the dialogue that follows the observation, the supervisor and teachers talk and listen, give and take. Often O/F is initiated by teachers, rather than supervisors, because teachers want a trusted and knowledgeable "third person" to help them see and hear what is going on with a particular child or group of children during a particular part of the day. For example, a teacher might say to a supervisor, "Large-group time isn't going well for some of the children lately. Jackson and Alyce, for example, lose interest after a few minutes and it's hard to get their attention back. Can you observe our large-group time next Tuesday? We have some ideas but would really appreciate another pair of eyes and ears." The supervisor would then observe Tuesday's large-group time, complete a narrative/notes form, and join the teachers at their next team planning meeting.

Team discussion results in mutually agreed-upon action. Once the team has examined what's happened in terms of the curriculum — especially the ingredients of active learning and KDIs — they generate solutions and decide which one(s) to try. They also schedule a follow-up visit to evaluate whether the solution is working and, if not, to further modify their strategy.

Note that the work of the adult team follows the same principles as does the work of the children in the program. In O/F, the *review* discussion results in a *plan* that the teachers *do*. Later, supervisors and teachers will repeat this cycle to see if the action is working or needs adjustment. (See p. 90 for an example of O/F in action.)

▲ Preschool Program Quality Assessment (Preschool PQA)

The Preschool PQA (see chapter 19) also uses observation as a tool for focusing team discussion — in this case, on the quality of program implementation. HighScope teaching practices, described in the preceding chapters, are reflected in the 39 classroom items in the PQA. (Another 24 items focus on agency-level factors.) The PQA enables the supervisor and teachers to record objective anecdotes about what they observe in the classroom. Because supervisors and teachers are both familiar with the PQA, there is nothing hidden or surprising about the content of the observation. Teachers know what to expect during the observation and contribute as equal participants during the discussion that follows the observation.

The PQA supports teamwork and professional development in several ways. Teachers might request that the supervisor, who is knowledgeable about the curriculum, look at a specific area or set of items that the teachers have identified as a concern. For example, teachers may want to know if children have adequate time to carry out their intentions in each part of the daily routine. The items on the PQA may also serve as a starting point for team discussion around questions such as "Where do we think we are most and least effective as a classroom?" or "Room arrangement is working pretty well. Now what can we do to improve adult-child interactions?" A supervisor might also initiate a complete or partial PQA observation to pinpoint strengths and areas for improvement across the agency's classrooms. The results could then lead to ideas for professional development workshops, mentoring or coaching activities, and so on.

❖

In summary, the purpose of staff supervision and support is to gather data about what teachers do in the classroom — not to pass judgment on them but to see how well the classroom is working for the children. When the class is going well, supervisors can make teachers aware of the practices they use that are effective and support children's development. If something is *not* going well (e.g., if children are wandering away when the message board is read), the supervisor-teaching team will collaborate to find a more engaging way to share the messages.

This way of thinking is similar to the attitude HighScope teachers adopt with children. When children are focused on a task, adults support and encourage their work. When children hit one another or run away during a conflict, it is not viewed as "misbehaving" but rather as children not having yet learned how to behave appropriately in that situation. Similarly, when a classroom situation does not go well, it is not seen as stemming from "bad" behavior by the teacher but, rather, that the teacher needs to examine his or her teaching practices — often with input from other trusted adults — to learn how to handle it better. HighScope teams assume good intentions and help teachers and supervisors achieve them. The children are the ultimate beneficiaries.

Try These Ideas Yourself

1. Think of a good experience you had as a member of a team or committee. What made it a good experience? Make a list, considering such things as the group's goals, the personalities and skills of its members, the qualities of the leader (if there was one), how you gathered information and identified resources, the division of labor, how disagreements were handled, and so on. How might your reflections help you to be a better member of a teaching team?

2. On a piece of paper or in a spreadsheet program, make a grid of staff members and activities in your program (or one where you can observe and interview staff). Across the top (in the columns), fill in the names of all the staff members. Down the left side (in the rows), list typical responsibilities. Include everything such as housekeeping chores (preparing materials and snacks, cleaning up what the children cannot do themselves), ordering supplies, communicating with families, conducting family meetings and workshops, making arrangements with community agencies for family services, completing children's health records, submitting licensing forms, recruiting families, taking prospective clients on a tour, leading various activities with children (such as music at large-group time), taking anecdotal notes on children and recording the information, making daily activity plans, and so on. Check off who does what, and underline the items where the team is working well (e.g., where tasks are getting done and labor is divided fairly based on job descriptions, interests, and skills). Circle or highlight problem areas. Think of how the teamwork could be improved in these areas to make the tasks more efficient or fairer or to better take advantage of the interests and skills of team members.

3. Observe in an early childhood classroom and take anecdotal notes. Focus on one child and one small-group time. Based on your observations, make a plan for the next day that includes (a) ways to support that child at work or choice time and (b) a small-group activity.

4. The following problems might make it difficult for team members to plan together every day:

- There is no free time in the daily routine; both teachers must be with the children at all times.
- There is only a brief overlap (15 minutes) in the shifts of staff caring for the same children.
- Parents are often late picking up children so teachers cannot plan at the end of the day.
- One team member has to run to catch the last bus of the day right after work ends.
- Team members do not speak the same language.
- There are personality conflicts; some team members do not like each other.
- One team member prefers to do things on his or her own.
- The administrator does not think planning is a good use of time.

Add any other problems you can think of to the list. For each problem listed, write down how you could solve or lessen it to make it easier for team members to plan together on a daily basis.

5. Think of someone, such as a teacher or a boss, who gave you useful feedback on your work. What made it useful? Now think of another person whose feedback was not helpful. Why not? What was different about the two people or situations? How might your reflections apply to the relationship between a supervisor and teacher(s) in an early childhood program?

Part 3

HighScope Curriculum Content

This part of the book describes the HighScope Preschool Curriculum content. Each content area, including children's development and adult teaching strategies, is covered in a separate chapter.

Chapter 10 discusses Approaches to Learning.

Chapter 11 addresses Social and Emotional Development.

Chapter 12 covers Physical Development and Health.

Chapter 13 is about Language, Literacy, and Communication.

Chapter 14 deals with Mathematics.

Chapter 15 examines the Creative Arts.

Chapter 16 explores Science and Technology.

Chapter 17 addresses Social Studies.

For more information on HighScope's curriculum content, see *The HighScope Preschool Curriculum* (Epstein & Hohmann, 2012) and eight accompanying KDI books (Epstein, 2012a–h) as well as the *Key Developmental Indicator (KDI) Scaffolding Charts* (HighScope Educational Research Foundation, 2013), a set of charts with examples of what children might do and say at early, middle, and later stages of development and how adults can scaffold their learning at each level.

What Is the HighScope Curriculum in Approaches to Learning?

Think About It

An article in The New York Times *(Janofsky, 2005) described a 10-year-old girl who was eager to enroll in an experimental school that was opening the following year. An avid learner, she read six books a month, played violin and piano, and "asked so many questions that her teachers sometimes got angry at her." Overjoyed at the prospect of attending the new school, the frustrated girl said, "A lot of times now, I ask three and four questions that are really complex, and the teacher stops and says, 'We're not getting into that. Let's go on to another subject.' At the [new] academy, I know I could ask whatever I wanted and the teacher wouldn't get mad."*

Imagine a preschooler in a similar situation who arrives full of ideas and is sent to the "thinking chair" for using masking tape to "caulk cracks" in his block tower, building a roof for his fort with towels, and jumping off the end of the slide to test his "magic cape."

Our nation's leaders, including corporate executives, often complain our society lacks creative thinkers and is losing its competitive edge. One source of the problem may lie in how our educational system responds to able and motivated students such as those described above. Eager to learn, they are often held back by adults who see their persistent curiosity and creativity as drawbacks rather than assets. In these settings, children are discouraged from asking questions, pursuing subjects that interest them, or using materials creatively. They may be criticized for not doing things the teacher's way. Both the individual and society suffer from the lost potential.

Children come to school with different abilities and styles of learning. The burden should not be on them to adapt to an insensitive and inflexible learning environment. Rather, it is up to the educational setting to create universal opportunities for success. This process can and should begin in early childhood. Encouraging children to express and explore their own interests and take on challenging problems will establish positive lifelong **approaches to learning.**

In this chapter we will discuss approaches to learning — how one acquires knowledge and skills — and how teachers can support and enhance children's motivation to learn.

Why Approaches to Learning Is Important

How young children approach learning shapes their educational experiences in all other content areas and affects academic success. Researcher Ross Thompson (2002) says that when young children are curious, interested, and confident about discovering the answers to their questions, they are best able to benefit from learning opportunities in reading, mathematics, and other subjects. This is reflected in their achievement scores through the primary grades and beyond.

Chapter Learning Objectives

By the end of this chapter, you will be able to

- Explain why children's approaches to learning are an important component of early development.
- Describe the HighScope key developmental indicators (KDIs) in the Approaches to Learning content area.
- Begin to apply the strategies adults use to scaffold (support and gently extend) early development in approaches to learning.

By encouraging children to explore their own interests and take on challenging problems, adults help them to establish positive lifelong approaches to learning.

What Approaches to Learning Means

The National Education Goals Panel says approaches to learning includes curiosity, creativity, confidence, independence, initiative, and persistence (Kagan et al., 1995). Psychologists call these **dispositions,** which are defined as "enduring habits of mind and characteristic ways of responding to experiences" (Katz & McClellan, 1997, p. 6).

Children also have different **styles of learning.** They may gravitate toward a particular sensory mode, for example, visual, auditory, or tactile; stick with one thing for a long time or switch back and forth between tasks (also known as pacing); or prefer working alone or with others (often referred to as social context). While we all use every learning style to some extent, depending on the situation, the preferences that appear in early childhood may continue throughout our lives.

Approaches to learning also involves being able to break down a task into its parts, organize a plan of work, and reflect on how successfully one's goals were achieved. In these respects, a child's approach to learning affects performance in other content areas. For example, it can determine whether the child asks a teacher for help writing a letter of the alphabet or finds one to copy or builds a small tower alone versus collaborating with others to construct a bigger or more complex one.

How Temperament Affects Approaches to Learning

One's approach to learning is partly shaped by **temperament** (Chess & Alexander, 1996). Babies are born with innate temperamental differences, such as their level of inhibition or emotional reactiveness, which persist into adulthood. The environment, however, plays a role in how these biological traits are expressed (Elias et al., 1997). For example, persistence helps a child solve problems, while stubbornness can lead to inflexibility and poor social relationships. By offering realistic choices and being alert to signs of frustration, adults can help children use the traits they are born constructively.

General Teaching Strategies for Approaches to Learning

▲ Establish a physical environment that is rich in options to explore materials, actions, ideas, and relationships

A classroom that is arranged and equipped for active learning allows children to do things on their own and in their own way. Choosing from among many options to match their interests and personalities lets children gain confidence in their ability to explore, answer their own questions, form

Terms Used in This Chapter

• approaches to learning • dispositions • styles of learning • temperament • initiative

meaningful relationships, and draw conclusions about how the world works.

▲ Create a daily routine that allows children to express a variety of learning styles and preferences

Predictable yet flexible routines establish a safe setting where children can approach learning in whatever ways feel comfortable to them. A combination of child- and adult-initiated activities, during individual and group times of the day, provides a range of experiences to suit children's needs, interests, and preferred modes of engaging with the world.

▲ Give children time to approach learning in their own way

Preschoolers need time and psychological space to try new things, make plans, solve problems, practice skills, and think about what they see and hear. Adults, therefore, need to be patient as children approach experiences in their own way. When adults step in too quickly, they deprive children of a chance to discover and create things for themselves.

Key Developmental Indicators in Approaches to Learning

HighScope has six key developmental indicators (KDIs) in Approaches to Learning: 1. Initiative, 2. Planning, 3. Engagement, 4. Problem solving, 5. Use of resources, and 6. Reflection. See "KDIs in Approaches to Learning" on this page.

The rest of this chapter describes and discusses children's early learning in each of these KDIs and the specific teaching strategies you can use to support their development in young children.

KDI 1. Initiative: Children demonstrate initiative as they explore their world.

Description: Children are eager to learn. They exhibit curiosity, independence, and self-direction as they learn about relationships, materials, actions, and ideas. They take reasonable risks as they investigate the environment.

KDIs in Approaches to Learning

1. **Initiative:** Children demonstrate initiative as they explore their world.
2. **Planning:** Children make plans and follow through on their intentions.
3. **Engagement:** Children focus on activities that interest them.
4. **Problem solving:** Children solve problems encountered in play.
5. **Use of resources:** Children gather information and formulate ideas about their world.
6. **Reflection:** Children reflect on their experiences.

How Initiative Develops

The landmark publication *Eager to Learn: Educating Our Preschoolers* (National Research Council, 2001) emphasizes that, from infancy onward, children are highly motivated to seek out new challenges. Young learners are inherently enthusiastic and engaged, and, with no need for external rewards, they explore, master new skills, and discover the effects of their actions (Hyson, 2008; Stipek, 2002).

Preschool children show **initiative** when they choose to participate in a variety of activities that, over time, engage all their senses. They are increasingly comfortable trying new things, taking risks, and generating their own ideas. Supported by adults, young children discuss a broadening range of topics, exchange observations, entertain open-ended questions, and solve problems.

Teaching Strategies That Support Initiative

▲ Focus on effort, not outcome

Celebrate children's attempts, not whether they succeed or fail in their efforts. Acknowledge when they try to master a new skill, solve a problem, or explain what they observe. Describe what you see children do or comment on their ideas, and use encouragement rather than praise to focus on children's actions. Ask open-ended questions so children know you are interested in their thinking rather than one correct answer.

▲ Acknowledge when children try new things

Encourage — but never force — children to explore new materials (e.g., scissors, the computer), try out their knowledge and skills (e.g., sort beads, ride a trike), or share an idea or opinion (e.g., about why ice melts, the feelings expressed in a painting). Taking the initiative requires confidence and trust.

Let children know that you see and value their courage as well as their curiosity:

> *At small-group time, the children are using finger paint. Jane is reluctant to touch "icky" things so the teacher offers her disposable gloves. After a few minutes, Jane removes a glove and dips a forefinger into the paint. She holds it up for the teacher to see. "You put your finger in the paint," the teacher acknowledges. Jane rubs the fingers on that hand together, wipes them with a towel, and continues dipping and wiping for the rest of small group.*

▲ Balance freedom and structure in the physical environment

An overly structured classroom can inhibit children afraid to make a "mess." On the other hand, a disorganized setting with too many materials can be overwhelming. Children should feel free to take reasonable risks while knowing the equipment and materials are safe to use. Initiative is also supported by giving children independent access to materials so they can act with autonomy while pursuing self-directed goals. Finally, make adaptations to support those with a wide range of abilities. See "Supporting Initiative in Children With a Wide Range of Abilities" on page 99.

Adults provide materials during teacher-guided times of the day but children choose how to use them.

▲ Encourage children's initiative during adult-initiated parts of day

During teacher-guided times of the day, adults provide materials and/or the originating idea, but the children use materials as they choose and suggest their own ideas. For example, at small-group time, you might introduce materials with a brief story or description but then let children explore them according to their own interests and curiosity (e.g., "Here are the pebbles, leaves, and twigs we collected yesterday. I wonder how you will arrange them on your paper"). Likewise, at large-group time, you might begin a movement, music, or story and then encourage children to contribute their own ideas on how to move (e.g., "Let's all hop up and down"), what to sing (e.g., "Do the boat song"), or how to add to the story (e.g., "We're fish monsters who eat up all the food").

KDI 2. Planning: Children make plans and follow through on their intentions.

Description: Children make plans and decisions, and express choices and intentions based on their interests. Their plans increase in detail and complexity. Children follow through on their plans.

How Planning Develops

Research shows the value of planning in early development (see, e.g., Epstein, 1993; Friedman & Martin, 2011), and many state standards, as well as the Head Start Program Performance Standards (Administration for Children and Families, 2002), include planning as a measure of program quality and child learning. Too often, however, planning is seen as simply making choices: "Planning is *choice with intention*. That is, the chooser begins

Supporting Initiative in Children With a Wide Range of Abilities

- Leave wide aisles for wheelchairs, walkers, and other mobility devices; make sure floors are nonsnag and nonskid (e.g., avoid area rugs and waxed surfaces).
- Provide adaptive equipment and materials for children who need mobility or sensory support.
- Modify materials and activities so children can participate as independently as possible (e.g., use large-type print, easily grasped materials with nonslip handles, enhanced volume, vibrations to accompany or replace sounds, classroom directions in more than one modality [such as telling and demonstrating]).
- Provide information and experiences in many sensory modalities (e.g., provide visual and auditory cues, use facial expressions and gestures, make daily routine charts tactile by using actual objects and raised shapes and letters, make models with clay and play dough).
- Use assistive technology specifically designed for preschoolers, in consultation with a child's medical or therapy team. As a general rule, aim for "low-technology" solutions that employ and enhance conventional toys and equipment, rather than electronic gadgets. Children with special needs, like all young children, learn best with hands-on experiences that take advantage of the natural sensory properties of real-world materials.
- Provide adult assistance as needed when children begin an activity and then reduce support as they show eagerness and the ability to act independently.
- Provide opportunities for interaction between peers of differing abilities throughout the program day; treat everyone equally as members of the classroom community.
- Engage children to act as models, helpers, and friends. Acknowledge when children provide assistance and encouragement to one another.
- Encourage children to suggest ideas on how to create or modify activities so they can participate.

with a specific goal or purpose in mind that results in the choice" (Epstein, 2003, p. 29).

Planning requires children to hold a mental image of objects and actions in mind. For younger children tied to the here and now, it helps to see or hold the options available to them as they plan. Older children can more easily picture the areas, objects, and people in the room; remember what they've done before; and think about what they will do next. Children's plans also become increasingly detailed and complex, involving more materials, steps, and/or people. They are better able to follow through on their plans, anticipate problems, and extend them over time.

Teaching Strategies That Support Planning

▲ Establish a consistent planning time in the daily routine

Set up a predictable schedule, with a designated planning time, in which children make plans and carry them out every day. Once they learn this routine, and know they will have the time and materials to act on their intentions, children sometimes even make plans on the way to school.

▲ Provide opportunities for intentional choices throughout the day

In addition to the scheduled planning time, HighScope programs encourage young children to make intentional choices and decisions throughout the day. For example, a child might have the following opportunities to make choices during a typical daily routine:

- *Greeting time:* Whom to sit with, what book to look at, whom to talk with, what to talk about
- *Planning time:* What to do at work time, what materials to use, how to use materials, where to use materials, whom to work with
- *Work time:* How to begin to carry out his or her plans, how to modify plans, how long to

stay with an activity, what materials to add, how to solve problems, what to do next

- *Recall time:* What to share, what details to include (who, what, where, how), how to share (gestures, words, drawings)
- *Small-group time:* Whom to sit next to, which materials to use, what to do with materials, what to say, whether and how to use backup materials, whether and how to interact with others
- *Large-group time:* What songs to sing, what verses to add, what movements to try, whether to be a leader, what happens next in a story
- *Outside time:* What equipment and materials to use, whom to play with, how fast or slow to move, how loud or quiet to be

▲ Show interest in the choices and decisions children make

Because many decisions are left to adults (e.g., for health and safety), it is important for children to set their own agenda whenever they can appropriately do so. Children can do this at school; teachers can also share ideas with family members about how to encourage child planning at home. Adults support children's intentions by commenting on their ideas, repeating and extending their thoughts, imitating their actions, accepting their suggestions, and letting them be the leaders.

KDI 3. Engagement: Children focus on activities that interest them.

Description: Children sustain involvement and concentration in their play. They are persistent, motivated, and able to stay engaged.

How Engagement Develops

Engagement is the "action-oriented dimension of approaches to learning" (Hyson, 2008, p. 17). It includes attention and persistence and is a critical process in *executive function*, the cognitive skills that help us "command and control" life's daily tasks (Rothbart, Sheese, & Posner, 2007; Zelazo, Muller, Frye, & Marcovitch, 2003). Typically, when adults talk about children and attention, they are often referring to "paying attention" (i.e., listening to someone else). HighScope prefers the term *engagement,* whereby children remain involved with activities and events that interest *them.*

Attention and persistence foster school readiness (Fantuzzo, Perry, & McDermott, 2004). They require self-regulation, which is children's "ability to act in a deliberate planned manner in governing much of their own behavior" (Bodrova & Leong, 2007, p. 127). The older children get, the longer they can sustain their attention while being less susceptible to distractions. The more they learn, the greater their curiosity to learn more. Engagement is thus self-reinforcing.

Teaching Strategies That Support Engagement

▲ Provide materials and activities that hold children's interest

Children pay attention when they have something worth attending to. By providing an abundance of diverse materials and scheduling a mix of individual and group activities, adults can guarantee that each child will find something to engage his or her interest every day.

▲ Give children ample time to carry out their intentions

Even if children do not initially stay with one thing, scheduling a work time of 45–60 minutes or allowing them to finish a small-group activity lets children know their ideas have value. Allow them to transition gradually instead of as a whole group (e.g., finishing a book before shelving it at cleanup or joining large-group time after finishing snack). Give notice when an activity is ending, and provide children with work-in-progress signs so they can continue a project the next day.

By the same token, be sensitive when children lose interest in a small- or large-group activity by modifying the activity (e.g., introduce backup materials or have restless children move instead of sing) or bringing the activity to an end. If children feel forced to continue, that time period may take on unpleasant associations. They may come to dislike group time in general and refuse to participate, even on days when the materials and actions would otherwise interest them.

▲ Minimize interruptions and transitions

While engagement increases over time, don't assume young children have short attention spans. A constant change of pace or novel stimulation may inadvertently hamper their concentration. To encourage sustained involvement, minimize interruptions and transitions. For example, don't set up special projects during work time that pull children away from their ongoing activity. Having fewer transitions ensures that children have the necessary time for each part of the day and lets them pursue their intentions.

KDI 4. Problem solving: Children solve problems encountered in play.

Description: Children are inventive and flexible in solving a variety of problems. They progress from using trial and error to more systematic attempts at problem solving.

How Problem Solving Develops

Psychologist Carol Dweck (2002) found children fall into two categories when it comes to solving problems: *performance oriented* or *learning (or mastery) oriented*. Those with a performance orientation focus on getting a positive evaluation from others, avoid situations that may result in failure or criticism, and give up easily. Children with a learning (mastery) orientation focus on increasing their abilities, regardless of feedback. They tackle new challenges even if their initial efforts are not successful. Although these two orientations are rooted in temperamental differences, they are influenced by whether adults emphasize outcomes (performance) or efforts (learning).

In addition to individual differences, there are also developmental changes. Younger children approach problems with more enthusiasm and self-confidence but with less persistence. Older children are more persistent and flexible and likely to offer their own solutions (Flavell, Miller, & Miller, 2001). Executive function also plays a role. Studies show older children are better able to regulate their attention and apply cognitive skills in problem-solving situations (Zelazo et al., 2003). The years between three to five are especially critical because of concurrent changes in a child's brain, particularly the frontal cortex, which governs regulating and expressing emotion (Shore, 2003).

To help children develop their problem-solving skills, give them time to come up with their own solutions.

Teaching Strategies That Support Problem Solving

▲ Encourage children to describe the problems they encounter

Give children time to recognize and describe problems without doing it for them. If their verbal skills are limited, make a simple statement (e.g., "So the problem is…") until they begin to do this on their own. Children may not see problems the same way as adults, but by using their own words, children begin to trust their skills as observers and analyzers as Cole demonstrates here:

> *Cole comes to his teacher Jackie and says, "The computer's not working." She asks him to tell her how it isn't working and follows him back to the computer. "See, it keeps going back to where I started," Cole explains. When Jackie asks Cole what he wants the computer to do, he says, "Go to the next part of the game." She then asks, "What have you tried to do to make it go to the next part?" Cole pushes the space bar and the enter key. Jackie looks at the screen, points to the arrow icons, and says, "I wonder what these do?" Coles tries clicking on the icons. When he clicks on the forward arrow icon, the game advances. Cole says, "Now I got it working!"*

▲ Give children time to come up with their own solutions

Just as you wait for children to identify problems, hold back so they can try to solve them. While your solution may be more efficient or effective, simply giving it to the child deprives the child of an opportunity to learn and develop confidence in his or her problem-solving abilities.

▲ Talk with children about what is and is not working

To help children move from trial-and-error to systematic (cause-and-effect) problem solving, encourage them to describe and think about the results of their actions. It is just as important for them to be aware of when a solution works as to recognize when a different approach is needed:

> *Raven shows her teacher Beth that her arm is stuck in her jacket sleeve. Beth comments, "Your mitten is on your hand and it won't fit through your sleeve. How have you done it before so your arm fits through?"*

▲ Assist children who are frustrated

Sometimes children do need adult help, especially when their inability to solve a problem keeps them from moving forward with their plans. When children have run into roadblocks they cannot get past, provide just enough assistance for them to continue problem solving on their own. A brief explanation of the solution can help them use the information independently at a later time.

KDI 5. Use of resources: Children gather information and formulate ideas about their world.

Description: Children use all their senses and a variety of tools to explore and gather information about the world around them. They ask questions and try to explain their ideas about the things they encounter.

How Use of Resources Develops

Children become increasingly adept at using resources — manipulable objects, readily observed actions and events, and human expertise — to gain knowledge and accomplish goals. The dispositions (also referred to as *habits of mind*) they bring to this endeavor include a desire to find things out, make sense of experiences, strive for accuracy, and seek proof that something works (Katz, 1993). Although temperamental differences affect children's willingness to try new experiences (Kagan, 2005), there is a developmental trend to greater openness. The more children know, the more they can extract knowledge from the resources at hand. There is also a shift in their questioning. Unlike the toddler's reflexive "*What* is that?" a preschooler's "*Why* is that?" is more reflective. Children may ask questions aloud (e.g., "Why does it get cold when it snows?") or question themselves (e.g., "I wonder if tape will work better than glue…I'll try it.").

The importance of providing young children with age-appropriate and hands-on resources to draw on during these investigations cannot be overstated. The HighScope Training for Quality study (Epstein, 1993) found that access to diverse materials was a significant predictor of early development. An international study of diverse programs in 10 countries (Montie, Xiang, & Schweinhart, 2006), coordinated by HighScope, also found that the availability of open-ended materials in the preprimary years significantly and positively predicted children's cognitive and language performance at age seven. These studies are consistent with brain research, which indicates that "the tasks for early years educators [is] facilitating the further articulation and application of that web of knowledge and verbal expression" (Catherwood, 2000, p. 33). In other words, our job is to provide resources that apply what scientists are learning about the language and cognitive connections developing in the young child's brain.

Teaching Strategies That Support Use of Resources

▲ Provide open-ended materials and experiences that appeal to all the senses

Children learn meaningful lessons when materials can be manipulated and experienced in many ways. Diverse materials also respect individual preferences for learning through one or more senses. Closed-ended materials, with one "correct" use, offer limited possibilities for exploration and discovery. Children quickly lose interest in them. By contrast, open-ended materials, which can be put to multiple uses, sustain children's attention and capture their imagination. They also offer more opportunities for learning. For example, children working with real clay were surprised to see it lighten in color as it dried, unlike play dough. This led them to feel other art materials and compare their moisture content.

▲ Talk with children about how they use materials

As noted previously, brain research indicates that verbalizing actions and observations helps children make lasting neural connections. It is therefore important to talk with children about the objects and people they choose to work with, how they problem-solve with these resources, what they observe, and the conclusions they draw. Do not talk so much, however, that you interrupt or intrude on children's play. Give children time to explore and observe on their own by simply sitting quietly alongside them; children may choose to initiate conversation at a later point when they are ready to share.

▲ Encourage children to use a variety of resources to answer their own questions

The questions children ask of others and themselves — rather than those we ask them — often lead to the most meaningful and lasting insights. Encourage children to ask questions and help them locate the resources that allow them to find answers. For example, say "I wonder what could you use to find out" as an invitation to look around the room or ask "How would that work?" to encourage a child to experiment with materials and observe the results.

KDI 6. Reflection: Children reflect on their experiences.

Description: Children use their experiences to draw conclusions about people, materials, events, and ideas. They make connections between what they already know and what they are doing and learning.

How Reflection Develops

Cognitive and language developments in the preschool years make children increasingly able to engage in reflection. As they begin to construct mental images (representations) of objects, events, and interactions, children become less tied to the here and now. They can review the past and anticipate the future. Words help them "encode" (form a mental image of) experiences, so they can remember the past or entertain "what if" ideas about things that have not happened.

Reflection involves more than "memory or a rote recitation of completed activities. Reflection is *remembering with analysis*" (Epstein, 2003, p. 29). Unlike rote memorization, reflection lets children discover and apply underlying concepts. For example, grasping the alphabetic principle that each letter has a unique appearance and sound allows children to apply this idea when they encounter a new letter. Being able to generalize information is an efficient way to learn.

Teaching Strategies That Support Reflection

▲ Establish a consistent recall time in the daily routine

When recall time predictably follows cleanup time, children develop the habit of reviewing and thinking about their work-time activities. Adults can also encourage children to be reflective by using recall-type questions and comments at other times of the day. For example, if children invite you to join their pretend-play scenario during work time, ask them what has happened up to that point (e.g., you might say, "So I'm the big sister who needs to make the baby brother stop crying. What have you tried so far?"). Reflecting throughout work time helps children recap and describe their activities in greater detail at recall time itself.

▲ Make comments and ask questions that encourage reflection

As you play alongside children, ask open-ended questions and share observations that promote reflection such as "How else could the story end?" "What if…?" "How else could you have…?" and "I wonder where else would this work." To build connections between previous and current experiences, ask "What does this remind you of?" or comment "You made a 'vroom' sound riding the trike outside. You're making the same sound while you move the car down the ramp."

▲ Use photos and mementos to help children remember and reflect on experiences

"A picture is worth a thousand words" means one image can evoke the entire story behind it. A sequence of photos helps children recall the order of events and also highlights if-then connections. For example, pictures of children building a block construction not only helps them recall the series of steps but also reminds them of how they had to add blocks to each wall after widening the base for balance. Likewise, an object representing an event, such as something brought back from a field trip, elicits memories and reflections:

The day after the class field trip to the art museum, the children look at the reproduction postcards they bought in the gift shop. One child studies a painting in somber tones and says, "It's gray because he was sad when he made it." Another child examines a metal sculpture of a large figure and comments, "It's so tall, you can't see its eyes. It's scary, like a monster." A third child, rather than reflecting on the art or the time in the museum, remembers the trip to the museum cafeteria. "Tommy spilled his juice on my shoe," the child recalls.

Try These Ideas Yourself

1. List what you consider to be the five most important things preschoolers need to know or be able to do in the Approaches to Learning content area when they enter kindergarten. Why are they important? How can teachers support their development?

2. What were your early school experiences like? For example,

- What made you feel confident or insecure about your abilities as a learner?
- To what extent did teachers encourage or discourage your initiative and independence?
- How did these early experiences affect your later attitudes toward school?
- How do you approach learning now?
- How might you apply your own early school experiences to working with young children?

3. Think about an important project you undertook recently and then answer the following:

- How much time and effort, if any, went into planning the project before you got started?
- How did you obtain information, materials, help, or other resources to carry it out?
- Did you reflect on how satisfied you were while working on the project and/or after it was completed?
- What, if anything, would you do differently before, during, or after undertaking a similar project?
- How might you apply this experience to supporting children in their work?

4. Think of a recent problem you faced at home, school, or work (e.g., juggling several deadlines, repairing or replacing broken equipment, or accommodating conflicting viewpoints).

- How did you approach solving this problem?
- Did you feel angry or excited about facing the challenge? Were you methodical or did you react moment by moment to each part of the crisis?
- How does your approach to problem situations vary? What determines your response in each case?
- What might you do to make your approach to solving problems more satisfying?
- How might you apply your problem-solving experiences to working with young children?

5. Observe children in a preschool setting. Record examples of them showing initiative, making plans, and solving the problems they encounter in play. What do your observations tell you about children's development and how to support their approaches to learning?

Chapter 11

What Is the HighScope Curriculum in Social and Emotional Development?

Think About It

Did you ever play "school" as a child? Whoever got the coveted role of "teacher" was eager to share his or her knowledge, for example, by reading aloud to the children playing "students" or giving them arithmetic problems to solve. Occasionally, the child playing teacher related some interesting bit of knowledge gleaned at "real" school, while the children playing students also shared information or skills they had learned at home, in class, or in the neighborhood.

Playing school, you also picked up more than academic knowledge. A great deal of social learning went on as the group set out the rules (debates about "how" to play school may have taken up more time than the game itself!). You may have practiced certain skills, such as writing or drawing. Depending on how the pretend teacher ran the class (often as an authoritarian), you may have sat still for long periods of time listening to lectures or instructions. The game also reflected and possibly developed attitudes toward school, what educational psychologists call ***dispositions toward learning.*** *In sum, the childhood social activity of playing school was a learning ground in many other areas of development — academic, creative, and physical.*

As this example shows, early social and emotional experiences shape children's lives in many ways. During these early experiences, children observe and try out different ways of interacting, rehearsing the types of relationships they will form with family members, teachers, classmates, friends, and (later) colleagues. Social exchanges also provide opportunities to gain knowledge and skills in other areas of development (e.g., conversations develop language; playing catch with a friend enhances physical skills). When these experiences are positive and supportive, children become engaged and motivated learners. When the context is harsh or punitive, children are more likely to turn away from school.

For these reasons, the HighScope Curriculum puts a high value on creating warm and nurturing environments in which young children can get a good start on schooling and life. In this chapter, we describe children's early social and emotional development and how educators can support it.

Why Social and Emotional Development Is Important

Social and emotional development has always been a focus of early childhood education. In recent years, however, the field has been pressured to increase its emphasis on academic subjects. Yet the importance of early social as well as intellectual development is receiving renewed attention. Landmark publications, such as *Eager to Learn* (National Research Council, 2001) and *From Neurons to Neighborhoods* (National Research Council & Institute of Medicine, 2000), cite evidence that social and emotional learning is a significant com-

Chapter Learning Objectives

By the end of this chapter, you will be able to

- Explain why early learning in social and emotional development is important.
- Describe the HighScope key developmental indicators (KDIs) in the Social and Emotional Development content area.
- Begin to apply the strategies adults use to support early learning in social and emotional development.

Early social and emotional experiences shape children's lives in many ways.

ponent of school readiness. In fact, it is largely through social interactions that children increase their overall competence (Katz & McClellan, 1997).

Accompanying the general spotlight on social and emotional development is a specific focus on the many benefits of play. In 2006, the American Academy of Pediatrics pleaded for the restoration of play to develop skills such as building resilience, managing stress, and forming relationships with adults and peers (within and outside the family). Their report advised the following: "As parents choose child care and early education programs for their children, pediatricians can reinforce the importance of choosing settings that offer more than 'academic preparedness.' They should be guided to also pay attention to the social and emotional development needs of the children" (p. 18).

Changing Ideas About Social and Emotional Development

In the late 1990s, psychologists Judy Dunn (1998) and Carolyn Saarni (1999) summarized research that challenged traditional beliefs about early social and emotional development, particularly the notion that young children are egocentric. Even toddlers are interested in how others' feelings and beliefs compare to their own. Young preschoolers begin to develop an increasingly complex *theory of mind* to explain how people's behavior is determined by internal thoughts and feelings (Wellman, 2002). Older preschoolers are aware that underlying personality traits affect thoughts, feelings, and behavior (Giles & Heyman, 2005a, 2005b). At this age, they can also identify a broader range of emotions and can explain their causes and consequences (e.g., "You're mad because it keeps falling down!"). See "Milestones in Social and Emotional Development" on page 107.

Factors That Affect Social and Emotional Development

The preschool child's developing capacity for relationships is affected by three characteristics (Epstein, 2009a):

A desire for friendship. Children are social beings. From late toddlerhood through preschool, they expand their desire for relationships with adults to include other children.

A struggle to resolve "me" versus "we." Sometimes children's individual needs or wants ("me") conflict with the desire to be part of the group ("we"). Understanding adults help them resolve this competition between individual and social desires.

Terms Used in This Chapter

• dispositions toward learning • "me" versus "we" • social competence • modeling • coaching • solitary play • parallel play • cooperative (collaborative or reciprocal) play • problem-solving approach to conflict resolution

Milestones in Social and Emotional Development

Infants

- Learn to regulate behaviors (e.g., crying, moving, focusing)
- Create bonds with primary caregivers and form a sense of trust from nurturing attachments

Toddlers

- Identify and gain control of their feelings
- Test their skills and begin to see themselves as capable
- Increasingly differentiate themselves from others and venture into the world of social interaction

Preschoolers

- Develop understanding of their own and others' feelings
- See themselves as doers, based on their ability to achieve self-initiated goals
- Widen their social network, developing preferences and forming friendships and associating with new communities at home and school

Source: Adapted from *Me, You, Us: Social-Emotional Learning in Preschool* (Epstein, 2009a, p. 13)

Their growing social competence. As young children experience the consequences of their actions, they can better choose between positive and negative social interactions. Language gives them a powerful tool to resolve conflicts in nonaggressive ways and further develop their **social competence.** While still largely self-centered, preschoolers become increasingly aware of the needs and feelings of others.

General Teaching Strategies for Social and Emotional Development

▲ Create a supportive environment

Children learn and thrive when they feel emotionally secure and are socially connected to adults who provide nurturance and positive opportunities for learning. You can establish a safe and secure setting by understanding the challenges children face when they find themselves among strangers, in an unfamiliar place, and with new expectations for behavior.

▲ Help children make the transition from home to school

Support children through separations until they can handle them on their own, and reassure children of your concern for their well-being. Encourage family members to stay as long as they can while a child settles in. It may help to set up a simple dropoff routine (e.g., child hangs up coat, gives three hugs, and waves to mom from window). Children may also benefit from having a family picture they can carry around with them as they join activities at their own pace. Be aware of family stresses that may cause anxiety. Reassure children of your concern for their well-being.

▲ Arrange and equip the classroom for social interactions

How the classroom is arranged influences the interactions that take place in it (Cummings, 2000). For example, one observational study (Hemmeter & Ostrosky, 2003) found that children interacted at higher levels when they worked in areas that accommodated several children and played with toys conducive to multiple users (such as dress-up clothes that inspire role play or multiwheeled vehicles that require two or more children to operate). Children in such settings engaged in more complex play, communicated more with peers and adults, and had fewer conflicts.

▲ Implement predictable schedules and routines to create a secure community

Predictability helps children feel secure and in control of the day's events. A balanced schedule, with relaxed time for each component, provides opportunities to work individually, in pairs, and in small and large groups. Further, a shared daily routine creates a sense of community.

▲ Foster specific skills through modeling, coaching, and providing opportunities for practice

Didactic whole-group instruction does not foster social and emotional skills, but individualized guidance from a warm and supportive adult can. Three techniques work well with preschoolers:

Modeling. "Teaching by example, or modeling, is the most powerful technique that educators employ, intentionally or otherwise" (Elias et al., 1997, p. 56). Modeling works best when embedded in the meaningful activities that happen during a child's day (Fox & Lentini, 2006). For example, while playing with a group of children, you might comment, "It looks like you need another big block. I'll share one of mine with you."

Coaching. Coaching social skills (also called *play tutoring*) is like instruction in other domains, such as literacy or sports. It involves breaking a behavior into its components, explaining how to perform and sequence them, creating opportunities for practice (see the following anecdote for an example), and giving feedback. Social coaching may be especially helpful with children who do not seem to be accepted by their peers and whose resulting anger only increases their rejection and ostracism.

To support children's social and emotional development, teach by example. Through modeling, adults can show children how to interact with each other.

At planning time, Joey says, "I'm going to the computer." When told both computers are in use, he frowns and tenses his body. Then he remembers what his teacher suggested the day before. "Maybe I can watch them," he says, "and then I can play." He pulls up an extra chair and watches the other children work with a drawing program. "You could put a dog there," Joey suggests, and one of them does. He moves over to make room for Joey at the keyboard and all three children share ideas, try them out, and comment on the results. At recall time, Joey announces proudly, "Me and Ali and Kevin all played on the computer."

Providing opportunities for practice. Social and emotional development entails learning new skills and "unlearning of habitual patterns of thought and behavior" (Elias et al., 1997, p. 55). For example, a child realizes that she can simply ask for what she wants rather than thinks that she needs to yell to get attention. Unlearning may be easier in preschool than later, after habits are ingrained. Once social skills become automatic, they can be generalized to new settings and people.

Key Developmental Indicators in Social and Emotional Development

HighScope has nine key developmental indicators (KDIs) in Social and Emotional Development: 7. Self-identity, 8. Sense of competence, 9. Emotions, 10. Empathy, 11. Community, 12. Building relationships, 13. Cooperative play, 14. Moral development, and 15. Conflict resolution. See "KDIs in Social and Emotional Development" on page 109.

The remainder of this chapter discusses each Social and Emotional Development KDI and the strategies you can use to support their development in children as you interact with them throughout the program day.

KDI 7. Self-identity: Children have a positive self-identity.

Description: Children are aware of the characteristics that make up their identity, such as gender, ethnicity, culture, and abilities. They perceive their uniqueness and develop a healthy self-image.

KDIs in Social and Emotional Development

7. **Self-identity:** Children have a positive self-identity.
8. **Sense of competence:** Children feel they are competent.
9. **Emotions:** Children recognize, label, and regulate their feelings.
10. **Empathy:** Children demonstrate empathy toward others.
11. **Community:** Children participate in the community of the classroom.
12. **Building relationships:** Children build relationships with other children and adults.
13. **Cooperative play:** Children engage in cooperative play.
14. **Moral development:** Children develop an internal sense of right and wrong.
15. **Conflict resolution:** Children resolve social conflicts.

How Self-Identity Develops

Self-identity is who we are (girl or boy, brown- or blue-eyed), rather than what we can do (see KDI 8). Healthy identity development is based on establishing trusting and secure relationships early in life. A sense of self first appears as infants realize that they and the people caring for them are not extensions of one another but, rather, separate beings (Post et al., 2011). Identity formation continues into preschool and proceeds positively thereafter if children learn to respect their personal characteristics.

Because preschoolers are concrete, they initially focus on one visible aspect of identity and already have well-established ideas about race, social class, culture, gender, and physical or mental ability (Ramsey, 2006). They tend to perceive their sameness to one another more than their differences. Older preschoolers look beyond appearance and behavior. Four-year-olds have a dawning understanding of their psychological selves, for example, as someone who approaches new things with gusto or caution (Marsh, Ellis, & Craven, 2002). They develop theories of mind about how unobservable thoughts and feelings affect behavior and apply these ideas to their self-perceptions (Pomerantz, Ruble, Frey, & Greulich, 1995). For example, a child may notice that a parent is more irratable at pickup time than after dinner, when the family is more relaxed. The child may then form a theory of mind that being hungry or tired makes people grouchy. Applying this theory to him- or herself, the child may further conclude that he or she will have more patience for problem solving after a snack or rest.

Teaching Strategies That Support Self-Identity

▲ Focus on children throughout the day

Spend most of your time interacting with the children, rather than arranging materials, cleaning up, or conversing with other adults. Never shout, shame, utter derogatory words, or use harsh language and actions with any child. Finally, address your comments directly to children. Do not talk about children in front of them, as though they were not there.

▲ Address diversity and differences positively

Answer children's questions about people in a straightforward manner, and use neutral labels to describe gender, skin color, family composition, religion, and other aspects of identity. Use common characteristics to sort children for transitions or games (e.g., "Everyone with a brother, put on your coat"). Display and discuss photos showcasing the diversity in children's families.

▲ Provide nonstereotyped materials, activities, and role models

Share books, stories, and songs in which people feel good about themselves and have positive relationships with others who are the same and different from them. Provide materials and plan activities that defy traditional stereotypes and represent a variety of backgrounds.

▲ Encourage family members to become involved in the program

Invite family members — parents, grandparents, siblings, and others — to be part of the program to affirm a child's emerging self-concept. Provide many options so family members can choose the type and level of participation that fits their work schedules and personal preferences.

▲ Establish ties with the community

Develop relationships with community members who can contribute their time and expertise to the children. Individuals and groups such as artists, tradespeople, business owners, tribal leaders, and senior citizens can serve as mentors and role models. Some can host visits at their workplaces; others can come to the classroom. Discuss with them ahead of time the things that interest your children and share ideas to make these exchanges hands-on and interactive for preschoolers.

KDI 8. Sense of competence: Children feel they are competent.

Description: Children make discoveries and solve problems with an expectation of success. They believe they can acquire the knowledge or skills they need.

How a Sense of Competence Develops

Competence is "the belief that one can successfully accomplish what one sets out to do" (Kagan et al., 1995, p. 16). A sense of competence is sometimes confused with self-esteem. However, *high* self-esteem is not the same as *healthy* self-esteem. If self-esteem is inflated, it can lead to poor academic outcomes and unreasonable risk-taking (Baumeister, Campbell, Kreuger, & Vohs, 2004). Healthy self-esteem is a realistic sense of one's competence and an acceptance of one's limitations without fear of failure. Children with healthy self-esteem are satisfied with their own efforts and do not need adult approval.

Adults are important, however, in helping children positively appraise themselves. For example, infants whose actions produce an effect feel a sense of self-efficacy (e.g., "If I coo, daddy coos back"). Likewise, as toddlers and preschoolers explore materials and activities, adult interest and encouragement supports both their intellectual development and their emerging sense of their own abilities (Meece & Daniels, 2007). Peers also become increasingly important. Children whose ideas are accepted and followed by others see themselves as competent individuals. Settings that promote collaboration rather than competition promote this sense of competence (Bandura, 1994).

Teaching Strategies That Support a Sense of Competence

▲ Encourage self-help skills consistent with children's abilities and developmental levels

Judge success by what children set out to accomplish, not by adult standards. Resist temptations to do something faster or better; letting children help themselves instills a sense of "I can do it!" Acknowledge how hard each child is trying, and recognize each step along the way to competence in a child's self-care.

▲ Scaffold learning by introducing the next level of challenge when children are ready to move on

Children sometimes lack the confidence or know-how to try something a little more difficult, so provide gentle encouragement when appropriate. Give indirect suggestions rather than explicit instructions; for example, you might say, "When I have trouble putting on my shoes, I try to loosen the laces first."

▲ Support children's ideas and initiatives

Encourage children to make choices, follow through on their intentions, and share their thoughts. Children develop confidence when they decide where to play, what materials to use, whom to play with, and how long to stay with an activity. They feel validated when others listen to their ideas. Referring children to one another for help acknowledges their competence to solve problems.

Imitate children's actions to show you value their efforts and ideas enough to try them yourself.

▲ Acknowledge children's efforts and accomplishments

Praise can make children depend on the judgment of others and prevent them from developing the tools they need to evaluate their own work (Katz, 1993; Kohn, 1999). By contrast, encouragement helps children review their growing knowledge and skills with positive self-regard. To encourage (rather than praise) young children:

- *Watch and listen* to communicate your interest.
- *Imitate children's actions and words* to show you value their ideas enough to try them yourself.
- *Comment on what children do* to help them engage in self-reflection.
- *Show children's work to others* to make them all feel equally valuable and capable.

For additional strategies on using encouragement rather than praise, see pages 32–33 in chapter 5.

▲ Provide opportunities for children to be leaders

Being the leader helps children see themselves as capable people whose ideas are taken seriously by others. Provide opportunities for children to lead throughout the day (e.g., ask them to suggest a way to move at large-group time or during a transition). Never force children to lead, but give everyone who wants to lead a chance and allow ample time for them to think of an idea.

KDI 9. Emotions: Children recognize, label, and regulate their feelings.

Description: Children identify and name their emotions, and recognize that others have feelings that may be the same as or different from their own. They regulate the expression of their feelings.

How Emotion Develops

Young children develop emotionally through *expression* (experiencing and showing emotions), *regulation* (controlling how emotions are expressed), and *knowledge* (understanding how emotions affect individual and interpersonal behavior) (Denham, 2006). A child's emotional growth is influenced by such factors as innate *temperamental differences* (e.g., whether one is predisposed to be content or anxious), *cognition* (how one perceives and understands emotions), *language development* (naming feelings and interpreting the emotional content of messages), and *socialization* (learning how to handle emotions in ways deemed appropriate by one's culture) (Raver, Garner, & Smith-Donald, 2007).

Preschoolers' growing vocabulary is especially useful in helping them differentiate emotional states. So is their ability to form mental representations, which allows them to imagine what might cause and solve an emotional problem (e.g., they can imagine the return of an absent parent). Children with better emotional knowledge are therefore more likely to form friendships because they can imagine how others feel and act to sustain satisfying relationships.

Teaching Strategies That Support Learning About Emotions

▲ Accept children's full range of emotions as normal

Do not judge emotions as good or bad. Stop harmful words and actions, but reassure children it is the behavior and not the underlying feelings you are limiting. Show you accept their emotions by your words, facial expressions, and gestures — make eye contact, get down on their level, and listen. Be sensitive to individual or cultural differences in how emotions are expressed, and never pressure children to show feelings in ways that are not comfortable to them.

▲ Name or label children's emotions as well as your own

By preschool, most children have learned the words for basic emotions such as *angry, happy,* and *sad*. Encourage them to use the labels they know, and gradually introduce new words in situations that are meaningful to them (e.g., being *disappointed* when a field trip is cancelled). Label your own emotions (e.g., "Grrrr, I'm getting frustrated because this area sign keeps falling off the wall"). Seeing how you deal with your feelings reassures children they can learn to do the same.

▲ Call attention to the feelings of others

Making children aware of others' feelings helps them understand that emotions are universal and may be the same as or different than their own. Learning to "read" other people's feelings is how children develop emotional literacy. Point out cues such as body language (e.g., clenched fists, jumping for joy), facial expressions (e.g., grins, downcast eyes), and verbalizations (e.g., growls, soothing hums). Adult interpretation is especially useful for children who are not (yet) adept at picking up these cues themselves or are too personally overwhelmed at the moment to notice them.

▲ Comment on and discuss feelings throughout the day

In conversing with children about their feelings, notice and remark on both positive and negative emotions. Casual remarks about feelings make them part of everyday life, and feelings that might otherwise be overwhelming are less scary when they are treated as manageable events (e.g., "Yes, the fire drill bell is loud and sometimes kids feel scared").

Preschoolers' growing representational capacity enables them to talk about emotions apart from when they are feeling them. For example, they can discuss the emotions portrayed in a storybook and relate it to something that happened to them or talk about the feelings depicted in their own or someone else's artwork.

KDI 10. Empathy: Children demonstrate empathy toward others.

Description: Children understand the feelings of others by drawing on their own experiences with the same emotions. They respond empathically by sharing the happiness of others and offering assistance when they see that others are emotionally upset or physically hurt.

How Empathy Develops

Empathy involves imagining how things look or feel to someone else. Empathy appears in infancy and toddlerhood and becomes increasingly sophisticated in preschoolers (Eisenberg, Spinrad, & Sadovsky, 2006). Babies are interested in looking at and listening to one another as early as two months of age. In the middle of the first year, they match their behavior to the emotional expressions of significant others. Toddlers display empathy by turning toward sounds of distress and trying to help or soothe others. Preschoolers make inferences about the thoughts, desires, and feelings of others (e.g., at snacktime, when a child sees another child crying, the first child asks, "Is he sad because he wants his mommy?").

Families are critical in developing a child's capacity for empathy, especially through modeling. The more parents fulfill their children's emotional needs, the better children can empathize with the needs of siblings, playmates, and others (Atance, Bélanger, & Meltzoff, 2010). As young children move into child care settings, interactions with teachers and peers and the cognitive development of perspective-taking skills also influence the course of empathic behavior.

Teaching Strategies That Support Empathy

▲ Model caring behavior

Use words, facial expressions, and body language to show you understand children's feelings and are there to help them deal with their emotions.

Describe what you see and the actions you are taking (e.g., "I'm moving over to make room for Taryn because she looks upset that she can't find a place to sit"). Individualize the type of comfort you provide based on what works with each child (e.g., a hug, a chat, or simply standing nearby). Respond positively to children who express their needs in annoying or harmful ways (such as clinging, pouting, or hitting). Your patience and understanding will help children learn more positive ways to express themselves.

▲ Acknowledge and label the feelings that children have in common

To help preschoolers become aware that others experience similar feelings, be concrete. Focus on the situation and the accompanying emotion (e.g., "Isabel is sad her mom is leaving. When you started school, you felt sad when your mommy left"). Recalling their experiences helps children understand, and even anticipate, others' emotional behavior.

▲ Create opportunities for children to act with empathy

Create situations where children are explicitly encouraged to listen and think about the feelings of others. For example, invite them during a field trip to choose a pumpkin for a child who is home ill. Encourage children to assist one another (e.g., holding a cup while another child pours, picking up something dropped by a child in a wheelchair). Taking care of plants and animals also help children appreciate how their actions affect the well-being of others.

Practice perspective taking in nonsocial situations

Since adopting other viewpoints is the cognitive basis of empathy, introduce perspective-taking activities that involve objects and actions as well as people. For example, at outside time, ask children what they notice about a bush when they view it from the side, top, and underneath. Encourage them to give movement directions using words so they have to think about what those receiving the instructions hear and understand. Many three-dimensional art activities also involve perspective taking. Encourage children to view it or take photos of structures from many angles.

KDI 11. Community: Children participate in the community of the classroom.

Description: Children act as members of the classroom community by participating in routines, cooperating with social expectations, and sharing responsibility for maintaining the classroom.

How Community Develops

The classroom is a community whose members share an age-range, activities, interests, time, and friendship. Preschoolers want to join this community, but balancing their own needs against those of others is a learning experience. The gratification of group membership helps children cross this bridge (Battistich, Solomon, & Watson, 1998).

As they transition from "me" to "we," children develop a sense of responsibility for the group. For example, when they use classroom materials, children observe what happens when resources are not taken care of (e.g., markers dry up when the tops are left off). An emerging capacity to connect cause and effect helps children alter their behavior and become responsible community members.

Teaching Strategies That Support Community

▲ Create an atmosphere that fosters mutual respect and responsibility

A positive community sets the stage for children to feel good about school and be successful learners (Randolph & Gee, 2007), and it is the adult's behavior that sets the tone for the classroom. Thus, although it should go without saying, adults should never shame students, blame or humiliate them in front of others, or criticize their personal attributes. When children make mistakes, adults use social problem-solving techniques that allow children to learn by working through their problems (Zeiger, 2007). Establishing a regular cleanup time also helps promote the sense that the classroom belongs to the children, not just the teacher. Finally, remember that listening is critical in a supportive community — not only how adults listen to children, but also how children listen to one another.

How adults treat each other and the children sets the tone for the classroom; adults create the atmosphere that fosters mutual respect and responsibility.

▲ Call attention to activities the whole class participates in

Daily whole-class activities include large-group time, greeting circle, transitions, cleanup, and outside time. Pointing out the togetherness of these periods increases children's awareness that everyone is participating as a group. Take photos of these times, and use phrases such as *our class, all of us,* and *our group* when describing and recalling whole-group activities. While planning such whole-group activities is important in creating a community, peer interactions should not be forced, for example, by assigning rotating play partners (DeVries & Zan, 2012). While well-intentioned, especially among children who rarely interact with others, such coercion can actually hinder their sense of belonging. Your role is to create inviting activities that children have the option to join.

▲ Involve children in the community outside the classroom

Preschoolers are becoming aware of the community beyond their homes and school, such as the library, parks, shopping malls, or movie theaters. Validate these experiences by showing interest, by encouraging children to share them with classmates in conversations and role-playing, and by bringing materials from these places into the classroom. Visit local establishments, such as the farmers' market, and take part in activities such as street fairs and parades that feature local culture. Invite guests from your community into the classroom so the children can act as hosts, which lets them display pride in and knowledge about how their classroom functions as a community.

KDI 12. Building relationships: Children build relationships with other children and adults.

Description: Children relate to others in the classroom. They refer to teachers and peers by name. Children develop friendships, seek out others, and engage in give-and-take interactions.

How Building Relationships Develops

Early relationships guide children's interactions with adults and peers throughout school. Children who get along well with others adjust better and score higher on measures of academic achievement than those who have difficulty establishing relationships (Ladd, Birch, & Buhs, 1999).

Relationships with peers are evident by age two, when children show preferences for whom they want to play with. The more children play together, the greater the complexity and compatibility of the play (Ladd, Herald, & Andrews, 2006). During preschool, peer relationships become more reciprocal and exclusive (Rubin, Bukowski, & Parker, 2006; Vandell, Nenide, & Van Winkle, 2006). Preschoolers can describe their reasons for liking friends (e.g., shared interests or traits such as being funny or kind) and disliking others (e.g., being too noisy or mean). Although friends have more opportunities to get into conflicts, they are likely to resolve them to maintain the relationship.

Relationships with adults are important during preschool, but the nature of these relationships changes from the infant-toddler years. Preschoolers become more selective about the kinds of interactions they want with grown-ups, be it seeking comfort, getting help, sharing a discovery, or simply having a conversation. These connections contribute to young children's sense of competence and well-being, especially when adults share control with children.

Teaching Strategies That Support Building Relationships

▲ Interact with children in a genuine and authentic manner

When adults treat children with warmth and respect, children respond in-kind. To foster authentic interactions with children, adults listen to what children have to say and avoid issuing questions or orders. Strive for real conversations with children by addressing them by name, placing yourself at their level, letting them direct the conversation, and giving them time to think and speak. Occasionally ask a real question (that you don't know the answer to), and respond honestly to children's questions.

▲ Maintain a stable group of children and adults

Children, like adults, get to know others through repeated and meaningful contact. To give them time to form relationships, HighScope programs maintain stable groupings — the same adult and group of children for small-group activities (ranging from 5 to 10 children, ideally 6 to 8 children per group; see chapter 7). This continuity also helps children feel emotionally and physically secure.

▲ Support the relationships that children establish with one another

When daily observations show children forming friendships, you can support them by, for example, putting two children in the same planning and recall group. You can also comment on what they do together at work time, small-group time, or outside time. Finally, if their play revolves around certain ideas, make sure they have the materials to carry them out together.

▲ Provide opportunities for children to interact with others with whom they are less familiar

Friendships among preschoolers develop spontaneously. However, you can create situations where they interact with peers they might not ordinarily play with, opening up possibilities to learn about classmates with different backgrounds and experiences (e.g., asking two children who were fascinated by the parachute to fold it up and put it away). By the same token, accept that it is also natural for children to play alone or with the same one or two friends. Never require children to "be friends," which negates their choice and independence. Children's relationships, just like those of adults, thrive when they are genuine and come from within.

▲ Refer children to one another

Support peer interactions by referring children to one another for help solving problems or as a source of play ideas. This gives children a reason to interact with each other while building trust and mutual respect. Children are then more likely to offer and ask one another for help without adult prompting.

KDI 13. Cooperative play: Children engage in cooperative play.

Description: Children involve adults and peers in their play. They engage in cooperative play with others by sharing materials, space, conversation, and ideas.

How Cooperative Play Develops

Cooperative play (also called collaborative play) means playing and working with others while sharing toys, space, friends, the attention of others, conversations, resources, skills, and ideas. It involves understanding the rights of others, interacting without being overly directive or submissive, differentiating intentional from accidental actions, treating others as you want to be treated, and balancing your needs with those of others (Szanton, 1992).

The foundations of collaborative play appear in infancy when babies imitate one another. While **solitary play** is most common at this age, by the second year children engage in **parallel play** (playing alongside one another) and, in the third year, **cooperative** (also called **collaborative** or **reciprocal**) **play.** During preschool, the length and reciprocity of these interactions increases, facilitated by language development (Vandell et al., 2006). Greater emotional self-regulation also helps children work through social problems and sustain interactions. This increased capacity for cooperative play does not come naturally to children, however, and adults play a very important role in structuring a learning environment that fosters cooperative play. If fact, research has found that higher quality child care is generally related to more competent peer relationships during early childhood and into the school years (Belsky, 2002; National Institute of Child Health and Human Development, 2006).

Teaching Strategies That Support Cooperative Play

▲ Encourage children to plan, work, and recall together

Planning together acknowledges the importance of children's collaboration and friendship. Work time lets them add jointly to the detail and complexity of their plans. Afterward, when children recall together, each one builds on the other's narrative and fills in additional pieces. Throughout the plan-do-review sequence, children experience the satisfaction of having their individual ideas respected, sometimes challenged, and often elaborated upon by one or more peers.

▲ Provide opportunities for collaboration at group times

Plan small- and large-group times that encourage collaborative play. For example, ask children to think of ways to pass balls to one another, take an imaginary voyage with children contributing items to take onboard, or provide opportunities for children to take turns leading and following during large-group time. As children share and extend one another's ideas, they will learn the essence of cooperative play.

▲ Help aggressive or withdrawn children join their peers

Some children need extra help before they can negotiate cooperative play on their own. You can help forceful or shy children in several ways. For example, coach children who enter a group too aggressively. Observe with them from the sidelines, validate their desire to join the play, and discuss noninvasive strategies (e.g., "Maybe if you help carry blocks, they'll let you build the tower with them"). Play as a partner with these children to model how to play with others. For children who may be fearful of joining ongoing play, regular group times let them play safely alongside peers without having to orchestrate it themselves. Withdrawn children benefit from an invitation (but never a requirement) to participate more actively. Even shy children rarely turn down a chance to offer an idea to the group when invited to do so. Seeing their peers accept their suggestions may embolden them to attempt cooperative play at child-initiated times of the day.

▲ Play as partners with children

Teachers model cooperation when they act as partners in children's play. To join in children's activities, get down on their level, imitate their use of materials, and talk with them about their interests and ideas. Let them take the lead and act out the roles they assign you. You can occasionally offer an idea, but be sensitive to the response and drop it if the child does not pick on it. See the following anecdote for an example of how a teacher lets the children direct and expand the play:

> *At work time in the house area, Gina and Lily declare their restaurant is open for business. Beth, their teacher, asks if she can order lunch. "What do you want?" asks Gina. Beth says she's hungry and orders a sandwich, salad, and large glass of lemonade. "We only have soup and cupcakes at this restaurant," says Lily. "What kinds do you have?" asks Beth. "Tomato soup and chocolate cupcakes," answers Lily. "Then that's what I'll order," says Beth. "Coming right up," says Gina, and she puts a bowl, a plate, and eating utensils on the table.*

KDI 14. Moral development: Children develop an internal sense of right and wrong.

Description: Children develop ethical behavior. They understand that there are moral principles that do not vary by situation (e.g., people should not hit others).

How Morality Develops

Research shows that moral development begins in toddlerhood and extends well into adulthood (Pinker, 2008). Piaget (1932/1965) was among the first psychologists to study moral development in children and his work was elaborated by Lawrence Kohlberg and his colleagues (Power, Higgins, & Kohlberg, 1991). They describe a child's progression in moral development from self-interest (what is best for me) to conformity with rules (a rigid division between right and wrong) to a more reciprocal system for judging behavior (based on people's intentions).

Preschoolers wrestle with questions about how to treat others. At this stage, moral development is characterized by concrete thinking and observation of results, but children gradually begin to consider the motivation behind the action and how it makes people feel (DeVries & Zan, 2012). They consider whether harmful behavior is accidental or intentional. The ability to differentiate intent is fragile at this age — preschoolers still focus primarily on the consequences of their actions. However, the difference becomes clearer as classification skills in general develop, that is, children are increasingly able to sort behaviors into those that were done "on purpose" and those that happened "by accident." Consider the following example:

At outside time, Casey runs into Maribelle while he is riding a bike. He gets off and says, "I'm really sorry. It was an accident." Then he gives her a hug. "It's okay. You didn't hurt me," Maribelle reassures him. Casey looks relieved. "Do you want to ride the bike now?" he offers.

Teaching Strategies That Support Moral Development

▲ Model moral behavior

Be consistent and fair-minded in your interactions with children. Emphasize problem-solving, not blame or punishment. When resolving social conflicts with children, avoid indefinite or abstract solutions; children need to see a direct relationship between their behavior and its result. Remember too that instructional strategies influence the development of moral reasoning. Top-down teaching conveys the message that morality derives from authority. By contrast, an active, inquiry-based approach to learning (shared control) encourages children to express ideas, try them out, and receive feedback from adults and peers in a reciprocal system that embodies moral principles.

▲ State situations that involve moral matters in simple cause-and-effect terms

Use simple explanations in concrete terms to describe moral situations (e.g., "Let's make sure every child who wants chicken gets a piece before we take seconds; it's not right if someone gets two pieces before every child has one") rather than stating abstract moral principles (e.g., "Greed is wrong"), which young children cannot understand. Children will pick up on these cause-and-effect statements and begin to use them on their own.

▲ Acknowledge children's moral behaviors

Adults often think that if children feel good about themselves, they will do the right thing. But moral development does not arise from self-esteem. In fact, says developmental psychologist William Damon (1990), it is the opposite. Children who do the right thing feel good about themselves. By acknowledging (not praising) children's moral behavior, we help them become more aware of what they did and its positive effect on others.

▲ Involve parents to achieve as much consistency as possible between home and school values

Support parents as they shape their children's moral behavior, especially as they try to counteract media messages that may differ from their own values. If home and classroom beliefs diverge, speak openly and honestly with parents about how to solve the problem. Often differences reflect variations in social conventions (such as whether food is eaten with utensils or fingers), rather than underlying moral principles (adults should feed children healthy food). Clarifying both commonalities and differences can help you reach a mutually acceptable resolution.

KDI 15. Conflict resolution: Children resolve social conflicts.

Description: Children engage in conflict resolution, or social problem solving, to settle interpersonal differences. They identify the problem, offer and listen to others' ideas, and choose a solution that is agreeable to all.

How Conflict Resolution Develops

Conflict resolution is the use of appropriate and nonaggressive strategies to settle interpersonal differences. Conflicts happen because children have not yet learned more acceptable ways to express their needs: "Children don't misbehave, they make mistakes" (Evans, 2002, p. 13). Seeing children's actions as mistakes rather than bad behaviors lets us respond with kindness and understanding, not punishment (Gartrell, 1995).

The capacity to resolve conflicts draws on a child's other emotional and social abilities. Because conflicts elicit strong feelings, children must be able to recognize and regulate emotions (KDI 9). Finding solutions involves seeing another's perspective, or empathy (KDI 10), preserving a sense of community (KDI 11), working cooperatively (KDI 13), and being guided by moral principles (KDI 14). Thus, mastering conflict resolution skills reflects the trajectory of growth in many areas.

Teaching Strategies That Support Conflict Resolution

▲ Establish a safe classroom with clear expectations

Children need to know that their bodies; their feelings; their thoughts, ideas, and words; and their work are safe (Levin, 2003). Reassure children that you will not allow them to be physically or verbally hurt and will immediately stop any harmful or dangerous behavior. Let them know they will never be punished, shamed, or deprived of basic needs.

Many strategies for establishing the learning environment and daily routine also create a safe classroom. Ample and diverse materials minimize conflicts over who plays with what. Open traffic patterns and lack of clutter keep children from colliding and knocking over one another's work, while too much openness (all the furniture up against the wall) encourages running and accidents. A consistent routine helps children know what to expect. Minimize waiting time and transitions to avoid the situations that lead to challenging behavior, and provide clear and consistent limits so children have a sense of control over what behaviors are and are not acceptable.

▲ Use a multistep approach to conflict resolution

To help children resolve social conflicts when they do occur, HighScope teachers receive training in a six-step **problem-solving approach to conflict resolution** (detailed in Evans, 2002). Each step is described below with an example. For a summary with additional examples, see chapter 5.

Step 1. Approach calmly, stopping any hurtful actions. When you remain calm, it helps children regain control. Place yourself between the children, get down on their level, use a calm voice and gentle touch, and do not take sides. If an object is involved, hold it yourself. This neutralizes the object so children can become engaged in solving the problem.

Emma and Joe are building a dinosaur house together. When Joe accidentally knocks part of it down, Emma pushes him, saying, "Get out!" Their teacher, observing this interaction, comes over and places herself between the children and the house they are building. She kneels down between the children and gently puts an arm around each of them.

Step 2. Acknowledge children's feelings. Emotions often run high during a conflict because children feel strong strongly about their desires. Helping children express their feelings allows them to let go of their emotions so they can begin to solve the problem. Use simple words to help children label their feelings (e.g., "You look really upset"). You may need to acknowledge feelings several times before you are ready to move on to the next step.

Adult: Emma, you sound angry with Joe. And Joe, you look sad.

Step 3. Gather information. It is important for all the children involved to express their points of view. You and other adults need the information, the children need to have their say, and everyone can benefit from listening to the others state what they need in the situation. You might start by asking an open-ended question such as "What's the problem?"

> **Adult:** *(Asks each child)* What's the problem? Tell me what happened?

Step 4. Restate the problem. Restating the problem ("So the problem is...") without taking sides or jumping in with your solution lets children know you are truly listening. Repeat the children's words, or rephrase them if the words are hurtful or unclear. For example, if a child says, "He's a dummy. He took my block," you might say, "You're upset because Vic took the block off the top of your tower." Check with the children to make sure you have stated the problem correctly, and allow them to add more information, if necessary.

> **Adult:** Joe, you don't want Emma to push you, and Emma, you don't want Joe to build because he is knocking the house down. Is that right? *(They nod their heads.)*

Step 5. Ask for ideas for solutions and choose one together. Begin by asking, "What can we do to solve this problem?" Encourage children to propose a solution, giving them ample time to think and respond. Accept their ideas, even if some are unrealistic. If the children draw a blank, offer an idea or two to get them started. Help children think through the consequences of implementing their ideas and encourage *them* to pick one. Sometimes, an idea that adults think is unworkable or unfair may end up working just fine for the children. Once the children choose a solution, make sure that each child is comfortable with it.

> **Adult:** You both still want to build the dinosaur house. What can we do to solve the problem?
>
> **Emma:** I want to build this part by myself. Joe can build over there.
>
> **Joe:** I want to build something for the dinosaurs too.

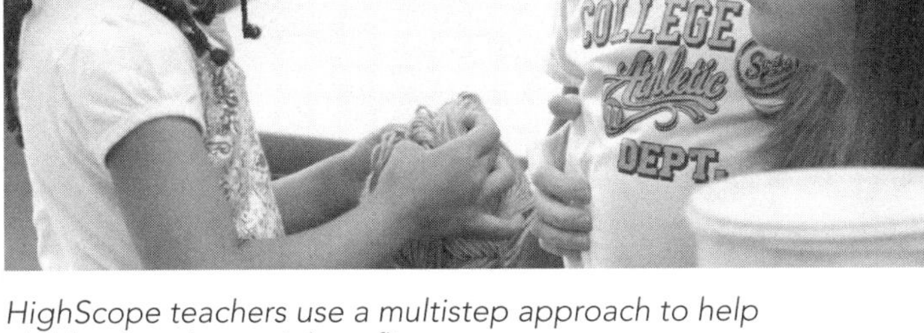

HighScope teachers use a multistep approach to help children resolve social conflicts.

> **Adult:** It sounds like Joe wants to build something for the dinosaurs too. What else do the dinosaurs need? What do you have at your house?
>
> **Joe:** I have a swimming pool at my house. I could build that.
>
> **Adult:** That's an idea.
>
> **Joe:** Hey, I can build the dinosaurs a swimming pool just like mine!
>
> **Emma:** Yeah!
>
> **Adult:** So, Emma is going to keep building the dinosaur house here *(points to the stack of blocks)* and Joe is going to build a dinosaur swimming pool in this space *(points to the area next to the dinosaur house). (Emma and Joe nod their heads yes and turn back to the blocks. Emma rebuilds the dinosaur house while Joe starts building the swimming pool.)*

Step 6. Give follow-up support as needed. Acknowledge that the *children* have solved the problem: "You solved the problem!" As children return to their play, stay nearby to make sure the solution is working and everyone is satisfied (you may also help carry out the solution). If a problem remains, repeat the process with the children to find another approach.

> **Adult:** Emma and Joe, you solved the problem! You both talked about ideas for solving your problem together. And you listened to each other carefully. I'd like to see the dinosaur house and pool when they are finished.

▲ Help children reflect on problem-solving strategies apart from actual conflict situations

Sometimes it is easier for children to process what they have learned after a conflict has passed, when emotions are not running so high. You can review the episode and acknowledge their success in resolving it later, for example, during snacktime or as you dig alongside them at outside time. You can also read books, share songs, and tell stories about people coping with similar social problems. Children also explore conflict resolution in their artwork and pretend play. Another useful technique is a *social story,* where an adult introduces a common problem during a time when children are together (e.g., at greeting circle), the children share their ideas about how to solve it, and then they agree on a solution to try. Typical problems addressed with social stories include children sharing toys, not letting others join their play, or unsafe situations such as children running or spilling water.

Try These Ideas Yourself

1. List what you consider to be the five most important things preschoolers need to know or be able to do in the Social and Emotional Development content area when they enter kindergarten. Why are they important? How can teachers support their development?

2. In the following scenario, identify the Social and Emotional Development KDIs. What kinds of learning are occurring in other areas of development? What could you as a teacher do to support and extend the learning? (Refer to the list of KDIs on p. 109.)

Brenda and Mikey are pretending to be kitty cats under one of the small-group tables. "We need bowls for milk," says Brenda. "I'll get some in the house area," replies Mikey. When he brings them back, Brenda says, "Those are too small. We're really thirsty!" When Mikey says those were the only bowls he could find, they decide they will have to make their own bowls. "I know," says Mikey. "They can be square bowls. Let's make them out of the big blocks." Brenda and Mikey go to the block area, and they each carry several blocks under the table. Greg comes over and asks what they are doing. "We're kitty cats and we're going to drink milk out of these big bowls," says Brenda. Greg asks if he can be a kitty cat too. "No," says Mikey. Greg watches them for a while and then gets some more large blocks. "Bring them under here," says Brenda. "You can be the guy who pours the milk for the kitties."

3. Think of the last time you had a disagreement with someone (e.g., a family member, friend, colleague). Did the other person acknowledge your feelings? How did you respond? Did you acknowledge the other person's feelings? How did the other person respond? What ideas do your reflections give you for working with children in the classroom?

4. Think of all the words you can use with children that have to do with feelings (e.g., *happy, angry, sad*). Share your list with another adult, and ask for additional ideas. Use these words to help children identify and express their feelings. Write down when you used them and how children respond. Notice if and when they begin to use these words themselves.

Chapter 12

What Is the HighScope Curriculum in Physical Development and Health?

Think About It

"Pick me, please pick me," the child silently pleads as his or her classmates choose up sides for a game. Those who are selected early walk with pride to their place in the lineup. Posture erect, heads held high, they high-five their teammates. Meanwhile, the children still waiting to be chosen grow progressively more stooped and despondent. Even standing still, their bodies seem to fall apart with rejection and shame. They'd rather be any place other than the playing field.

Decades later, we can still remember which group we belonged to and the feelings it evoked. If we were among the first children picked for the team, we felt it not only meant we were physically well coordinated but also, by extension, popular, smart, and an all-around good student. We were bound for success, whatever endeavors we undertook. By contrast, if we were chosen near the end, we took it as a negative reflection not only of our athletic prowess but also of our general intelligence and likableness. This familiar ritual could also work in the opposite direction; that is, children who were not particularly talented at hitting a ball or scoring a basket but were well-regarded otherwise (for being smart or friendly) might be selected early for a sports team. Knowing they were well thought of, regardless of their athletic ability, allowed them to play with gusto and self-confidence. They had fun in the gym and on the field!

At what point in our development does our self-image become so tied to our physical abilities? Very young children learning how to crawl or walk do not think in these terms. Their bodies are their own and they practice using them, gaining satisfaction at the same time they gain skill. No one has to watch or give approval for infants to roll over or for toddlers to heedlessly hurl themselves across the room in pursuit of a toy. "Look at me" only comes later, when children sense that others (parents, siblings, caregivers) attach value to their physical accomplishments. Before then, the sheer joy of moving and mastering are sufficient to propel physical development for its own sake.

A curriculum that supports physical development and health aims to sustain the determination and delight of the young child's earliest experiences. It recognizes that physical development is not a contest or a means for gaining approval. All children need to see themselves as competent explorers, not as winners or losers. Young children use the parts of their bodies, and their bodies as a whole, as primary tools in learning about the world. To shake their confidence in their ability to move with increasing purpose and skill is to discourage an important desire and pathway to discovery. By contrast, encouraging children to see what their bodies can do as they handle materials and move around their environment gives them a valuable self-image and a tool kit they will own for life. The HighScope emphasis on *active participatory learning* promotes children's physical involvement with the world as central to early growth and development.

Chapter Learning Objectives

By the end of this chapter, you will be able to

- Explain why early learning in physical development and health is important.
- Describe the HighScope key developmental indicators (KDIs) in the Physical Development and Health content area.
- Begin to apply the strategies adults use to scaffold (support and gently extend) early learning in physical development and health.

Why Physical Development and Health Is Important

The idea that children need to be "taught" to develop physically seems odd. Provided children have adequate nutrition and opportunities to use their large and small muscles in safe settings, there is a natural biological progression to their gross- and fine-motor development (Copple & Bredekamp, 2009). However, it is a mistake to view these changes as purely maturational. Many factors at home, in school, and in the culture at large affect healthy physical development. In fact, research confirms that young children do not learn basic motor skills simply through unguided play (Manross, 2000). Stephen Sanders (2002), a pioneer in the development of preschool movement curricula, says that "play provides children with the opportunity to practice movement skills in a variety of contexts. [However], some structuring of physical activity is necessary to help children maximize their movement experiences" (p. 31).

Physical and Health Benefits of Movement Education

Movement education has received increasing attention due to the rise in childhood obesity. According to the White House Task Force on Childhood Obesity (2010), one in five children is overweight or obese by his or her sixth birthday. The preschool years are crucial to prevent obesity, since ages three to seven are when fat tissue is laid down (fat cells remain in the body for life). Poor diet and physical inactivity, which have been tied to obesity, are the primary reasons for the increase in early-onset health problems. By contrast, children who develop basic motor skills and are physically active are less likely to become obese and more likely to become healthy adults (National Center for Health Statistics, 2004).

Studies cited by the American Academy of Pediatrics, Committee on Public Education (2001) show a significant correlation between time spent watching media and being overweight. Instead of children being sedentary, the National Association for Sport and Physical Education (2009) recommends preschoolers get *at least* one hour a day of vigorous physical activity (combined for home, school, and other settings), yet studies show most children fall far short of this goal.

Physical development also promotes learning in other areas. Children who are physically competent are seen positively by peers and adults and gain knowledge and skills through social interactions. They are more willing to tackle intellectual challenges and do better in school than those who are physically insecure (Gallahue & Donnelly, 2003). Rae Pica (1997), a children's movement specialist, makes no distinction between physical and academic learning: "Not only does movement stimulate learning physiologically, but it also helps young children to experience concepts so they can process them cognitively" (p. 4). Brain research also shows children's minds and bodies are inextricably connected — moving increases heart rate and circulation, sending more oxygen to key areas of the brain (Jensen, 2000).

Developmental Stages and Principles in Physical Development

Children generally progress through four developmental stages or levels of proficiency in their

Terms Used in This Chapter

• movement education • gross-motor skills • fine-motor skills • self-help skills • nonlocomotor (anchored) movement • locomotor (nonanchored) movement • hand-eye coordination • self-other boundary • steady beat • rhythm physical abilities (Graham, Holt/Hale, & Parker, 2004). There is great individual variability, but preschoolers are typically at the first two levels:

1. Precontrol level (beginner): Children's actions often lack coordination and fluidity. They need many opportunities for exploration and feedback to discover what their bodies can do.

2. Control level (advanced beginner): Children's movements are less haphazard but they still require practice. To learn a new skill, they must experience success at least 80 percent of the time (Sanders, 2002).

3. Utilization level (intermediate): Children's movements are increasingly automatic. They no longer have to think before taking action and can join one movement skill with another.

4. Proficiency level (advanced): Children's movements begin to seem effortless. They are able to refine specific skills and are now ready to participate in formal games.

Two underlying principles are important for classroom practices in physical development and health. First, motor development is sequential; later learning builds on earlier skills (Gallahue, 1995). Second, **movement education** and youth sports are different (Pica, 2013). Children lack the skills to participate in formal sports until age six or later. By contrast, early movement education emphasizes self-improvement, involvement, and cooperation instead of competition. There are no winners and losers.

General Teaching Strategies for Physical Development and Health

▲ Provide space to explore and practice motor skills

To develop **gross-motor skills,** young children need large open spaces. Classrooms should have unobstructed areas for large-group time as well as for construction and other projects at work time. Children also need freedom to move outdoors, in an onsite play yard or nearby playground. If weather or safety conditions make this difficult, a gym or multipurpose room can substitute.

Young children also need quiet and protected spaces to practice **fine-motor skills** and hand-eye coordination. Uncluttered tables at a child's height provide flat surfaces for working with small toys, writing tools, and art materials. Other work spaces include the floor, easels, paper tacked to the wall, outdoor pavement, sand and water tables, and flower gardens and digging areas.

Children need large, open spaces to develop their gross-motor skills.

▲ Provide equipment and materials to explore and practice motor and self-help skills

Developing gross-motor skills requires equipment for climbing, riding, sliding, and balancing as well as objects children can manipulate while moving (e.g., balls, beanbags, scarves, hoops, ropes). Young children's fine-motor skills are honed using art materials, writing tools, dress-up clothes, household utensils, blocks and other construction toys and tools, puzzles, stacking and nesting toys, beads, and items that can be taken apart and put back together. Some items are best purchased (and worth the investment), such as a sturdy set of wooden blocks. Others can be made or collected at minimal cost, contributed by children's families and local businesses.

▲ Provide time to explore and practice motor and self-help skills

Movement activities most often occur during large-group time and outside time. However, other times of the day also provide opportunities for preschoolers to exercise muscles, learn about their bodies, take care of their physical needs (and develop their **self-help skills**), and engage in health-promoting practices. For example, children can exercise large-motor skills by making a train at planning time and jumping off in the area where they want to play. They can move in different ways during transitions or toss beanbags into a basket at small-group time. At work time, children may draw, do puzzles, or turn the pages of a book, and at snacktime they can pour juice or use utensils — all fine-motor activities.

▲ Model and guide emerging physical skills and healthy behaviors

Although preschoolers' abilities have come a long way since toddlerhood, their bodies are still changing. Likewise, their capacity to take care of their own needs and adopt healthy behaviors is evolving. Demonstrate healthy behaviors yourself, and encourage children's attempts to take care of their own needs, rather than judging the outcomes of their efforts. Remember to keep your expectations reasonable.

▲ Add language to describe behavior related to physical development and health

Describing and encouraging children's efforts to describe their movements and health-related behaviors makes them aware of their bodies, actions, spatial relations, and self-care competence. Verbal labels also increase vocabulary, which helps children master new challenges. For example, a child who understands putting one foot *in front of* the other can respond to the directions to do so when learning to throw a ball. Words such as *beginning, end*; *top, bottom*; *fast, slow*; or *straight, bent* can also be applied to other content areas, such as Language, Literacy, and Communication; Mathematics; and Creative Arts.

Key Developmental Indicators in Physical Development and Health

HighScope has five key developmental indicators (KDIs) in Physical Development and Health: 16. Gross-motor skills, 17. Fine-motor skills, 18. Body awareness, 19. Personal care, and 20. Healthy behavior. See "KDIs in Physical Developement and Health" on this page. The rest of this chapter discusses the Physical Development and Health KDIs and the strategies you can use to support their development in young children.

KDIs in Physical Development and Health

16. **Gross-motor skills:** Children demonstrate strength, flexibility, balance, and timing in using their large muscles.
17. **Fine-motor skills:** Children demonstrate dexterity and hand-eye coordination in using their small muscles.
18. **Body awareness:** Children know about their bodies and how to navigate them in space.
19. **Personal care:** Children carry out personal care routines on their own.
20. **Healthy behavior:** Children engage in healthy practices.

KDI 16. Gross-motor skills: Children demonstrate strength, flexibility, balance, and timing in using their large muscles.

Description: Children use nonlocomotor (stationary) movements (e.g., bending, twisting, rocking) and locomotor (traveling) movements (e.g., walking, climbing, running, jumping, hopping, skipping, marching, galloping). They coordinate gross-motor movements in throwing, catching, kicking, bouncing balls, and using a swing.

How Gross-Motor Skills Develop

As children's bodies become more proportional (e.g., their heads are less outsized relative to their torsos, their limbs lengthen), preschoolers' movements become steadier and more surefooted (Tomlinson & Hyson, 2009). However, because their nervous and muscular systems are still not fully mature, preschoolers' reaction time is generally slower than that of early elementary-school-aged children. They may, therefore, sometimes appear hesitant or uncoordinated.

Preschoolers develop several types of gross-motor skills. **Nonlocomotor** or **anchored movement** involves an upper or lower body movement performed in one's personal space (without moving around) that does not involve a weight transfer (Weikart, 2000). Examples of nonlocomotor movements include tapping the head while sitting, rocking back and forth in place, or twisting the upper body while one's feet remain on the floor. **Locomotor** or **nonanchored movement** involves a weight transfer or moving through space, such as walking, running, galloping, and jumping. Both sets of skills may be performed alone or with objects (such as standing and waving a scarf over one's head or marching while beating a drum).

Teaching Strategies That Support Gross-Motor Skills

▲ Encourage children to explore a wide range of positions and movements

To explore nonlocomotor movements, encourage children to think of ways to move their arms, legs, head, or torso while remaining stationary (e.g., children might stand in place and swing their arms to music at large-group time or observe their shadows as they twist back and forth). For locomotor movements, plan group times and transitions in which children run, jump, and use other active motions. Also be alert to their spontaneous movements during work time.

▲ Build movement skills in sequence

Preschoolers work up to a more complex movement by gradually mastering its components, for example, from striking a stationary object with their hand to hitting one gently thrown at them with a bat.

Sequencing also applies to following movement directions. Begin with one simple movement (e.g., pat the head), and then add a second movement after children are comfortable with the first one (e.g., pat the head and touch the shoulders). When giving movement directions, separate the verbal and visual components (Weikart, 2000), that is, demonstrate a movement without talking *or* describe it without moving. Then ask the children to try it. After they master it, combine the verbal and visual directions.

These children are exploring nonlocomotor movements by moving their arms and torso while they remain stationary.

▲ Provide interesting materials to accompany children's movements

Think of equipment and materials children can use in different ways when they move, including *things to move with* (e.g., pinwheels, paper fans, containers filled with sound-making materials), *things to move on and in* (e.g., paper plates to slide on, "caves" made by draping sheets over a table, low balance beams), and *things to make move* (e.g., wagons, balled socks, wheelbarrows, foam balls).

▲ Provide experiences and materials for children to explore movement concepts

To explore the weight and force of their movements, provide children with experiences and open-ended materials, such as empty appliance boxes, tires, sections of logs, or flexible tubing. Comment on their level of effort (e.g., "You are carrying a heavy box") and amount of force (e.g., "You are swinging the tire in a wide arc").

KDI 17. Fine-motor skills: Children demonstrate dexterity and hand-eye coordination in using their small muscles.

Description: Children use the fine-motor movements (e.g., molding, squeezing, poking, smoothing, positioning, writing, cutting) needed to manipulate materials and tools. They have hand-eye coordination (e.g., stacking blocks, assembling puzzles, stringing beads, pouring juice, pounding nails).

How Fine-Motor Skills Develop

Between the ages of three and five, children gain in strength, **hand-eye coordination,** and endurance (using their whole hand, and their thumb together with their index or middle finger). They grow more adept at manipulating age-appropriate materials such as scissors, pencils, screwdrivers, paintbrushes, fasteners, and gears. Despite these advances, there are physical limits to children's abilities. They cannot make fully circular wrist motions because the cartilage does not harden into bone until age six (Berk, 2011), and writing, drawing, and precise cutting remain difficult. Although right- or left-handedness is generally established by age four, children at this age still try to use their nondominant hand. Keep these limits in mind to maintain realistic expectations.

To support fine-motor skills, offer children materials and support activities that involve using their hands and fingers.

Teaching Strategies That Support Fine-Motor Skills

▲ Provide materials and activities that involve the use of fingers and hands

Make sure there are appealing materials in each classroom area that engage children in using their fine-motor skills, such as scissors (art area), thin rods (block area), magazines (book area), small figures (toy area), egg beaters (house area), measuring spoons (sand and water table), and chalk (playground). Provide hard and soft materials that children can transform with their hands and fingers and that require varying levels of effort, such as play dough with different amounts of flour to change its thickness and moldability. The same holds true when you plan small- and large-group times. Vary both the materials and the content of these activities so children can use their hands and eyes to make and build, transform, investigate cause and effect, and represent things (write, draw, sculpt).

▲ Provide similar objects in a range of sizes and shapes that children can handle

Provide the same types of materials in graduated levels of difficulty: Duplo and Lego blocks, knob puzzles and flat jigsaw puzzles, pegs and pegboards with large and small holes, figures and animals in different sizes, paintbrushes with thick and thin handles and different width bristles, fat and skinny crayons and markers, and doll clothes with different types of fasteners. This allows children with varying levels of dexterity to carry out their plans in increasingly complex ways.

KDI 18. Body awareness: Children know about their bodies and how to navigate them in space.

Description: Children recognize the names and locations of body parts. They are aware of their own bodies in relation to people and objects around them. Children feel, and move their bodies to, a steady beat.

How Body Awareness Develops

Body awareness in preschool involves two components. First is the **self-other boundary,** differentiating the space one occupies from the space shared with other people and objects. Early preschoolers tend to bump into things, but they gradually get better at navigating space. Second is learning the names and functions of body parts. Young children are intrinsically interested in their own bodies and what they can do with them.

A preschooler's body image often lags behind reality. Clumsiness is sometimes the result of children's body awareness not catching up to their increased size. Perceptual development also affects body awareness. Young children perceive sensory information but may not adjust their movements accordingly. Eyesight also plays a role, as preschoolers are far sighted and have trouble switching focus between near and far items (Tomlinson & Hyson, 2009). Their binocular vision is still developing and limited depth perception means they may run into things and each other (Pica, 2013). And, although preschoolers' hearing is more developed than sight, a distracting noise easily throws them off target.

Teaching Strategies That Support Body Awareness

▲ Create environments and activities to explore personal (self) space and general (shared) space

Young children need clearly marked spaces, such as a cubby or a coat hook, they can call their own. Large-group activities can also help them define their space. Begin with simple movements, such as rocking or bending, where children stay in their own place, and use visual markers, such as carpet squares. Once children have a sense of their bodies' boundaries, encourage them move through a space shared by other people and objects. Again, begin with a simple locomotor movement, such as crawling or walking, and say something like, "Let's see how we can move to the other side of the room without touching anyone or anything else." Encourage them to move in their own ways.

▲ Provide opportunities to move through different types of space in different ways

Give children opportunities to move through different types of space — narrow and wide, low and high, straight and twisted, short and long, and smooth and bumpy. Encourage them to move their bodies in, around, and through these spaces in different ways. Let them experiment with movements when they are alone in a space and also when they share that space with others.

▲ Provide opportunities for children to feel and move their bodies to a steady beat

"Steady beat is the consistent, repetitive pulse that lies within every rhyme, song, or musical selection" (Weikart, 2000, p. 122). (Note that steady beat is different from rhythm; "rhythm is superimposed on the steady beat of the rhyme or song" (p. 124). A sense of **steady beat** begins with a sense of steady movement, which is why movement activities are important in preschool. (**Rhythm** activities may begin in second grade.) Movement in steady beat helps children develop a basic sense of timing, contributing to speech fluency and reading fluency (Haraksin-Probst, Hutson-Brandhagen, & Weikart, 2008).

To help young children make steady movements and feel a steady beat, provide equipment with regular, predictable motions and sounds (e.g., rocking chairs and horses, swings, metronomes, wind-up kitchen timers) and offer them materials and activities so they can create their own steady beat such as patting to a song or chant, pounding a ball of clay, or clapping under water.

▲ Help children learn the names and functions of body parts

Preschoolers learn about body parts in the context of play, not rote memorization. Name body parts when you introduce or imitate children's movements (e.g., "Cara says to tap our *shoulders* with our *thumbs*"). Literature and the arts offer many opportunities to focus on the body:

> *At work time in the art area, Senguele draws a picture of Sue, her teacher. The figure has a face, arms, and legs. "What else do you see when you look at me?" asks Sue. Senguele adds fingers, feet, shoes, pants, and hair to her drawing.*

Read books, recite nursery rhymes, and sing songs that feature body parts (such as "The Hokey Pokey"). Describe, and encourage children to describe, the actions they perform using different parts of their bodies.

KDI 19. Personal care: Children carry out personal care routines on their own.

Description: Children feed themselves, dress, wash their hands, brush their teeth, use tissues, and use the toilet.

How Personal Care Develops

Young children enjoy taking care of themselves. Adults are sometimes amazed at how long and intently children work at mastering a self-help skill such as zipping up their jacket and the satisfaction on their faces when they succeed. The development of children's fine-motor skills (KDI 17) enables them to assume more self-care responsibility. As children learn to take care of themselves, they often show interest in taking care of others too. For example, they may help a friend fasten a shoe or change the water in the guinea pig's bowl.

Teaching Strategies That Support Personal Care

▲ Let children do things for themselves

Adults are often tempted to do things for children because it is faster, easier, or neater. However, children cannot learn to care for themselves unless they are permitted to do so. Build enough time into the schedule to clean up or get ready for outside time so children can practice without feeling rushed. Unless an issue involves health or safety, let them achieve the goals they set for themselves. When you improve upon or correct children, they may give up on further attempts.

▲ Provide activities and equipment to practice the skills needed for personal care routines

Provide tools and activities so children can develop the manual dexterity needed to button a jacket, steady a pitcher, or loop a shoelace. Examples include beads and string, pegs and pegboards, scissors, staplers, screwdrivers, hammers, and brooms. Preschoolers practice many self-help skills during pretend play, such as preparing food when playing house or dressing up as firefighters. Art and building activities also allow them to exercise the fine-motor abilities needed to care for themselves. Even turning the pages of a book is practice for separating the top paper towel from the stack.

KDI 20. Healthy behavior: Children engage in healthy practices.

Description: Children participate in active, physical play. They know that some foods are healthier than others. Children carry out behaviors that are healthy (e.g., cough into their elbow, wash their hands after toileting, use their own fork) and safe (e.g., wear a bike helmet, not walk in front of a moving swing, walk around a spill).

How Healthy Behavior Develops

According to pediatrician Susan Aronson (2012), physical activity and good nutrition are essential to healthy development and are inextricably linked: "Activity has a lot to do with appetite and nutritional status. Active children need more calories than inactive ones; this means they have a better chance of getting all the required nutrients. Adequate physical exercise year-round, preferably on a daily basis, is important to a child's development because it: stimulates healthy appetites, uses calories and maintains muscle tissue, improves coordination, and encourages children to express themselves and develop social skills" (p. 79).

As children learn to take care of themselves, they often show interest in helping to take care of others.

Early childhood programs play a vital role providing healthy foods and time for vigorous activity. Because children's stomachs are small, they need several smaller meals and snacks, rather than one or two large ones, during the day. Variety is also important. Preschoolers, like adults, enjoy food from different groups, provided they are introduced gradually and never forced upon a child. Good exercise habits are also established when children enjoy a variety of large-motor activities. Be sure to enjoy healthy food and exercise alongside the children to send the message that good nutrition and an active lifestyle are desirable and routine for adults too.

Teaching Strategies That Support Healthy Behavior

▲ Model healthy behavior yourself

The more you engage in healthy behaviors as a regular part of your day, the more preschoolers are apt to adopt these behaviors themselves. In addition to modeling the behavior itself, you also convey your attitude toward it. If you express displeasure, children will internalize these negative sentiments as well. If you express pleasure in exercising your body, sampling different foods, and practicing good hygiene, children will develop these positive attitudes instead.

▲ Provide opportunities for children to engage in healthy behavior

Opportunities for exercise, healthy eating, and good hygiene abound throughout the day: moving at large-group time, washing before and after meals, putting on bicycle helmets, or wiping noses with a tissue. Children's interest and pride in mastering self-help skills is a natural motivator for them to develop these habits.

Learning about food and nutrition can also be easily integrated into the daily routine. Plan meals and small-group times so children can describe and discuss the properties of healthy foods (including their appearance, sound, smell, feel, and taste), and cook with children. Many teachers shy away from cooking because they worry about accidents, transmission of germs, or other hazards (Colker, 2005). However, there are many simple steps you can take to protect children's safety and health: use dull knives, heavy potholders, and warm rather than hot water; keep foods at the recommended temperatures; and discourage nibbling during cooking. Preschoolers have the self-control to wait if you keep the preparation time short and provide a concrete measure (such as a timer) of when it will be done.

Try These Ideas Yourself

1. List what you consider to be the five most important things preschoolers need to know or be able to do in the Physical Health and Development content area when they enter kindergarten. Why are they important? How can teachers support their development?

2. What health concerns do you think confront young children today? How can a program of age-appropriate physical education help to address these problems? What would you say to a school board to convince them to fund such a program?

3. In the following scenario, identify the Physical Development and Health KDIs taking place.

What other educational opportunities are occurring? What could you as a teacher do to scaffold (support and gently extend) the learning experience?

Melanie and Liza are playing a game in which they dig a small hole under one tree, run to a second tree, put both hands on the trunk and say "dino bobo," and run back to the first tree. Then they repeat all four steps. After Melanie takes a turn, Liza says, "You didn't use both hands. You have to do it all over again." Melanie repeats the part where she runs to the second tree and says "dino bobo," this time putting both hands on the tree trunk. Liza says, "No, you have to do the whole thing again!" Melanie refuses.

4. List all the words you can think of to use with children that have to do with the position of the body relative to other things (e.g., *above, underneath, next to,* and so on). Share your list with a coworker, classmate, or friend and ask for additional ideas. Make a plan for how you will use these words the next time you are involved in a movement experience with children.

Preschoolers learn about food and nutrition through hands-on activities, including cooking.

Chapter 13

What Is the HighScope Curriculum in Language, Literacy, and Communication?

Think About It

Imagine you are traveling in a foreign country named Paminiland. Not only do residents speak another language (called Pamini), but they also use a different written alphabet. At first, you depend on your tour guide for everything: reserving hotel rooms, ordering food, arranging transportation, and dealing with vendors at the market. A word that keeps coming up in these transactions is kindalay*, so you figure out this is the name of the local currency. By midweek, you notice all the signs in the marketplace have a number followed by the same set of marks. What at first looked like squiggles resolves into three distinct shapes — a square with a dot in the middle, a half-moon, and a vertical line with a curlicue on top. This is the written word for the currency, and the three marks stand, respectively, for the sounds in kin/da/lay. On the fifth day, you buy a piece of mellani, the local pastry, on your own. You ask your tour guide to write the letters for mellani on the corner of your map, and later that day you copy them on a postcard to your family. You vow not to leave Paminiland before getting the recipe for this wonderful confection.*

The connection between language and literacy is powerful. In the above anecdote, the aha moment connecting the spoken and written word for *kindalay* came only after you heard and saw it many times. You recognized this particular word because of its importance to you — it allowed you to get the services, and especially, that delicious pastry you wanted. Later in your travels, you would probably pick up other words and phrases that were especially useful as you journeyed around Paminiland, such as words corresponding to *bathroom, too expensive,* and *stop and rest.*

The development of literacy in young children follows a similar course. Before they can read, children need many rich experiences hearing and speaking the language represented in print. The first letters and words they read and write are personally meaningful to them and are usually their own names. The HighScope Curriculum honors and promotes this connection between language and literacy, recognizing that children are powerfully motivated to communicate with others.

Why Language, Literacy, and Communication Is Important

Early literacy is one of the most important factors in school readiness because so much learning depends on knowing how to read. Reading, in turn, depends on language skills, particularly a sizable vocabulary. Language is also the basis for cognitive development because it allows us to represent ideas in words. Social and emotional development too depends on language skills. For example, naming feelings helps children manage their emotions (Raver et al., 2007), and verbal interactions help build positive relationships (Denham, 2006). The Joint Position Statement of the International Reading Association and the National Association for the Education of Young Children

Chapter Learning Objectives

By the end of this chapter, you will be able to

- Explain why early learning in language, literacy, and communication is important.
- Describe the HighScope key developmental indicators (KDIs) in the Language, Literacy, and Communication content area.
- Begin to apply the strategies adults use to scaffold (support and gently extend) early learning in language, literacy, and communication.

Literacy is an important school readiness skill because so much learning depends on reading. Reading, in turn, depends on language skills, especially vocabulary.

notes that "although reading and writing abilities continue to develop throughout the life span, the early childhood years — from birth through age eight — are the most important period for literacy development" (Neuman, Copple, & Bredekamp, 2000, p. 3).

How Early Literacy Skills Develop

Oral language is the foundation of early literacy, and its development begins at birth (Dickinson & Tabors, 2002). Infants listen to caregivers talk and sing to them. Older infants and toddlers talk to communicate their needs to the people around them. By the time children are in preschool, there is a significant increase in their use of conversation to create and sustain relationships. Three- and four-year-olds ask questions, listen, refer to things that are not present, and talk about desires and imaginary situations. Their vocabularies grow, and they master the basic rules of grammar. Young children are also beginning to read and write, at first in unconventional ways (such as "reading" pictures and drawing horizontal lines of scribbles) and later in more conventional ways. **Emergent literacy** research (Snow, Burns, & Griffin, 1998) shows the connection between spoken and written language and proves that literacy skills develop gradually in the early years; thus, we no longer wait until first grade to begin reading instruction.

Key Components in Early Literacy

Touchstone publications, such as those by the National Reading Panel (2000) and the National Early Literacy Panel (Strickland & Shanahan, 2004), identified four key components of literacy development: **comprehension, phonological awareness, alphabetic knowledge,** and **concepts about print.** Researchers and educators added to this list the role of *speaking* (conversation) and *vocabulary* in comprehension, specific *book knowledge* as a subset of concepts about print, the importance of valuing and enjoying *reading*, and the role of *writing* to facilitate learning to read and communicating (Dickinson & Tabors, 2002; Indrisano & Squire, 2000; Schickedanz & Collins, 2013). In addition, researchers and educators are paying increasing attention to the 10 percent of today's students who do not speak English as their pri-

Terms Used in This Chapter

• oral language • emergent literacy • comprehension • phonological awareness • alphabetic knowledge • concepts about print • English language learners (ELLs) • Growing Readers Early Literacy Curriculum • interactive reading • contextualized and decontextualized language • co-narration • receptive (listening) vocabulary • productive (speaking) vocabulary • phonemic awareness • rhyming • alliteration • segmentation • alphabetic principle • letter links

mary language (National Center for Education Statistic, 2013). **English language learners (ELLs)** face the challenge of communicating in two or more tongues simultaneously.

General Teaching Strategies for Language, Literacy, and Communication

▲ Have real conversations with children

In a real conversation, adults *listen patiently* while children organize their thoughts, *communicate their interest nonverbally and verbally* (i.e., get down on the children's level, look at them, use facial expressions), and *let children dominate the conversation* (i.e., follow their lead, make comments, ask an occasional open-ended question). Children say little when commanded to talk (if you ask, "Did you like this story?" a common response will be "Uh-huh"). Children talk when they have something to say and a responsive partner to say it to.

In addition to verbal conversations, some programs employ sign language for all children as a way to communicate. Signing helps children recognize that words are symbols and can be combined following the rules of grammar, just like the connection between speech and print (Brereton, 2008; Daniels, 2001).

▲ Have fun with language

Enjoy sounds and words with children, rather than drilling them on vocabulary or grammar. Preschoolers love to hear and make up stories, rhymes, and chants. They repeat words, including big ones, even if they don't yet know their meanings. Preschoolers also enjoy making up words and combining sounds, using existing skills and developing new ones. For example:

> *"I jumped up and down, and guess what I said?" Jonah asks his teacher. "Bang-a-wang!"*
>
> ◆
>
> *"Beth," Jessa tells her teacher, while getting ready for outside time, "you're standing on my mitten." Beth moves her foot. Jessa holds up her mitten and says, "Squished to death by teacher Beth!"*

▲ Provide a print-rich environment

Preschoolers need to engage with print in many ways to understand that print can be used to *give and receive information* (e.g., area signs, message board, book about dinosaurs), *express ideas and opinions* (e.g., poem about a tree, song book of class favorites), *create and maintain relationships* (e.g., thank-you note, party invitation, turn-taking list), and *conduct business and accomplish tasks* (e.g., restaurant menu, set of instructions for a machine). Signs and labels should be meaningful to the children, posted at children's eye level and written in large print. Books should have their front covers facing out and be put on low shelves or in bins children can reach. Children also need to "touch" print, so make sure three-dimensional letters, books, magazines, and writing tools are handy and sturdy. Finally, don't go overboard; remember that print-rich does not mean print-cluttered.

▲ Use and enjoy print yourself

Think of your own excitement opening a book to meet a character, have an adventure, answer a question, or learn how to do something. Remember the satisfaction of recording your thoughts and feelings to share with people you care about. Let children see your pleasure reading and writing throughout the day to inspire them to become literate adults.

Key Developmental Indicators in Language, Literacy, and Communication

HighScope has 10 key developmental indicators (KDIs) in Language, Literacy, and Communication: 21. Comprehension, 22. Speaking, 23. Vocabulary, 24. Phonological awareness, 25. Alphabetic knowledge, 26. Reading, 27. Concepts about print, 28. Book knowledge, 29. Writing, and 30. English language learning. See "KDIs in Language, Literacy, and Communication" on page 134.

The rest of this chapter describes early learning in these KDIs and the teaching strategies you can use throughout the program day to support their development. For specific activities, see the **Growing Readers Early Literacy Curriculum** (HighScope Educational Research Foundation,

KDIs in Language, Literacy, and Communication[1]

21. **Comprehension:** Children understand language.
22. **Speaking:** Children express themselves using language.
23. **Vocabulary:** Children understand and use a variety of words and phrases.
24. **Phonological awareness:** Children identify distinct sounds in spoken language.
25. **Alphabetic knowledge:** Children identify letter names and their sounds.
26. **Reading:** Children read for pleasure and information.
27. **Concepts about print:** Children demonstrate knowledge about environmental print.
28. **Book knowledge:** Children demonstrate knowledge about books.
29. **Writing:** Children write for many different purposes.
30. **English language learning:** (If applicable) Children use English and their home language(s) (including sign language).

[1]Language, Literacy, and Communication KDIs 21–29 may be used for the child's home language(s) as well as English. KDI 30 refers specifically to English language learning.

2010) and other literacy resources on the High-Scope website (www.highscope.org).

KDI 21. Comprehension: Children understand language.

Description: Children understand (comprehend) conversations, signing, stories, books, songs, poems, and/or chants. They listen; respond; connect information to their own lives; predict what will happen next; and recall real and fictional people, materials, actions, events, and ideas.

How Comprehension Develops

Children have to understand the words they hear before they can make sense of the words they see in print. They progress from comprehending simple spoken (or signed) words and phrases to more detailed information (e.g., from "dog" to "the dog is running" to "the big dog is chasing the cat around the tree"). They respond to a simple statement with an action (fetch a cup), gesture (nod), or word ("No"). Children's understanding of oral and written stories undergoes a similar progression. First they remember a single character or event; later, they create a narrative sequence (e.g., from "boy" to "the boy cried" to "the boy was playing with his truck and when the truck broke, he cried").

Later still, children draw on their own experiences to understand a character's motivation and make predictions (Paris & Paris, 2003). Engaging preschoolers in conversation and **interactive reading** (i.e., encouraging the child to participate by making connections between the story and the child's life) of increasingly complex texts further develops their comprehension (Sulzby, 1986). They begin to use the same narrative devices found in storytelling and books. Instead of being confined to **contextualized language** ("here and now"), they use **decontextualized language** ("there and then") to imagine what is not visible ("Once upon a time" or "In a faraway land").

Teaching Strategies That Support Comprehension

▲ Engage in extended back-and-forth conversations

Leisurely discourse — a two-way conversation — encourages children to share their thoughts and feelings and gives adults a window into their perceptions and reasoning. The primary purpose of conversations, therefore, should not be to issue commands ("Put on your jacket") or elicit simple information ("Do you want more juice?"). Compare how much the child talks, and what the adult learns, in these two conversations:

Brief adult-dominated talk. A teacher walks up to a child who is painting at the easel.

> **Teacher**: *(Points at a flower in the painting)* What color is this?
>
> **Child**: Red.
>
> **Teacher**: *(Points to another flower)* How about this one?
>
> **Child**: Yellow.
>
> **Teacher**: Tell me the names of the other colors in your painting.
>
> **Child**: *(Stops painting)* I'm done painting. *(Takes off smock and goes to sink to wash up.)*

Extended two-way discourse. A teacher kneels silently beside a child who is painting at the easel.

> **Child**: *(After teacher has been watching for a minute)* It's my mommy's garden.
>
> **Teacher**: Your mommy has a garden.
>
> **Child**: *(Points at painting)* Flowers.
>
> **Teacher**: There are flowers in your mommy's garden.
>
> **Child**: Vegetables too. *(Points)* The yellow are daisies and the red circles are tomatoes.
>
> **Teacher**: There are daisies and tomatoes in your mommy's garden and also in your painting.
>
> **Child**: Now I'm going to do the beans. I helped pick beans for supper last night.

In the second example, the adult neither questions nor gives directions, but rather listens, repeats, clarifies, and extends the child's words. The child controls the conversation and, thus, talks more.

▲ Create stories with children

One particular type of conversation that supports children's comprehension involves partnering with them to make up stories, often referred to as **co-narration** (Moran & Jarvis, 2001). As children use their experiences and imaginations to invent stories with adults, their narratives become more detailed and make more sense. Adults scaffold children's ideas with prompts, such as "I wonder what will happen next" or "Then what did they do (say)?"

Back-and-forth conversations with children encourage them to share their thoughts and help them develop their comprehension skills.

Storytelling (which includes co-narration) promotes *listening* comprehension. Listening is the communication skill that develops earliest in life and is the source of up to 80 percent of the information we obtain (Jalongo, 2008), yet schools rarely promote active listening. Children are more apt to listen when they are part of the process of creating a story to listen to.

▲ Read and discuss books with children

Reading stories with children may seem like second nature to us, but there is a surprising amount of cognitive skill behind the pleasure children take in being read to. In fact, "children enjoy listening to stories so much that we may not realize how much effort it requires" (Hohmann & Adams, 2008, p. 5). To comprehend stories, children must recognize characters and recall the sequence of events, applying what they know from personal experience to understand the pictures and the text. To foster children's comprehension during book reading, adults can help children:

Learn new vocabulary words. Look for unusual words. Use synonyms (words children

When speaking with children, model appropriate speech: talk clearly; use standard vocabulary, pronunciation, grammar, and syntax; and, when children make errors, restate their ideas using conventional language rather than correct them.

already know), and give simple definitions to help children understand the new words.

Make connections in a story. Talk with children about what they see on the book's cover and pages, and ask them about similar things they have seen or experienced at home, in school, or in other books the class has read.

Retell (remember) a story. From time to time (without breaking the story's flow), help children reflect on what has already happened (without looking at the pictures).

Make predictions in a story. Before you begin reading, ask children to look at the cover and say what they think the book is about. As you read, pause now and then to ask children what they think a character might do next and why, based on the story so far.

Incorporate ideas from stories and books throughout the day. Provide materials, including art supplies, props (dress-up clothes, woodworking and kitchen tools), puppets, and simple instruments, for children to represent ideas from stories and books. At transitions, ask them to move to the next activity like a character in a story, book, poem, or song. Talk about books and stories at times other than when they are being read or told, such as during meals or related field trips. For example, if a child mentions eating hot cereal for breakfast, you might talk about Goldilocks and the three bears eating porridge.

KDI 22. Speaking: Children express themselves using language.

Description: Children share observations, experiences, ideas, explanations, feelings, preferences, and needs. They progress from making gestures to using sentences of increasing length and complexity.

How Speaking Develops

Children use speech to express needs, describe feelings, indicate preferences, ask questions, engage in pretend play, relay information, tell jokes, and establish relationships. During the preschool years, children's speech changes noticeably; the length of their sentences grows, their words are more intelligible, and their narratives become more sequenced and coherent (Curenton & Justice, 2004). Children also add detail and complexity to their speech. They use adjectives (*soft* blanket), position words (*under* the chair), negatives (do *not*), and compound sentences (*and, but,* and later on, *if-then* constructions) (Hoff, 2005). Although they still make errors, preschoolers also pay more attention to grammar (verb tense, accurate pronouns) because of their desire to communicate effectively (Chapman, 2000).

As their facility for speech grows, children are increasingly able to sustain a dialogue. Younger preschoolers can maintain a conversation for one or two turns. Older preschoolers talk for several turns and take more responsibility for keeping a conversation going. By age five, they understand how conversations work and master the social rules governing communication.

Teaching Strategies That Support Speaking

▲ Model appropriate speech

When speaking with children, talk clearly and use standard vocabulary, pronunciation, grammar, and syntax. Expand children's one- and two-word utterances. For example, if a child says "Book," you might say, "You want us to read this book." When children make errors, don't correct them because this can discourage them from speaking. Instead, restate their ideas using conventional language. For example, if a child says, "I goed to the barbershop. He cutted my hair," you might say, "That's exciting! You went to the barbershop and the barber cut your hair."

▲ Listen to children speak

Don't take over conversations with children. The more you talk, the fewer opportunities they have to voice their ideas. By being a patient listener, you not only encourage children to speak but also model how they can listen attentively and become better conversationalists themselves.

▲ Use questions sparingly

When children are bombarded with questions, they tend to stop speaking. By contrast, comments that reflect or gently expand what children say show you are interested in their ideas. "Where?" and "what?" questions often elicit a one-word reply ("Yes," "No," "Blue"). An occasional open-ended question (e.g., "How did you do that?") is more likely to evoke a phrase or a sentence from the child.

▲ Encourage children to talk instead of using gestures

While nonverbal interactions are a basic form of communication, children who can speak may become overly dependent on them. For example, a child may hold out a cup to an adult instead of asking that adult for more milk. If you think children can use words instead of only motions, encourage speech by not immediately complying with a request communicated by gesture alone. Tell children when you don't understand a vague gesture, and ask for an explanation so you can better meet their needs.

▲ Encourage children to act as leaders in group activities involving verbal directions

Take advantage of opportunities (e.g., large-group time, transitions) when children can be leaders and communicate their ideas using speech. Encourage them to relate their ideas in words, not just demonstrate them. Restate their suggestions to make sure you and the others have it right, and if not, ask them to use more precise words. Examples of leader-describer games include:

Simon says (variation). Instead of having Simon say, "Do this," have a child think of and describe the action (e.g., "Put your legs far, far apart," "Slap your hands on the floor").

Little foxes. Have a child think of and describe a place for all the foxes to run to (e.g., "Run to the stone steps," "Hop to the log").

"Let's be...." Ask each child to take a turn describing something for everyone else to pretend to be (e.g., "Let's be...a man painting," "Let's be...a dog licking his feet").

▲ Encourage children to talk to one another

Provide materials and plan activities that promote collaboration (e.g., props that support pretend play and big or heavy equipment, such as boards or a wheeled bus, that take two children to use). Or plan a small-group activity where children work in pairs (e.g., one hides an object and gives clues for the other to find it). To further support peer conversations, refer children to one another for ideas or help solving problems.

KDI 23. Vocabulary: Children understand and use a variety of words and phrases.

Description: Children learn and use new words and phrases in conversations, activities, written materials, and play. They ask the meaning of unfamiliar words. Children use multiple parts of speech to describe, clarify, and elaborate their experiences and ideas.

How Vocabulary Develops

Receptive (listening) vocabulary is the number of words a child understands. **Productive (speaking) vocabulary** is the number of words a child says and uses correctly. Not all children have the same receptive and productive vocabulary; in fact, researchers found that the number of words children hear by the time they enter school varies widely by socioeconomic background (Hart & Risley, 1995, 1999). The more words children hear and know, the more competent they are as speakers and readers in the early grades and beyond (National Reading Panel, 2000). Especially important are rare words, those that go beyond what is needed to carry out everyday tasks (e.g., spatula, snug, downpour). The more adults use rare words in conversation, the better children do on later literacy measures (Dickinson & Porche, 2011).

Children learn new words when they are *word conscious,* that is, when they are interested in the meaning of a word because it relates to what they are doing or thinking at the time (Christ & Wang, 2010). In addition, children's vocabulary growth is cumulative: "The more frequently they encounter a new word, the more attuned they become to its multiple meanings and shades of meaning" (Hohmann, 2010, p. 16). Their vocabulary growth is also active; they do not acquire new words by memorizing vocabulary lists but by exploring materials, having real conversations, reading books, and telling stories.

Teaching Strategies That Support Vocabulary

▲ Describe and encourage children to describe their experiences and thoughts

Comment on what children do as you observe their actions and play alongside them. Use basic vocabulary words they may not have heard before, and introduce less common words. Children are more likely to understand and remember new words when they hear them in a context that is meaningful to them. For example, while talking with a child about his or her painting, use common words such as *color* or *brush,* and introduce new terms such as *shade* or *texture.*

Children expand their vocabulary by saying as well as hearing words. Encourage them to share their ideas, describe materials and how they use them, and talk about their interactions with others. If they misuse or mispronounce a word, say it correctly yourself, but do not correct them.

▲ Read books and tell stories with basic and unusual vocabulary words

Because books and stories use more complex language than conversations, they can broaden children's vocabulary. As you choose books for the classroom, look for unusual words (such as *enormous* rather than *big* or *swift* instead of *fast*). Help children understand new words by asking what they think a word means, using nonverbal cues (e.g., imitate the object or action) and connecting new words with terms and situations the children are familiar with.

▲ Provide opportunities for children to experience new materials and ideas

New words come from new experiences. Children are curious about what something is called, and they seek words to describe new sensations, actions, and feelings. To enrich their vocabulary, provide preschoolers with many opportunities to explore new materials and tools (first introduce them at small–group time) and to discover new properties about familiar materials (reintroduce materials children have stopped using or have been using in the same way for a long time). Go on walks, take field trips, and visit places in the community (e.g., artist's studio, corner store). All these activities create opportunities for children to hear and practice using new words and phrases.

KDI 24. Phonological awareness: Children identify distinct sounds in spoken language.

Description: Children recognize the beginning and ending sounds of words, including rhymes (same ending sounds) and alliteration (same initial sounds). They recognize separate syllables in words (segmentation).

How Phonological Awareness Develops

Phonological awareness is recognizing the sounds that make up words. The ability to think about the sound of language separate from its meaning is crucial in learning to read; it helps children understand the alphabetic principle (KDI 25), the association between a letter and its sound (Bishop, Yopp, & Yopp, 2000).

Spoken language is made of sound units from greater to lesser complexity: words, syllables, sub-syllables (beginning and ending sounds), and phonemes (the smallest unit of sound). Phonological awareness refers to all speech sounds in general; **phonemic awareness** refers to the smallest sound unit in words.

Children become aware of the largest units of sound and then increasingly attend to the smaller ones (Anthony, 2002). They can detect initial phonemes (such as the sound of the first letter in their names), then final phonemes, and lastly the sounds in the middle of a word. Blended sounds in a phoneme cluster (e.g., /pl/ in *plop*) are especially difficult to distinguish.

Preschoolers need experience with three aspects of the word-sound connection to develop phonological awareness:

- **Rhyming** refers to word endings that sound the same, such as the /at/ in *cat* and *hat*. Some of the earliest word parts that preschoolers can distinguish are rhymes, and they find rhyming fun.
- **Alliteration** is two or more words with the same initial sound, such as the onset of *b*ig and *b*oy. Children enjoy repeating alliterative words in stories, songs, chants, and nursery rhymes.
- **Segmentation** involves breaking words into syllables. Many children do not master this task until kindergarten. However, preschoolers can begin to detect the syllables in their names or other familiar words, especially when they are chanted or sung (e.g., "An-drew, din-ner!").

Songs and chants that feature rhymes not only delight children but also help them to identify word endings that sound the same.

Teaching Strategies That Support Phonological Awareness

▲ Explore and identify sounds with children

Experiences with environmental sounds (voices, appliances, vehicles) lay the groundwork for discriminating among the discrete sounds that make up words. To support and extend children's sound recognition, try the following:

Explore sound-making materials inside the classroom. Provide musical instruments, timers, wooden blocks, carpentry tools, and things that make noise during filling and emptying.

Explore sound-making materials outside the classroom. Listen for sounds on the playground, in nature, throughout the school, and around the neighborhood.

Identify sounds. Ask children to close their eyes and guess what is making a particular sound.

Locate sounds. Encourage children to guess where a sound is coming from.

Identify voices. Record children's voices and those of familiar adults. Play them back, and have children guess who is speaking.

Listen for a word or phrase. At transitions, give the children a word or phrase to listen for as a signal to move to the next activity.

▲ Build rhyme awareness

Have fun — and build children's phonological awareness — using the following rhyming strategies:

Share songs, poems, books, stories, nursery rhymes, and chants that feature rhyming. Emphasize the rhyming words as you say them (e.g., "down the **stream**," "but a **dream**").

Identify rhymes. Use the word *rhyme* when one occurs (e.g., say "**Dock** and **clock** rhyme"). Encourage children to identify rhymes.

Make up rhymes. Have children fill in the missing rhyme to a familiar verse (e.g., "Hickory, dickory, **dock**. The mouse ran up the ____"). Later, they can substitute a different word at the end (e.g., "Hickory, dickory, **door**. The mouse ran up the _____").

Substitute nonrhyming words. After children are familiar with a rhyme, substitute a nonrhyming word to get a reaction (e.g., "Jack and Jill went up the **road**").

Play games and plan activities using rhymes. Pair a child's name with a rhyme at transitions (e.g., "Red Ted, go to the snack table") or to make cleanup fun (e.g., "I spy something that rhymes with **flock** that needs to be put away").

▲ Build alliteration awareness

The strategies that support alliteration awareness parallel those used with rhyming, including:

Share songs, poems, books, stories, nursery rhymes, and chants that feature alliteration. Emphasize the initial sound as you say the alliterative words (e.g., *bouncing ball*).

Identify alliteration. Point out common beginning sounds, and use the word *alliteration* to describe them (even children who cannot say the word will begin to recognize what it means).

Make up alliterative phrases. Substitute the initial sound in familiar phrases (e.g., *mee millie minkie*). Ask children to add alliterative words; for example, ask, "What other /r/ words go with *red* and *riding*?" You can *also use alliterative phrases during the daily routine* (e.g., "We're having **c**runchy **c**rackers for snack"), and alliterate children's names at transitions (e.g., "Bouncy Becky get your coat").

Substitute nonalliterative words. Occasionally use a nonalliterative word in a phrase to see if children catch the error (e.g., *Wee, Willie, Robin*).

Play games and plan activities that involve alliteration. At transitions, have children move to the next activity when they hear their name paired with a word beginning with the same sound. At large-group time, create stories that feature alliteration (e.g., a "**b**ig **b**oat with **b**ells").

▲ Build syllable recognition

To help preschoolers break words into syllables, try the following:

Call and sing name syllables. "Sing-song" or "yoo-hoo" the syllables in children's names. For example, as you call Ibrahim on the playground, sing-song "Ib-ra-him," singing each syllable on a different or alternating pitch.

Call and sing word syllables. Use the same sing-song technique when saying familiar words in books and stories and during the daily routine (e.g., *mark-er, re-call*).

Sing and chant pitch syllables. Sing songs and nursery rhymes in which the words are broken into syllables to fit the notes of the melody (e.g., "Ring Around the Ros-ie").

Play guessing games that separate and combine word sounds. Use children's names or familiar words. For example, you might say to the children, "I'm thinking of someone whose name begins with the /d/ sound and ends with the /on/ sound."

KDI 25. Alphabetic knowledge: Children identify letter names and their sounds.

Description: Children know letters are a category of symbols that can be individually named. They name a growing number of letters and associate them with their sounds (often beginning with the initial of their first name and/or other familiar words).

How Alphabetic Knowledge Develops

Alphabetic knowledge first means understanding the **alphabetic principle,** that there is a systematic relationship between letters and their sounds. Children then acquire increasing knowledge about these specific connections, that is, the sound(s) associated with each letter. The gateway to this understanding is often the child's own name, beginning with the first letter. Children achieve this recognition because their names are important to them. If you try to teach children the names and sounds of letters by rote (e.g., by the "letter of the day"), the connection is likely to be lost on them (Wasik, 2001).

Once they grasp the alphabetic principle, children often ask adults about the names and sounds of other letters. They make informed guesses at

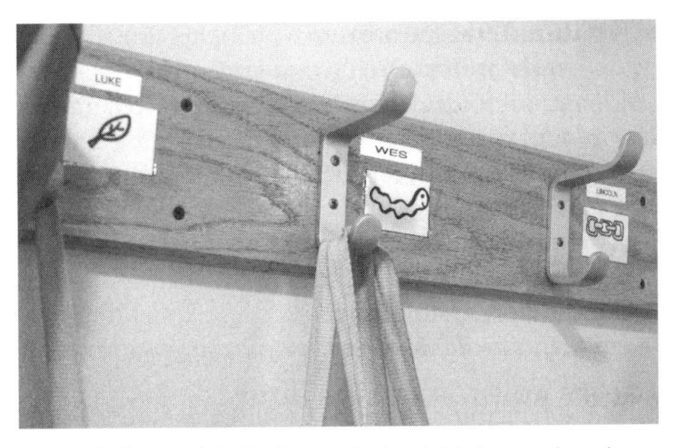

Letter links are labels that pair the initial sound and letter of a child's name with those of a familiar object.

reading and writing familiar words, such as reading *mom* when they remember that *m* makes the /m/ sound. Thus, to fully develop alphabetic awareness, children need both phonological (sound) awareness and knowledge about how spoken sounds are represented by letters in print. HighScope's **letter links,** which are labels that pair the initial sound and letter of a child's name with a familiar object (such as Evan and egg), help children make this connection (DeBruin-Parecki & Hohmann, 2003). Children use letter links on their cubbies, sign-up lists, art projects, and so on. They soon learn not only their own letter links but also those of their peers.

Teaching Strategies That Support Alphabetic Knowledge

▲ Build letter recognition

To help children learn letter names in meaningful (not rote) ways:

Provide alphabet materials. In addition to seeing letters in print, children need concrete hands-on experiences with them. Provide three-dimensional letters made of different materials; alphabet blocks, cookie cutters, pretzels, puzzles; and interactive letter-recognition software.

Make alphabet letters and books. Children can make letters with clay, dough, pipe cleaners, sticks, and shells. They can cut around large letters (e.g., in recycled newspaper ads) and sort or glue them onto paper. Then, encourage the children to make a book of their letter collections.

Identify alphabet letters indoors and outdoors. Identify letters throughout the classroom and outside. Give children one or more letters from their names to carry so they can match them with those they see around the room or on a neighborhood walk.

Draw, scribble, and write letters. Encourage children to write alphabet letters (e.g., a child may draw a few letters to indicate a material or person at planning or recall time or he or she may write and draw about a field trip). Help children incorporate writing into their pretend play, for example, by writing shopping lists or party invitations. Encourage different mediums for writing letters, such as writing letters in the sand with a stick.

▲ Build letter-sound awareness

To help preschoolers build letter-sound awareness:

Identify the initial letter sounds in children's names and other familiar words. Pair a child's name with the sound of its first letter when writing names or letter links, during transitions, and commenting on familiar words (e.g., "Box and Bobby both start with the /b/ sound").

Say the names of letters and sound them out in the words children read, write, and dictate. Pronounce single letters and letter strings (e.g., say *"p-i-z-z-a"* while helping a child write *pizza* on a menu).

Search for letters by their sound. Look for letters that make a certain sound; for example, say "Let's find all the letters on this page that make the /s/ sound" or play letter I spy: "I spy something in the house area that begins with *S* and makes the /s/ sound."

Connect sounds to the letters children write to stand for whole words or invented words. Read back what children write (e.g., "I see *H* for the /h/ sound in *happy*"). Sound out children's made-up spellings.

KDI 26. Reading: Children read for pleasure and information.

Description: Children look at a variety of printed materials for enjoyment and knowledge. They ask adults to read books to them, and they "read" books to others. Children tell or retell stories based on pictures. They read aloud a word, simple phrase, or short sentence.

How Reading Skills Develop

Learning to read involves two abilities. The first is *decoding*, or converting words into their spoken form, for example, seeing the written word *picture* and saying "pik-chur." The second is *understanding the meaning of words*. The more words and meanings children know, the easier it is for them become fluent readers (Snow et al., 1998).

Young children are involved in the process of reading long before they actually read. They "read" pictures, stop signs, product logos, screen icons, and their own scribbles. Because reading plays such a critical role in future school success, adults are understandably eager for young children to learn to read. Pressuring them to read like adults, however, can discourage intrinsic motivation. Supporting emergent readers, on the other hand, while it takes time and patience, results in children who eventually not only read but want to read and take pleasure in doing so.

Teaching Strategies That Support Reading

▲ Provide materials children are interested in reading

Include printed materials in every interest area. Create an inviting reading or book area stocked with storybooks, wordless board books, nonfiction (information) books, nursery rhymes and poetry, picture dictionaries, magazines, atlases, and catalogs. Make sure they reflect the home languages and cultures of the children in your program. In other parts of the classroom, keep printed materials appropriate to that area (e.g., cartons with writing on them in the block area, plastic containers with printed labels at the sand and water table). Outside the classroom, call attention to environmental print such as traffic signs, street names, and window displays.

▲ Read interactively with children every day

As you read with children, pause to talk about the pictures and words they notice. Commenting on the illustrations and text helps children connect their experiences to the book's characters, objects, and events (McGee & Richgels, 2000). Read with children one on one, in pairs, and in small groups. Make sure all the children can see and point to the pictures, turn the pages, hear the story, and comment and ask questions. Personal interactions add a social component that makes reading pleasurable, a benefit that cannot be accomplished by reading with children in large groups. Encourage parents to read with their children every day at home, just as you do in class.

▲ Encourage children to read to adults and to one another

Begin with wordless picture books or simple illustrated text which children can "read" by turning pages, looking at pictures for clues, and reciting remembered phrases. Eventually, they will begin to recognize and sight-read specific letters and words and make educated guesses based on the letters and sounds they know.

Children also enjoy reading their own writing or dictation. "For many children, writing is the path to reading — once they begin to figure out the alphabetic principle, and start writing words phonetically, they often begin to sound out words that *others* have written" (Ranweiler, 2004, p. 136). Encourage children to read the labels on their artwork, what they write at planning or recall time, and the things they write during pretend play.

KDI 27. Concepts about print: Children demonstrate knowledge about environmental print.

Description: Children learn about the function of print. They understand the connection between spoken and written words. They recognize that a word is a unit of print, letters are grouped to form words, and words are separated by spaces. As they experience various forms of environmental print (e.g., signs, newspapers and magazines, lists, messages, menus, packaging), children learn about print conventions such as directionality (English is read top to bottom and left to right).

How Concepts About Print Develop

Concepts about print means knowing how print is organized on the page and used in reading and writing. Understanding how print works involves four basic concepts, which appear in preschool. First is knowing the *difference between pictures and words*. Second is recognizing the principles governing the *composition of print*: print is made of letters arranged to compose words; words are ordered to make sentences; there are spaces between words; and a period marks the end of a sentence. The third concept, *orientation of text*, refers to holding printed material right-side up (without relying on pictures). Fourth is understanding the *direction in which text is read* (in English, top to bottom and left to right).

Young children gain an understanding of how print works through experiences with books and environmental print, which is defined as "print that is encountered outside of books and that is a pervasive part of everyday living" (Neuman et al., 2000, p. 123). Acquiring print concepts is significantly associated with later reading performance (Adams, 1990; Clay, 2000; Snow et al., 1998). Above mere print exposure, children need what Baker, Serpell, and Sonnenschein (1995) call *personal literacy events* at home and at school, including seeing adults read and write, being read to, reading text on containers or advertisements, signing their names on cards, and using computers. The more frequent such events in their own experiences, the higher children's motivation to read.

Teaching Strategies That Support the Development of Concepts About Print

▲ Provide diverse examples of the forms and functions of print

Most children associate print with storybooks and the pleasure of being read to. However, it is important for them to realize that print takes other forms and serves other functions. As children encounter various types of print, point out the purpose(s) they serve. For example, comment "That sign says 'Don't walk.' We have to wait until it says 'Walk.'" When labeling a child's picture, say, "I'm writing your name (or letter link) so we'll know who made it." Before snacktime, say "Let's check the snack chart to see whose turn it is to pass out the cups." During work time in the house area, ask children to help you find the list of ingredients on a package of food. Point out words such as *up* and *down* on a computer screen.

▲ Help children distinguish between pictures and words

As you look with children at illustrated text (e.g., storybooks, signs, posters, maps), talk about the pictures and then say something like, "Let's look at the words." Point to the text as you read it aloud and connect it to the pictures (e.g., "These words say that the monster had blue hair!"). Call attention to picture-word distinctions when you add names or captions to children's artwork, as Chris's teacher demonstrates here:

> *At small-group time, after completing his drawing, Chris says to his teacher, "Write that it's a bird." After checking on the exact phrase he wants, the teacher says, "I'm writing the words 'Chris made a bird' on a sticky note and attaching it to the top of your picture." After some consideration, Chris adds, "Say that the bird is blue." When the teacher asks where to write those words, Chris says on the bottom, so she adds another sticky note with those words at the bottom. At the end of the day, when his father comes to get him, Chris shows his dad the picture and points to the words: "This says I made a bird. And down here, it says it's blue."*

▲ Help children understand the composition, orientation, and direction of text

Use these strategies to help children understand the mechanics of how text works:

Composition. Text is composed of letters grouped into words, and words are ordered to create sentences, paragraphs, and pages. To help children grasp these ideas, emphasize how letters make up a word; for example, you might say, "*C-A-T* — that's how you write the word *cat*." Point to each word as you read a sentence, and use the word *sentence* while reading with children (e.g., "Let's find the sentence that says what he ate"). If children are interested, describe how other print features work, such as uppercase letters and punctuation marks.

Orientation. Orientation refers to the upright position in which print is held. Ask children to hand you a book to read with them. If they hand it to you upside down or sideways, turn it the right way. Now and then hold print the wrong

To help children distinguish between pictures and words, point to the text and connect it with the pictures as you read aloud.

way. If children don't correct you, say "Oops, it's upside down" and turn it upright. Play with orientation on a rectangular message board: read messages from top to bottom when the message board is turned so the longest side is vertical, and read from left to right when the message board is turned so the longest side is horizontal (Gainsley, 2008).

Direction. Direction refers to how text flows (from page to page, left to right, and back to the beginning of the next line). To help children become aware of these mechanics, make comments such as "Let's turn the page to see what happens next," put your finger at the top of the next page, and occasionally run your finger along a line of print while reading. Let children turn the page so they get a feel for how text progresses.

KDI 28. Book knowledge: Children demonstrate knowledge about books.

Description: Children know how books work, for example, they hold a book upright and face-forward, read it front to back, and differentiate text and pictures. Children identify the parts of a book.

How Book Knowledge Develops

Book knowledge is understanding how books, as one category of print, work. Books have unique features such as a title, author, illustrator, front and back covers, and pages. Preschoolers are ready to identify the parts of a book, and appreciate how books work, for example, that the title indicates what the book is about. As they handle, read, and make books, children recognize which general concepts about print apply specifically to books (Clay, 2000). Young children also need to gain familiarity with different types of books, including storybooks, information (nonfiction books), poetry and song collections, alphabet and counting books, art books (photos and reproductions), and instruction manuals.

Teaching Strategies That Support Children's Book Knowledge

▲ Explore the parts of a book with children

As you look at books with children, point out one or two features. (Do this before or after reading so you don't interrupt the story.) For example, before beginning, say "Let's look at the picture on the front cover to see if we can figure out what this story is about." Explain the idea of author and illustrator (e.g., "I'm going to read the book _____. It was written by _____ and _____ drew the pictures"). When you're done reading, say "That's the end of the story."

Children also learn about book parts by making their own books. Leave published books on the table for them to refer to while they draw, write, and fasten their books. Display handmade books, and put them in the reading area so children can look at their own books and one another's. Invite them to "read" their books aloud at small-group or recall time, and describe how they made each part.

▲ Help children understand books' composition, orientation, and direction of text

Ask children to hand you a book to read with them. Then either accept it in the position they give you or reorient the book as needed. Occasionally pick up or hold a book the wrong way yourself and see how children react. If a book is turned the wrong way, make a visual and vocal point of turning it right-side up. Apply the other strategies regarding composition, orientation, and directionality that are described under concepts about print (KDI 27) to working with books.

KDI 29. Writing: Children write for many different purposes.

Description: Children write to represent ideas, use writing in their play and/or ask adults to take dictation, and read what they and adults have written. They use writing tools such as crayons, markers, pencils, and computers. They copy or write letters, and progress from scribbles to letterlike forms to recognizable letters.

How Writing Develops

Children "write" before they read, in the sense that they scribble and draw prior to recognizing letters (Clay, 2000). Learning to make letters and words (and numbers) is another step along the writing continuum (Ferreiro & Teberosky, 1982; Sulzby, 1986, 1987). Children begin with pictographs in which drawing and writing are similar and may only be interpretable by the child. Later, they make letterlike marks that resemble real letters in form (lines and curves) and length (longer strings of marks stand for longer words) and adopt the directionality of their culture's writing. Eventually, children write real letters, often with reversals (e.g., Ǝ) or other mistakes until second grade. Next they string letters together to make words, using developmental or invented spelling, which "results from a beginning writer's initial attempts to associate sounds with letters" (Neuman et al., 2000, p. 123). It is important to encourage children's inventive spelling rather than correcting them, or children may write simpler words rather than risk being wrong. The desire to communicate accurately will motivate children to learn conventional spelling on their own.

Teaching Strategies That Support Writing

▲ Provide a variety of writing and drawing materials

Provide writing materials throughout the classroom, and encourage children to carry them from one area to another to support their play (e.g., for making construction signs in the block area, labeling a drawing in the art area, tracing shapes in the toy area, printing party invitations in the house area). Look for interactive computer programs that allow children to create pictures, letterlike forms, and actual letters.

▲ Expect and support various forms of emergent writing and developmental spelling

"The single most important element children need to grow as writers is the belief that they are writers" (Calkins, 1997, p. 58). Thus, adults should respect and support each attempt on the continuum of learning how to write. Match your help to children's developmental levels. For example, if they know how to write letters, say each letter's sound and spell the word. For children who have phonemic awareness, say, for example, "Let's figure out what the first letter is. It makes the /m/ sound" and wait for the child to identify the letter. You can also write letters or find examples for children to copy and refer children to one another for help.

▲ Encourage children to write for a wide variety of reasons

Children write when and because they want to, for example, to caption a picture, create a menu during pretend play, or send a get-well card. When children become adept social problem solvers (KDI 15), writing can help them with turn-taking. Planning and recall provide daily opportunities for children to write down their ideas and experiences. Mathematics and science activities also lend themselves to writing. For example, after collecting and sorting natural objects on a field trip, children might record on a chart the names and quantities of the objects they found.

▲ Take dictation from children

While children enjoy doing their own writing, sometimes they want to dictate their ideas to adults. This is true of children who do not yet write, as well as those who have begun writing independently. You can take individual or group dictation (captioning a painting, or writing what the class saw on field trip, respectively). Be sure to *write down and read back exactly what children say* without correcting grammar or word

Adults can support young children's developing writing skills by expecting and supporting different forms of emergent writing and spelling.

order. This strategy helps children connect the spoken word to the written word and shows children that you value what they say.

KDI 30. English language learning: (If applicable) Children use English and their home language(s) (including sign language).

Description: Children understand and use English and their home language(s). They adjust the language they use to the person with whom they are communicating. Children know there are different writing systems (alphabets).

How English Language Learning Develops

Preschoolers first learning English as a second language typically progress through several stages (Tabors, 2008):

Stage one. Children attempt to communicate in their home language but gradually realize they are not being understood and must adapt their strategies. This phase can last days or months, depending on the child's awareness and the responsiveness of the setting.

Stage two. Children actively attend to the new language, often silently. This quiet period does not mean they are "tuning out" but are instead busy listening. Meanwhile, they try to communicate nonverbally using gestures, facial expression, and nonlanguage vocalizations.

Stage three. Having mastered the rhythms and a key few words or phrases, children are ready "go public" with their English. They use *telegraphic speech* (a word to stand for a phrase, such as "Up!" to mean "Look up at the bird!") and *formulaic speech* or memorized phrases (e.g., "I want ___" may be said with "I want apple" or "I want go").

Stage four. Children express themselves in their own words. They apply the general rules of English, although they still make errors, much as a young native speaker might. The ability to transfer the rules of grammar depends on how similar their native language is to English.

Children learning another language are also learning another culture, including when and how it is appropriate to speak (Rogoff, 2003). Given all these variables, a child's movement through the four stages may take anywhere from six months to two years, depending on the amount of language at home, verbal interactions in preschool, and exposure to English in other settings.

Teaching Strategies That Support English Language Learning

▲ Encourage children to communicate regardless of which language they use

The more children know their home language, the better their ability to learn a second language (Cheatham & Ro, 2010). When possible, pair non-English-speaking children with bilingual peers to help them make the bridge. Sing songs, read books, and tell stories from children's home languages as well as English. Encourage English language learners (ELLs) to share familiar songs, fairy tales, and rhymes from home, and to teach common words to the class. These practices enhance the retention of the home language, contribute to learning English, and validate the child and his or her family.

▲ Use pretend play to expand the vocabulary of ELLs

Pretend play offers ELLs opportunities to combine verbal and nonverbal skills in a nonpressured setting. By adding in actions and props, ELLs can accompany their home language with gestures and materials to be better understood. This reduces their frustration trying to communicate. Children whose first language is English will frequently fill in missing words spontaneously, thereby providing a natural learning opportunity for the English learners.

▲ Use narrative to enhance the fluency of ELLs

Children learn English from storytelling, even if they cannot yet produce an English narrative (Cheatham & Ro, 2010). Think of storytelling broadly. For example, a plan is a story about what children intend to do; recall is a story about what they've done. Reading the message board is telling a story about what will happen that day. Children often accompany their work-time activity with a story or share a story about what happened on the way to school or an event they are looking forward to. The more opportunities ELLs have to share "stories" about people and events in their lives, the more motivated they will be to master their new language.

Try These Ideas Yourself

1. List what you consider to be the five most important things preschoolers need to know or be able to do in the Language, Literacy, and Communication content area when they enter kindergarten. Why are they important? How can teachers support their development?

2. Look at the illustrations or photos in a book or magazine you have not read before. Make up a story from the pictures. What personal experiences did you draw on for your story? How might children draw on their interests and experiences to make up stories from pictures?

3. When Becca was three, her mother cautioned her about big kids in the neighborhood playing "rough." Puzzled, Becca asked her mother, "Do little kids play smooth?" How does the use of language in the following statements reveal preschoolers' understanding of the world?

If I spread out my crackers, it will take me longer to eat them.

When I put my jacket outside me, the wind can't get inside me.

When I grow up, I'm going to have more letters in my name.

I can't go to France with my parents because I don't know how to fly yet.

How can you apply your understanding of preschoolers' use of language to your interactions with them in the classroom?

4. In the following scenario, identify the Language, Literacy, and Communication KDIs. What types of learning are occurring in other areas of development? (See the list of KDIs on p. 134.) How could a teacher support and extend the learning?

> *Jared and Evan sit next to one another, each looking at a book. Jared says to Evan, "Do you want me to read you this book about bears?" When Evan says* yes, *Jared moves closer so they can both look at the pictures. Jared turns the pages and "reads" to Evan, making up a story about what the bears are doing. "Now you read your book to me," says Jared. Evan knows his book, which is about a family car trip, by heart. As he recounts the tale, he occasionally points to a word as he says it. "That was a good book," says Jared when Evan is finished.*

5. Think of a familiar nursery rhyme, song, or chant. Invent a rhyming game using a pair of rhyming words. Invent an alliteration game using the common beginning sound in a series of two or more words. How might you introduce each game to children in a preschool classroom?

6. Think of all the words you can use with young children to describe books and how books work (e.g., *title, author, first page, the end*). Share your list with a colleague, and ask for additional ideas. Use these words the next time you read a book with children.

Use play dough and plastic knives to provide children with a tactile experience in making alphabet letters.

Chapter 14

What Is the HighScope Curriculum in Mathematics?

Think About It

It's likely you have heard the phrase, "Let's look at the numbers!" in reference to a budget, sports statistics, polling results, and so on. Whether you like working with numbers, or they fill you with anxiety, mathematics is part of our everyday lives. And mathematics is much more than numbers. Arranging the furniture in a room, for example, involves shapes and space, which is geometry. Dividing a problem into steps and working through each one methodically is similar to solving a series of algebra equations. Figuring how much mulch to buy for your garden requires measurement. Deciding where and when to celebrate the holiday season with your extended family requires data analysis (i.e., who is available when and where everyone wants to go). All these activities draw on the mathematical properties of common objects and events.

For children, as for adults, mathematics is about ordering and comparing quantities, discovering patterns, and moving our bodies and possessions from place to place. Because these activities are so basic, HighScope believes all children and adults can and should be capable mathematicians.

Why Mathematics Is Important

Educators now recognize that early mathematics learning merits the same attention as literacy. The National Research Council's (NRC's) Committee on Early Childhood Mathematics (2009) says that mathematics belongs at "the top of the national policy agenda" (p. 1) and that mathematics education should precede kindergarten entry. In fact, children's early mathematical abilities, even more than their reading abilities, significantly predict success in all areas of the school curriculum (Duncan et al., 2007).

The **National Council of Teachers of Mathematics** (NCTM, 2000) identifies five content areas appropriate to all age groups: number and operations, geometry, measurement, algebra, and data analysis. The first three areas, or *focal points,* are especially important in early childhood (National Council of Teachers of Mathematics, 2006). HighScope's **Numbers Plus Preschool Mathematics Curriculum** (Epstein, 2009b) is based on NCTM's recommendations, as are the mathematics key developmental indicators described in this chapter.

Early Mathematics Learning

Young children's mathematical experiences "should build largely upon their play and the natural relationships between learning and life in their daily activities, interests, and questions" (Clements, 2004b, p. 59). When researchers Herbert Ginsburg and his colleagues observed preschoolers' free play, they were amazed at how much children used mathematics to express their ideas (Ginsburg, Inoue, & Seo, 1999). In fact, children aged three to five "are predisposed, perhaps innately, to attend to numerical situations and problems" (Baroody, 2000, p. 61).

Chapter Learning Objectives

By the end of this chapter, you will be able to

- Explain why early learning in mathematics is important.
- Describe the HighScope key developmental indicators (KDIs) in the Mathematics content area.
- Begin to apply the strategies adults use to scaffold (support and gently extend) early learning in mathematics.

Educators also confirm that early mathematics is more than rote counting (i.e., saying "1, 2, 3"). Preschoolers understand how numbers work by counting real things. When children build a road with blocks of different shapes and sizes, they are doing geometry. Figuring out who jumped farther involves comparing distances, or preliminary measurement. Looking for patterns in a design or a series of movements is preparation for middle-school algebra. And finding out whether the class wants more pretzels or raisins in the trail mix applies data analysis to real-life decisions.

How Young Children Learn About Mathematics

Opportunities to engage children in mathematics occur all day, but this learning cannot be left to chance. Adults must systematically and intentionally involve preschoolers in working with materials, pursuing investigations, and using mathematical thinking to draw conclusions. One important aspect of teaching mathematics is understanding that children learn sequentially (Campbell, 1997; Clements, Sarama, & DiBiase, 2004); that is, each new concept or skill builds on what children have learned before. While most mathematics curricula have a fixed sequence of activities that all the children proceed through together, an alternative approach (used in Numbers Plus) offers open-ended

Young children understand how numbers work by using them in everyday situations, such as counting with one-to-one correspondence to set the table for mealtime.

activities that allow children to engage with the materials and ideas at their own level in the learning sequence.

General Teaching Strategies for Mathematics

▲ Provide a wide variety of mathematics materials in every classroom area

You need not set up a separate mathematics area but do create an environment where children "bump into interesting mathematics at every turn" (Greenes, 1999, p. 46). Include items such as kitchen timers, spinners, and number books (for number words and symbols); figures and pegs with pegboards (for counting with one-to-one correspondence); sets of small objects children can combine and separate (for part-whole relationships); two- and three-dimensional shapes (for geometry); large climbing structures (for spatial awareness); measuring cups and spoons (for measuring); lengths of string and rulers (for unconven-

Terms Used in This Chapter

• National Council of Teachers of Mathematics (NCTM) • Numbers Plus Preschool Mathematics Curriculum • cardinal number • ordinal number • number sense • subitizing • one-to-one correspondence • part-whole relationships • spatial awareness • spatial orientation • spatial visualization • unit

tional and conventional measuring units); beads and noise makers (to create visual and sound patterns); and paper and markers (to record and analyze data). When using computers and other interactive media, choose open-ended programs and applications that promote discovery, not rote drill and practice.

▲ Use mathematics words and terms

Children come to understand number words when they hear *number talk* from adults (Levine, Suriyakham, Rowe, Huttenlocher, & Gunderson, 2010). Examples of number talk include referring to the number of people and objects (e.g., "There are only six people at small group today because Katie isn't here"), commenting on relative amounts (e.g., "More children ate apple slices than pear slices at snacktime"), using measurement terms (e.g., "We need to add one cup of flour"), and using mathematics to answer questions that arise in play (e.g., "How could we find out which is bigger?").

Although children often use mathematics spontaneously, they may not be aware of this unless adults inquire about their reasoning (Zur & Gelman, 2004). So, for example, ask how a child *divided* the cars so each person had the *same* number. You can also scaffold children's thinking by referring children to one another to learn from what their more advanced peers have to say (Campbell, 1999; Kirova & Bhargava, 2002). In fact, disagreements during peer dialogue more often prompt reflection and reconsideration than comments from adults (Baroody, 2000).

▲ Encourage children to use mathematics to answer their own questions and solve their own problems

Preschoolers begin to replace trial-and-error problem solving with more systematic methods and logical thinking. Children can develop these cognitive skills through mathematics activities that encourage manipulating materials, observing outcomes, and trying to explain the results. To support the use of mathematical reasoning, do not jump in with the answer or hurry children to figure out a specific solution. See, for example, how this teacher supports the children as they use mathematics to solve their problem:

> *At outside time, Leah, Jacob, and Perez argue about who is taller. "How could you find out?" asks their teacher. "We could measure!" says Perez. Leah gets a piece of chalk and asks the teacher to mark where the tops of their heads come on the side of the tool shed. "I'm tallest," announces Jacob. "Only a little," says Perez. "When I'm five, I'll be tallest," declares Leah.*

Let children self-correct their thinking to match what they observe. It may take longer for them to arrive at an answer, but their brains will construct a better understanding of how mathematics works (Copley, 2010).

▲ Pose challenges that encourage mathematical thinking

Challenges should engage children in the fun of mathematics, not test or trick them. Preschoolers enjoy challenges that originate in their interests, for example, "How many beads can I fit in the jar before they spill over?" To set the right tone, make comments ("I wonder what would happen if…") and occasionally ask an open-ended question ("How could you make it fit a different way?").

Key Developmental Indicators in Mathematics

HighScope has nine key developmental indicators (KDIs) in Mathematics: 31. Number words and symbols, 32. Counting, 33. Part-whole relationships, 34. Shapes, 35. Spatial awareness, 36. Measuring, 37. Unit, 38. Patterns, and 39. Data analysis.[1] See "KDIs in Mathematics" on page 152.

In this chapter, we discuss early learning in each of these KDIs and the strategies you can use to support their development. For specific activities, see the Numbers Plus Preschool Mathematics Curriculum (Epstein, 2009b) and, for additional resources and publications, see HighScope's website (www.highscope.org).

[1]The Mathematics KDIs align with the NCTM content areas and Numbers Plus Preschool Mathematics Curriculum as follows: The first three KDIs encompass number sense and operations; the next two are within geometry; the following two are part of measurement; and the last two fit, respectively, within algebra and data analysis.

KDIs in Mathematics

31. Number words and symbols: Children recognize and use number words and symbols.
32. Counting: Children count things.
33. Part-whole relationships: Children combine and separate quantities of objects.
34. Shapes: Children identify, name, and describe shapes.
35. Spatial awareness: Children recognize spatial relationships among people and objects.
36. Measuring: Children measure to describe, compare, and order things.
37. Unit: Children understand and use the concept of unit.
38. Patterns: Children identify, describe, copy, complete, and create patterns.
39. Data analysis: Children use information about quantity to draw conclusions, make decisions, and solve problems.

KDI 31. Number words and symbols: Children recognize and use number words and symbols.

Description: Children recognize and name numerals in their environment. They understand that cardinal numbers (e.g., one, two, three) refer to quantity and that ordinal numbers (e.g., first, second, last) refer to the order of things. They write numerals.

How Knowledge About Number Words and Symbols Develops

Through everyday experiences, children learn **cardinal number** words (e.g., zero, one, two) and **ordinal number** words (e.g., first, last, second, third) and develop **number sense** (i.e., awareness that numbers represent quantity and can be manipulated). Most preschoolers learn cardinal number words by repeating them until memorized and can count up to 20 by kindergarten, although they often say numbers out of order or repeat them (Clements, 2004b). Combining number words with objects or actions helps establish one-to-one correspondence and the idea that the last number counted tells how many are in the set.

Learning to read numerals depends on how often children encounter them and adults point them out (Clements & Sarama, 2007). Two- and three-year-olds recognize some, and most four-year-olds can read the numerals 1 to 10 (National Research Council, 2009). As they learn number names and numerals, preschoolers begin to write them. As with letter-writing, children often begin with numeral-like marks and gradually produce recognizable numerals, sometimes with reversals (such as 3 and 5).

Teaching Strategies That Support Children's Use of Number Words and Symbols

▲ Use number words to describe everyday materials and events

Hearing number words in context makes more sense to children than merely reciting them. With respect to cardinal numbers, for example, comment at greeting time that there are two new dolls in the house area. For ordinal numbers, say things such as "We got on the first boot. Now let's do the second boot" or "Let's turn to the first page." For English language learners, use number words in their home languages.

▲ Call attention to numerals (number symbols) in the environment

Point out written numerals on equipment and materials, such as toys, tools, books, timers, and snack charts. Use numerals on the message board, for example, indicate that there will be two visitors by drawing two stick figures and writing the numeral 2. You can also talk about the numerals on the clock and play board games that include spinners with numerals. At small-group time, plan activities in which children search for numerals in the classroom, outdoors, in the building, and in the neighborhood.

▲ Encourage children to write numerals

Apply letter-writing strategies (KDI 29) to numerals. Provide a wide array of materials to write and construct numerals, such as markers and paper, sand and sticks, shaving cream, pipe cleaners, and Popsicle sticks. Accept children's number-like forms as well as errors such as reversals. Encourage them to write or dictate numerals during pretend play and at planning and recall times.

KDI 32. Counting: Children count things.

Description: Children count with one-to-one correspondence (e.g., touch an object and say a number). They understand that the last number counted tells *how many.* Children compare and order quantities (e.g., more, fewer/less, same). They understand the concepts of *adding* to and *taking away.*

How Counting Develops

A child's understanding of counting develops quite early. Older toddlers, for example, can eyeball and recognize up to three items (called **subitizing**) long before can count, and three-year-olds have a basic understanding of higher and lower numbers (Zur & Gelman, 2004). Older preschoolers recognize that two sets are equal if they share the same number name, despite any differences in their physical appearance. Even more advanced is being able to say by how many one set is larger or smaller than another. At first, young children may compare by aligning two sets and counting the extra ones in the larger set. Later, they use their fingers or other manipulatives to do simple addition and subtraction problems and, for very small numbers, they can do the arithmetic mentally (Sophian, Wood, & Vong, 1995).

Teaching Strategies That Support Counting

▲ Count and compare everything

"Preschoolers see the world as an arena for counting. Children want to count everything" (Gardner, 1991, p. 75). Young children also love big numbers, such as a *thousand* or a *gazillion*, even

Support children's use of numbers by calling attention to them in the environment (e.g., on the message board).

without knowing what the words mean (Ginsburg, Greenes, & Balfanz, 2003). Be creative in looking for opportunities to count with children during typical activities (e.g., blocks in a tower or steps up the ladder) as well as in unusual or silly ways (e.g., mosquito bites or ways to move backward). Note that children can count objects before actions and actions before events (Campbell, 1999).

▲ Provide materials to explore one-to-one correspondence

Provide children with materials such as nuts and bolts, dominoes, and dot cards to explore one-to-one correspondence, and encourage them to create their own (e.g., one ball of clay in each paper cup). Participating in the classroom community (such as distributing cups at snacktime) also supports **one-to-one correspondence** because social activities are important to children (Mix, 2002). To help children keep track while counting, separate objects in a line and touch or move each object as it is counted. Rather than correcting miscounts (double counting or skipping a number), model correct counting.

▲ Engage children in simple numerical problem solving

Pose mathematical challenges that are interesting to children. For example, when they set the table, remind them to look at the sign-in sheet to see if anyone is absent. Encourage them to count to answer their own questions, for example, how many treats they need to bring to class to celebrate their birthday. Refer children to one another for help with simple number problems (e.g., "Maybe Jane can help figure out how many blocks you need to make your wall one row higher"). Encourage children to reflect on their solutions rather than saying if they are right or wrong; for example, you might say, "There are still some empty spaces. How many do you think you'll need to fill them?" or "Mr. and Mrs. Rodriguez are joining us at snacktime. How many more chairs do we need at the table?"

KDI 33. Part-whole relationships: Children combine and separate quantities of objects.

Description: Children compose and decompose quantities. They use parts to make up the whole set (e.g., combine two blocks and three blocks to make a set of five blocks). They also divide the whole set into parts (e.g., separate five blocks into one block and four blocks).

How an Understanding of Part-Whole Relationships Develops

Understanding **part-whole relationships** is the basis for performing simple operations such as addition, subtraction, division, and multiplication. Children explore these relationships by combining (composing) and separating (decomposing) sets of objects in different ways. As early as age three, children care about dividing such things as pieces of candy or minutes per turn at the computer into "equal shares" (Clements, 2004b). After many hands-on experiences, preschoolers can begin to visualize part-whole relationships in their minds, beginning with two parts that make up a whole (e.g., five is made up of two plus three), and, later on, three or more parts (e.g., five can also be made up of two plus two plus one).

Teaching Strategies That Support an Understanding of Part-Whole Relationships

▲ Provide materials that can be grouped and regrouped

Many classroom items can be grouped and regrouped in various ways. These include small toys (e.g., counting bears and blocks), writing and drawing materials (e.g., colored pencils and pieces of paper), and natural items (e.g., shells and rocks). Let children determine how to create and rearrange groups of objects. Once they have completed making their sets, encourage them to count and compare the quantity (number) of items in each.

▲ Provide materials that can be taken apart and put back together

Many art and construction materials lend themselves to being subdivided and combined in new ways, such as lumps of clay, unit blocks, and Legos. In addition to work time, plan opportunities for children to work with these materials. For example, at small-group time, distribute baskets of buttons and say "I wonder how many ways you can make five with your buttons." Later on, increase the total (e.g., ways to make eight) and ask children to make combinations made of more than two parts (such as combining three groups of buttons to make a total of eight).

KDI 34. Shapes: Children identify, name, and describe shapes.

Description: Children recognize, compare, and sort two- and three-dimensional shapes (e.g., triangle, rectangle, circle; cone, cube, sphere). They understand what makes a shape a shape (e.g., all triangles have three sides and three points). Children transform (change) shapes by putting things together and taking them apart.

How Knowledge About Shapes Develops

An awareness of shapes emerges early; young children have an innate ability to recognize and match shapes before they know shape names

(Clements, 2004a). At first, children form general categories for shapes based on their experiences rather than their distinctive properties (a figure is a rectangle "because it looks like a door" rather than because it has four sides). The next step is when children recognize the parts of a shape (sides or edges and angles or points). Finally, they understand how the unique properties of each shape make it different from other shapes. By the end of preschool, most children can accurately name many two- and three-dimensional shapes, even when a shape varies in size or orientation (Sarama & Clements, 2009).

Teaching Strategies That Support Naming and Using Shapes

▲ Provide shapes that children can see and touch

To create a "shape-rich" environment:

Add two- and three-dimensional shapes to your classroom. Provide opportunities for children to explore these shapes in a variety of sturdy materials such as wood, cardboard, Styrofoam, and fabric. Offer many examples of each type of shape, including narrow and wide rectangles and triangles with equal and unequal angles.

Encourage children to draw shapes. Even if their drawings are inexact, children actively consider the properties of shapes as they create them.

Encourage children to sort shapes and provide reasons for their groupings. Ask children to describe why shapes are alike and *not* alike and to say why something is or is *not* a shape.

Provide and encourage children to explore unconventional or less common shapes, such as trapezoids and octagons. Even if they do not immediately recognize them, children enjoy hearing the names of unusual shapes and exploring the variety of shapes.

Offer materials with vertical symmetry (left-right halves are identical) and horizontal symmetry (top-bottom halves are identical). Point out symmetry in the things children make.

Use printed materials to focus on shape. Print out photos from the web (or cut out photos from magazines) that feature shapes, and encourage children to sort them. Create a shape scrapbook for the book area.

▲ Encourage children to create and transform shapes and observe and describe the results

Children often transform materials in ways that involve shapes (e.g., combine two square blocks into a rectangle or flatten a ball of clay into a circle) (Chalufour & Worth, 2003). To support these actions:

Provide materials to create and modify shapes. Children enjoy working with toothpicks, play dough, and yarn. Talk about what defines the shape children make.

Talk with children as they create new shapes. As children combine and take apart shapes to create new shapes, talk with them about these transformations. Encourage them to say what is the same and/or different after each change.

Look for interactive media that allow children to manipulate shapes. Use computers as a supplement to using hands-on materials by choosing interactive programs that allow them to slide, rotate, and flip shapes.

Wooden blocks that come in different geometrical shapes help young children learn about basic shapes and their properties.

▲ Name shapes and the actions children use to transform them

To provide children with the vocabulary of shapes and their transformation:

Identify and label shapes throughout the environment. Apply the games used to find letters and numerals to two- and three-dimensional shapes. Go on a shape hunt or play shape I spy (e.g., "I see something shaped like a triangle in the book area. What do you think it is?").

Label, describe, and discuss shape attributes. Repeat children's words and add others (e.g., *sides* and *edges; points, angles,* and *corners; straight* and *curved lines*).

Describe and encourage children to describe their actions and outcomes as they transform shapes. Talk about the shape(s) children start with (e.g., two squares) and the one they end up with (e.g., a rectangle). Label their motions, using words such as *slide, turn; twist, flip;* and *rotate, reverse.*

KDI 35. Spatial awareness: Children recognize spatial relationships among people and objects.

Description: Children use position, direction, and distance words to describe actions and the location of objects in their environment. They solve simple spatial problems in play (e.g., building with blocks, doing puzzles, wrapping objects).

How Spatial Awareness Develops

Spatial awareness involves **spatial orientation** (knowing where your body is and how to get around objects and through space) and **spatial visualization** (the ability to manipulate and "move" images in your mind). A young child can picture where a block is located; an older child can mentally move that block to decide if it fits in a given space. Spatial awareness is important in motor development and understanding the orientation of print.

Spatial awareness begins at birth as newborns turn toward food and stimulation. Toddlers implicitly use spatial knowledge to get around, and preschoolers explicitly understand position, distance, and direction (Copley, 2010). Children acquire the language of spatial relationships early, which, interestingly, develops in a consistent order across cultures (Bowerman, 1996). First children learn direction words (e.g., *up, down*); followed by position words (e.g., *in, on, under; beside, between; in front of, behind*); and, finally, distance words (e.g., *near, far*), although these are subjective (near to or far from oneself). Children do not learn the words *left* and *right* until the early elementary grades.

Teaching Strategies That Support Spatial Awareness

▲ Provide materials and plan activities that encourage children to create spaces

To create an environment where children can explore space:

Provide a large space indoors and small spaces outdoors. Early childhood settings typically have small spaces indoors and large spaces outdoors. Children also need to experience the reverse, for example, a large space to build block structures or a small grassy area under a tree.

Give children opportunities to work with two- and three-dimensional objects in different spatial contexts. We usually think of spatial awareness as three dimensional; for example, arranging doll furniture or crawling inside a cave. However, children also explore space with two-dimensional materials, such as making all the letters fit across the page. Provide materials and plan activities that allow for both.

Provide materials that let children fully and partially cover an area of space. At small-group time, for example, give children small tiles and a large board or different-sized presents to wrap in various containers. At large-group time, have children move their bodies in ways that occupy a small space (a carpet square) and then travel over a large space (across the room).

▲ Encourage children to handle, move, and view things from different perspectives

Young children rarely notice how their actions affect spatial relationships unless adults call it to their attention in the following ways:

Encourage children to observe familiar things from a variety of unfamiliar viewpoints. For example, children can look at a table from underneath, mount the climber to look down on the garden, or put their heads between their knees to look behind them.

Help children solve spatial problems by looking at things from different angles. Pose spatial challenges that help children view people, objects, and situations from other positions:

> *At work time in the block area, Sylvan becomes frustrated when he pushes a long cylinder through an opening in the front wall and it knocks down the back wall. His teacher stands behind the walls and says, "I wonder what is making your back wall fall down. Maybe if you come around to where I am, it will help you solve the problem." Sylvan goes to the other side and instantly sees the cylinder is longer than the distance between the two walls. He rebuilds the second wall farther back and then reinserts the cylinder in the front wall.*

Take photos of children from different perspectives during the daily routine. As you discuss the photos, talk about the position they were shot from and how the children can tell.

Use books to explore spatial concepts. Many storybooks illustrate one setting from different perspectives. Encourage children to describe the position or distance of characters and objects in relation to one another.

Use interactive media as an aid in the development of spatial concepts. Computers can supplement manipulatives in exploring spatial relationships. Using a mouse, touchpad, or touchscreen makes it easy for children to move objects onscreen and observe the result of their actions.

▲ Use and encourage children to use words that describe position, direction, and distance

To help children understand and use words related to space, try these ideas:

Find and create opportunities to use position, direction, and distance words. At planning and recall times, encourage children to describe their intentions in spatial terms (e.g., "Where did you hide from the giant?"). At work and group times, comment on what children do using spatial concepts. For example, you might say, "I wonder how many of you can fit underneath the blanket" or "I spy something pink inside the doll carriage."

Encourage children to give directions to one another. For example, at large-group time, in addition to demonstrating a movement, ask children to say what they want others to do. As you play alongside children, ask them to explain how they did something so you can imitate them (e.g., "Where on the lace I should sprinkle the sequins?").

Sing songs and act out favorite stories and rhymes that involve movement. Encourage children to make up their own words and motions to favorite songs, such as "The Hokey Pokey."

KDI 36. Measuring: Children measure to describe, compare, and order things.

Description: Children use measurement terms to describe attributes (i.e., length, volume, weight, temperature, and time). They compare quantities (e.g., same, different; bigger, smaller; more, less; heavier, lighter) and order them (e.g., shortest, medium, longest). They estimate relative quantities (e.g., whether something has more or less).

How Measurement Knowledge and Skills Develop

The motivation to measure comes from children's interest in making comparisons: Who runs faster? Which tower is taller? Which rock is the heaviest? Their conclusions are initially influenced by perception (a long snake of clay looks like it has more than the same amount rolled into a ball), but preschoolers increasingly overcome misconceptions with mathematical thinking (Sarama & Clements, 2009).

Children's ideas about quantity, volume, weight, length, and time develop gradually. They recognize length as an attribute beginning around age three. By age four, children compare lengths by holding objects next to one another or with simple measuring tools (both conventional and unconventional measuring tools). They also begin to measure correctly (using the same unit, starting at the baseline, measuring without gaps or

By age four, children can use simple measuring tools to compare lengths.

overlaps), although they still make errors (Lehrer, 2003).

Understanding area and volume also begins in preschool, but because these measurements involve two and three dimensions, respectively, a full understanding of them does not emerge until the early or middle elementary grades. Children's developing number sense helps them with measurement (Clements & Stephan, 2004). For example, if they can count length or area units, or read the numerals on a scale or timer, they can compare properties more accurately and verify differences.

Teaching Strategies That Support Measuring

▲ Support children's interest in identifying and comparing measurable attributes

Begin with materials and experiences that enable children to compare things on length, such as longer and shorter, wider and narrower, higher and lower, and how far around (circumference). Then provide opportunities to measure and compare area (covers more or less space); volume or capacity[2] for solids and liquids (holds more or less); weight (heavier or lighter); temperature (hotter or colder); sound (louder or softer); and two aspects of time — duration (lasts longer or shorter) and speed (goes faster or slower). After children have many experiences comparing two items, they can begin to compare three or more items and put them in order (most to least, or vice versa).

▲ Encourage children to estimate quantities

Encourage children to estimating relative amounts, such as whether one thing is taller or holds more than another. It does not matter if their predictions are correct, only that they consider the reasoning behind their estimates. For example, you might say, "I wonder why you think the red bowl holds more than the blue bowl." Have children verify their estimates to learn from any discrepancies (e.g., "Why do you think it was more [or less] than you expected?").

▲ Use and encourage children to use measurement words

Children need experience with three types of measurement words. First are terms for *attributes* that can be measured, such as length, height, and time. Second are *comparison words* (to make two-way comparisons and to order or seriate three or more items), such as faster and slower or tall, taller, and tallest. Third are common *measurement units*, such as inches, days, and teaspoons. Here are some additional vocabulary words to introduce in different measurement domains:

Length terms. Length, long, tall, short, wider, narrower, width, inch, foot, ruler, yardstick (and for distance as a measure of length between two points: near, far, closer together)

Capacity and volume terms. Volume, empty, fuller, holds more, holds fewer or less, pint, quart, gallon, liter, measuring cup, measuring spoon

Weight terms. Weight, heavy, lighter, heft, scale, balance, ounce, pound, ton

[2]*Volume* is sometimes used to refer to solids and *capacity* to refer to liquids (Copley, 2010); however, these terms are also used interchangeably.

Time terms. Time, speed, fast, quicker, slower, soon, later, last longer, minute, hour, day, year, clock, timer, stopwatch

Temperature terms. Temperature, hot, heat, warmth, cool, colder, freezing, melting, thermometer, degree

KDI 37. Unit: Children understand and use the concept of unit.

Description: Children understand that a unit is a standard (unvarying) quantity. They measure using unconventional (e.g., block) and conventional (e.g., ruler) measuring tools. They use correct measuring procedures (e.g., begin at the baseline and measure without gaps or overlaps).

How an Understanding of Unit Develops

The two concepts children need to learn about **unit** is that measuring involves repeating equal-sized units and that one counts the number of units to arrive at the total quantity (Sophian, 2004). Most children grasp these principles by the end of preschool. They also begin to understand how a unit functions — they use the same unit, begin at the baseline, and measure without gaps or overlaps (Clements, 2004b). Preschoolers use both unconventional units (e.g., string, scoops, sand timers) and conventional units (e.g., rulers, measuring cups, stop watches). Materials that strike a balance, such as unit cubes, help them transition between the two types of tools.

Teaching Strategies That Support an Understanding of Unit

▲ Support children's use of conventional and unconventional measuring tools

Unconventional tools can be engaging because they are novel and quirky. It is fun, for example, to measure how many shoes long the teacher is compared to each child. On the other hand, the conventional tools used by adults are also intriguing. Encourage children to choose their own measuring devices and to explain why something would (or would not) be useful to measure the attribute they are interested in.

▲ Model accurate measuring techniques

Measuring accurately does not come naturally to children; they learn by observing adults. When children make errors, do not correct them. Instead, measure correctly and describe what you are doing. Take advantage of situations where children measure the same thing and are surprised when they arrive at different results. For example, say "Joshua says the table is two boards wide and Eliza measured it at three boards wide. I wonder why your measurements aren't the same."

KDI 38. Patterns: Children identify, describe, copy, complete, and create patterns.

Description: Children lay the foundation for algebra by working with simple alternating patterns (e.g., ABABAB) and progressing to more complex patterns (e.g., AABAABAAB, ABCABCABC). They recognize repeating sequences (e.g., the daily routine, movement patterns) and begin to identify and describe increasing and decreasing patterns (e.g., height grows as age increases).

How Pattern Awareness Develops

Children learn two important principles about patterns. The first principle is *stability* — the elements stay the same with each repetition (e.g., elements remain red and blue). Second, children learn that *order* matters; once a pattern is established, it determines what follows (e.g., blue always follows red).

In preschool, children develop the ability to recognize, describe, duplicate (copy), extend (add to and fill in), and create their own patterns. First they identify the core unit (the repeating part), which allows them to predict what comes next and fill in or extend it (Klein & Starkey, 2004). Later, as they get older, they create their own patterns. Young children begin by working with simple two-element patterns such as ABABAB or AABBAABBAABB and then move to creating more

Provide children materials and opportunities that encourage them to create patterns, such as pegs and pegboards.

complex patterns that have two elements (AABAABAAB) or even three elements (ABCABCABC).[3] In addition to working with repeating patterns, preschool children begin to recognize and predict patterns that increase (e.g., height increases with age) and decrease (e.g., as children leave the planning table one by one, the number left decreases correspondingly).

Teaching Strategies That Support an Understanding of Patterns

▲ Provide opportunities for children to recognize and describe patterns in the environment

Begin with the simplest two-element patterns and gradually introduce more complex patterns with two or three elements. Refer to them as *patterns,* and say what makes a pattern a pattern (the same elements in the same order). Point to the elements in a pattern and say their order aloud (e.g., "The jewels on the crown go red, yellow, red, yellow, red, yellow all around the king's head"). Encourage children to point and name the elements together with you. Help children identify when something is *not* a pattern because the elements appear in random order (e.g., red, yellow, red, blue, blue, green) or the sequence changes after two repetitions (e.g., red, blue, red, blue, red, green).

Most children find it easiest to begin with visual patterns (unless they have visual limitations), but there are many patterns that occur and appeal to the other senses, such as sounds in the environment (such as the high-low pitches in a siren) and movement sequences (such as pumping legs in and out on the swing). Recurring events, such as the daily routine, are another type of repeating pattern.

In addition to repeating patterns, help children identify increasing and decreasing patterns. For example, they are fascinated by the idea of getting bigger as they get older. Likewise, they can see decreasing patterns in many parts of the daily routine (e.g., the level of napkins in the basket goes down by one each time the number of napkins on the table increases by one).

▲ Provide materials and opportunities that lend themselves to creating patterns

Materials that encourage pattern-making include beads, sticks, blocks, small animal and people figures, pegs and pegboards, drawing and collage materials, and interactive media. Look for books that feature patterned illustrations and craft magazines with photos of patterned quilts, weaving, and woodwork. Include patterns in classroom furnishings and dress-up clothes, and collect patterned objects from nature such as shells, fallen leaves, and bark. Plant a garden with alternating rows of crops, and arrange fruit and vegetable slices in a pattern at snacktime. Finally, provide opportunities at group times and transitions for children to create sound and movement patterns (alternating two body parts to pat the beat or singing at high and low pitches).

[3]Mathematicians require at least three repetitions for a pattern to be established since elements may change (expand, drop, rearrange, or reverse) after two repetitions. Therefore, always provide and describe at least three repetitions when introducing a pattern to a child.

▲ Look for opportunities to have fun with patterns

For many children, making patterns has the same attraction as doing puzzles or building with blocks. To extend this interest as you work alongside children, create patterns and encourage them to add the next element or fill in a blank. Occasionally make an error for them to find and correct. Call attention to increasing or decreasing patterns that emerge in play, for example, as children systematically transfer toys from one pile to another.

KDI 39. Data analysis: Children use information about quantity to draw conclusions, make decisions, and solve problems.

Description: Children collect, organize, and compare information based on measurable attributes. They represent data in simple ways (e.g., tally marks, stacks of blocks, pictures, lists, charts, graphs). They interpret and apply information in their work and play (e.g., how many cups are needed if two children are absent).

How Data Analysis Knowledge and Skills Develop

Doing simple data analysis helps preschoolers develop their thinking and reasoning abilities. They learn how to ask questions in ways that can be answered by collecting and tabulating information. Once they have gathered the relevant data, children gain practice interpreting and applying the results to problems that interest them: How many rows should the garden have? Who is going to kindergarten next year and not returning to preschool? Who has milk and who has juice in their lunch bag?

Young preschoolers do not automatically categorize the information they gather. They will generate a list but will not group the data in a way that allows interpretation. Later, with emerging numerical knowledge and adult guidance, older preschoolers begin to sort and count data. For example, here is how children might list what they collected on three nature walks, taken at an earlier, middle, and later time during the school year:

What We Collected on Our Nature Walk		
Developmental Level		
Earlier	*Middle*	*Later*
Sue: Pinecone John: Stone Isaac: Leaf Paula: Pinecone Sammy: Acorn Fiona: Stone Ozzie: Pinecone	Pinecone: Sue, Ada, Ozzie Stone: John, Fiona Acorn: Sammy Leaf: Isaac	Pinecone: /// (3) Stone: // (2) Acorn: / (1) Leaf: / (1)

Teaching Strategies That Support Data Analysis

▲ Provide opportunities to sort and count things and to describe and apply the results

Provide materials that children can group according to the attributes that interest them (e.g., size, color, texture, weight, sound, speed, pattern). Use mathematical language when talking about their sorting, using both general terms (e.g., *none, some, all*) and specific numerical values (e.g., "Two in this pile, five in that pile"). Encourage children to think about what the numbers mean and how to apply them to answer their own questions or solve problems they encounter in play:

> *After the first few snowfalls of the year, children in Miss Kay's class comment that outside time is getting shorter because they have to put on snowsuits and boots. Miss Kay asks the children how they could solve the problem. Rachel suggests they could get dressed faster if those who were ready first helped the others. "How can we be sure that way is faster?" asks Miss Kay. Milo suggests she time them with a stopwatch and the others agree. That day, without children helping one another, Miss Kay times and writes down "15 minutes." The next day, when children help one other, she times and writes "10 minutes." "Ten is smaller than 15," says Ben. The children conclude their solution works and help one another after that.*

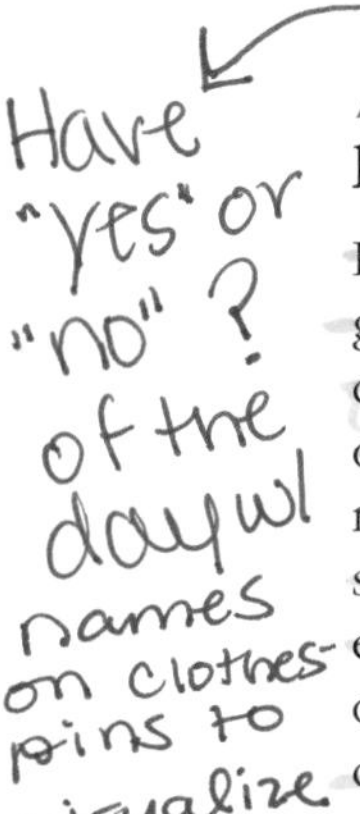

▲ Help children represent data using lists, tabulations, charts, and graphs

Recording information on simple lists, charts, and graphs helps make data gathering and analysis concrete for young children. They can move small objects into columns or make marks (checks, hash marks) to represent each piece of data. Use large sheets of paper or clipboards that children can easily see and use for data entry. Begin with a one-column list and then divide the data into two columns or more as children become more skilled at categorizing and counting. Once they get in the habit of charting things that interest them (how many played in an area, the number of people in their families), children will generate many recording ideas themselves!

▲ Ask and encourage children to ask questions that can be answered by gathering data

Begin by asking data-based questions yourself about things of interest to children. For example, if their reading and pretend play involves different types of vehicles, plan a neighborhood walk and wonder whether you'll see more cars or more trucks. Bring a clipboard and writing tools to record their observations. Back in the classroom, help children count how many of each vehicle they saw. At first, children may need your help to rephrase their questions into ones than can be answered by collecting and analyzing data. For example, if children wonder who brought a juice box in their lunch and who has milk, you might say, "So your idea is to count how many children have juice and how many have milk." Children also need your guidance to interpret and apply the results (e.g., "How many juice boxes and milk cartons should we bring for lunch on our field trip?"). This last step gives added reason — in addition to sheer curiosity — for asking the question in the first place and helps children appreciate the relevance of mathematics in their lives.

Try These Ideas Yourself

1. List what you consider to be the five most important things preschoolers need to know or be able to do in the Mathematics content area when they enter kindergarten. Why are they important? How can teachers support their development?

2. In the following scenario, identify the Mathematics KDIs (see p. 152) taking place. What types of learning are occurring in other areas of development? How could a teacher support and extend the learning?

> *Mark and Jennifer are building a race track with blocks for their toy cars. "Let's make it really long," says Jennifer. "All the way from one end of the room to another." Their teacher says, "I wonder how many blocks you'll need to reach from the door to the back wall." Mark answers, "A hundred!" Jennifer says she isn't sure. They decide to build their track and then count the number of blocks. They carry the big blocks together, and when they run out of big blocks, they finish with small ones. "Good," says Mark. "Now our track will have even more blocks."*

3. Write down all the things you do in a week that involve mathematics, such as balancing your checkbook, adapting a recipe to feed half or twice as many people, calculating your car's gas mileage, or fitting everything in your suitcase. Next, think about how children use simple mathematics in their daily lives.

4. Make a list of all the words you can use with children that have to do with number, other than actual numbers (e.g., *some, many, large amount, fewer than, as much as, for each person*). Share your list with a colleague and ask for additional ideas. Plan ways to use these words the next time you are involved in a number experience with children.

5. Walk around your house or outside. List all the things you see with patterns (e.g., curtains, linoleum tile, leaves, brickwork). Now think about a typical week in your life. List all the patterns or repeated sequences you can identify in these events (e.g., your morning routine, errands done in a particular order). Next, list the patterns young children are likely to come across in their belongings, surroundings, and day-to-day activities. How can you help children become more aware of (and create) patterns and repeated sequences in their experiences?

Chapter 15

What Is the HighScope Curriculum in Creative Arts?

Think About It

After attending a parent workshop on young children and art, one parent recalled:

> *After an audition to determine our voice range for the class chorus, I was one of several children told we would be "listeners." We stood silently in the back row to appreciate everyone else's voices. Another time, we took an art placement exam. The teacher played the music "Ebbtide," and we painted whatever came to mind. My picture must have gotten washed away with the tide because I never had an art class that year.*

Another parent shared a very different memory:

> *My fourth grade teacher told us we were all artists. First thing every morning, we spent 15 minutes playing with art materials. Every child succeeded and felt confident tackling math, reading, or whatever subject came next. I still think of myself as an artist. Whether I'm choosing clip art or rearranging furniture, I keep that sense of playfulness.*

These contrasting stories show that early experiences shape how we see ourselves as artists. Like the teacher in the second example, HighScope believes an artist lives inside each of us. Adults often marvel at children's inventiveness, yet we fail to credit our own creativity and exclude art appreciation from the curriculum because we doubt our artistic judgment. Yet art has a language anyone can understand. Once we learn to speak it, art can become a welcome part of daily life.

Why the Creative Arts Are Important

Children who participate in art activities benefit throughout their school years in all areas of learning (Fiske, 1999). For young children in particular, the creative arts provide an inner sense of competence and control: "As they engage in the artistic process, children learn that they can observe, organize, and interpret their experiences. They can make decisions, take actions, and monitor the effect of those actions" (Arts Education Partnership, 1998, p. 2).

Artistic Development in Preschool

Developmental changes during preschool make children especially open to learning in the creative arts. Language opens up new avenues for expression. Preschoolers can also form mental images. "Being able to think about something not present and then find a way to express it is a major cognitive accomplishment for young children" (Seefeldt, 1995, p. 40). This ability lets them engage in various forms of **artistic representation.** They can paint a picture of their family (art), make up a song about an upcoming birthday party (music),

Chapter Learning Objectives

By the end of this chapter, you will be able to

- Explain why early learning in the creative arts is important.
- Describe the HighScope key developmental indicators (KDIs) in the Creative Arts content area.
- Begin to apply the strategies adults use to scaffold (support and gently extend) early learning in creative arts.

glide like a cloud floating across the sky (movement), or role-play making dinner (pretend play).

The creative arts provide preschoolers with an inner sense of competence and control.

Stages in Making and Appreciating Art

The stages of artistic development do not have clear beginnings and endings (Taunton & Colbert, 2000). Like adult artists, children move back and forth between levels when they encounter a new medium. Nevertheless, their ability to *make art* progresses along with the growth of related abilities (Epstein & Trimis, 2002; Kerlavage, 1995):

From accidental to intentional representation. Younger children accidentally create a form or movement and then decide it's like something (e.g., roll on the floor and say "I'm a ball"). In older children, this order is reversed; they choose materials or actions to match their mental image.

From simple to elaborate models. Initially, children hold one or two characteristics in mind. Later, their representations become more detailed. A younger child may pretend to be a baby by going "Waa!" An older child crawls, sucks on a bottle, and reaches out to be picked up.

From randomness to deliberation. Children initially explore a medium without regard to the effects. As they gain more control over art materials and tools, their actions become more deliberate. For example, after randomly singing notes, they try to reproduce a specific pitch.

From unrelated elements to relationships. Children gradually become aware of how marks, sounds, movements, and play themes relate to one another. For example, they make marks wherever their hand lands, but later consider how marks or colors look next to one another.

Likewise, the ability to *appreciate art* follows a progression that reflects overall development:

Sensorial. Very young children like artwork that appeals to their senses (e.g., bright colors and bold patterns, music with a strong beat). They engage with art emotionally and focus on one detail. They do not differentiate between artistic forms (such as a painting and a photo).

Concrete. As children begin to work with symbols, their preferences are based on the subject matter. They like realistic art that relates to their own experiences and see the purpose of art as telling a story with images, sounds, or actions. Children at this stage can sort art by medium (e.g., painting versus sculpture; vocal versus instrumental music).

Expressive. By late preschool or early kindergarten, children think about the artist's point of view (what the artist wants to show or say). They still prefer realism but they now pay attention to

Terms Used in This Chapter

• artistic representation • process versus product • beat, rhythm, tempo (rhythmic qualities) • pitch, melody, harmony (tonal qualities) • sociodramatic play • action dialogue • aesthetic choices

HighScope teachers emphasize effort — rather than results — and give children a lot of time for experimentation with artistic materials and processes.

how artists use the features of a medium (i.e., composition, speed, plot) to express an idea or feeling. Children in this stage recognize different artistic styles and how culture affects artwork.

General Teaching Strategies for Creative Arts

▲ Provide open-ended art materials and experiences

Provide a variety of open-ended materials for children to transform in their artistic exploration and creative play. Materials should be hands-on to encourage sensory exploration but may include open-ended (interactive) media that allow children to create their own drawings, music, and so on. In addition to providing materials, be intentional about engaging children to use them and plan group-time activities that help children discover and reflect on the cognitive and social possibilities embodied within the creative arts. "Art educators agree that the intention to teach and respect art is vital to creating a climate in which art learning can thrive" (Epstein, 2007, p. 110).

▲ Establish a climate that supports creative risk-taking and emphasizes process over product

Children's artistic creativity thrives when they feel supported and know they will not be judged. Don't praise artwork as "pretty" or second-guess artistic opinions. Children may play it safe in search of rewards or refrain from expressing their views if they fear correction, disagreement, or ridicule.

Emphasize effort rather than results and allow time for experimentation. Cutting the creative process short or introducing too many materials at once can stunt the flowering of early creativity (Thompson, 1995). In addition, encourage collaboration, and don't be afraid children will "copy" one another. When children work together, originality actually increases (Taunton & Colbert, 2000). Children build on the ideas of their peers and incorporate more details in their own artwork.

▲ Encourage children to represent real and imaginary experiences through the arts

Young children readily express themselves using artistic media. However, their play can be quite stereotyped and unvarying unless adults extend it (Kindler, 1995). Try these scaffolding strategies to help children expand their choice and manipulation of materials as well as opportunities to represent their ideas and feelings:

- At small-group time, provide art materials and suggest children use them to share what they remember from the field trip the day before.
- At large-group time, provide opportunities for children to imitate animals, machines, or other familiar things. Encourage them to describe their movements.
- Take advantage of experiences that occur throughout the daily routine, and ask children how they could draw, build, sing, move, or otherwise represent the people, material, and events.
- Take photos of the children engaged in various activities in the classroom and outside. Talk with them about the pictures and the sounds or movements that went along with the activity.

KDIs in Creative Arts

40. **Art:** Children express and represent what they observe, think, imagine, and feel through two- and three-dimensional art.
41. **Music:** Children express and represent what they observe, think, imagine, and feel through music.
42. **Movement:** Children express and represent what they observe, think, imagine, and feel through movement.
43. **Pretend play:** Children express and represent what they observe, think, imagine, and feel through pretend play.
44. **Appreciating the arts:** Children appreciate the creative arts.

▲ Talk with children about the arts

Encourage children to talk about the arts in their own words. Don't, however, presume to know what they have created or think because you might be wrong and may deprive them of the chance to describe and reflect on their own artwork and that of others. While too many adult questions or comments can end a conversation, a well-timed remark can begin to a satisfying exchange. Here are some conversational openers that can lead to a meaningful dialogue with children about art:

- How does the (material) feel (smell, sound, or other appropriate sense)? For example, "How do the beads feel?" or "How does the clay smell?" or "How does the tambourine sound?"
- What does the (sound, image, movement) remind you of? For example, "What does this slow music make you think of?" or "I wonder if this jagged shape reminds you of anything on the playground?" or "I'm thinking of something we saw on our walk that moves this way."
- I'm curious about how you will (make, be, do) that. For example, "What will you use to build the boat?" or "I wonder what you will use to be the guy who puts out the fires."
- Tell us what you found out about the _____ (material or tool). For example, "Jason, what did you learn about using the garlic press with the play dough?"
- Why do you suppose the artist (painter, composer, dancer) made/did it that way? For example, "I wonder why this artist paints big pictures and this one makes small pictures?" or "The first composer wrote fast notes and the second one wrote slow notes. Why do you suppose they each wrote their music a different way?"

▲ Draw on the artistic forms in the cultures of children's families and communities

Before arriving at preschool, children encounter the arts at home, in the community, and in the broader culture. To deepen this exposure, include representative artwork from every medium in your program's furnishings, materials, and activities, and encourage families to share their interests and talents at work time and group times. You can also contact local arts groups to find out what resources are available for young children. In addition, go on field trips and/or invite visitors to the classroom, working with parents and local artists to ensure that the sessions include hands-on activities and are appropriate for all children.

Key Developmental Indicators in Creative Arts

HighScope has five key developmental indicators (KDIs) in Creative Arts: 40. Art, 41. Music, 42. Movement, 43. Pretend play, and 44. Appreciating the arts. See "KDIs in Creative Arts" above.

The remainder of this chapter discusses the early learning in each KDI and the ways that adults can support their development. For specific activities, see the resources on HighScope's website (www.highscope.org).

KDI 40. Art: Children express and represent what they observe, think, imagine, and feel through two- and three-dimensional art.

Description: Children explore and use a variety of materials and tools to draw and paint, mold and sculpt, build and assemble. They use the properties of art materials (e.g., shape, color, texture) to represent their ideas. Children's representations and designs develop from simple to complex and from accidental to intentional.

How Art Develops

A young child's interest in making art is universal (Thompson, 1995). Florence Goodenough (1926), an early art theorist, emphasized that "to little children, drawing is a language — a form of cognitive expression — and its purpose is not primarily esthetic" (p. 14). In other words, children care more about the **process** of creating rather than about making a **product.**

While artistic development varies somewhat according to cultural norms (e.g., whether it is acceptable to represent the human form), there is a general progression from treating art materials the same as other objects to exploring their actions and properties to naming scribbles and other visual signs to trying to capture (represent) the basic features of objects to striving for greater representational accuracy (Wolfe & Perry, 1989). Changes in cognitive, social and emotional, perceptual, and physical growth affect children's visual art. As children develop, they can hold images in mind, take more than one perspective, recognize feelings, identify colors and shapes, and use greater motor control and eye-hand coordination in handling materials and tools.

Teaching Strategies That Support Art

▲ Provide diverse examples of visual art throughout the classroom

In addition to paintings and sculpture, remember that art is also present in everyday objects, such as the colorful design of a sweater, the shape of a hand-carved bowl, the texture of a porcelain plate, the scenic background in a vacation photo, or the molded metal hinge on a wooden box. Nature also abounds in artistic elements. Call children's attention to these items throughout the room and outdoors. Select books illustrated in different styles and media, such as collage, line drawings, photographs, intense colors, and pastels. Offer colorful scarves to move with at large-group time. Now and then, arrange snacks artfully on a plate and discuss the patterns and textures with the children. Almost any material or experience can be approached with aesthetics in mind!

▲ Give children time to explore art materials and tools in depth

Introduce art materials slowly to children, rather than inundate them with many different options. If children are continually presented with new materials, they "are never able to gain control over, or develop skill in, the use of any one medium and may not be able to acquire the skills and techniques necessary to actually use these materials to create art" (Seefeldt, 1999, p. 209). For example, at small-group time, begin with one primary color — red, blue, or yellow. Let children thoroughly explore that color and how it changes when they add white or black to it. Then they can mix two colors.

Use the same gradual process with tools. Children should begin by using just their using hands to experience the medium: "Does the paint feel wet or dry?" "Is the clay hard or soft to squeeze?" "How much strength does it take to tear paper?" Then offer children tools such as brushes, sponges, or items for making impressions.

Periodically reintroduce familiar materials for children to investigate in new ways, and provide safe areas to store unfinished projects with work-in-progress signs. Finally, have fun exploring art materials and tools yourself. Copy children's actions and try out their ideas. When adults work alongside children, they tend to use art materials for a longer time, use them in more varied ways, and spontaneously talk about what they are doing (Kindler, 1995).

▲ Display and send home children's artwork

Display children's artwork on walls and shelves throughout the room. Keeping these at eye level helps children notice them and increases the likelihood they will talk about their intentions and ideas. Taking dictation can further spur young children to talk about their art. Write the dictation on a sticky note rather than directly on the artwork to show you respect what the child has done.

Send children's creations home regardless of its artistic content or skill level. If parents pressure children or you to have them produce "refrigerator-ready" artwork, help parents understand and appreciate the value of exploration rather than production at this age. Explain that art benefits children intellectually, socially, emotionally, and physically, as well as creatively.

KDI 41. Music: Children express and represent what they observe, think, imagine, and feel through music.

Description: Children explore and experience sound through singing, moving, listening, and playing instruments. They experiment with their voices and make up songs and chants. Children explore and respond to musical elements such as pitch (high, low), tempo (fast, slow), dynamics (loud, soft), and steady beat.

How Music Develops

Musical understanding develops along four lines (Stellaccio & McCarthy, 1999). Children first learn about *rhythmic qualities*, or time elements, including **beat** (underlying pulse), **rhythm** (sound duration), and **tempo** (speed). This awareness grows from toddlerhood to preschool, especially when children are exposed to music with a prominent beat (Metz, 1989; Weikart, 2000).

Children next understand *tonal qualities*, including **pitch** (the highness or lowness of a note), **melody** (tune), and **harmony** (the interval between pitches). Infants try to match the pitch of their voice to a range of sounds. Toddlers can reproduce melodic intervals (match singing one note and then another higher or lower note). By age three, children can sing with a lyrical quality, and by age five, tonal stability is well established.

Music also has *emotional qualities* that can have a powerful effect on our feelings. Preschool children respond to the emotional components of

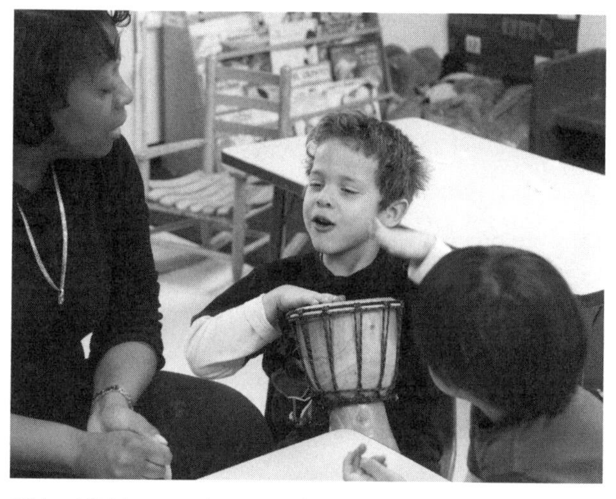

This child invents his own chant while beating on a drum.

different musical styles. Finally, children explore *musical creativity* by inventing chants and songs and playing simple instruments. Toddlers create melodies and experiment with timing, while preschoolers use musical vocalization to describe events, act out roles, and express their feelings (Tarnowski & Leclerc, 1994).

Adults often feel uneasy about teaching music, but "young children engage in music as play. Though many early childhood educators may not consider themselves musicians or music educators, they generally do feel comfortable with the medium of play" (Kemple, Batey, & Hartle, 2005, p. 25). To help young children play with music, use the teaching strategies described here.

Teaching Strategies That Support Music

▲ Look for opportunities to listen to, identify, and create sounds with children

Call attention to naturally occurring environmental sounds, indoors and outdoors, such as bird songs, wind, traffic, bells, doors, rain, or phones. Provide noise-making materials, such as instruments, music players, timers, or talking computer programs and other interactive media. Children also enjoy creating sounds, especially during pretend play (e.g., the "waa" of a baby, the "jing" of a machine). Listen to and imitate their sounds, and ask the children what other sounds the person, creature, or machine makes. Anticipate sounds; for example, you might say, "I wonder what we'll hear if we're quiet outside." Encourage children to name and describe sounds, and expand their vocabulary with new words (e.g., *clank, shriek, throb*).

▲ Sing with children

Young children enjoy singing many types of music including nursery rhymes (e.g., "Rain, Rain, Go Away"), traditional children's songs (e.g., "The Wheels on the Bus"), simple folk songs (e.g., "She'll Be Coming 'Round the Mountain"), and songs for special occasions (e.g., "Happy Birthday"). Introduce a song by first patting the beat, and repeat songs often so children have time to learn them. Read books that illustrate these familiar songs, singing the words as you share them.

Create opportunities for children to sing throughout the day. Use singing to alert children (e.g., "Five minutes until cleanup time") or describe what they are doing (e.g., sing "Blue, blue, blue square here. Red square over there" to the tune of "Row Your Boat" as they sort blocks). Children can also sing their plans or recall what they did at work time. You can also initiate singing games. For example, in pitch-matching, sing or play two notes and invite children to repeat them, listening to whether their voices go higher or lower on the second note.

▲ Play a wide variety of recorded and live music

Children benefit from hearing a wide range of musical styles, such as folk music; classical music; jazz music; contemporary music; march and circus music; and waltzes, tangos, and ballets. Include music that is representative of local cultures and communities. Play primarily instrumental rather than vocal music, because the brain attends to language (words) first, which prevents children from hearing other musical features, such as tempo or instrumentation. Incorporate live music by playing yourself, inviting parents and local musicians to the classroom, or arranging a field trip to hear a school or community band or orchestra.

Just as singing can occur throughout the day, so can listening to music — while moving at large-group time, painting at small-group time, using headphones at work time, and during transitions. Do not, however, play music as background noise, because it distracts children from their own thoughts and actions, interferes with conversation, and lessens music appreciation.

▲ Provide simple instruments

Preschoolers enjoy playing simple musical instruments, especially percussive ones that involve active hand and body movements. Examples include wooden blocks and sticks, drums, bells, xylophones, tambourines, triangles, maracas, washboards, and pots and spoons. Be sure to provide instruments that reflect the children's cultures, such as simple stringed instruments or gourds. Children can also create noisemakers by filling containers and taping the ends or the lids shut (e.g., fill metal, wooden, cardboard, or cloth containers with beads, pebbles, sand, metal washers, or wood chips). Children will enjoy using these instruments during pretend play, to plan and recall, to signal transitions, and to play stop-and-start games at group times.

KDI 42. Movement: Children express and represent what they observe, think, imagine, and feel through movement.

Description: Children explore moving their whole bodies, or parts of their bodies, with and without music. They respond to the features and moods of music through movement.

How Movement Develops

As young children gain greater motor control (see chapter 12), they use their bodies in more than functional ways. They also take great pleasure in expressing themselves through creative movement, that is, "taking a familiar movement and changing it in some way" (Sawyers, 2010, p. 32). Nevertheless, while children enjoy testing the boundaries of their bodies, their range of creative movements can be quite limited — up and down, side to side, or circular (Sims, 1985). The variety of children's movements increases, however, if adults intentionally model and encourage experimentation with body postures, actions, and hand gestures as a means of creative expression (Stellaccio & McCarthy, 1999).

Preschoolers are able to turn their mental images into creative movements during play, for example, stomping like a giant, turning a pretend steering wheel, or flying like a kite. Expressing feelings, experiences, and ideas through movement builds children's confidence in their ability to communicate with their bodies. This sense of bodily comfort and creativity in movement spills over into other areas of learning and strengthens children's belief in themselves as academically capable, socially competent, and imaginative young people (Centers for Disease Control and Prevention, 2010).

As movement educator Phyllis Weikart (2000) notes, "expressing creativity through movement is not a one-time experience....Rather, it evolves over time when children are in the care of adults who consistently promote and support [it] as children explore, plan, make choices, initiate ideas, lead other children, work cooperatively, and solve problems" (p. 111).

Teaching Strategies That Support Movement

▲ Describe and encourage children to describe their creative use of movement

Comment on children's expressive movements throughout the day. For example, during work time, say "You're stepping slowly so the scarf doesn't fall off your head." At cleanup time, note how children carry objects to put them away (e.g., "Justin is walking tippy-toe to the puzzle shelf"). At large-group time, label and encourage others to imitate children's movements. You might say, for example, "Josie and Luke are flapping their arms like birds. I'm going to try that too." Encourage children to describe their creative movements in their own words (as demonstrated in the following anecdote), and add new words (e.g., *glide, crouch, whirl*):

> *At large-group time, Julie (a teacher) plays the guitar, stops, and then plays again. While she plays, the children move their arms to the music. When she stops playing, they stop moving. When she resumes playing, the children move their arms a different way. During the "stop" time she comments, "You moved your arms in all kinds of ways!" The children respond as follows: "I waved mine around." "I bounced mine up and down like you played the guitar." "My arms bended like a straw." "I made mine go faster than anything!" "I waved to you!"*

▲ Encourage children to solve movement problems at group times and transitions

Preschoolers enjoy meeting interesting movement challenges from adults and often incorporate any new ideas that emerge during adult-initiated times into their spontaneous (child-initiated) play. You can invent movement problems at any time of the day, but they are especially appropriate at small- and large-group times, to build on children's explorations at outside time, and as a useful strategy to smooth transitions. Here are a few examples:

Cleanup. Ask children to put away the blocks using just their elbows.

Recall. Have children show what they did at work time by motioning with their hands.

Transitions. Encourage children to move to the next activity someway other way than walking.

Small-group time. Ask children what they can use (other than their hands) to carry their projects to their cubbies.

Outdoor large-group time. Ask children how many ways they can move in, out, over, and around a row of tires.

▲ Provide opportunities for children to represent their experiences through movement

Because preschoolers are capable of representation, they can reflect their experiences and convey things they imagine using movement. Encourage children to use their bodies to express emotions (e.g., "How do you move when you feel happy?" or "Let's move to the snack table as though we're tired and sleepy"). Ask children to move in ways that match how characters feel at key points in a story, for example, how Max (in *Where the Wild Things Are* by Maurice Sendak) might move when he comes home and finds his dinner is still warm. Have children represent a field trip with movement, for example, the movements of the animals they saw when visiting a farm.

▲ Encourage simple ways of moving creatively to music

Play a variety of musical styles to encourage different types of movement. Imitate children, call their attention to the creative movements of their peers, and comment on how it is connected to the quality of the music (e.g., "Sammy is swinging his arms back and forth in time to the lively beat"; "Eleanor is sliding across the floor to the smooth-sounding music"). Create simple movement sequences. For example, take a song with two parts (such as "Yankee Doodle"), and encourage children to do a different movement for each part (march to the verse; wave arms to the chorus). Provide props (e.g., scarves, streamers, paper plates, rhythm sticks) to further encourage the children to move creatively as they listen to music that varies in tempo, pitch, and volume.

KDI 43. Pretend play: Children express and represent what they observe, think, imagine, and feel through pretend play.

Description: Children imitate actions, use one object to stand for another, and take on roles themselves based on their interests and experiences. They use figures to represent characters in their pretend scenarios (e.g., having a "family" of toy bears talk to one another). Their play themes develop in detail and complexity over time.

How Pretend Play Develops

Pretend play, also called **sociodramatic play,** involves both imitation and imagination. When young children imitate, they use gestures, sounds, words, and props to represent the world they know. In imaginative play, they express ideas about the world of "what if." Research shows that pretend play strengthens children's skills in attention, memory, reasoning, language, imagination, emotional understanding, and self-control (Tomlinson & Hyson, 2009). Children's social behavior is more mature in pretend than nonpretend play (Chafel, 1984) and also more complex when scaffolded by adults (Bodrova & Leong, 2007).

During this large-group time, the teacher offers the children scarves to encourage them to move creatively to the music.

Pretend play begins at about 18 months, as children imitate familiar actions and sounds. Parallel play (playing *alongside* others) arises in the second year and becomes social (playing *with* others) at around age three. During preschool, pretend play also becomes more imaginative. Children use props and advance from using one object to stand for something (e.g., pretending a small block is a phone) to creating objects that support complex play themes (e.g., building a doghouse with blocks and pillows). By age four, children collaborate with peers to create a scene with multiple roles and story lines (e.g., a mother takes her sick baby to the hospital where the doctor gives it a shot and medicine). During these pretend-play scenarios, children's interactions last longer, involve more partners, and are more cooperative than in other social situations (Creasey, Jarvis, & Berk, 1998).

Teaching Strategies That Support Pretend Play

▲ Support children as they imitate what they see and hear

Children use their bodies and voices to imitate what they see around them. Support this type of pretend play by imitating what they do, which may lead to an **action dialogue** — communication carried out with gestures instead of words

— as demonstrated by Gary and Jaye in this anecdote:

At work time in the block area, Jaye announces she is leading an exercise class. She stretches her arms high over her head. Her teacher, Gary, imitates her stretching action. When Jaye kicks one foot and then the other forward, Gary does the same. After she performs each part of the exercise routine — bending, twisting, and so on — Jaye pauses and looks at Gary to see if he will imitate her. Only after he reproduces each of her actions does Jaye go on to the next one.

Take advantage of other opportunities for imitation throughout the day. At recall, ask children to pantomime what they did at work time. They can also imitate the actions in a familiar book or song. Finally, recreating actions and sounds from a field trip helps children reflect on the experience.

▲ Watch for and support imaginative role play throughout the classroom

Provide space and materials for pretending and role play. Encourage children to create their own props, and seek donations from families and local businesses. Pretend play often overlaps areas so arrange the room with large and fluid spaces. It also occurs outdoors. Wheeled toys may serve as buses, spaceships, or boats, and climbing structures become forts, tents, and igloos. Small items from nature (e.g., pebbles, leaves) are a feast for a banquet. Bringing indoor materials, such as scarves, dolls, and cooking utensils, outside further helps children extend their imaginative play ideas.

▲ Participate as a partner in children's pretend play

Adults who participate as partners in children's play are better observers, understand children more, and communicate with them more effectively (Paley, 1990). However, partnering must be done with sensitivity so children retain control of the play. Observe first to understand their intentions and follow this set of guidelines:

- Continue with the play theme set by the children, for example, be another dog rather than adding a new type of character.
- Stay within the play situation when offering suggestions, for example, if the children are pretending to visit the doctor's office, do not suggest an emergency ambulance trip to the hospital.
- Match the complexity of the play by supporting children's current developmental levels.
- Acknowledge and accept children's responses to your gentle ideas to extend their play. If they do not pick up on your suggestion, let it go and return to the play that was happening previously.

KDI 44. Appreciating the arts: Children appreciate the creative arts.

Description: Children express opinions and preferences about the arts. They identify the pieces (e.g., a painting or musical selection) and styles they do or do not like and offer simple explanations about why. Children describe the effects they and other artists create and develop a vocabulary to talk about the arts.

How Art Appreciation Develops

Understanding the meaning and aesthetics of art sounds abstract, but young children are more capable of art appreciation than we give them credit for (Gardner, 1991). With their senses open to experience, preschoolers are aware of artistic features around them, such as the emotions evoked by color, the messages delivered through sound, the explosive energy of a movement like leaping, and the emotional tension between characters in a dramatic scene.

While preschoolers initially focus on subject matter rather than aesthetics, they can be sensitive to the quality of artwork if adults engage them in meaningful conversation about it. Preschoolers are capable of sorting artwork based on style, not just content, because they naturally categorize things according to their perceptual attributes. If asked open-ended questions, children can state what they think the artist wants to convey or how a work of art makes them feel. In fact, says art educator Marjorie Schiller (1995), young children enjoy talking about art and identifying the characteristics of artists and their work.

Teaching Strategies That Support Appreciating the Arts

▲ Focus on specific aspects of artwork when you explore it with children

Young preschoolers attend to one dominant feature of a work of art. As their cognitive and aesthetic abilities mature, older preschoolers can focus on the overall work and the relationships between parts. To help children maintain and expand their artistic focus, begin with artwork that has a limited number of features, such as a painting with bold colors, an instrumental selection with a strong beat, a single movement, or a story with a simple repetitive action. Encourage children to talk about what they observe. Gradually increase the complexity of the art to encourage children to reflect on more elements and how they relate to one another, for example, the contrast between colors or the change in mood from one section of music to the next.

▲ Encourage children to make and explain simple aesthetic choices

Children express **aesthetic choices** when they look at one picture longer than another, pick their favorite song from the song book, demonstrate a movement for others to imitate, or choose which character to be in a scenario. However, while younger preschoolers may have clear preferences, they cannot state the reason behind their choices. Older preschoolers are capable of saying why they do (or do not) like something based on aesthetics (e.g., "Yellow is a happy color") or personal relevance (e.g., "My grandpa says that too. It's funny!"). To help children become aware of what and why artistic attributes appeal to them, provide a wide variety of artistic materials and styles so they can find something they are drawn to. As you provide children with a language for talking about the arts, encourage them to use that vocabulary to describe their aesthetic preferences.

▲ Discuss the feelings expressed through artwork

As children's verbal abilities increase, they become more adept at identifying and describing the emotional elements in a work of art. For example, they can say whether a line drawing is happy or sad, a piece of music sounds busy, a movement conveys being tired, or a dramatic incident is scary. Children can also represent the underlying emotion of a work of art through their own facial expressions, gestures, and whole body movements. In fact, the creative arts are an especially potent vehicle for children with limited verbal skills to express emotions. They are also a bridge for English language learners to communicate with teachers and peers in meaningful ways.

Older preschoolers, who are beginning to take another person's perspective, can say what they believe an artist is thinking or feeling. They can also articulate the emotions that art evokes in them. To support this development, comment on the emotional content of art. For example, when commenting on an illustration in a book, you might say, "This pale green looks soothing, like a soft baby blanket." In addition, use descriptive language in your conversations with children. When talking with a child, for example, you might say, "Whenever I wear this shiny red dress, it makes me want to dance!"

▲ Expose children to the materials, tools, and techniques used by artists

To expand preschoolers' experiences in a wide range of artistic media, provide the following:

- **Art.** Illustrated storybooks with artwork in different styles; reproductions of fine art, such as postcards and posters, depicting a range of media and subject matter
- **Music.** Musical selections featuring classical, jazz, opera, folk songs, and other genres; sounds and images of music being performed by individuals, small groups, choirs, and orchestras; a variety of percussion and string instruments for children to play
- **Movement.** Music that inspires children to move in response to tonal quality, tempo, or pitch; sounds and images that illustrate dance styles and performance settings from around the world
- **Pretend play.** Props for children to develop play themes based on familiar television shows and movies; encouragement to expand the complexity of the play beyond scripted lines

Share with children illustrated storybooks and nonfiction books that include pictures of different artists' artwork.

▲ Plan local field trips to introduce children to the creative arts

Look for arts venues in your community — museums, studios, galleries, performance spaces — that welcome young children. Art fairs, botanical gardens, landscaped parks, and public performances of music and dance also offer settings where young children can actively view art. Invite visitors to the classroom, but talk with them beforehand so they know the children's interests and what they are likely to say and do. Provide hands-on activities ahead of time too (e.g., explore clay at small-group time before a ceramist visits; read or tell the story children will see dramatized).

To extend a visit or field trip, encourage children to represent them with a variety of media and group writing activities. Provide materials and ask artists to donate supplies the children can use to create their own artwork or reenact the experience (e.g., yarn, clay, carving tools, dance and theater programs, ticket stubs). Finally, let people know how much you and the children value their contributions. Take dictation for a collective "thank you" letter. Send photos and samples of the artwork children create and how they incorporate what they learned into their play.

Try These Ideas Yourself

1. List what you consider to be the five most important things preschoolers need to know or be able to do in the Creative Arts content area when they enter kindergarten. Why are they important? How can teachers support their development?

2. Think back to your experiences with art, music, movement, and pretend play as a child. Did you feel you were gifted and creative or that you lacked talent and imagination? What affected how you saw yourself as an artist? Consider the importance of each of the following: exposure to the arts, access to materials and tools, the interest and attitudes of adults toward your efforts. How can you make the creative arts a positive experience for the children in your program?

3. List the words you can use with children to describe the features of art (e.g., *color, white space, line, shading, shape*). Now list words that describe styles of music (e.g., *fast, slow, loud, soft, tinkly, booming, jumpy, smooth*), types of movement (e.g., *high, low, straight, zigzag, bouncy, gliding*), and the emotions and actions in pretend play (e.g., *mysterious, exciting, character, role, dialogue, comedy, drama*). Share your lists with a colleague and ask for additional ideas. Select one or two words to use each time you talk to children about the creative arts.

4. What types of art, music, dance, and drama (movies, television, theater) do you enjoy? Why? How did your experiences growing up influence your aesthetic preferences as an adult? How can you introduce children to a variety of creative media and artistic styles?

5. Visit an art museum with someone you trust. Tell each other what you see and how you feel about the artwork, including how it looks (its color, shape, size), how it was made (the medium and technique used), the subject matter (whether it is realistic or abstract, what the artist is trying to say), and the emotions it evokes in you (curiosity, delight, confusion, joy, sorrow). Take time to find the words to express your own thoughts and feelings. Listen to what your companion says. What ideas does this give you for fostering art appreciation with young children?

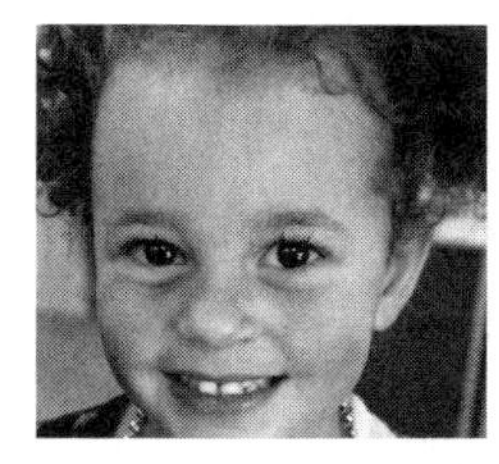

Chapter 16

What Is the HighScope Curriculum in Science and Technology?

Think About It

"I wonder what would happen if...?" "They're the same but also different." "Let's try it both ways and see which works better." These familiar statements show how much we use the principles and methods of science in our daily lives. For example, we sort clothes by color and fabric before laundering them. Likewise, biologists observe and sort plants and animals according to a classification system. Cooking involves chemistry — solid and liquid ingredients are transformed by mixing, beating, heating, or chilling. When we play sports, we use our knowledge of the natural world (how bodies move) and the physical world (what happens when objects collide) to help us score. Carpentry and knitting involve figuring out the tools and materials needed to carry out a specific project. Laboratory research involves similar scientific processes — making a prediction (hypothesis), designing an experiment to test it, observing the result, and drawing a conclusion.

We act as scientists when we gather information and form hypotheses about objects, people, and events. We make predictions by analyzing the past and reach conclusions to predict the future. Science is rooted in curiosity, a trait young children possess in abundance. They pose questions about how the world works, make observations, and use the information they collect to answer their questions. Children are thus natural scientists, although their knowledge and skills will become more sophisticated over time. In this chapter we will discuss how the HighScope Curriculum encourages this process of investigation and discovery in young scientists.

Why Science and Technology Is Important

Young children are immersed in science "by which we mean the process of developing explanations about how the world works — and are developing useful and quite powerful scientific theories" (Landry & Forman, 1999, p. 133). For preschoolers, science is not about memorizing facts, but is rather about the process of observing, predicting, experimenting, verifying, and explaining. Science draws on young children's *perceptual abilities*, develops their *critical-thinking skills*, and promotes *language development* as they communicate their ideas. Scientific inquiry also involves *social collaboration*. In fact, resolving the conflicting explanations of peers can motivate young children to change their theories more than comments or questions from adults (Tudge & Caruso, 1988; Vygotsky, 1978).

How Scientific Thinking Develops

Science and technology learning occurs all the time in early childhood settings as preschoolers use their senses to observe, sort things into cat-

Chapter Learning Objectives

By the end of this chapter, you will be able to

- Explain why early learning in science and technology is important.
- Describe the HighScope key developmental indicators (KDIs) in the Science and Technology content area.
- Begin to apply the strategies adults use to scaffold (support and gently extend) early learning in science and technology.

egories, attempt to answer their own and others' questions, try to make sense of the world around them, discover contradictions in their thinking, and employ tools and technology to carry out their intentions (Neill, 2008).

"Doing science" involves three interrelated strands of development (Gelman & Brenneman, 2004). The first is recognizing that something that was expected to happen did not occur. Very young children may simply accept what they see. However, as they accumulate knowledge, children set up expectations, become aware of discrepancies, and ask themselves, "What's wrong here?" This leads to the second strand of development. Recognizing they need to adjust their thinking, preschoolers next ask, "What is happening here?" Based on their observations, they construct an alternate theory. It may not be accurate, but they will be satisfied if it "fits" their experience.

In the final step of development, young children ask, "Where's the proof?" On their own, preschoolers are not likely to test their theories, but with adult support, they can be more systematic and refine their ideas. The adult's role is *not* to give the answer but to provide materials and support "so children can test and find out on their own whether their ideas are correct or not" (DeVries & Sales, 2011, p. 2).

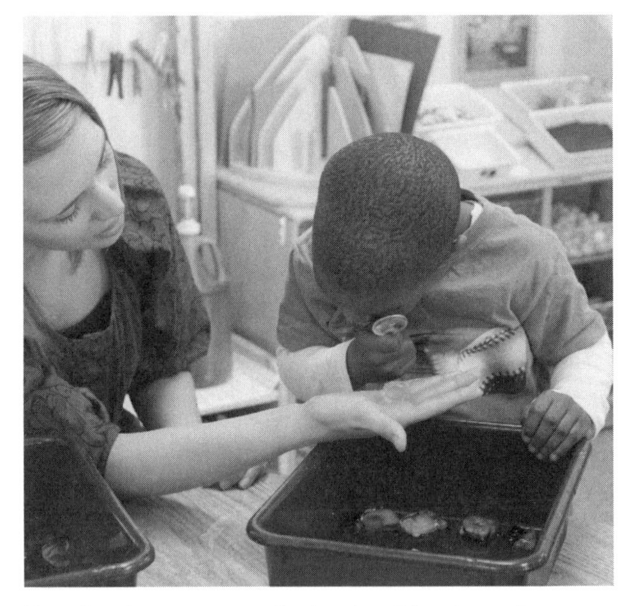

Preschoolers are natural scientists. They investigate materials and actions, pose questions, make observations, and construct ideas about how the world works.

General Teaching Strategies for Science and Technology

▲ Introduce children to the steps in the scientific method

Young children use the same processes as adult scientists, but HighScope refers to this as the "**preschool scientific method** [because] preschoolers engage in their investigations in a much more random and spontaneous fashion" (Neill, 2008, p. 2).[1] To help children become familiar with this process, use the words of science to label each step. Rochel Gelman and Kimberly Brenneman (2004) suggest that teachers introduce preschoolers to "the vocabulary and methods of *observe*, *predict*, and *check*" (p. 153). They give an example in which children explored an apple and the teacher wrote down what they said (it's red, round, smooth, and cold) "because [explained the teacher] scientists record their observations." Next,

[1]The six components of the preschool scientific method comprise the first six science KDIs, described later in this chapter.

Terms Used in This Chapter

• preschool scientific method • cognitive discrepancy • *no* and *not* language • trial and error • assimilation • accommodation • if/then language

the children made a prediction, which the teacher described to them as "something like a guess" about what was inside (it's white, it has seeds). Finally, after cutting open their apples, the children checked their predictions against what they found (it is white and it has seeds; it's also wet).

▲ Encourage reflection

Children's curiosity is often satisfied by taking action and observing what happens. However, science also means asking *how* or *why* to explain the results. Science educators Karen Worth and Sharon Grollman (2003) say it is up to teachers to establish these inquiring habits of mind:

> "Direct experience with materials is critical but it is not enough. Children also need to reflect on their work. They need to analyze their experiences, think about ideas such as patterns and relationships, try out new theories, and communicate with others. These processes allow children to think in new ways about what they did, how they did it, and what is significant to them." (p. 5)

Working and recalling with children creates openings for you to encourage their reflections with comments such as "Show (tell) me how you did that," "How could we make it happen again?" "I wonder why that happened," or "What do you suppose would happen if…?"

▲ Create opportunities for surprise and discrepancy

Young children's scientific ideas develop when they encounter **cognitive discrepancy,** that is, when they observe something they did not expect. Create natural (not contrived) opportunities for children to have these types of experiences. Simply providing many types of materials and tools for children to explore guarantees they will encounter surprises by chance. You can also intentionally provide new materials that behave differently from familiar ones, for example, by introducing irregularly shaped blocks so children can explore how they fit and balance in ways that differ from rectangular blocks. Try using clay outdoors where it dries faster than indoors, or cover ramps with smooth and rough materials so children can see how the texture affects the speed of racing cars.

▲ Encourage documentation

Preschoolers focus on what they see and hear in the moment and may forget what they observed earlier. Fortunately, three- and four-year olds are able to create and interpret representations of their experiences. This allows them, with adult assistance, to record data by drawing pictures or making and interpreting simple charts and graphs (Katz & Chard, 1996). Teachers can also take photos or make videos of objects and children's actions upon them. This documentation acts as a visual reminder as children construct their scientific explanations.

▲ Encourage collaborative investigation and problem solving

Social interaction doesn't just help children construct ideas; it also deepens their understanding. As

Create a natural opportunity for children to observe something they did not expect, for example, by adding shaving cream to the sand and water table.

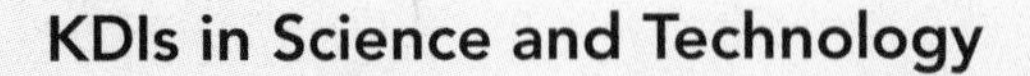

KDIs in Science and Technology

45. **Observing:** Children observe the materials and processes in their environment.
46. **Classifying:** Children classify materials, actions, people, and events.
47. **Experimenting:** Children experiment to test their ideas.
48. **Predicting:** Children predict what they expect will happen.
49. **Drawing conclusions:** Children draw conclusions based on their experiences and observations.
50. **Communicating ideas:** Children communicate their ideas about the characteristics of things and how they work.
51. **Natural and physical world:** Children gather knowledge about the natural and physical world.
52. **Tools and technology:** Children explore and use tools and technology.

they attempt to tell others what they see and think, children pay attention to more details and try to articulate the reasons behind their observations. Children learn from one another and, as noted previously, are more likely to change their thinking when challenged by a peer rather than an adult:

> *At small-group time, the children plant tomato seedlings in their vegetable garden. Fiona and Gabriella disagree over how much water to use. Fiona fills half a pail, but Gabriella, who has planted a garden at home with her mother, says it's too much. When Fiona pours the water on a tomato plant, she sees it lean to the side, while the one Gabriella put less water on is still standing upright. Fiona does not say anything, but for the next seedling she uses less water.*

Key Developmental Indicators in Science and Technology

HighScope has eight key developmental indicators (KDIs) in Science and Technology: 45. Observing, 46. Classifying, 47. Experimenting, 48. Predicting, 49. Drawing conclusions, 50. Communicating ideas, 51. Natural and physical world, and 52. Tools and technology. See "KDIs in Science and Technology" on this page.

The rest of this chapter discusses early learning in each KDI and how you can promote its development in young children. For activities supporting Science and Technology, see the resources on the HighScope website (www.highscope.org).

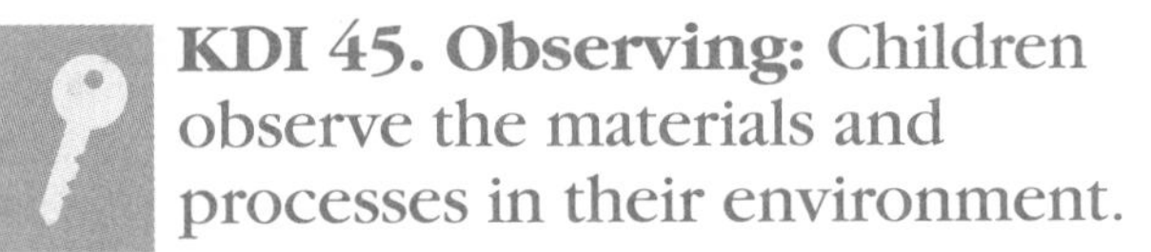

KDI 45. Observing: Children observe the materials and processes in their environment.

Description: Children are curious and use all their senses to learn more about the natural and physical world. They gather information by observing what others do and discovering how tools and materials work.

How Observing Develops

Unlike casual looking, "observing is paying close attention to something to learn more about it" (Neill, 2008, p. 10). Being a careful and accurate observer is the single most important ability in becoming a good scientist. This ability develops gradually. For example, preschoolers are able to observe an increasing number of details. Younger children focus on one or two things (e.g., the color of a block, whether a car goes fast down the ramp). Older ones make multiple differentiations (e.g., light, medium, and dark colors; slow, faster, even faster, and fastest speeds).

Children also develop a growing ability to describe their sensory impressions and the properties of objects and actions. Their observations become increasingly verbal (Gronlund, 2006). As children's vocabularies grow, they attach simple words to describe what they see, hear, feel, taste, and smell. Later still, excited by their expanding awareness, children are eager to describe in more complex language what they observe and the discoveries they make about the world.

Teaching Strategies That Support Observing

▲ Provide a sensory-rich environment

Incorporate different sensory properties in your indoor and outdoor learning environment. For example, provide things that create light and shadow (e.g., flashlights, cellophane taped to windows, flying banners, wind spinners, sheets hung up or draped over tables and chairs); distinctive textures (e.g., bark, straw, gourds, cotton, leather); aromatic materials (e.g., spice jars, beeswax, open windows that let in the smells of plants and rain, herb garden); things that make noise (e.g., musical instruments, ticking clocks and timers, workbench tools, pebbles and beads to pour into and out of containers, running water, bird feeders that attract song birds outdoors); and snack foods with a variety of tastes, smells, and textures.

▲ Establish a safe environment for children to observe with all their senses

Equally important to providing diverse sensory materials is creating a climate in which children are free to explore, take risks, make a mess, and try things that may not work. At the same time, children must also have the right to refuse to taste, smell, touch, or otherwise experience the materials provided. In other words, children should be granted autonomy and guaranteed safety.

▲ Provide the vocabulary to help children label, understand, and use their observations

In addition to labeling objects (nouns) and actions (verbs), add descriptive words (adjectives and adverbs) to enhance children's observational skills. Provide, and encourage children to provide, verbal explanations of what they sense (e.g., "How does it feel?" "What does that sound remind you of?"), what they do (e.g., "How did you get it to stick?" "What should I do to make mine look the same as yours?"), and the outcomes they observe (e.g., "I wonder why it got bigger?" "Why do you think it smells more when you crush it?"). Match your language to children's developmental levels. Label clearly observable cues (e.g., color, loudness) and gradually introduce less obvious properties (e.g., dampness, temperature). After focusing on how things look (sound, feel, taste, or smell), talk about how things change; for example, you might comment, "When the sun came out, it melted the snow."

Bring some of the outdoors inside (in this case, dirt) to help children explore different textures and smells.

KDI 46. Classifying: Children classify materials, actions, people, and events.

Description: Children group similar things together. They identify relationships between things and the categories they belong to. Children look for new ways to organize the knowledge they already have and for ways to fit new discoveries into familiar categories.

How Classifying Develops

Children classify — they sort objects, people, or actions — spontaneously when they play (Langer, Rivera, Schlesinger, & Wakeley, 2003). At first they group things that share one attribute (e.g., all the red beads), although they may not be able to state the reason and are not always consistent. At the next level, children sort consistently and use the words *same* and *different,* followed by *some, none,* and *all.* Next children sort things based on more than one attribute (such as color and size). The highest level of sorting is when children can recognize and describe the reason behind the sorting even when someone else has done it. Children at this level can also describe whether and what type of object can, and cannot, be added to each group.

Teaching Strategies That Support Classifying

▲ Encourage children to collect and sort things

There are many opportunities throughout the day and in the learning environment for children to indulge their passion for collecting and classifying. Inside the classroom, labeled areas with an abundance of organized and diverse materials help children think in terms of categories. Nature also provides many materials for sorting — small and large stones, things that fly or crawl, trees with leaves or needles.

Neighborhood walks and field trips provide added opportunities to make interesting collections. Give each child a container to gather items. Once back in the classroom (at small-group time), encourage children to sort and label their collections. Then make the items available at work time in whatever area(s) are appropriate. For example, acorns can go in the house area for pretend cooking or the art area for gluing on paper, or they can be hidden in the sand table.

▲ Call attention to *same* and *different*

As you create a daily plan, think of opportunities to introduce the idea of *same* and *different*. For example, after reading a favorite book, provide art materials for children to draw characters that are the same or different from those in the story. At work and small-group times, provide games such as Concentration and bingo to help children match shapes, numbers, and letters. During cleanup time, play I spy (e.g., "I spy something in the toy area that's the same shape as this [hold up a circle] and needs to be put away"). During large-group time, go on a treasure hunt to find things that are the same and different; begin with one attribute (e.g., rectangular) and then increase it to two or three properties (e.g., rectangular and blue). With movement activities during large-group time, challenge children to imitate the same movement as another child and to suggest a different one when they are the leader. You can also use same and different as the basis for transitions (e.g., "Everyone with gloves go outside…now everyone with mittens…"). Finally, at snacktime, serve a variety of foods for children to compare. Talk about the similarities and differences in the foods that children in diverse families and cultures enjoy eating.

▲ Use *no* and *not* language

To develop the concept of ***no*** and ***not***, children need to hear those words many times. Take advantage of opportunities to highlight this idea throughout the day. For example, when children dress to go outside, note whose jacket has a hood and whose does not. At snacktime, comment on who does and does not want juice. When children make collections, encourage them to identify the attributes that items in a group do not have (e.g., "These beads are shiny; those are not shiny"). At large-group time, challenge children to move in a way that does not involve their feet. Transition using the no/not concept (e.g., "If your name does *not* begin with the letter B, go to the rug").

Introduce the universal no symbol (a red circle with a diagonal line superimposed on an image of an object or action). An example is the work-in-progress sign children put on a project

Classification involves knowing what something is and what it is not. HighScope encourages children to use the concepts of no and not, such as this sign that means "Do not touch."

they want to continue working on the next day. The image of a hand with a line through it signifies "Do not touch" and sets the object apart from that category of items that it is okay to handle.

KDI 47. Experimenting: Children experiment to test their ideas.

Description: Children experiment to test whether an idea is true or a solution will work. They may encounter problems with materials that they do not have answers for. They experiment by manipulating materials, using trial and error, and then approaching the problem with possible solutions in mind.

How Experimenting Develops

Young children experiment for two reasons — out of curiosity and to solve problems they encounter in play:

On the field trip to the children's museum, in the boys' rest room, James alternately moves his hands under and away from the automatic dryer to make it turn on and off.

◆

At small-group time, Erin grinds apples in a food mill for applesauce. She looks underneath and sees that nothing is coming out. "You have to grind it harder," says Mike, demonstrating with his grinder. "I think it's stuck in the holes," says Erin. Sandra calls from across the table, "You got to scoop out the peel." Erin tries this and the ground apples flow freely again.

In the process of experimenting, children observe cause-and-effect relationships. At first this happens accidentally. For example, babies waving their arms hit a mobile and the shapes jiggle; they repeat the action without understanding the connection. By contrast, preschoolers are increasingly aware that a specific action produces a predictable outcome, and they strive to bring about a desired result. Their efforts are still largely **trial and error** at this stage, but with adult scaffolding, children's experiments can become more systematic.

Preschoolers are also increasingly aware of the role of time (Van Scoy & Fairchild, 1993). They pay attention to sequence; the cause comes first followed by the effect. Children also observe duration, whether an effect lasts or fades. Finally, they notice the pace of events (e.g., puddles fill quickly in a heavy rainstorm; snow melts slowly in the sun). Older preschoolers may notice delayed effects (e.g., water dripped on paper spreads to the edges after a few minutes). When children become aware of these factors — cause and effect, sequence, and timing — their experiments become more sophisticated and they conduct them to answer more complex questions.

Teaching Strategies That Support Experimenting

▲ Ask and answer "What if...?" "Why?" and "How?" questions

Children develop higher-order thinking skills when you follow up their investigations with open-ended how and why questions (e.g., "How did you get the top to spin?" "Why do you think it kept falling?"). In addition to asking questions, make comments that prompt children to question you and themselves. By welcoming their inquiries, you support and stimulate children's natural curiosity (Gronlund, 2006). If you express interest and surprise (e.g., you might say, "Wow! It bubbled over the top when we added vinegar to the baking soda!"), the children will be inspired to ask why or how something happened on their own. You can then ask follow-up questions to help them experiment, test out their ideas, and try to answer their own questions.

▲ Encourage children to gradually replace trial-and-error exploration with systematic experimentation

To scaffold (support and gently extend) learning through experimentation, talk with children about what they are doing and the results of their actions. Use small-group times to carry out simple hands-on experiments with easily observed results (e.g., mix different amounts of flour and water and compare the consistency; paint with water outdoors and watch the pavement dry). Introduce novel materials and tools, and encourage children to consider alternative ways of using familiar materials. Ask what is different about what they did this time and the effect(s) their actions produced. Offer challenges involving step-by-step or systematic changes. For example, you might ask a child who is racing her cars down a ramp, "Could you make it go just a little bit faster? How about a medium amount faster? What if you wanted it to go really fast?"

▲ Provide materials and experiences for investigating how things change with time

Many aspects of the natural and physical world change with time — kittens grow bigger, leaves turn brown, sand compacts as it is walked on day after day. Draw children's attention to the role that time plays in these transformations. Encourage them to notice how long it takes for things to happen, and ask open-ended questions that prompt them to test their theories about time (e.g., "Yesterday we played the cleanup music two times before we were done. How many times do you think we will have to play it today?"). Since time is abstract to preschoolers, make it concrete with materials such as tools to signal stopping and starting (timers, stop signs, instruments) and things children can set in motion (wheeled toys, metronomes, balls, tops, pinwheels).

KDI 48. Predicting: Children predict what they expect will happen.

Description: Children indicate through words and/or actions what they expect an outcome to be. They think about what happened in similar situations and anticipate what might happen. Children make predictions based on experimentation.

How Predicting Develops

A prediction is more than a guess or a wish. Predicting uses prior knowledge to anticipate what is likely to happen in the future. Because of their growing cognitive capacities, preschoolers can "begin engaging in a hallmark of the scientific process — posing *hypotheses,* or explanations for sets of facts that can be verified through further exploration" (Neill, 2008, p. 15). Predicting helps preschoolers think in ways they might not do otherwise. Instead of focusing on the here and now (what is occurring in the present), they think about the there and then (using what occurred another place and time to imagine what has not yet happened). The more opportunities children have to engage in this type of thinking, the better they get at reflecting on their experiences and observations to make predictions (Church, 2003).

Teaching Strategies That Support Predicting

▲ Help children reflect on the similarities between their past and present experiences

Encourage children to recall what they observed and whether the same thing might happen with similar objects or actions. You might say, for example, to a child, "Think about how you got the wood to stick to the paper. I wonder if that might also work to attach the wood to the cloth." Use children's interest in classification to help them determine whether objects in the same category might behave the same way (e.g., materials that are sticky can both be used to attach things), while those in separate categories might act differently (e.g., "You squished the soft clay to fit inside the hole. What about this hard block?").

▲ Encourage children to say what they think will happen

Encouraging children to state their predictions creates an opportunity for them to think about and apply their experiences. For example, when his teacher asked Rajiv why he predicted, "There's going to be lots of leaves at outside time," Rajiv pointed out the window and replied, "It's really windy and the wind makes them fall down. When I help my auntie rake leaves, she lets me jump in them." Asking children to voice their predictions gives adults insights into their reasoning and helps us avoid making incorrect assumptions about their ideas and intentions.

▲ Encourage children to verify their predictions

Having voiced their belief, children generally accept its truth. Adult encouragement, however, can make them curious about whether their expectations are accurate. To help children test their scientific predictions, make comments and ask questions such as "Let's check it out" and "How can we be sure?" Discuss which observations did (or did not) match their predictions and why they think this is so. You don't have to know the answer yourself (so don't worry if you're not a "scientist"); satisfy your own curiosity along with the children.

KDI 49. Drawing conclusions: Children draw conclusions based on their experiences and observations.

Description: Children attempt to fit their observations and reasoning into their existing knowledge and understanding. They construct knowledge in their own way as they collect data to help them form theories about how the world works (e.g., "It's night because the sun goes to bed").

How Drawing Conclusions Develops

Preschoolers use the scientific processes discussed previously to draw conclusions. Piaget (1950) used the term **assimilation** to describe when children take in new information that matches their current thinking. He used the term **accommodation** to describe when children alter their understanding to take account of contradictory information.

Young children draw conclusions by generalizing their observations to similar objects and events (Gelman, 1999). Initially, their conclusions are based on concrete perceptions and immediate experiences (Bruner, Olver, & Greenfield, 1966). They then begin to think more broadly, although their generalizations may be in error; for example, they may think that if one bird lays blue eggs, then all birds lay blue eggs. An erroneous theory may actually influence what young children observe and conclude; for example, if they think gooey things smell bad, they'll declare honey smells yucky rather than sweet. It may take many instances of contradictory information before they adjust their thinking. Being in a safe environment where they feel free to change their mind helps them to think more flexibly.

Teaching Strategies That Support Drawing Conclusions

▲ Provide materials and experiences that work in similar but not identical ways

Provide opportunities for preschoolers to encounter things that are sometimes, but not always, the same (e.g., play dough changes properties depending on the amount of water in it; only some bushes have berries on them). To help preschoolers draw conclusions from several sources of evidence, make comments and ask open-ended questions that encourage them to explore alternatives: What else could you do (or look at) to find out? What about that other one? Do you think it will do the same thing or something different? How are they the same? How are they different?

▲ Encourage children to reflect on the processes and outcomes they observe

Drawing conclusions is a thoughtful process. To promote children's reflection, make comments, for example, you might say, "I notice that the water isn't going down the drain," and ask open-ended questions, such as "Why does a heavy block on top make the tower fall down?" Call attention to things that contradict children's expectations: "You thought the bigger one would weigh more, but it weighed less than the little one. Hmm...." You need not know the answers to encourage children to consider the questions. Act puzzled, surprised, and delighted as you and the children make discoveries together — a sense of wonder and curiosity is contagious!

KDI 50. Communicating ideas: Children communicate their ideas about the characteristics of things and how they work.

Description: Children share their questions, observations, investigations, predictions, and conclusions. They talk about, demonstrate, and represent what they experience and think. They express their interest in and wonder about the world.

"Where will you add the second wing to your airplane," this teacher asks, "so it won't tip over?"

How Communicating Ideas Develops

Young children are eager to share their scientific discoveries. The very act of talking can make children more observant and attend to more details. Conversation encourages them to use **if/then language** and think in terms of cause-and-effect relationships. Symbolic communication (drawing, writing, demonstrating, and role playing) helps children document their observations and recognize patterns (Chalufour & Worth, 2003). By looking at and listening to how children communicate, adults gain insight into their thinking. For example, a child may twist the play oven dial to the right to demonstrate the knowledge that the cookies need high heat to bake. Likewise, a child may ask the teacher how to spell *stick* while making a simple chart comparing materials that are and are not attracted to a magnet.

Teaching Strategies That Support Communicating Ideas

▲ Use scientific language as you talk with children about their actions, observations, and discoveries

"Science, for children as well as adults, is not done in a vacuum but in a social realm within which ideas are discussed, debated, and take shape" (Landry & Forman, 1999, p. 137). To help children talk about their explorations in science, listen closely to what children say and share your own observations and discoveries to introduce new words (e.g., use the word *frost* as you describe scraping the ice off your windshield before school). Building a vocabulary to talk about science takes time so use the same words repeatedly. Children will eventually understand and use these terms themselves.

At least as important as what you say are the words children use to ask their own questions, raise doubts, and voice surprise when their observations do not match their expectations. Demonstrate your interest with gentle questions that ponder what, where, when, how, and why. Be patient so children have time to frame their answers and to think about your comments and questions.

▲ Provide opportunities for children to symbolically represent their scientific experiences

Support the many ways children document and represent their scientific ideas, including:

Artwork. Provide drawing and modeling materials so children can represent their understanding of such things as how houses are built, how animals look and act, and what makes things go fast:

> *At work time in the toy area, Josie puts shells and marbles on the balance scale. She gets paper and markers and tells her teacher, "I'm going to draw a picture with two shells here (she points to one side), a line down the middle, and six marbles here (she points to the other side)." Her teacher comments, "You are going to draw a picture of how you got the shells and marbles to balance on the scale."*

Pretend play. Provide prop-making materials and play as a partner in children's scenarios. For example, while pretending to bake a cake in the house area, a teacher asks a child for something to stir with. Handing her an electric mixer (with the cord removed), the child says, "You can't really plug it in. You have to pretend it works." To extend the child's idea, the teacher replies, "You need a cord so electricity can run the motor that turns the beaters."

Writing. Provide writing tools such as clipboards and markers to encourage children to record their ideas. Reading books about science will also inspire children to communicate their ideas by "writing" communications of their own.

Lists, charts, and graphs. Making a simple chart lets children reflect on the steps in the scientific method as they decide what categories to create (e.g., "How should we label the columns?"); what symbols to use (e.g., "Should we make hash marks or write numerals?"); and most significantly, how to interpret the results (e.g., "I wonder why there are more in this column than the other column").

KDI 51. Natural and physical world: Children gather knowledge about the natural and physical world.

Description: Children become familiar with characteristics and processes in the natural and physical world (e.g., characteristics of plants and animals, ramps and rocks; processes of growth and death, freezing and melting). They explore change, transformation, and cause and effect. They become aware of cycles that are meaningful to them.

How Knowledge About the Natural and Physical World Develops

Children's ideas about how the world works seem naive, but they are often quite sophisticated when viewed within their system of logic (e.g., "Sun makes things warm. If the sun's out, it must be warm, even in the winter"). Children hold onto their theories because they make sense to them and help them organize their observations (Landry & Forman, 1999). Only after repeated experiences do they begin to adjust their thinking. Children, therefore, don't learn about the natural and physical world by memorizing a series of facts. Nevertheless, there are certain areas of knowledge that preschoolers are ready to get acquainted with. This information builds on their interests and observations of nature (their own bodies, plants and animals, weather patterns) and the physical world (how machines operate, why objects of the same size have different weights, why things change color or make bubbles when mixed together). Adults can support children's learning about the natural and physical world by *listening* to the questions children ask to find out what interests them.

Teaching Strategies That Support Learning About the Natural and Physical World

▲ Provide materials and experiences for children to gather knowledge about the natural and physical world

Assemble collections of living and nonliving things that children can compare (plants, animals, shells, seeds, salt and fresh water, soil, rocks, hardware fasteners). Supplement real objects with printed materials and realistic replicas. Encourage children to sort these collections, using all their senses, to discover similarities and differences in their properties. Observe how the materials change over time or as a result of their actions (e.g., a wet towel is heavier than a dry towel; colored leaves turn brown and crumble if you squeeze them; flowers decay and lose their smell).

Use objects and experiences, including field trips, to build an awareness of animal and plant needs (air, food, water, light, rest); natural and urban environments (bodies of water, forests, beaches, hills, farm land, meadows, deserts, snow-covered mountains, towns and cities, parks); and cycles such as birth, growth, and decay and changing seasons and weather patterns. Weather in the abstract holds little meaning for preschoolers, but they do care about how short-term changes affect them (e.g., whether they can play outside, what clothes they should wear).

▲ Encourage children to make connections to explain how the world looks and functions

Build on the objects and events children gravitate toward indoors and outdoors. Ask how and why questions, for example: "Why are some stones smooth while others are rough?" "I wonder how birds fly?" "Why does pumping your legs make you go higher on the swing?" You do not have to know the answers to these questions yourself.

Generate theories and seek answers together with the children, and refer them to one another for ideas as they are more inclined to construct their own theories after hearing what their peers think (Campbell, 1999):

> *At greeting time, Ian says his family is making an ice rink in their backyard. "We're going to shovel snow, put water on it, and wait one minute for it to turn to ice," Ian explains. His teacher comments to the group, "I wonder how snow turns into ice." The children offer various theories: "When the water dries, the snow gets hard"; "The water makes the snow cold"; "It takes more than a minute. You have to wait all night"; and "When the water freezes, it gets slippery."*

KDI 52. Tools and technology: Children explore and use tools and technology.

Description: Children become familiar with tools and technology in their everyday environment (e.g., stapler, pliers, computer). They understand the functions of equipment and use it with safety and care. They use tools and technology to support their play.

How Use of Tools and Technology Develops

Young children use tools and technology in two ways. They are interesting *ends in themselves* (mastering the use of a stapler or pushing the buttons on a recording device). Tools and technology can also be a *means to an end* (stapling two pieces of ribbon together to make a longer leash or listening to a favorite song on a music player). Children initially explore tools as materials in their own right, but as they become more competent with them, they think about how a tool can help them accomplish a goal or solve a problem. Problem solving with tools builds young children's conceptual awareness because it involves "planning, sequential thinking, and predicting what specific actions with a tool might do" (Haugen, 2010, p. 50).

Technology can play a useful role in early science learning (as well as literacy and mathematics) when used appropriately (National Association for the Education of Young Children & Fred Rogers Center for Early Learning and Children's Media, 2012); it should supplement rather than replace hands-on learning with real materials (Hyson, 2003). Young children benefit from becoming familiar with the mechanics of hardware (turning a machine on or off, using touchscreens and touchpads) and using programs and applications that are interactive, open ended, and promote discovery learning rather than emphasizing drill and practice (Clements, 2002). Computers can also serve as social catalysts. Preschoolers can work together at the computer to solve problems, talk about what they are doing, help and teach friends, and create rules for turn-taking and cooperation (Clements, 1999). [*Note:* There is no evidence, however, that individually used devices promote social interaction, and there are concerns that they may isolate young users (Rosen & Jaruszewicz, 2009). As new technologies are developed, therefore, their cognitive and social appropriateness for young children must be evaluated on an ongoing basis.]

Teaching Strategies That Support Exploring and Using Tools and Technology

▲ Provide a variety of tools in all areas of the classroom

Don't be restricted to typical "science" tools (e.g., magnifiers, binoculars, magnets, balance scales gears, plastic thermometers). Many other items lend themselves to experimentation and discovery, for example, paint jar pumps, kitchen utensils, carpentry tools, rubber bands, mesh strainers, ropes, and gardening tools. Bring tools and gadgets from home, and encourage families to contribute old and unused items, such as wind-up clocks and cell phones (with batteries removed). Visit garage sales and flea markets to add to your classroom's collection. Encourage children to think about what the tools and gadgets are and how they can be used.

▲ Help children consider how and why to use tools in various ways

In addition to supporting children's spontaneous discoveries about tools during work and outside time, plan activities with tools at other times of the day. For example, children might hammer into different surfaces at small-group time, make sounds with tools at large-group time, bring a tool they used at work time to recall time, use tools to prepare and serve snacks, or take a field trip to the hardware store. Look for opportunities to explore tools as children engage with other content areas, for example, modeling tools for clay (Creative Arts), books about scientists and inventions (Language, Literacy, and Communication), conventional and unconventional tools to measure (Mathematics), or timers to resolve social conflicts (Social and Emotional Development).

▲ Choose and mediate children's use of appropriate technology

Computers and other electronic equipment should take a back seat to hands-on learning with manipulatives and direct social interaction. However, because children's exposure to technology outside the program varies widely, making it available in the classroom can provide an important experience for those whose family income or other factors limit their access (Lee & Burkham, 2002). To support the balanced and appropriate use of technology:

Model safe and careful use of technology. Help children learn to use technology in ways that will neither hurt them nor damage equipment, just as they do with other classroom materials.

Choose child-friendly hardware. Innovations make technology easier for young children to use; choose devices that are appropriate for young children's perceptual and physical capabilities. Encourage children who already know how to use the equipment to help their peers.

Select appropriate programs or applications. Emphasize interactive and open-ended learning, not drill and practice. Introduce each program or application to a few children at a time, for example, as a small-group activity, before making it available at work time.

Locate classroom technology so that it facilitates social exchanges. Allow space for children, as well as adults, to use devices together. Classroom technology should be visible from other areas of the classroom so children can wander over and join in.

Encourage children to verbalize their thinking as they solve technology problems. Help children reflect on their solutions (e.g., How do I turn up the sound? How should I turn the puzzle piece to fit?). Be available so they do not get frustrated or discouraged when something is not working.

Computers can serve as social catalysts.

Try These Ideas Yourself

1. List what you consider to be the five most important things preschoolers need to know or be able to do in the Science and Technology content area when they enter kindergarten. Why are they important? How can teachers support their development?

2. Write down typical things you do in a week that involve scientific reasoning (e.g., looking at the sky to anticipate the weather, packing groceries to protect fragile items, rehanging a shelf so it doesn't fall down again). How do children use simple scientific thinking in their daily lives?

3. In the following scenario, identify the Science and Technology KDIs. What types of learning are occurring in other areas of development?

If adding computers to your learning environment, locate the technology so that there is ample space for children (and adults) to use it together.

How could you as a teacher support and extend the learning? (The Science and Technology KDIs are listed on p. 178.)

> *At outside time, Heidi makes a campfire with sticks that she sorts into short, medium, and long lengths and says, "You have to start with the littlest ones so they catch fire. That's how my daddy does it." She invites George, Ben, and Fae (a teacher) to sit by the fire. Heidi pretends to make s'mores by putting one small twig between two big, flat stones. She makes four, one for each person (including herself) at the campfire. Then she fills a bucket and puts water on the fire, explaining that "water makes the fire go down."*

4. Here are some typical why and how questions children might ask:

- Why does water make bubbles when you blow through a straw?
- How do you make icicles?
- Why does the screen light up when you push this button but not that one?
- Why don't the wheels on the toy car turn in the mud?
- How come we're not the same size if we're the same age?

Choose one of these questions, or another one you've heard a young child ask, and decide how you would help children be "scientists" and answer their own questions.

Chapter 17

What Is the HighScope Curriculum in Social Studies?

Think About It

A preschool child went to his older brother's wrestling matches and got several classmates interested in playing "wrestling" at work time. They used an area rug as their mat, pushed up their sleeves, and got down to wrestle. The game went on for several days, becoming more elaborate. The children gave themselves wrestlers' names and developed a scoring system.

In the second week, however, a few children complained that the play was too rough. The teachers also worried about them getting hurt but did not want to stop a game that many clearly enjoyed and that promoted learning in many ways, including gross-motor skills, cooperative play, conflict resolution, counting, spatial awareness, pretend play, and predicting. So one day, when the wrestlers were setting up their game, a teacher voiced her concern. She said, "We need to make some class decisions so children will not get hurt." She wrote down the children's ideas and posted them on the wall above the mat. Here is what they came up with:

1. Take off your shoes (but not your socks).
2. No hitting.
3. No punching. (The children debated whether punching was the same as hitting, but decided it deserved its own rule.)
4. No pinching.
5. You can't call someone a bad name.
6. No spitting.
7. No head butts.
8. ~~Only boys can play~~. (Several girls protested this rule and it was dropped.)
9. At least three people have to play so one can be the referee and make sure the fight is fair.
10. The referee has to be able to count to 10. (After a count of 10, the match is declared over.)
11. You can't wrestle if you don't have a wrestler name.
12. You can't have the same wrestler name as someone else.
13. Everyone who wants to wrestle gets a turn. The referee decides who goes next.
14. People who want to watch have to stand behind the line. (After some debate, they decided the edge of the block shelf would mark the "watching line.")

The children referred to their ideas in subsequent weeks as their interest in wrestling continued. If one child did not comply, the others were quick to point out the infraction.

The above anecdote shows young children participating in a democracy. While preschoolers are often self-centered, when teachers brought potential problems to their attention, the children demonstrated genuine sensitivity to the safety and feelings of others. Their creative solutions balanced their personal enthusiasm for the wrestling game with a keen desire to preserve the sense of community in their classroom.

Chapter Learning Objectives

By the end of this chapter, you will be able to

- Explain why early learning in social studies is important.
- Describe the HighScope key developmental indicators (KDIs) in the Social Studies content area.
- Begin to apply the strategies adults use to scaffold (support and gently extend) early learning in social studies.

HighScope views the classroom as a community in which children form their identities both as individuals and members of a group. While the members may differ in significant ways, they still find commonalities that let them bond with and respect one another. Everyone has a voice. In short, classrooms operate on the same principles on which a democracy is founded. Experiencing and learning these basic principles defines the content of social studies at this age.

Why Social Studies Is Important

"The aim of social studies is the promotion of **civic competence** [boldface added] — the knowledge, intellectual processes, and democratic dispositions required of students to be active and engaged participants in public life" (National Council for the Social Studies, 2010, p. 1). This statement by the National Council for the Social Studies underlies the kinds of learning occurring daily in the preschool classroom, where we strive to help children develop basic ideas about community, justice, and democracy. The importance we, as a society, attach to these subjects explains why social studies is now a distinct content area in the early childhood curriculum standards of most states (Gronlund, 2006). The challenge for educators is translating these lofty ideals into concrete experiences that make sense to practical-minded preschoolers.

For preschoolers, social studies means developing a sense of community. The classroom is a community in which children share common experiences, routines, interests, and conversations.

Young Children's Interest in Social Studies

Children study their social world from the moment of birth and are quite sophisticated about observing and interpreting group behavior by the time they enter preschool. Their knowledge of social studies builds on their interactions with diverse people (teachers and peers with different interests and skills and from varied backgrounds), wide-ranging materials (pretend-play props, books), and daily and special activities (field trips, celebrations, group decision making, responsibility for the classroom play space). "In the preschool and primary years, social studies offer a structure for content [with] multiple entry points and significant opportunities for investigation. For children, such content serves as a training ground for acquiring problem-solving skills as well as a laboratory for the development and elaboration of interpersonal coping skills and strategies" (Mindes, 2005, p. 16).

Social Studies in the Early Childhood Curriculum

As with other areas of development, social studies learning moves from simple to complex; shifts from a focus on oneself to taking the perspectives

Terms Used in This Chapter

• civic competence • socialization • multicultural education • classroom decisions versus class rules

of others; and involves learning specific content, in this case, in areas such as history, geography, and ecology (Seefeldt, Castle, & Falconer, 2013). Two components are especially important in preschool. *Social knowledge and understanding* is the awareness of social norms and customs. Acquiring this knowledge is called **socialization** or becoming a member of the community. To join the group, children must give up some individuality ("me") for the greater good ("we"). *Social skills* are strategies for interacting with others. Cognitive developments in perspective-taking facilitate their acquisition. Early classification skills also help preschoolers appreciate how they are like and not like others, which shapes later ideas about diversity and tolerance.

General Teaching Strategies for Social Studies

▲ Build on concrete experiences to help children construct general principles for social understanding and behavior

Preschoolers apply their knowledge of the *here and now* to the *there and then* of unfamiliar situations (Seefeldt et al., 2013). They understand stories about real people living in settings they have never seen, or imaginary creatures doing things they have never done, by drawing on differences in their own families (e.g., experiencing that the preferences and habits of their parents differ from those of their grandparents) and concrete cues (e.g., clothing, facial features, furniture, plants, transportation). Talking and playing with teachers and classmates exposes children to families with different living arrangements, languages, jobs, celebrations, beliefs, routines, and tastes. To further raise awareness, make comments (e.g., "Juan's daddy is a teacher. Malcolm's daddy paints houses. People have different jobs") and ask an occasional question (e.g., "Why do you think the other animals didn't help the little red hen?").

▲ Help children recognize that their personal actions can have a positive effect on the world

When young children share control of the classroom with adults (see chapter 5), they learn that their choices and actions have observable outcomes. It is especially important for adults to focus on the positive outcomes of children's behavior. Too often when adults talk about "consequences," the message is that unsocial actions have negative effects. However, if we want children to feel empowered, we need to acknowledge their capacity to bring about positive changes. Therefore, comment when children assist others (e.g., "Carl stopped crying when you held his hand"), recognize when they solve social problems (e.g., "You found a way to use the dump truck together), and acknowledge their voluntary attempts to help (e.g., "You wiped up the water so no one would trip").

Key Developmental Indicators in Social Studies

HighScope has six key developmental indicators (KDIs) in Social Studies: 53. Diversity, 54. Community roles, 55. Decision making, 56. Geography, 57. History, and 58. Ecology. See "KDIs in Social Studies" on page 192.

The following is a discussion of early learning in the Social Studies KDIs and how you can support their development as you play and interact with children in your program. For specific activities supporting Social Studies, see the resources on the HighScope website (www.highscope.org).

KDI 53. Diversity: Children understand that people have diverse characteristics, interests, and abilities.

Description: Children see similarities and differences in personal attributes (including gender, culture, age, religion, family structure, ability levels, and appearance) as natural and positive. They are interested in how people are the same and/or different from themselves and their families.

How Knowledge About Diversity Develops

Children apply the thought processes they use in classifying objects and events to forming ideas about people (Epstein, 2009a; Levin, 2003). At this

KDIs in Social Studies

53. **Diversity:** Children understand that people have diverse characteristics, interests, and abilities.
54. **Community roles:** Children recognize that people have different roles and functions in the community.
55. **Decision making:** Children participate in making classroom decisions.
56. **Geography:** Children recognize and interpret features and locations in their environment.
57. **History:** Children understand past, present, and future.
58. **Ecology:** Children understand the importance of taking care of their environment.

age, children tend to focus on one attribute at a time, especially a visual one. They may not be clear on which attributes are fixed (e.g., gender or ethnicity) and which are changeable (e.g., job or food choices). Young preschoolers think in dichotomies; to them, people are either the same or different. Older preschoolers realize people can be both.

Children need adult help to live in an increasingly pluralistic society (Gonzalez-Mena, 2013). As teachers, we can help children learn and adapt by respecting their emerging attempts to understand diversity and not forcing our ideas or ideals on them (Derman-Sparks & Edwards, 2010). How children think about and react to diversity is influenced by their families and, increasingly, by popular media (Carlsson-Paige, 2008). Although we often romanticize children's acceptance of everyone, they internalize stereotypes and may adopt negative attitudes quite early (Aboud, 2005). Early beliefs tend to persist, which is why early childhood educators have the best opportunity to positively influence children's lifelong racial and ethnic attitudes (Soto, 1999).

Teaching Strategies That Support Learning About Diversity

▲ Model respect for diversity

If we want children to treat others equally, we must demonstrate this behavior ourselves when interacting with adults (colleagues and parents) and children. Disrespect for differences is rooted in fear, and children, like adults, may be uncomfortable with unfamiliar people and practices. If you make exploring diversity part of everyday interactions, young children will not automatically equate "different" with "bad." Understanding human variation will be another area of learning.

To create an emotionally safe environment for this, use factual words to describe differences (e.g., "Kulani has curly hair; Frank has straight hair"). If children make hurtful comments (e.g., "Crystal has dirty skin"), reframe them. For example, you might say, "Crystal's skin is darker than yours and mine. Skin comes in many different colors." While young children do not intend harm by such statements, it is okay to gently challenge their reasoning (Levin, 2003). Instead of correcting them, point out something at odds with what they've said. For example, if a child says "old people smell bad," ask children how their grandparents smell. The responses of peers can prompt children to rethink their ideas.

▲ Focus on similarities and differences without judgmental comparisons

Use children's curiosity about differences as a learning opportunity. Comment on attributes or behavior without labeling one as better than another. For variations that are not present in your classroom (e.g., people using canes or speaking other languages), find meaningful and concrete ways to introduce them. Examples include picture books, photos, artwork, computer programs and other interactive technology, field trips, and visitors. Remember that diversity includes similarities as well as differences, that is, what people share as well as what distinguishes them. Since preschoolers are concrete thinkers, comment on characteristics they can see, hear, taste, touch, and smell in common.

When adults model respect for diversity, children can then positively explore their similarities and differences with awareness and openness.

▲ Include diversity in every classroom area and activity

Many well-intentioned programs introduce *diversity* in connection with holidays or traditional foods or clothing. However, such experiences, while valuable if they are meaningful to the children, do not help them understand that diversity is an everyday and everywhere occurrence. To help include diversity in the learning environment, teachers can turn to a growing body of resources on **multicultural education,** whose "underlying premise is that exposing children to a wide range of values and life styles will help them appreciate their own and other groups" (Ramsey, 2006, p. 280). Thus, it is better to show the diversity of daily life instead of adopting a "tourist curriculum" (Gronlund, 2006, p. 86). To do this, make sure the program's equipment and materials reflect children's homes and community. Families can often contribute many of these items. For example:

- In the house area, add work clothes and tools used in various jobs, cooking utensils and empty food containers from various cuisines, and equipment for people with disabilities.
- At snacktime and meals, serve food from different cultures on a regular basis, not just as special treats associated with holidays.
- Stock the reading area with publications illustrating diverse cultures and nonstereotypical role models. Interactive media available in the classroom should also reflect human diversity.
- Take field trips to local stores and markets, and attend street fairs, concerts, and festivals that represent the community's diversity.

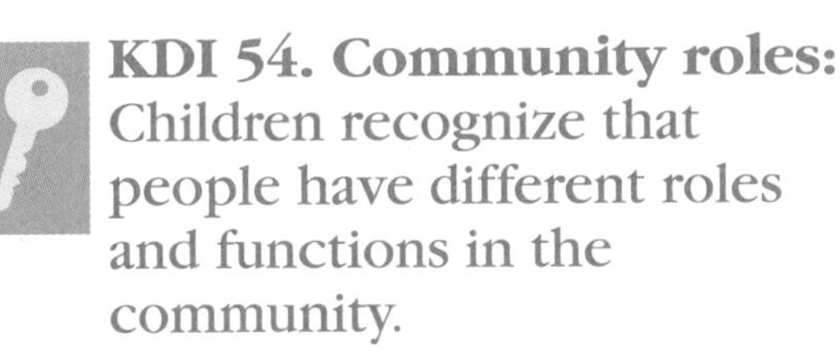

KDI 54. Community roles: Children recognize that people have different roles and functions in the community.

Description: Children know about familiar roles in the communities they belong to (e.g., family, school, neighborhood). They understand that people depend upon one another. Children know that people need money to buy goods and services.

How an Understanding of Community Roles Develops

Preschoolers first become aware of the roles within their families. They are initially preoccupied with actions that involve their well-being at home, but as they become less egocentric, children pay attention to the roles family members play in the community. Finally, young children take an interest in the services performed by people outside the family, such as doctors, firefighters, and bus drivers. This focus is apparent in their pretend play. Over time, they include more roles and expand the number of details they act out.

Preschoolers also develop rudimentary ideas about reciprocity between roles, including the exchange of money between people for the goods or services they provide one another (Jantz & Seefeldt, 1999). While *economics* may seem an abstract term, preschoolers, in fact, know many things about this aspect of social studies. For example, they understand that people work to make money to buy food, medicine, and movie tickets and that money or its equivalent comes in various forms. Preschoolers are also able to make simple choices about how to spend money. They know certain goods and services are more valuable than others, although they are likely to judge something's worth by its importance to them, rather than its actual market value.

Teaching Strategies That Support an Understanding of Community Roles

▲ Provide opportunities for children to learn about and act out different community roles

To support children's interest in family roles, provide pretend-play materials (e.g., dress-up clothes, housewares, shop and garden tools). Talk about what family members do at home and outside. For example, you might say, "Sean's daddy and Mattie's daddy both cooked dinner last night" or "Jerome's aunt is a teacher like me." Make a class book with photos of children's families engaged in different work or volunteer roles. Encourage children to write or dictate captions describing what their family members are doing (e.g., "That's my daddy. He sells plants" or "My mommy teaches grown-ups"). For parents who are able, encourage them to bring their children to work.

Provide opportunities for children to solve problems and make decisions as a group. Here the children and teacher discuss what would be the best home for the earthworm one child found.

Field trips and visitors also give children firsthand encounters with roles outside the family. Walk around the neighborhood so children can see people at work, and visit places of work that appear in children's pretend play (e.g., fire station, supermarket). Bring back materials (e.g., grocery bags, receipt pads) children can add to their pretend-play scenarios. You can also invite family and community members to share their experiences and work tools (be sure to talk with visitors ahead of time to make the visit hands-on and appropriate for the children).

▲ Provide opportunities for children to learn about and act out relationships that involve exchanging money for goods and services

To help children connect basic economics to their own lives, build on their family experiences purchasing goods and services (e.g., groceries, appliances, babysitting). Read books whose stories include people going to stores and markets as well as buying and selling things. Join as a partner when children play restaurant, barbershop, or doctor's office. Help them recognize the relationship between work and money. For example, you might ask, "Doctor, how much do I have to pay you to give my baby a shot?" Children enjoy using play money in these scenarios, but they also like to make their own, for example, with strips of paper or small items such as rocks and beads.

KDI 55. Decision making: Children participate in making classroom decisions.

Description: Children understand that everyone has the right to share ideas and be heard. They participate as leaders and followers. With adult guidance, they join in class discussions, help make decisions, and share ideas to resolve group problems.

How Decision Making Develops

A growing capacity for self-regulation and empathy (perspective taking) allows preschoolers to participate in the decision-making process (Harter, 2006). As they begin to see themselves as members of a community, preschoolers strive to make the group work better to achieve common goals (Thompson, 2006). **Classroom decisions** (which are developed with the children's input) are *not* the same **class rules,** however. Rules are limits that adults place on children's behavior for their safety and well-being (e.g., "No running with scissors"). Rules are generally outside the children's control and are made without their input. Unlike following classroom rules, decision making offers children options and allows them to be part of solving a problem (e.g., "How can we stop the markers from getting dried out?") or expressing a preference (e.g., "Which path should we take on our walk today?"). When children are included in such decisions, they are more likely to go along with them and also to remind their peers to comply (Elias et al., 1997).

Young children invited to contribute to classroom decisions typically go through three stages (DeVries & Zan, 2003). At first, they *parrot or repeat others' ideas.* Often they agree without fully understanding the topic under discussion, yet they want to be part of the process. Next, children will *elaborate on someone else's idea.* Although these contributions are not wholly the children's creation, they reflect a growing sense of autonomy and power. They also indicate that children have listened to and reflected on what someone else has said. Finally, preschoolers *invent original ideas.* This skill reflects their growing ability to think about the matter at hand and imagine (mentally represent) how their suggestion will play out. It also involves having the words to express their thoughts so that others can understand and respond to them.

Teaching Strategies That Support Decision Making

▲ Provide opportunities for children to solve problems and make plans as a group

Begin with simple classroom matters, such as where to post the list for passing out cups and napkins. Make sure all the children understand the issue being discussed, and clarify any limits that apply (e.g., "It has to be low enough for everyone to see"). If necessary, offer a couple of suggestions to get the discussion started. Anticipate areas of disagreement or identify them early in the process, before emotions run high and ideas or patterns of behavior become fixed (Gartrell, 2006). To help children consider the outcomes of their choices, ask questions such as, "What you do you think would happen if...?" and "Is there another way we could try to do that?" Be sure that you commit yourself to trying out children's ideas (provided they are safe and feasible). Finally, involve the children in evaluating the success of group decisions and, if needed, in generating alternatives.

▲ Encourage children to consider how their choices and decisions affect others

Acknowledge when a decision has added to the classroom's efficiency (e.g., "Since we decided to race the timer at cleanup time, we've been able to play outside longer"), enjoyment (e.g., "By turning down this street, we got to see the bulldozers"), or a sense of camaraderie (e.g., "We felt proud of ourselves when we wrote the thank-you letter to Mr. Haley"). Likewise, help raise awareness of a decision's unintended negative effects (e.g., "No one is using the small boxes since we moved them to the block area. Where else could we put them?"). When children realize their choices affect others, they can choose to use their decision-making skills for the good of the community.

KDI 56. Geography: Children recognize and interpret features and locations in their environment.

Description: Children identify familiar landmarks (e.g., home, school, park) and navigate simple routes between them. They match objects and events to their locations (e.g., scissors/art area; outside time/playground) and represent physical features (e.g., buildings, roads, bridges) in their play. Children use simple maps to describe and locate things in their environment (e.g., classroom areas, playground features).

How Knowledge of Geography Develops

Although *geography* sounds abstract, early education is compatible with its definition in the Geography Education Standards Project (1994): "A field of study that enables us to find answers to questions about the world around us — about where things are and how and why they got there" (p. 11). As early as 1934, Lucy Sprague Mitchell's influential book *Young Geographers* emphasized the need to build on preschoolers' here-and-now world to expand their understanding of the near-and-far universe.

When preschoolers become competent at navigating familiar spaces, that is, their "personal geography" (Hewes, 2007, p. 94), they develop a foundation for formal study in this area. Access to opportunities to explore their environment is particularly important for children living in urban settings, where safety concerns may restrict their freedom of movement. In fact, studies show that children who grow up in rural areas do better on measures of geographic (spatial) reasoning than their city-raised peers (Hewes, 2007).

Using our knowledge of early cognitive and social development, we can identify three appropriate areas for geography learning in preschool (Jantz & Seefeldt, 1999):

Simple mapping. Spatial awareness expands rapidly during preschool (Liben & Downs, 1993). Children as young as three spontaneously draw maps, and preschoolers can use an aerial photo to plot a route. Beginning with familiar landmarks, they extend spatial thinking to places beyond their experience. Between four and five, children consider a spatial problem from more than one perspective (e.g., how a map looks to someone sitting on the opposite side of the table).

Familiar locations. Young children learn *place geography* using their own experiences as the springboard (Mayer, 1995). They apply knowledge about the environments where they live to understand those that are different (e.g., "Behind my house there are mountains and it snows. My nana lives near a huge ocean with sunny beaches"). Emerging classification skills allow children to compare and contrast the characteristics of geographical regions they have not directly observed. That is why books like *The Snowy Day* by Ezra Jack Keats appeal to children living in warm climates and rural landscapes as much as to those from northern urban settings.

Natural features. Natural features include the earth's atmosphere, its surface, and how the sun affects conditions on earth. Young children are genuinely curious about the weather (Huffman, 1996). A daily weather chart will *not* make sense to them, but children care about how weather affects playing outside, what clothes they wear, or how the garden grows. Those whose parents' work is affected by climate (farmers, fishers) may be especially attuned to the weather. Children enjoy looking at cloud formations and (if they live on the water) observing tidal patterns. In short, when children study these features in relation to their own lives, they "behave very much like geographers, not only investigating their world and learning facts but also, more importantly, relating each fact to others and forming generalizations" (Jantz & Seefeldt, 1999, p. 173).

Teaching Strategies That Support Knowledge of Geography

▲ Acquaint children with familiar locations in their community

Talk with children about the places familiar to them and their families (e.g., homes, schools, parks, libraries, stores, restaurants). Encourage them to share when and how they get to and from these places. Walk around the school building to locate the front door, office, sibling's classroom, and other locations important to the children, and point out interesting neighborhood places (e.g., "Lila and her dad eat breakfast there before school"). Help children create simple maps on which they can locate familiar landmarks using symbols, flags, stickers, or other markers.

▲ Use concrete representations to connect children to places beyond their own experience

Books, photos, artwork, songs, and puzzles help young children become aware of people and places beyond their own lives. By relating these materials to matters of interest to them — food, clothing, houses, toys, animals — children will enjoy learning about experiences that parallel and differ from theirs. For example, while reading *The*

Three Snow Bears by Jan Brett, a book about the Far North, compare the clothes the children wear to keep warm with those worn by the characters. Preschoolers also enjoy examining globes, road and contour maps, aerial photos, and compasses. Connect these to their personal experiences. Talk about familiar landscapes (e.g., the river that winds through town) as you look at representations of other locations with comparable features.

KDI 57. History: Children understand past, present, and future.

Description: Children talk about what happened in the past (e.g., "Yesterday, when I was a baby...") and what will occur in the future (e.g., "When I'm bigger, I'll go to my sister's school"). They describe a sequence of events (e.g., "First I painted a picture, and then I built a tower").

How an Understanding of History Develops

Children's understanding of history is closely tied to their ideas about time (Wyner & Farquhar, 1991). At first, time is personal and intuitive, associated with the order and length of events in their daily lives. By late preschool, children begin to apply logic to understanding time. They know time moves forward and can reason backward to construct what happened before. They see how the recent past affects the present (e.g., they can wear the new jacket they bought yesterday to school today). Mental representations help children picture events farther in the past and future (Povinelli, Landry, Theall, Clark, & Castille, 1999).

A growing vocabulary (e.g., *before, after*; *first, last*; *then, next*) also helps children develop a sense of time (Thornton & Vukelich, 1988). Although shaky on specifics, preschoolers begin to grasp that a minute is shorter than an hour, and a day is shorter than a year. They understand that something that occurred many years ago is farther in the past than an event from yesterday. Older preschoolers also use visual cues, such as clothing or technology, to judge whether images are from long ago or closer to the present (Jantz & Seefeldt, 1999).

Teaching Strategies That Support an Understanding of History

▲ Support children's awareness of present, recent past, and short-term future events

The HighScope daily routine (see chapter 7) is an ideal structure to help children develop ideas about time. Use pictures, photos, cards, and objects to help children visualize and sequence the parts of the day. Planning and recall in particular provide opportunities to anticipate and review activities. The message board also provides concrete reminders of the recent past (e.g., a new material introduced at small-group time yesterday that is available for work time today) and near future (e.g., counting down the days until a field trip). Sequencing activities are another way to explore time and attach relevant vocabulary words. For example, when planning a large-group activity doing two movements in order, ask the children to first tap their ears and next tap their shoulders. Give children the opportunity to be leaders and to tell as well as show the movement sequence to their classmates. Do the same thing with music activities (sing two notes that vary in pitch or loudness). As children become adept at these movement and music activities, increase them to sequences of three or more motions or notes.

▲ Use concrete representations to make children aware of the distant past and far future

To support children's interest in time periods other than their own, read books (e.g., Tomie dePaola's *Mother Goose*) and sing songs (e.g., "Oh Susannah") that are clearly set in different times. Bring in artwork depicting other eras. Talk about historical characters and how their lives compare to how people live today (e.g., "Susannah traveled in a covered wagon instead of a car"). Do the same with stories set in the future. As you share these materials and partner in children's pretend play, use and encourage them to use a vocabulary of time and sequence words. Begin with terms such as *before, after*; *first, last*; and *yesterday, tomorrow*. Then introduce expressions such as *once upon a time, then and now, a long time ago*, and *when you grow up*. Hearing and using these words will help children think about the passage of time within the broader sweep of history.

KDI 58. Ecology: Children understand the importance of taking care of their environment.

Description: Children share responsibility for taking care of their environment inside and outside the classroom (e.g., picking up litter, watering plants, sorting things into recycling bins). They understand that their actions affect the well-being of the environment.

How Knowledge About Ecology Develops

Ecology is about people taking responsibility for the environment. While it entails learning about the natural world (KDI 51), ecology is part of the Social Studies content area because it involves understanding our roles as caretakers of the planet. As stated by the World Forum Nature Action Collaborative for Children (2010, para. 1):

"We believe that regular connections with the natural world encourage children to develop:

- Respect for local cultures and climates and for themselves as part of nature.
- Feelings of unity, peace and well-being as global citizens."

Children's ideas about ecology develop together with their social skills, notably empathy (the capacity to care for other people and wildlife [KDI 10]) and a sense of community (taking responsibility to maintain shared spaces [KDI 11]). In addition, as preschoolers learn about the natural world, they apply this knowledge to the environment. They identify what living things need to survive (food, water, shelter, warmth) and understand simple transformations (e.g., heat melts ice; flowing water moves things in its path). Because preschoolers use resources to accomplish their goals (e.g., paper to draw, clay to build), they develop an awareness that resources may be in limited supply and run out.

Emotions, attitudes, and values about nature are formed early in life (Kellert, 2002). Children must develop a love for nature before they can

Developing children's awareness of and appreciation for nature helps them become stewards of the earth as they get older.

think about the earth academically and become its guardians (Sobel, 2008). Therefore, "during early childhood, the main objective of environmental education should be the development of empathy between the child and the natural world" (White & Stoecklin, 2008, para. 11). This includes opportunities to play in nature, take care of plants, and cultivate relationships with animals — both real and imaginary.

Teaching Strategies That Support Learning About Ecology

▲ Develop children's awareness of and appreciation for nature

The more young children enjoy the sensations of the natural world, the more meaningful their concerns about ecology will become as they get older. Except for extreme weather conditions, include time in your daily routine for children to go outside every day, encouraging them to feel the sun and wind on their faces. Support young children's appreciation for nature by examining the plants and animals native to your area, planting a garden, and making a bird feeder. Walk around the neighborhood and go on field trips to experience different nearby environments (farm, forest, beach, lake, waterfall, or urban garden). Explain to parents why it is important for children to engage in less screen time and more outdoor time.

▲ Provide opportunities for children to take care of the indoor classroom and outdoor learning environment

Appropriate ways preschoolers can assume responsibility for the environment include:

- Taking care of materials and using them properly to avoid breakage and other damage (e.g., putting tops on markers, not banging or throwing mechanical tools or electronics)
- Cleaning up (putting away) materials in their designated places so others can find them
- Helping with simple repairs (e.g., gluing a wooden letter back on an area sign)
- Taking care of pets (e.g., feeding them, shredding paper for their cages)
- Planting, labeling, watering, and weeding the class garden
- Picking up litter in the hallway and on the playground (under adult supervision and with appropriate safety measures)
- Being careful not to damage plants or the habitats of the animals on the playground

▲ Connect children's personal environments to the world environment

As preschoolers' sense of the environment expands beyond their home, school, and community, comment on how their actions contribute to the well-being of the planet (e.g., turning off lights and water saves energy so there is enough for everyone to use). Focus on positive actions so as not to worry or frighten children about environmental problems they are too young to understand or unable to control. Encourage parents to model ecologically sensitive behaviors at home, and solicit their ideas on how their actions within the family can be applied to the classroom.

Try These Ideas Yourself

1. List what you consider to be the five most important things preschoolers need to know or be able to do in the Social Studies content area when they enter kindergarten. Why are they important? How can teachers support their development?

2. Consider what the phrase *tolerance for diversity* means to you.

- How did your early experiences at home and school help to make you more or less tolerant of others?
- Have you ever shared an experience with people whose backgrounds or beliefs differ from yours? What did you learn from that experience?
- How might your reflections help you understand and work with children in the classroom?

3. Think about what it means to create a *community* in the home, workplace, or classroom.

- How do people build community in each of these settings?
- How long does it take?
- What supports the process of community-building? What threatens it?

4. In the following scenario, identify the Social Studies KDIs. What types of learning are occurring in other areas of development? How could you as a teacher support and extend the learning? (The Social Studies KDIs are listed on p. 192.)

On the message board, Nell (a teacher) draws a female stick figure with a line through it, writes the letters P-O-L-L-Y below it, and tells the children that Polly (another teacher) will not be there today because she is sick. At planning time Maureen says she is going to make a picture for Polly, and at work time she draws a house with a big sun and flowers "so Polly will get better and come back tomorrow." Then Maureen goes to the message board and copies the letters of Polly's name on the top of her picture. She folds the paper in half; draws a stamp on the outside; and says, "I'll put it in the mailbox later on the way home from school."

Part 4

HighScope Assessment

This part of the book provides a comprehensive look at how HighScope assesses children and programs that serve them.

Chapter 18 explains the value of authentic assessment tools in evaluating and planning for children and describes HighScope's research-based and validated child assessment tool, COR Advantage.

Chapter 19 looks at the value to children, teachers, families, and agencies of valid and reliable program assessments and describes HighScope's research-based and validated assessment tool, the Program Quality Assessment (PQA).

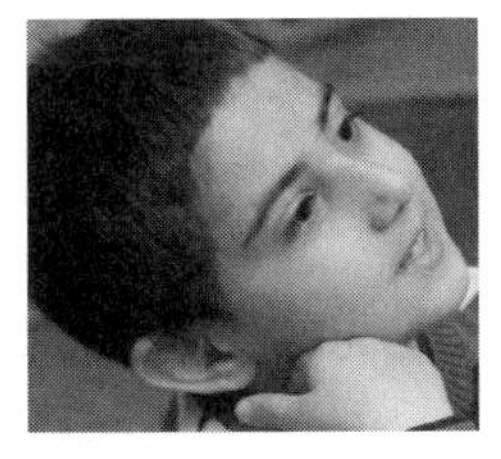

Chapter 18

How Does HighScope Assess Children?

Think About It

Lucy and her doctor are going over the blood tests from her annual physical exam. "Your total cholesterol level is 275, which is too high," says the doctor. "Anything over 240 puts you at risk for heart disease. I'm going to suggest some lifestyle changes and prescribe medication to lower your cholesterol level." The doctor explains the difference between "bad" and "good" cholesterol and shows Lucy her numbers on the lab report. She tells Lucy to reduce the amount of fat in her diet and gives her an information sheet on healthier eating. She also recommends that Lucy exercise at least 30 minutes a day, and together Lucy and her doctor discuss different options (walking, swimming, using the treadmill machine) and how Lucy can fit this regular activity into her schedule.

In the above scenario, both Lucy and her doctor are concerned about a potentially serious medical condition. By testing Lucy's blood before and after she makes the recommended changes, they can assess whether the new diet, regular exercise, and prescribed medication are having the intended effect of lowering her cholesterol level. If the results are good, Lucy can continue the new behavior pattern. If not, she and her doctor can explore additional options, such as trying a new medication.

In addition to simply being concerned about her own patient, Lucy's doctor, like other medical researchers, wants to know how different treatments work for the population as a whole. Does an old drug continue to be effective for many patients or for the same patient over time? Do new drugs work without having potentially dangerous side effects? Are different medications effective for different people? How can doctors help patients understand and follow recommended lifestyle changes? Should other family members be included in the treatment plan?

Even in other types of situations where there is not a "problem," we may want to know if our day-to-day behavior is good for us, our associates, and our possessions, leading us to seek objective answers about our actions and their consequences. Sometimes the answer is obvious (e.g., stepping on the scale tells us if we are losing weight), but other times we are not sure what questions to ask or how to measure the response. Also, though we may be able to assess changes in our own behavior, there are times when we want or need to know how we compare to others. In this chapter's opening scenario, for example, it is not enough for Lucy and her doctor to know whether her cholesterol has gone down. They need to know whether it is at or below the safe level recommended by experts in the field.

Similarly, good early childhood assessment tools provide all these types of information about children and their progress in our programs. They help us focus on important child behaviors, especially in areas where we may not have expertise. For example, detailed measures in specific curriculum content areas can help us know what mile-

Chapter Learning Objectives

By the end of this chapter, you will be able to

- Define authentic assessment and describe its benefits.
- Describe COR Advantage, a comprehensive measure of child development, and how it is used.

stones to look for in early language development or emerging relationships between children. Appropriate, comprehensive instruments also allow us to step back and take a broader view of the young children in our programs and whether we are meeting their needs. Looking at the children as learners thus helps us to look at ourselves as teachers.

Systematic assessment can help us organize our impressions and use them to create objective, numerically based reports. Although numbers do not replace the words in detailed anecdotes, they are handy for summarizing data gathered over time about one individual or for grouping information about the class as a whole. Numerical summaries also make it easier to communicate with others, especially those who are not familiar with the individuals being assessed. Systematic assessment is especially useful for communicating with administrators, funders, policy makers, taxpayers, and others who care about the effectiveness of the program overall.

Because HighScope is concerned about individual children and teachers in the classroom, as well as system-level public policy makers, HighScope's child assessment tool serves multiple purposes. It is designed to look at meaningful educational outcomes, gather information in ways that are natural and comfortable for children and adults, and provide accurate data that can be used for individual child planning and policy-level decision making. Also, because HighScope is an advocate for sound early childhood practices in general, its assessment tool is designed for use by non-HighScope programs as well as by those that do use the HighScope Curriculum.

Because HighScope teachers work closely with individual children, they can accurately assess their development. Looking at children as learners helps us look at ourselves as teachers.

The Benefits of Authentic Assessment

"If I could change one thing about teaching here, it would be to limit the busywork of evaluating children. I feel like I spend the whole first month out in the hall testing one child at a time, when I should be in the classroom with all the children. To top it off, once I've finished the testing, the information that I'm left with is not that useful in my teaching. What I need is something meaningful that doesn't take much time."

— Head Start Teacher, Detroit, Michigan

Educators assess young children to see how they are developing and to measure how the programs the children attend contribute to the children's growth. Traditional **testing** — such as a series of multiple-choice questions — is one way to measure children's learning. But, as expressed by the teacher in the previous quote, this type of test provides only limited information. It typi-

Terms Used in This Chapter

• testing • authentic assessments • reliability • validity • standardized • COR Advantage

Advantages of Authentic Assessment

- Based on real performance of the child, rather than an artificial testing situation
- Can focus on a broad range of developmental areas
- Assesses thinking and problem-solving abilities, not just factual knowledge
- Produces a profile of change and development over time
- Helps adults develop objective observational skills
- Helps adults become more knowledgeable about child development
- Encourages programs to become more child oriented (view learning from a child's perspective)
- Provides child-focused information adults can use to plan activities
- Makes adults pay attention to the "invisible" child
- If done as part of regular ongoing activities, does not add to program time or cost
- Can be done by all staff, including aides and assistants, with proper training
- Provides feedback to program administration and funding agencies
- Provides valuable and meaningful information for staff and parents to share

cally looks at learning for which there is one right answer. It does not indicate how children solve problems or collaborate with others. Moreover, it only shows how children do in the testing situation, not how they perform in real educational settings and everyday life.

Another way to measure children's development is with **authentic assessments.** These include objective observations, portfolios of children's work, and teacher and parent ratings of children's behavior. Authentic assessments are more naturalistic. They take place in the real world or duplicate a familiar situation instead of creating an artificial testing environment. As such, they provide a more accurate picture of what children normally do and reflect their true capabilities.

Authentic assessments add to what we can learn from tests. They provide teachers with valuable and practical information to understand and plan for the developmental needs of their students. Authentic measures can look at a broader range of children's behavior than can tests, which tend to focus on a single area of learning. With authentic assessments, the assessment process itself is more open ended — that is, it can allow for multiple answers and may even look at how children arrive at them. Finally, authentic measures often assess children over a longer period of time than a single test, so results do not depend on how children feel or their willingness to perform on a particular day.

HighScope recognizes that tests can be informative and are sometimes necessary (e.g., for research or diagnostic purposes). Tests may be the only feasible option in large-scale program evaluations and are often required by a funding source. However, HighScope is a strong proponent of authentic assessment, especially with young children. It therefore uses an authentic tool to measure overall development as well as learning in specific curriculum content areas.

The assessment instruments HighScope develops are always validated, meaning they meet the same rigorous scientific standards for **reliability** and **validity** as do conventional tests. A reliable assessment produces the same results when completed by different observers or at two closely spaced points in time. A valid instrument measures what it claims, is consistent with findings from similar measures, and may also predict future behavior. When developed according to these strict requirements, authentic measures can and should be as **standardized** as conventional tests. See "Advantages of Authentic Assessment" on this page.

This chapter describes the authentic assessment tool developed by HighScope, **COR Advantage,** the latest version of the Child Observation

Record (COR). Because this authentic measure assesses the universal characteristics of children's development, COR Advantage can be used by any early childhood program, not just those implementing the HighScope Curriculum.

COR Advantage

▲ COR Advantage overview

COR Advantage (Epstein et al., 2014) is an observation-based instrument for systematically assessing the knowledge and abilities of children from birth through kindergarten in nine areas of development (see "Categories and Items in COR Advantage" on p. 207). Each content area is composed of items that address key concepts in early learning, for a total of 36 items (including two for English language learners). Based on objective anecdotal notes about the child, recorded over time by an observer (such as a teacher, caregiver, parent, or researcher), each item is scored using an eight-level scale ranging from 0 (lowest) to 7 (highest). To help observers score COR Advantage reliably, and interpret and apply the results, this assessment tool provides notes for each area, item, and level, along with two anecdotal examples for each level.

COR Advantage is one continuous measure from birth to kindergarten. This developmental continuum allows programs that serve children over many years to track their progress throughout the length of their enrollment. Multiple levels also help assess children with special needs, whose developmental ages may differ across one or more dimensions.

Teachers record objective anecdotal notes while observing children in their learning environment.

▲ COR Advantage components

COR Advantage is designed to assist users in collecting and scoring observation-based child assessment data and is available online at www.coradvantage.org. A *User Guide* (Epstein, Marshall, & Gainsley, 2014a) provides the rationale for this tool, instructions for its completion (i.e., how to enter and score anecdotes as well as compile summary forms), and answers to frequently asked questions. A *Scoring Guide* (Epstein, Marshall, & Gainsley, 2014b) provides descriptions of all the content areas, items, and developmental levels, along with examples at each level to help users score COR Advantage reliably. In addition, there are forms for creating reports to summarize child- and classroom-level data. Administrators also have the option of creating other summary forms (e.g., by children's age or family background characteristics) to assist in meeting their reporting requirements or program planning needs. Other features of COR Advantage include a secure Family Network component that connects families to the anecdotes and photos that teachers enter for their child and tools to help teachers and parents support children at different developmental levels. However, the *User Guide*, *Scoring Guide*, and other materials are not intended as a substitute for COR Advantage training, which HighScope strongly recommends and makes available through numerous courses and workshops (see chapter 21).

▲ COR Advantage content

COR Advantage assesses development from infancy through kindergarten in nine areas: Approaches

Categories and Items in COR Advantage

Approaches to Learning
- A. Initiative and planning
- B. Problem solving with materials
- C. Reflection

Social and Emotional Development
- D. Emotions
- E. Building relationships with adults
- F. Building relationships with other children
- G. Community
- H. Conflict resolution

Physical Development and Health
- I. Gross-motor skills
- J. Fine-motor skills
- K. Personal care and healthy behavior

Language, Literacy, and Communication
- L. Speaking
- M. Listening and comprehension
- N. Phonological awareness
- O. Alphabetic knowledge
- P. Reading
- Q. Book enjoyment and knowledge
- R. Writing

Mathematics
- S. Number and counting
- T. Geometry: Shapes and spatial awareness
- U. Measurement
- V. Patterns
- W. Data analysis

Creative Arts
- X. Art
- Y. Music
- Z. Movement
- AA. Pretend play

Science and Technology
- BB. Observing and classifying
- CC. Experimenting, predicting, and drawing conclusions
- DD. Natural and physical world
- EE. Tools and technology

Social Studies
- FF. Knowledge of self and others
- GG. Geography
- HH. History

English Language Learning (if appropriate)
- II. Listening to and understanding English
- JJ. Speaking English

to Learning; Social and Emotional Development; Physical Development and Health; Language, Literacy, and Communication; Mathematics; Creative Arts; Science and Technology; Social Studies; and (for children whose first language is not English) English Language Learning. For a more detailed list, see "Categories and Items in COR Advantage" on this page.

▲ Completing COR Advantage

Using COR Advantage is a continuous process. Adults record objective anecdotal notes on children throughout the year (see chapter 9) and use them to score COR Advantage at periodic intervals. Raters may also use information from portfolios, photos, or other types of documentation to score COR Advantage. Although teachers do not record an anecdote on every child, every day, in every category (which would not be feasible), they do make several observations per week per child. They periodically review their collection of anecdotes to make sure each child's behavior is documented in each of the COR Advantage categories. If they notice a gap, they pay special attention to that child and area over the next few days and record what they observe.

Using the notes or other documentary evidence relevant to each item, raters score or "level" the entries on a scale of 0 to 7 to reflect each child's current level of development. Depending on a program's needs and reporting requirements, the anecdotes are used to complete and score COR Advantage two or three times a year, for example, at the beginning, midpoint, and end of the program. Less frequent measurement does not permit one to track development over time. More frequent measurement does not allow sufficient time between assessments for any changes to show up.

▲ Using COR Advantage

COR Advantage can be used by different people and for different purposes. Anyone who is familiar with the child (or children) being observed and who has been trained to record and score anecdotal notes can complete COR Advantage. This tool is primarily used by teachers and caregivers responsible for daily planning and regular reporting on their program. It is also used extensively by researchers and evaluators studying child development and how it is affected by program participation. COR Advantage may also be completed by parents, program volunteers and paraprofessionals, curriculum supervisors, and other program or administrative staff directly involved with the children. Training by a designated HighScope trainer is necessary to ensure that all these individuals use COR Advantage correctly and obtain reliable and valid results.

Of particular value to those who use COR Advantage for planning (i.e., adults who work directly with children) are suggested activities based on observations of children at different developmental levels. These activities help teachers scaffold (support and gently extend) early learning in all the content areas. For more information on these planning resources, visit the HighScope website at www.higscope.org.

In addition to providing teachers with the basis for daily planning, COR Advantage information can be shared with a variety of audiences. During formal conferences, as well as with the secure Family Network, teachers share anecdotes (but not scores) with parents to involve them in their child's program experience and to educate them about how to extend their child's learning at home. Administrators use COR Advantage results to monitor their programs and identify areas for staff inservice training. Finally, policymakers and funders, interested in holding programs accountable for their effectiveness, can rely on this assessment tool to provide accurate and objective information about how children are learning and developing.

Try These Ideas Yourself

1. Write three anecdotes about children in your own program or one you arrange to observe. (See chapter 9 for more information on observing children and writing anecdotes.) Review your anecdotes to see whether they are objective. Do they factually describe the behavior (e.g., "Rachel frowned and threw the puzzle on the floor") or make subjective judgments (e.g., "Rachel tested the teacher's patience by hurling the puzzle to the floor"). When necessary, rewrite the anecdotes to objectively describe the children's behavior. (*Variation:* Write three anecdotes about a family member or friend. Review them to see if they are objective. Rewrite them as necessary.)

2. Although researchers perform sophisticated statistical analyses, teachers and administrators often have to interpret simple data. The chart below lists the midyear scores of five preschoolers on the Social and Emotional Development items for COR Advantage. What can you say about the children individually and as a group?

Social and Emotional Development Items	Lisa	Don	Ari	Molly	Nema
D. Emotions	4	3	4	5	3
E. Building relationships with adults	4	3	4	5	4
F. Building relationships with other children	3	3	2	4	3
G. Community	3	3	3	4	4
H. Conflict resolution	4	3	2	4	3

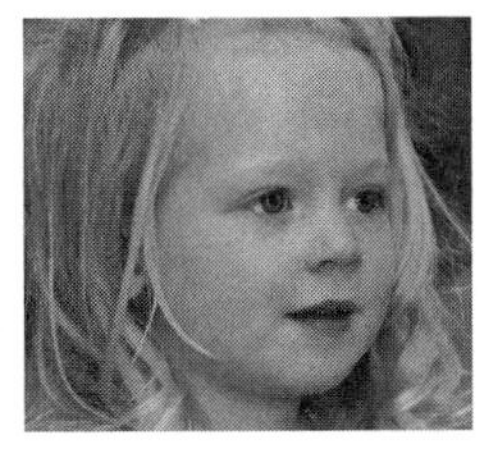

Chapter 19

How Does HighScope Assess Programs?

Think About It

Consider the following two scenarios:

Scenario #1: *Jeanne teaches second grade. Every spring at Jeannie's school, staff are given an annual performance review to see if they qualify for a merit increase in next year's salary. They are not told ahead of time which day their evaluation will take place.*

One morning in mid-April, Mr. Beaudette, the principal, comes to Jeanne's classroom. It is his first visit since last fall, when he had stopped by briefly to welcome the students back. This time, Mr. Beaudette goes directly to the back of the room without saying hello. For 30 minutes, he fills out a form while Jeanne conducts her regular reading lesson. The students keep turning around to watch him. Ten days later, Jeanne finds a copy of the form in her mailbox. Mr. Beaudette has marked "Satisfactory" on grooming, clarity of speech, accuracy of information presented, and assigning homework. He has checked "Needs to Improve" on maintaining order in the room, following curriculum standards, allowing sufficient time for each subject, and neatness of student desks. Jeanne will get a letter in two months saying whether she has received a raise.

Scenario #2: *Pat teaches second grade at a different school. On a mutually decided day in the fall, Mrs. Lowell, the curriculum supervisor, spends a morning observing Pat's classroom. The students know that Mrs. Lowell, a familiar figure, will be visiting. When she arrives, they greet her and go back to work. As she observes, Mrs. Lowell takes notes on the materials available to students, how Pat interacts with them, how much students contribute to class discussions, the amount of time allotted to required subjects, and what happens during "open" times of the day.*

After dismissal, Pat and Mrs. Lowell go over the notes and ratings. Mrs. Lowell tells Pat her room is well stocked with interesting materials, and she suggests additional items other second-grade teachers have found helpful. She says Pat is on target to cover reading, mathematics, and social studies but might have trouble meeting the science requirement. Together Pat and Mrs. Lowell brainstorm ideas for adjusting the schedule to allow more time for science, and Mrs. Lowell says she'll drop off some program brochures from the new hands-on children's museum.

Pat says her main goal this year is to get more student participation, especially during book discussions. Pat and Mrs. Lowell review several ways Pat might do this, such as supplementing the required reading with students' book choices and letting them lead the discussions. They agree Mrs. Lowell will observe a book discussion in two months, using the sections of the observation form that address teacher-student interaction and student participation.

A performance review can make anyone nervous, even an experienced and respected employee. Yet an evaluation like that in the second scenario above would be much less anxiety

Chapter Learning Objectives

By the end of this chapter, you will be able to

- List the components of program quality.
- Describe the importance of program assessment.
- Describe the features and uses of effective program quality measures.
- Describe the features of the Preschool Program Quality Assessment (PQA) and explain how this validated instrument is used.

HighScope staff use the results of ongoing program assessment to highlight program strengths, identify areas for improvement, and plan effective staff development strategies.

provoking for most of us than that of the first. For one thing, we'd know *when* we would be observed. Additionally, the supervisor would look at meaningful educational practices that could be objectively measured, such as the number and variety of materials we provided our students. We wouldn't be judged according to arbitrary and subjective factors, such as grooming (suppose the supervisor just didn't like our taste in clothes or hairstyle!). The observation would be followed by a meeting in which the supervisor acknowledged what was working well. After this encouragement, we'd discuss potential problems and how to address them. There would time to share our own goals for professional growth and receive support in reaching them. Follow-up observations during the year would show what was effective and what still needed fine tuning.

In sum, this teamwork approach to evaluation would be much more comfortable and certainly more informative. Its purpose would not be to judge us as passing or failing some test but, rather, to *collaborate* on achieving what was best for the children in our program.

The HighScope approach to assessing programs is consistent with the second scenario. HighScope recognizes that valid assessment relies on objective information collected on meaningful variables. Whether we are evaluating teachers or administrators, the underlying concern is always *what will help children and families*.

In this chapter, we discuss why this approach to program assessment is an important component of any comprehensive curriculum model. You will read about the **Preschool Program Quality Assessment (PQA)** (HighScope Educational Research Foundation, 2003), an instrument used to objectively measure how well programs meet the needs of children, families, and staff. Because it is based on documented best practices, the PQA and its online version, **OnlinePQA** (HighScope Educational Research Foundation & Red-e Set Grow, 2012), can be used by any developmentally based early childhood program, not just those using the HighScope Curriculum.

The Importance of Program Assessment

Decades of research, summarized in the report *Eager to Learn* (National Research Council, 2001), make it clear that program performance is positively and significantly related to child performance. To evaluate and understand children's performance and progress (see chapter 18), we need

Terms Used in This Chapter

• Preschool Program Quality Assessment (PQA) • OnlinePQA • program quality measure or quality rating systems • program quality • structural components • process • interrater reliability • self-assessment • developmentally appropriate practice • monitoring

to measure the educational experiences that the programs they attend are providing. Put another way, *programs,* rather than children, should be held accountable for learning. To help programs meet their obligation to teach children, early childhood educators need valid tools to assess how well their programs promote learning in all areas of development. Such tools are typically referred to as **program quality measures** or **quality rating systems.** Their purpose, quite simply, is to answer the question, "Does it work?" (Gilliam & Leiter, 2003).

To learn how such tools are developed, we first need to look at what we mean by **program quality.** Dedicated professionals want to do what is best for children, families, and society as a whole. But program quality, like child development, is complex and has many dimensions. It includes the **structural components** of the classroom — how the learning environment is set up and what happens during the program day. Additionally, quality is especially dependent on **process** — notably, how adults interact with children and plan and carry out meaningful learning experiences. The ways in which staff relate to parents, one another, and the community can also affect children and are part of quality processes. Finally, agency-wide factors influence what happens in the classroom and directly or indirectly affect children. These include how staff are recruited and trained and how the program is financed and managed overall.

While we know all these quality components are important, we are still faced with the challenge of defining and measuring them. Only valid assessment instruments can guarantee we are looking at the right ingredients of quality in an honest and accurate manner. They give us the information to evaluate whether we are achieving appropriate levels of quality, and if not, where and how we can improve. Good assessment tools also give us a common language with which to share this information with parents, administrators, researchers, and policymakers. An objective program evaluation tool is essential to encouraging self-assessment and promoting communication among everyone concerned about program quality and its implications for early childhood development. Above all, "the desired outcomes should be attainable" so that assessment results in acknowledging successes and developing a feasible improvement plan (Gilliam & Leiter, 2003, pp. 8–9).

The Characteristics of Effective Program Quality Measures

With these goals in mind, HighScope developed and validated the Preschool PQA. There is also an Infant-Toddler PQA (Epstein et al., 2013; Hohmann, Lockhart, & Montie, 2013) and a Family Child Care PQA (2009). To determine the most effective format and content for these instruments, HighScope examined other widely used program quality measures, including the Early Childhood Environment Rating Scale (Harms, Clifford, & Cryer, 2005) and the Classroom Assessment Scoring System (Hamre & Pianta, 2007). This review allowed us to identify the following characteristics as being essential for an effective and user-friendly program quality measure.

The most effective program assessment tools define quality along a continuum. In talking to practitioners and researchers, we found many were frustrated by assessment instruments that permitted only yes-no (pass-fail) scoring. Such measures were often used to measure compliance with regulations but did not allow for the fact that quality is achieved in stages. An assessment tool that rates quality along a continuum helps practitioners see where their programs are now and what steps they need to take to continue making improvements.

Program assessments are most helpful if they provide users with many examples. For the assessment tool to be used accurately and objectively, it should clearly describe typical behaviors at each level of quality. Concrete examples allow different raters to interpret and score the same behavior in the same way, which is what researchers call **interrater reliability.** Multiple examples also help staff to see what level they fit into and to know by example what they are striving to achieve.

Program assessments are most informative if they are comprehensive. HighScope has identified two aspects of comprehensiveness. First, *assessment tools should look at both the structure and the process of a program.* Most instruments cover structural qualities (e.g., safety, diversity of materials), but many fail to pay equal — if not more — attention to processes (e.g., adult-child and child-child interactions). Yet research (see, e.g., National Research Council, 2001) shows that these program features are crucial to defining quality and promoting child development.

The second aspect of comprehensiveness refers to *looking at the program from multiple perspectives*. Although our top concern is children, we should also pay attention to how programs serve families and staff. A complete program assessment tool should, therefore, look at how teachers interact with parents, how staff work together to plan for the children, how supervisors support staff development, and how management secures adequate resources. In other words, a program quality assessment should look at the classroom, the agency, the home, and the community — and the activities and experiences of the participants in each.

Program assessments make the greatest contribution to the field if they have been tested and validated. Because we each want to capture our program's uniqueness, it is tempting to create our own assessment tools. The problem with this approach is that we end up talking only to coworkers and a few others who know our program well. We cannot communicate or share successful models outside our own agencies or understand how our program fits within the broader scheme of early childhood initiatives. Moreover, "reinventing the wheel" by creating our own measurement tools fails to make use of decades of valuable research. If we instead build assessment systems on standard best practices, we can advance the field as a whole and use its knowledge to our own benefit as well. For that reason, HighScope concluded that the most effective assessment tools can and should be applied across program settings, including those using other developmentally based curriculum models.

Supervisors and teachers use findings from the PQA to improve the learning environment, daily routine, adult-child interaction, and team planning.

The Uses of Effective Program Quality Measures

Good program quality measures offer the following options and benefits across a wide array of uses and in different types of settings.

Effective program quality assessments also serve as training tools. Evaluation highlights program strengths and identifies areas to be improved through staff training. Concrete examples define good practice for new teachers. They help experienced ones reflect on what they do and encourage them to continue growing as professionals.

Effective assessment tools allow supervisors to observe individual staff members and provide them with constructive feedback. Assessment can be anxiety provoking if the rules are arbitrary and the intention is judgment rather than improving performance. But a well-constructed tool can provide the person being assessed with clear expectations and opportunities for growth. Properly used, a good assessment tool allows a supervisor and a teacher to work as a team, as in the second scenario at the beginning of this chapter.

Valid program quality measures are essential for research and program evaluation. We often evaluate our programs to meet individual funding requirements. Beyond that, practitioners share a responsibility to contribute to the field as a whole. Assessments should serve both local and broad interests. They should meet rigorous scientific standards and produce results that are clear and concise. Instruments that work for researchers and practitioners build bridges between them. Researchers can ask meaningful questions and practitioners can use the results in their programs.

Effective program assessment tools communicate to many audiences. Good assessment tools avoid jargon. They speak to professional and lay audiences, including teachers, administrators, parents, researchers, and policy makers. If all these audiences understand the language used in an assessment tool, they are in a better position to collaborate on achieving high program quality.

❖

With these principles in mind, HighScope developed, field-tested, and validated the PQA tools, a comprehensive set of assessments to examine all meaningful aspects of program quality. By collect-

Effective Program Quality Measures...

Have the following characteristics:

- Define quality along a continuum, not just "yes" or "no"
- Provide users with many examples
- Are comprehensive
- Have been field tested and validated

Can be used in the following ways:

- To support the curriculum implementation of teaching teams
- To plan and carry out a program of staff development
- To carry out research and program evaluation
- To communicate to many audiences

ing feedback from many programs in both HighScope and non-HighScope settings, HighScope has refined and revised the measure over a period of several years.

The Preschool Program Quality Assessment (PQA)

▲ Preschool PQA overview

The PQA is a rating instrument designed to evaluate the quality of early childhood programs and identify staff training needs. It is a comprehensive assessment that examines all the components of program quality. These range from the activities and interactions in the classroom, to relationships with families, to the policies and practices of agency managers. Because the PQA is based on best practices in the early childhood field as a whole, it is appropriate for use in all early childhood programs, not just those using the HighScope Curriculum. For example, the PQA is suitable for use in the quality rating and improvement systems being adopted in many states.

The PQA allows raters to systematically collect information through classroom observations and interviews with teachers and administrative staff. The PQA can be implemented by trained outside evaluators or used as a **self-assessment** — that is, by an individual or team to evaluate their own program. Based on objective evidence (including anecdotal notes, diagrams, and interviews), PQA raters complete a series of five-point scales describing a broad array of program characteristics. To ensure reliable and valid ratings, the endpoints and midpoint of each scale are defined by behavioral indicators and illustrated with examples. Unlike compliance measures that permit only yes-no scores, PQA ratings are made along a continuum, which results in more accurate information. It also helps raters pinpoint a program's current level of quality and, if necessary, a path for moving up to a higher level.

▲ Preschool PQA components

The PQA has several components. It includes an administration guide, forms with items for observing the classroom and teaching behaviors, forms with items for assessing agency-level factors, and summary scoring forms. The items of the PQA align with the Head Start Program Performance Standards (Administration for Children and Families, 2002). The PQA can also be aligned with state and local program performance standards, and with quality rating and improvement systems. (See the HighScope website at www.highscope.org for PQA alignment information.)

Although the PQA contains instructions for conducting and scoring the assessment, HighScope recommends that raters receive training in using the instrument (see chapter 21). Training results in the most effective, reliable, and valid use of the measure.

▲ Preschool PQA content

The PQA has a total of 63 items, divided into seven sections. Each item is scored on a five-point scale from a low (1) to a high (5) level of quality. The first form (also known as Form A: Classroom Items) includes sections on the learning environment, daily routine, adult-child interaction, and curriculum planning and assessment. The second

Sections and Items on the PQA

Form A — Classroom Items

I. Learning Environment

A. The classroom provides a safe and healthy environment for children.

B. The space is divided into interest areas that address basic aspects of children's play and development.

C. The location of the interest areas is carefully planned to provide for adequate space in each area, easy access between areas, and compatible activities in adjacent areas.

D. An outdoor play area (at or near the program site) has adequate space, equipment, and materials to support various types of play.

E. Classroom areas and materials are systematically arranged, labeled, and accessible to children.

F. Classroom materials are varied, manipulative, open ended, authentic, and appeal to multiple senses.

G. Materials are plentiful.

H. Materials reflect human diversity and the positive aspects of children's homes and community culture.

I. Child-initiated work (work designed and created by children) is on display.

II. Daily Routine

A. Adults establish a consistent daily routine. Children are aware of the routine.

B. The parts of the daily routine include time for children to do the following: plan, carry out their plans, recall and discuss their activities, engage in small-group activities, engage in large-group activities, have snacks or meals, clean up, transition to other activities, play outside, and nap or rest (if applicable).

C. An appropriate amount of time is allotted for each part of the daily routine.

D. The program has time each day during which children make plans and indicate their plans to adults.

E. The program has time each day during which children initiate activities and carry out their intentions.

F. The program has time each day during which children remember and review their activities and share with adults and peers what they have done.

G. The program has time each day for small-group activities that reflect and extend children's interests and development.

H. The program has time each day for large-group activities that reflect and extend children's interests and development.

I. During transition times, children have reasonable choices about activities and timing as they move from one activity to the next.

J. The program has a set cleanup time with reasonable expectations and choices for children.

K. The program has time each day for snacks or meals that encourage social interaction.

L. The program has an outside time each day during which children engage in a variety of physical activities.

III. Adult-Child Interaction

A. Children's basic physical needs are met.

B. Children's separation from home and daily entry to the program are handled with sensitivity and respect.

C. Adults create a warm and caring atmosphere for children.

D. Adults use a variety of strategies to encourage and support child language and communication.

E. Adults use a variety of strategies to support classroom communication with children whose primary language is not English.

F. Adults participate as partners in children's play.

G. Adults encourage children's learning initiatives throughout the day (both indoors and outdoors).

H. Adults support and extend children's ideas and learning during group times.

I. Adults provide opportunities for children to explore and use materials at their own developmental level and pace.

J. Adults acknowledge individual children's accomplishments.

K. Adults encourage children to interact with and turn to one another for assistance throughout the day.

L. Children have opportunities to solve problems with materials and do things for themselves.

M. Adults involve children in resolving conflicts.

Sections and Items on the PQA (cont.)

IV. Curriculum Planning and Assessment

A. Staff use a comprehensive and documented curriculum model or educational approach to guide teaching practices.

B. Staff use a team teaching model and share responsibilities for planning and implementing program activities.

C. Staff maintain records on children and families.

D. Staff record and discuss anecdotal notes as the basis for planning for individual children.

E. Staff regularly use a child observation measure of proven reliability and validity to assess children's developmental progress.

Form B — Agency Items for Infant-Toddler and Preschool Programs

V. Parent Involvement and Family Services

A. The program provides a welcoming environment for families and a variety of opportunities for parents to become involved in the program.

B. Parents are represented on program advisory and/or policymaking committees.

C. Parents are encouraged to participate in program activities with children.

D. Staff and parents exchange information about the curriculum and its relationship to children's development.

E. Staff form partnerships with parents and interact informally to share information about the day's activities and children's experiences.

F. Staff and parents exchange information about how to promote and extend children's learning and social development at home.

G. Staff members schedule home visits and formal parent conferences to share information with parents and seek input from parents about the program and their children's development.

H. The program or its host agency provides diagnostic and special education services for children with special needs.

I. Staff provide parents with referrals and access to supportive services as needed.

J. Program activities are coordinated within the program and/or with community agencies and/or public schools to facilitate children's smooth transitions at each age level.

VI. Staff Qualifications and Staff Development

A. The program director has the appropriate education, training, and experience.

B. Instructional staff have the appropriate education, training, and experience for the age group they are working with.

C. Support staff (e.g., cook, bus driver, secretary) and volunteers receive the appropriate orientation and supervision.

D. Staff participate in ongoing professional development activities such as conferences, inservice training, professional workshops, college-level courses and seminars, online training, compiling or consulting a resource library, teacher exchanges, observation, mentoring, and coaching.

E. Inservice training involves participants in topics specific to young children's development and practice.

F. Instructional staff are regularly observed in the program setting and provided with feedback by someone familiar with the curriculum's goals, objectives, and methods for working with each age group of children in the program.

G. The director and teachers are affiliated with a local, state, and/or national early childhood professional organization.

VII. Program Management

A. The program is licensed based on regulations passed by the state and/or local licensing agencies.

B. Program policies promote continuity of care by classroom adults (paid staff who work directly with children).

C. Staff regularly conduct a program assessment and use the results to improve the program.

D. The program has a child recruitment and enrollment plan.

E. The program has a fully developed set of operating policies and procedures.

F. The program is accessible to those with disabilities.

G. The program is adequately funded.

— Excerpted from the Preschool PQA (Form A [HighScope, 2003] and Form B [Epstein et al., 2013])

form (known as Form B: Agency Items) covers parent involvement and family services, staff qualifications and staff development, and program management. PQA sections and items are listed on pages 214–215.

Completing the PQA

When the PQA is used as a self-assessment, or by a supervisor to support teachers' curriculum implementation (see chapter 9), one or more sections can be completed during a single session. If a comprehensive self-assessment is being conducted with the entire PQA, each section may be completed at a different time. However, to get an accurate picture of the program at a single point in time, this period should be limited to several days or a week at most.

Using the PQA

The PQA can be completed by a trained independent rater such a researcher, program evaluator, outside consultant, or agency administrator. It may also be done as a self-assessment by those directly involved with the program, such as center directors, curriculum specialists, education or parent coordinators, individual teachers or teaching teams, or parents. Students who are preparing to become early childhood teachers and caregivers may also conduct a PQA on someone else's classroom or as a self-assessment of their own student teaching. They can then discuss the results with their instructor and classmates as part of their training and professional development.

Uses for the PQA include training, monitoring, staff support and supervision, and research and evaluation. Results can be shared inside the program with instructional and support staff, administrators, parents, and funders and can also be presented to practitioners, researchers, and policy makers in the field as a whole. Findings from the PQA can be used to define and illustrate best practices and to focus attention on program enhancement in training. Statistical analyses can examine the relationship between program practices and child development and shape policies for improving the quality of early childhood programs. These multiple uses are described below.

Professional development. Both preservice and inservice training are enriched by the PQA. It can be used in its entirety to provide trainees with a comprehensive picture of quality. Individual sections can be used to focus on specific program components. The detailed examples in the indicators for each item offer concrete illustrations of best practices. Users often comment that the PQA defines the term **developmentally appropriate practice** by translating an idea or ideal into specific implementation strategies. Even experienced teachers find the PQA's depth and specificity helps them reconsider long-established practices from a new perspective.

Self-assessment and monitoring. The PQA is a valuable tool for administrators and teachers to assess their own practices and identify areas for growth. It can also be used by those responsible for quality control to monitor program implementation at a single site or across multiple sites. Because the PQA is objective and quantitative, it can be used to set program goals in one or more areas and to provide a numerical and anecdotal record of progress. HighScope also uses the PQA to certify teachers and accredit programs based on rigorous performance standards (see chapter 21).

Staff support and supervision. Supervision can be effective and nonthreatening when the PQA is used to conduct observations and the results are discussed as a team. A teaching team and a supervisor familiar with the curriculum and the instrument agree to focus on a particular aspect of implementation (e.g., the learning environment). The supervisor then uses the relevant PQA section(s) to observe, record anecdotes, rate the items, and discuss the results with the practitioners. Together, they acknowledge strengths and identify areas for improvement, using the PQA's concrete examples to develop a plan of action. They arrange a time for a follow-up observation to review how the plan is working.

Research and evaluation. The PQA has been used extensively as a research tool administered by trained outside observers. Researchers and evaluators can design studies to document program practices, compare quality in different program settings, evaluate whether and how staff training improves quality, and examine the relationship between program quality and young children's development.

Information and dissemination. With its straightforward language and detailed examples, the PQA can be used to explain research-based practices to a variety of audiences. These include administrators and policymakers, particularly those who may not know the elements of high-quality programs. The PQA can also help support staff understand the actions and requests of the instructional staff. Further, it is an effective tool for explaining the program to parents and for suggesting ways they can carry out similar practices at home. Additionally, PQA results can be easily communicated to researchers. Finally, the many concrete examples help others replicate proven practices in their own settings.

Try These Ideas Yourself

1. Make up a five-point scale for some behavior or skill. For example, a scale for cooking might range from low (1) for "Has at least three takeout restaurants on cell phone's contact list" to high (5) for "Prepares gourmet dinner for eight guests once a month." List the behavioral indicators that define each level of the scale. Use the scale to take anecdotal notes and rate five people you know. (*Variation:* Put each level of your scale with its indicators on a different index card. Do not number them. Scramble the order of the cards. Give them to a friend or colleague. See if he or she can identify the behavior you are scaling and put the cards in order.)

2. The chart below lists the scores of four teachers on the adult-child interaction items of the Preschool PQA. Identify each person's strengths and areas for improvement. What inservice workshop(s) would you recommend for the staff as a group?

Preschool PQA Adult-Child Interaction Items

Adult-Child Interaction Items	Teacher/Classroom Number			
	#1	#2	#3	#4
A. Children's basic physical needs are met.	5	5	4	5
B. Children's separation from home and daily entry to the program are handled with sensitivity and respect.	4	3	2	3
C. Adults create a warm and caring atmosphere for children.	5	5	4	5
D. Adults use a variety of strategies to encourage and support child language and communication.	3	3	3	3
E. Adults use a variety of strategies to support classroom communication with children whose primary language is not English.	2	3	2	3
F. Adults participate as partners in children's play.	4	5	3	4
G. Adults encourage children's learning initiatives throughout the day (both indoors and outdoors).	5	5	3	4
H. Adults support and extend children's ideas and learning during group times.	4	3	2	3
I. Adults provide opportunities for children to explore and use materials at their own developmental level and pace.	5	5	3	4
J. Adults acknowledge individual children's accomplishments.	4	5	4	4
K. Adults encourage children to interact with and turn to one another for assistance throughout the day.	3	3	2	3
L. Children have opportunities to solve problems with materials and do things for themselves.	5	4	3	5
M. Adults involve children in resolving conflicts.	4	3	1	3

A valuable monitoring tool for both administrators and teachers, the PQA can be used for self-assessment as well as for sharing information about program implementation with funding and regulatory agencies.

Part 5

HighScope Professional Development

This part of the book provides a brief overview of HighScope's approach to the professional development of staff. It describes how HighScope works with teachers and child care providers, and those who supervise them, to guarantee program quality. While this information presents HighScope's approach to professional development, it is not meant to substitute for actual training by the staff and designated HighScope representatives.

Chapter 20 explains how HighScope applies the principles of active participatory learning to training the adults who work with young children.

Chapter 21 describes HighScope professional development courses and its certification and accreditation procedures.

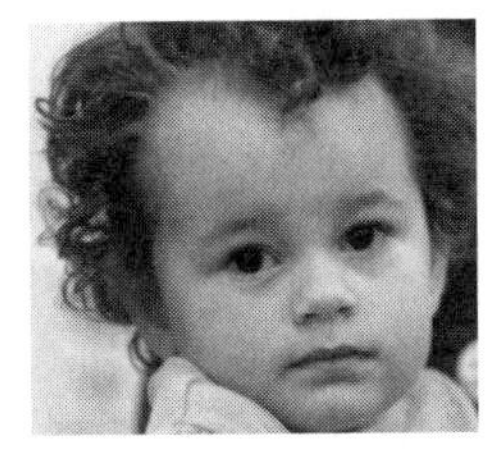

Chapter 20

How Does HighScope Apply Active Participatory Learning to Adults?

Think About It

Rachel liked natural sciences. In her sophomore year of high school, she enrolled in a biology class, taught by Ms. Schaeffer. For the unit on plants, students gathered samples from nearby woods and fields. They generated lists of similarities and differences, grouped them according to their observations, and compared their categories with official scientific classifications. To help answer their own questions, Ms. Schaeffer taught students to use a spreadsheet to organize and analyze their data. The class entered a group project in the school's annual science fair and was invited to present the results at a student auditorium and an evening session for parents.

In Rachel's junior year, she signed up for a botany course, taught by Ms. Zenda. Instead of collecting and comparing their own samples, students were given lists of plant similarities and differences to memorize. There was little laboratory work. Classes were primarily lectures whose content repeated the information in the textbook. Students were permitted to ask questions during the last five minutes of class. The teacher always answered them, but Rachel missed gathering data and researching the answers herself. That spring, only one student entered the school science fair.

Senior year, Rachel was ready to abandon science, but when she saw Ms. Schaeffer was teaching a course on environmental fieldwork, she signed up. Students collected water samples along the river and tested it for pollutants. The worst levels were at a manufacturing plant built 10 years ago, north of the city. When the class studied wildlife records, they found that plant and animal counts had decreased significantly over the past decade. They wrote their state representative and were invited to speak to the Department of Natural Resources. Ms. Schaeffer coached them on organizing and presenting the information. As a result, their state's legislature drafted an antipollution bill. Proponents were optimistic about its passage. When Rachel began college that fall, she signed up for natural sciences courses and eventually majored in environmental studies.

What made Rachel's experiences so different each year? In her first class, students were engaged in **hands-on learning.** They worked directly with materials, made observations, posed questions, and collected data to answer them. They were *active learners*. In the second class, the teacher fed students information; lectures replaced laboratory work. Rachel and her classmates were *passive learners*. Fortunately, the third class not only replicated the hands-on discovery of the first one but also enabled students to apply what they learned toward making a real difference in the world.

The HighScope model for adult training reflects the principles and strategies that characterized Rachel's first and third classes. It promotes active learning for adults as well as children. Adults not only gain an understanding of *what* the curriculum is and *why* it is grounded in theory and research but also emerge knowing *how* to imple-

Chapter Learning Objectives

By the end of this chapter, you will be able to

- Explain why active participatory learning is as important for adults as it is for children.
- Describe the HighScope principles of active participatory learning for adults.
- Discuss how the structure and content of HighScope professional development is related to the principles of active learning.

ment its practices. While scripted lessons may also provide teachers with how-to instructions, HighScope further respects them as thoughtful individuals who want to know the reasons behind their actions and interactions with children.

Why Active Participatory Learning Is Important for Adults

Research shows a strong and positive relationship between teachers' qualifications and young children's learning (Barnett, 2003; National Research Council, 2001). The higher their level of formal education and specialized training, the more likely adults are to use appropriate teaching strategies in their classrooms. In addition, they work more effectively with families and forge lasting team relationships with their coworkers. Teacher training is also associated with lower turnover rates, which provides essential continuity for children and parents as well as stability for the agencies that employ them and invest in their training (Bloom & Sheerer, 1992).

The best professional preparation encourages teachers to reflect on what they learn and apply it meaningfully in their jobs (Katz, 1995). The goal of reflection is to discover how what we *learn* translates to what we *do* in the child care setting. A thoughtful teacher does not rely on scripted lessons, which may not fit a particular child or group.

Active participatory learning is as important for adults as it is for children. Adults learn how to implement the HighScope Curriculum in hands-on courses, workshops, and online trainings.

Instead, teachers with appropriate education and training use what they have learned to guide their practice and make decisions about what works best for each child and the class as a whole.

Early childhood teacher education and training take place through courses at two- and four-year colleges (Early & Winton, 2001) and through workshops sponsored by early childhood agencies or professional organizations (National Institute on Early Childhood Development and Education, 2000). Formal education is sometimes referred to as **preservice training,** while on-the-job training is considered **inservice training.** However, professionals may participate in either or both at any point in their teaching careers. In fact, ongoing education and training is considered a hallmark of an effective early childhood professional. As the

Terms Used in This Chapter

• hands-on learning • preservice training • inservice training • integrated content • articulated curriculum • distributive learning • mentoring or coaching

field continues to learn about young children's development and how adults can best support early learning, staying up to date with the latest research and practical lessons is a necessity for a committed and competent teacher.

In addition to when and where ongoing preparation takes place, the *how* of such education and training is vital. Research shows that active learning is as important for adults as it is for young children (Mezirow, 2000). While grown-ups can deal with ideas and abstractions, they also need to work with materials, connect the information and skills they are learning to their own lives, and observe for themselves the direct effects of their actions on their students and coworkers. All too often, however, training for early childhood staff covers a series of disconnected topics, is not tied to a theory or the curriculum they are using, lacks practical information, and fails to provide follow-up as teachers attempt to implement new ideas in the classroom (Bloom & Sheerer, 1992).

By contrast, a core position of the National Board for Professional Teaching Standards (2012) is that teachers should think systematically about their practices and learn from experience. Its early childhood generalist standards state that "accomplished teachers engage in purposeful and systematic reflection on their teaching to enhance their professional knowledge and skill and to benefit young children's development and learning" (p. 17). This sentiment about the means of professional growth is echoed by other organizations, including the National Association for the Education of Young Children (NAEYC) and the Council for Exceptional Children/Division for Early Childhood.

The HighScope adult training model rests on these principles too. HighScope advises program administrators to "allocate staff time for monthly inservice training sessions and assure these sessions lead to systematic application of child development principles in the classroom" (Schweinhart, 2004, p. 22). This recommendation is based not only on philosophy but is also grounded in research. The HighScope *Training for Quality* study (Epstein, 1993), summarized in chapter 4, identified the characteristics of professional development programs that produce real changes in teaching practices and real benefits for young children and their families. The rest of this chapter describes how those critical features are embodied in the HighScope training model.

The Value of High-Quality Professional Development

The National Association for the Education of Young Children, in its book *Preparing Early Childhood Professionals* (Hyson, 2003), says the value of high-quality teacher education and training is greater than learning specific skills or teaching techniques. As practitioners engage in professional development, "they become better able to make connections:

- between research and daily practice
- between challenging content standards and children's positive outcomes
- between a curriculum and an individual child
- between homes and schools
- between prior knowledge/experience and new information
- between national and state policies and their effects on children's lives
- between the program and diverse cultural communities
- between program staff and other professionals who can serve as sources of expertise and resources." (p. 4)

HighScope Principles of Active Participatory Learning for Adults

HighScope provides professional development programs for teachers and caregivers as well as for the supervisors who train and support these practitioners. HighScope has been training teachers since the 1960s and has worked with supervisors in a training of trainers model since the 1980s. Curriculum courses for teachers and caregivers train them to implement the infant-toddler and/or preschool educational approach. Professional development courses for supervisors include curriculum information as well as strategies to prepare and support staff as they implement HighScope programs with young children and families. These training courses and procedures for certifying trainers and teachers and accrediting programs are described in chapter 21.

HighScope staff designed these courses to address the shortfalls commonly found in early child-

Effective Professional Development Programs

Effective professional development programs apply the principles of active participatory learning to training adults. The following chart compares the characteristics of effective and ineffective professional development programs in preparing good teachers.

In *effective* professional development programs...	In *ineffective* professional development programs...
Inservice training follows a progression of interrelated topics, resulting in knowledge that is cumulative over the course of training.	Topics are not connected in any logical or cumulative fashion.
Training procedures are based on current knowledge about how adults learn. Trainers interact with teachers during group workshop presentations and make individual onsite visits to the classroom for observation and feedback.	Disconnected topics often mean a series of one-time presenters, and their methods of presentation may not be geared toward adult learning styles.
Training uses a curriculum model based on child development principles. The curriculum serves as a framework for applying and implementing new knowledge.	The information presented by trainers is not related to a curriculum or program philosophy, and it is not connected to daily program practices. Consequently, staff may emerge with a few interesting ideas but since they cannot readily fit them into the context of the overall program goals, there is no motivation to implement the ideas in any sustained manner.
Inservice training sessions explore strategies for practical application. Strategies then become practices in the actual work setting.	Theory is not accompanied by practical information. Staff are given no how-to guidelines for applying what they have learned.
Training is spread out over many months; staff alternate one week of workshop sessions with several weeks of application at their sponsoring agency. This cycle promotes adaptation and problem solving, and it highlights the progression of skills over time.	Discovery and application are disconnected. There is no natural cycle that alternates learning new ideas and trying them out in an interactive process over time.
The regularity of training and supervision means that follow-up opportunities are built into the model. Trainees can explore issues individually with their trainer as well as in group sessions with their peers.	Follow-up is absent. The real questions surface when staff attempt to implement what they have learned. With no forum for addressing their questions to individuals or groups, staff do not receive the ongoing help they need to apply the lessons of inservice training.

Source: *Training for Quality* (Epstein, 1993, pp. 6–7)

hood teacher preparation initiatives (see "Effective Professional Development Programs" on p. 224). The *Training for Quality* study, conducted with participants in 80 adult training courses and 366 HighScope and non-HighScope teachers nationwide, confirmed the value of active participatory learning for adults as well as children (Epstein, 1993). These features, described below, contribute significantly to improvements in program quality and thereby enhance young children's development.

▲ Integrated content

Adults understand and use information when the learning builds on itself. Therefore, professional development works best as a course of study in which teachers and caregivers systematically add to their knowledge and skills. Too often, inservice training jumps from one topic of the month to another; the focus and presenter change with each session. By contrast, when topics follow a logical sequence, participants can connect what they have already learned with new information and construct an overall framework to guide their work with children and families.

Each HighScope training course is organized to result in this type of cumulative knowledge and skill (also known as **integrated content**). The curriculum is introduced one topic at a time. Participants then gain in their depth of understanding as each succeeding topic refers to, builds on, and is connected to what has come before. Moreover, because the participants meet and/or interact online with the same trainer (or team of trainers) over time, there is continuity in what and how the content is presented. Trainees also have an opportunity to discuss and problem-solve ongoing implementation issues in person and/or an online forum.

▲ Presentation geared to adult learning

Just as HighScope teachers share control with children, HighScope trainers also encourage participants to take the initiative in their own learning (see "Principles of Adult Learning" on p. 226). Teachers and caregivers in HighScope training courses therefore make plans, carry out course assignments and activities, and reflect on what they have learned, as this teacher from Dayton, Ohio, attending a HighScope training reflects:

Just as children plan, do, and review in the HighScope classroom, adults in HighScope professional development courses make plans, carry out assignments and activities, and reflect on what they have learned.

> *I have decided HighScope training is like being a grandmother for the first time. When you let children satisfy their natural curiosity, give them time to explore their world, and nurture them, you are giving them what they need to learn now and also encouraging lifelong learning. The same is true of my own training. We were encouraged to voice doubts and ask questions, try things for ourselves, and enjoy the support of our trainer and peers. This course turned us all into lifelong HighScope Curriculum learners. We will continue to use and grow in our knowledge of this successful child- and adult-initiated program.*

To accommodate different learning styles, course work includes oral and visual presentations, individual projects, small- and large-group work, practice activities and role playing, and discussion and sharing in person and/or online. Local supervisors who are certified to conduct HighScope training use the same methods to mentor staff at their own agencies.

HighScope workshops are a good example of how training helps teachers and caregivers connect the lessons learned to their own work and home lives. Adults, like children of all ages, learn by doing. Courses therefore include many opportunities to explore concepts and try out ideas during workshop sessions. The principles apply equally well to workshops for parents, who also want to understand the curriculum and extend their children's learning at home.

Principles of Adult Learning

1. Learning is enhanced when it is immediately applicable to real-life contexts.
2. Learning is enhanced when adults have control or influence over the learning experience.
3. Learning depends on past and current experience.
4. Learning depends upon active involvement of the learner.
5. Learning depends upon a climate of respect and comfort.
6. Learning is enhanced when learners achieve self-direction.
7. Learning is enhanced when adults make connections.
8. Learning should account for individual differences in learning style.

Each HighScope workshop begins with an *opening activity.* Like the "Think About It" section that opens each chapter in this book, the opening activity helps people remember an experience or share an activity as a way to stimulate or even "shake up" their thinking about the topic.

The second part of the workshop is called *central ideas and practice.* Through a combination of presentations, handouts, group activities, and discussion, participants learn the main concepts about child development and teaching practices that are the focus of that session. This workshop component is analogous to the chapter sections in this book that explain why the topic is important and then detail the relevant HighScope principles and practices.

In planning the session, trained facilitators identify the major learning goals and objectives for participants (just as we identify learning objectives for each chapter of this book). Sometimes the sessions validate for participants what they already believe and do. At other times, the workshop challenges and expands their current way of thinking. Although changing attitudes and practices may be anxiety provoking for staff, it can inspire and reinvigorate them.

The third workshop component is the *application activity.* This process allows participants to further internalize the new information by applying it in a related situation, role play, or other hands-on activity (just as the teaching strategies in this book are elaborated with examples and anecdotes).

Finally, because the ultimate goal of training is to improve teaching practices, participants make *implementation plans* to use what they have learned when they return to work. For teachers and caregivers, the plan will focus on working with children and/or parents. For supervisors, the implementation plan may be a strategy for introducing curriculum ideas to staff during an onsite workshop or observation/feedback session. The "Try these Ideas Yourself" sections at the end of each chapter in this book likewise help readers solidify what they have learned and explore ways to apply these lessons to their current situation as a student, teacher, or supervisor.

▲ Articulated curriculum

A national survey of 671 NAEYC members (Epstein, Schweinhart, & McAdoo, 1996) revealed that most programs do not use a single, coherent curriculum. They either use a combination or no curriculum at all. Yet as chapter 1 of this book emphasizes, programs achieve the highest quality when they implement a unified curriculum model — an **articulated curriculum** — proven to be effective. The curriculum should have written documentation of its philosophy, a set of child development principles, and specific teaching strategies to promote and assess children's learning. HighScope's comprehensive curriculum model, as explained and practiced in training, meets all these requirements.

▲ Distributive learning

A commonplace observation is that "change is hard." Doing what we already know is easier. Even when people are open to altering their behavior, desire often exceeds ability, especially at first. Real change is gradual rather than sudden. HighScope, therefore, practices **distributive learning** and spreads out its training courses over several weeks or months. Days that participants

"As I plan workshops, I balance presenting information with involving participants. Just as we create active learning environments for children, we need to create them for the adults we are training."
— Supervisor, Milwaukee, Wisconsin

spend attending workshops alternate with weeks at their home site. This distribution allows training participants to try out what they have learned, to see what is or is not working, and to bring their successes and questions back to the group. Each session begins with an opportunity to troubleshoot issues and to review previous material, and concludes with a plan for implementing new ideas and solutions. In this way, the HighScope adult learning model employs the plan-do-review sequence that is also a key characteristic of the children's daily classroom routine.

Follow-up mechanisms

Participants in HighScope courses ask follow-up questions (in person and online) between and during subsequent sessions. But what happens when a training course ends? HighScope's website, additional in-person and online courses, publications, and electronic contact via e-mail and other social networking options provide ongoing information and technical support. In addition, regional, national, and international conferences provide opportunities for updating and networking.

HighScope recognizes that teachers and caregivers also benefit from immediate onsite assistance. Because it cannot directly reach tens of thousands of HighScope practitioners, HighScope began to offer a training-of-trainers approach in the early 1980s (see chapter 21). This method of training, in which in-house supervisors learn both the curriculum and how to train adults to implement it, empowers local agencies. HighScope Certified Trainers are able to conduct observation and feedback with teaching teams in the classroom and plan group workshops that are responsive to the specific professional development needs of their agencies.

Another type of onsite follow-up is **mentoring** or **coaching** by HighScope Certified Teachers who work with less experienced or untrained staff, especially in agencies without in-house trainers. Agencies do not always have sufficient resources to enroll all their teachers in training courses. Turnover also means that new staff enter the program after the agency's contracted training with HighScope is completed. In these situations, certified teachers who have demonstrated high levels of curriculum knowledge and implementation skills can mentor or coach assistants, coteachers, or other instructional peers in the organization. They can also be available to answer questions and help new staff work their way through online training courses. As mentors and coaches observe, provide feedback, and work alongside teachers-in-training, they use the same supportive strategies as do HighScope-trained supervisors (see "Mentoring" on this page).

Mentoring

The successful mentor...

- Is willing to listen
- Is sensitive to the coteacher's needs
- Is able to initiate and maintain the relationship
- Communicates feelings of acceptance
- Demonstrates willingness to share ideas and materials
- Is receptive to learning from the coteacher
- Is nurturing and supportive
- Respects the uniqueness and strengths of the coteacher
- Is confident, secure, flexible, altruistic, warm, and caring

Source: "Mentoring in the HighScope Preschool Classroom" (Ranweiler, 2001, p. 383)

Try These Ideas Yourself

1. Write down all the ways children learn. Write down all the ways adults learn. How are they the same? How are they different? (*Variation:* How did you learn best as a child? How do you learn best as an adult? What has remained the same? What has changed as you have gotten older?)

2. Think of a time you taught or mentored someone (e.g., teaching a sibling to ride a bike,

coaching a classmate for a science test, showing a friend how to knit or change a tire). In what ways were your strategies successful or unsuccessful? Based on what you learned in this chapter, how would you change your approach to better enable the other person's learning?

3. Keep a daily journal describing a recurring situation in the classroom in which you'd like to change your behavior (e.g., to help a child who runs away whenever it is cleanup time, to plan large-group times that will result in increased student attention and participation). What training, mentoring, or other support would help you handle this situation better? How could you go about getting the help and support you need? *(Variation:* Think of a problematic situation at home. What type of outside help or perspective would help you change your behavior?)

4. Share what you've learned from this book with another student or coworker who has never studied HighScope. What can you do to make the curriculum "come alive" for this person?

5. Below is a list of training methods that can add interest and variety to a presentation or workshop. Which have you experienced or used? Which were successful or unsuccessful?

Brainstorming	Press conferences
Case histories	Problem-solving
Contests	Projects
Debates	Guest speaker
Demonstrations	Quizzes
Whole-group discussions	PowerPoint presentations
Exercises	Role playing
Handouts	Skits
Field trips	Small-group work
Games	Songs and poems
Interviews	Storytelling
Lectures	Humor (cartoons, jokes)

Can you think of other strategies? Describe them and why/how you think they will work.

Mentoring or coaching by a HighScope Certified Teacher helps provide continuing support to less experienced staff.

What Professional Development and Certification Does HighScope Offer?

Think About It

A city building inspector has just informed you that the wiring in your house is outdated and is a fire hazard. To retain your homeowner's insurance, the house must be rewired — a substantial investment. You need to hire an electrician. How will you find someone to do the job?

Word-of-mouth from someone you know and trust is one option, but if things turn out badly, it could rupture family harmony or end a friendship. Another tactic is to check online listings or classified ads. You could get one or more bids and choose an electrician based on the one who returns your call or e-mail, is cheapest, and/or promises to do the job fastest.

Alternatively, you could consult a trade association for a list of licensed electricians in your area. You could contact several, ask for references, and question past clients about their work. A licensed electrician may cost more than a general or unlicensed contractor. However, according to the wise old expression, "the best is cheapest," spending more at the beginning to get the job done right ends up saving money in the long run.

When it comes to the safety of young children, qualified professionals are worth the price too! The "work" that early childhood teachers perform has lifelong implications for the health and development of those in their care. Children's well-being, in turn, affects family functioning. And, as the HighScope Perry Preschool Study and other research shows, the well-being of children and families determines their ability to become satisfied and contributing members of society.

The importance of hiring qualified professionals is recognized by the government agencies that license child care facilities. Although standards are not uniform and may not be sufficiently rigorous, most licensing codes contain requirements about staff degrees and training. Appropriate teacher training and **credentialing** is also the goal of institutions of higher education that design courses of study and seek accreditation through the National Council for Accreditation of Teacher Education (NCATE). Other professional organizations, such as the National Association for the Education of Young Children (NAEYC) and the National Association for Family Child Care (NAFCC), set objective standards for professional development and program accreditation as well. These organizations base their criteria on child development research and best practices.

As an advocate for high-quality early childhood programs, HighScope also feels an obligation to provide professional development that benefits staff, families, and children. It further seeks to ensure that the staff and programs who claim to use HighScope do in fact have the appropriate training and actually deliver the expected level of quality.

When a skilled worker holds a license from a recognized organization, this means he or she has received proper training, undergone an apprenticeship, and passed objective assessments

Chapter Learning Objectives

By the end of this chapter, you will be able to

- Describe why professional development and certification are important.
- Identify organizations with professional standards in early childhood education.
- Describe the types and structure of professional development courses offered by HighScope, what participants learn from them, and what type of follow-up support participants receive.
- Describe the levels and process of HighScope certification and accreditation.

of knowledge and skill. A customer hiring that worker has good reason to believe this person will do the job correctly. Likewise, when an early childhood program has the proper documentation from a recognized government or professional group, then parents and others can feel reassured that staff members and the agency meet critical minimal guidelines for safety and education. If the credentials further verify in-depth training, hands-on apprenticeships, and observed best practices, it is even more likely that the agency and its staff will provide high-quality services.

Why Professional Development and Certification Are Important

In Marilou Hyson's introduction to NAEYC's *Preparing Early Childhood Professionals* (2003), she summarizes decades of research with the following statement:

"If early childhood practitioners have higher levels of formal education and specialized training, they are much more likely in their work with young children and families to use the evidence-based practices and possess the ongoing professional commitment we know are necessary to make a positive difference in children's lives." (p. 3)

The previous chapter focused on the training *process*. This final chapter emphasizes why training *content* is also critical. Studies conclusively show that the overall level of teachers' formal education is positively and significantly related to program quality and child learning (Barnett, 2003; National Research Council, 2001). For example, cross-national analyses of the HighScope IEA Preprimary Project found that the level of their teachers' education when children were four years old was significantly related to the children's language performance at age seven (Montie et al., 2006).

Beyond this general educational requirement, however, teacher training must also be *specific and specialized* to achieve maximum impact. That is, early childhood teachers are most effective when the courses and inservice workshops they attend specifically address early childhood development, early childhood curriculum and assessment, and early childhood teaching practices.

Further, it is not sufficient to just provide appropriate content in training courses. The field must also assess whether teachers *understand and use* the specialized information to implement high-quality programs. A valid system for *credentialing* teachers should be based on their grasp and application of developmental knowledge and best practices. Without proof of high quality, as implemented by practitioners, there is no guarantee that the immediate and lifelong benefits of early childhood education will be realized. This is the enduring message of the HighScope Perry Preschool Study and HighScope's ongoing work (Schweinhart et al., 2005).

Hyson (2003) continues in discussing NAEYC's standards for professional development:

"The kind of professional development that provides that sound base is not accomplished cheaply or easily. Degrees matter, but a degree alone...is not a guarantee of professional competence. What does matter is what early childhood professionals know, what they are able to do, and the dispositions or "habits of mind" they possess to nurture and promote children's development and learning

Terms Used in This Chapter

• credentialing • curriculum courses • training of trainers (TOT) course • curriculum evaluation • training evaluation • HighScope Certified Teacher • HighScope Certified Trainer • HighScope Accredited Program as a result of their preparation and continuing development." (p. 4)

Toward that end, organizations such as NAEYC, the National Board for Professional Teaching Standards, and NCATE have advocated for establishing professional standards in early childhood education. They emphasize knowledge and practice, attempt to define standards in measurable terms, and provide guidelines on how to evaluate whether teachers have met them.

Likewise, HighScope professional development includes content specific to early learning and program practice, and entails systematic procedures to assess whether participants understand *and* use the information they learn in their interactions with children, families, and colleagues. Because quality is determined by what takes place in the classroom, training room, and office, HighScope certifies teachers and trainers and accredits programs. To qualify, participants must meet objective and rigorous criteria encompassing active involvement in the training; completion of site-based assignments; reflective writing; and observed behavior while teaching children, training adults, and/or administering programs.

❖

In this chapter, you will learn about the types of courses HighScope offers and its system for credentialing practitioners, supervisors, and agencies.[1] HighScope conducts training onsite around the country and the world and at its headquarters in Ypsilanti, Michigan. Many courses are also available online, with active facilitation by HighScope staff or field consultants. In addition to the courses described here, HighScope trainers can customize onsite training to meet specific programmatic needs, while its online training provides the flexibility that allows practitioners to fit training into their busy work and family schedules. HighScope continually updates the scope and content of courses and the delivery systems available to students of the HighScope Curriculum.

HighScope Professional Development Courses

HighScope's inservice training and professional development programs in early childhood are organized into two basic categories. HighScope offers multisession **curriculum courses** for teachers and caregivers at both the infant-toddler and preschool levels. These courses provide comprehensive coverage of the HighScope Curriculum, including its underlying philosophy and approach to adult-child interaction, the learning environment, the daily routine, teamwork, parent involvement, curriculum content (key developmental indicators [KDIs]), and child and program assessment. These courses are available in person and/or online.

The second type of course offering is its **training of trainers (TOT) course.** For participants who have completed the curriculum training, the TOT course prepares them to train and support others to implement the HighScope educational approach. The strategies learned in this course apply not only to curriculum training but also to performing many other adult education and support activities. Further, learning effective presentation techniques also gives participants confidence in public speaking and leading sessions at professional development conferences. Those who enroll in the TOT course are typically in supervisory positions, such as center directors, education coordinators, or curriculum specialists. However, many HighScope Certified Teachers also take this level of training to mentor and coach their colleagues in the classroom.

HighScope courses are aligned with the Child Development Associate (CDA) requirements and undergraduate (two- and four-year) and graduate degree programs. Students who successfully complete HighScope Curriculum and TOT courses can earn continuing education units (CEUs) and undergraduate and/or graduate college credit through reciprocal arrangements between institutions of higher education and HighScope.

[1]This chapter describes course offerings for programs serving preschool-age children. HighScope offers comparable courses at the infant-toddler level as well as training in the use of the Ready Schools Assessment (HighScope Educational Research Foundation, 2006) for elementary schools. In addition, HighScope regional, national, and international conferences offer additional seminars and workshops on other specialized topics such as grant and proposal writing, working with children having special needs, working with children who are English language learners, designing and evaluating state prekindergarten programs, aligning HighScope with state and professional standards, and using HighScope in other countries and cultures.

▲ Curriculum courses

HighScope offers multisession, multiweek courses in the infant-toddler and preschool curriculum. These courses are geared toward practitioners. Supervisors who wish to become HighScope trainers also take the curriculum courses. The workshops and hands-on practice give them a solid grounding in the curriculum's principles and methods so they can effectively transmit it to others.

HighScope curriculum courses provide in-depth coverage of the topics presented in the second and third parts of this book, namely teaching practices and curriculum content. The sessions on teaching practices focus on adult-child interaction strategies appropriate for that age group, indoor and outdoor learning environments, daily routines and schedules, teamwork, and working with families. Workshops and readings focus on early childhood development and KDIs for the age range covered. Students in these courses also become acquainted with HighScope's observation-based assessment tools and practice writing objective anecdotes.

Course participants engage in hands-on learning in small- and large-group activities during workshops and in the training assignments they complete at their home agencies. Training sessions are distributed over time so participants can practice what they are learning in the weeks between sessions. Participants receive a library of texts, audiovisual materials, study guides, and assessment tools. They develop a working knowledge of the HighScope approach through the following course activities:

HighScope courses include workshops, online training, practice, reflective writing assignments, and mentoring.

Workshops. Face-to-face and online sessions cover theory, practice, and assessment with ample opportunities for sharing and reflection. Teachers are actively involved in group work during training weeks, facilitated by the in-person or online trainer.

Practice implementation. In the weeks between sessions, teachers apply what they have learned in their own classrooms. At the beginning of each week, they review implementation and assessment issues with their trainer and coteachers and share problems and solutions, face-to-face or online.

Training assignments. Participants complete reading and reflective writing assignments during and between training sessions. Through these assignments, they learn and internalize the central components of the HighScope early childhood curriculum. They receive face-to-face or online feedback on the assignments they submit.

Site visits and ongoing mentoring. The HighScope trainer visits each classroom to observe and provide feedback on implementation. An agency-based trainer, certified through the TOT course, continues to provide this support after the training ends. Resources available on HighScope website's also assist practitioners and mentors.

▲ Training of trainers (TOT) course

The HighScope TOT course is designed for those who have completed extensive training in the curriculum (infant-toddler and/or preschool) and want to extend their skills to training others in the educational approach. Like the curriculum courses, the TOT course is a multisession, multiweek endeavor in which active learning workshops and seminars alternate with practical learning assignments at the participants' home agencies.

The TOT course covers in-depth the principles of adult learning and strategies of adult supervision and support. Participants learn how to design and present workshops and conduct observation and feedback with staff. They study the HighScope program and child assessment instruments (i.e., Program Quality Assessment [PQA] and COR Advantage) in greater detail and practice using them to reach standard levels of reliability and validity. One of the most important lessons participants learn is that change can be difficult and that teachers require understanding along with instruc-

HighScope certification guarantees not only that teachers know about early development and best practices but also that they can apply this knowledge in working with children in the classroom.

tion. The TOT course therefore explores strategies to bring about gradual but authentic change in teaching practices, as noted by this supervisor from Dayton, Ohio:

> *I have altered my attempts to change it all, teach it all. HighScope has provided me with the information to decide which content is most relevant, appropriate, and useful in any given situation rather than trying to force all the change in a short period of time. Select a slice, a modifiable issue, then give support and allow time for change.*

In addition to gaining knowledge and skills, participants network with colleagues throughout the training course. These associations extend well beyond the training period. Because HighScope's onsite training projects bring together agencies in close geographic proximity, participants may establish arrangements to share and exchange training resources and expertise. When participants are drawn from the same source, such as Head Start education coordinators or a statewide prekindergarten initiative, training helps them coordinate implementation and dissemination efforts.

Each participant in the TOT course identifies a *training classroom,* usually at his or her home agency, and works with teachers at that site to train them in the use of the HighScope Curriculum. Throughout the course, participants keep extensive notes (called *trainer reports*) to document their work with staff in the training classroom. Near the end of the TOT course, participants answer "questions from the field" to show their mastery of the curriculum. They also make daily routine demonstration videos in their training classroom, which they review with their trainer, to document their implementation skills and ability to reflect on their own strengths and modifiable issues. In addition, each participant presents a workshop to his or her peers and conducts observation and feedback sessions with staff in the training classroom. These activities are observed and evaluated by the HighScope trainer. Finally, course participants complete a child study by writing extensive anecdotal notes on one child in the training classroom and developing plans based on these observations.

At the end of the TOT course, the HighScope trainer evaluates participants on both their curriculum and training knowledge and skills. For the **curriculum evaluation,** the HighScope trainer grades the child study, accurate administration of the PQA, and demonstration daily routine video. The trainer's assessment of the participant's peer workshop, observation/feedback session with staff, and trainer reports are the components of the **training evaluation.** Participants who meet HighScope's rigorous requirements on both the curriculum and training evaluation become HighScope Certified Trainers.

▲ Follow-up

After participants complete their training, they can update their knowledge and skills by visiting the HighScope website (www.highscope.org), where they will find video clips demonstrating the HighScope Curriculum in action, information and resources about the HighScope Curriculum, teaching and training strategies, current course offerings, and research reports. Finally, practitioners are updated through HighScope's annual international conference in Michigan and regional conferences throughout the country. HighScope Institutes in other countries also hold annual conferences for their members.

HighScope Certification and Accreditation

To guarantee quality, HighScope awards *certification to teachers and trainers* and *accreditation to programs* that meet a set of rigorous standards. Certification and accreditation are good for three years, after which they must be renewed through another application and evaluation process.

The following is a summary of the standards and qualifications at each level of recognition.

▲ Teacher certification

To become a **HighScope Certified Teacher,** a practitioner must attend a curriculum course (or equivalent training) and complete all the assignments. Applicants are then observed in their program setting and must achieve high scores on the classroom sections of the PQA. They also collect anecdotal notes and complete two child observations over several months, complete a series of planning forms, and document and reflect on their implementation practices. Depending on the curriculum course attended, certified teachers and caregivers also receive an endorsement in a specific developmental level (infant-toddler and/or preschool). A HighScope Certified Teacher is qualified to use that title and teach in a HighScope program in his or her area(s) of endorsement.

▲ Trainer certification

To become a **HighScope Certified Trainer,** an individual must complete both a curriculum course (or equivalent training) and a TOT course. As noted earlier in this chapter, applicants are evaluated on their knowledge and skills with regard to both curriculum implementation and adult training practices. Evaluation involves reports and assignments completed during the course, administration and scoring of the PQA and COR Advantage, a peer workshop presentation, and successful mentoring and observation/feedback with staff at the training site. HighScope Certified Trainers are qualified to use that title and to train staff in their own or an affiliated agency in the use of the HighScope Curriculum. They can also prepare and recommend teachers for certification and present HighScope workshops at conferences.

▲ Program accreditation

For a site to become a **HighScope Accredited Program,** it must have a HighScope Certified Teacher in each classroom and the agency must have an ongoing relationship with a HighScope Certified Trainer (either within the agency or close enough to provide regular site visits and support). In addition, programs must achieve high scores on both the classroom and agency sections of the PQA. HighScope Accredited Programs are qualified to use that title and operate as HighScope demonstration programs in the area(s) where staff have curriculum endorsements.

Try These Ideas Yourself

1. What do you consider the minimal standards an early childhood program should meet? What would make a program moderately good? What would characterize a high-quality program? Get a copy of your state's child care licensing standards. Do you consider these standards descriptive of minimal, moderate, or high-quality programs? What (if any) changes would you recommend?

2. Pick an area or topic from this book you are particularly interested in applying to your work or personal life (e.g., using encouragement rather than praise [see pp. 32–33]). Set a goal to achieve high-quality knowledge and practice in this area. How will you measure whether you have achieved your goal (i.e., what attitudes and behaviors will you look for)? How long will it take to reach your goal? Self-assess your knowledge and skills now. After the amount of time you identified as necessary to reach your goal has elapsed, do another self-assessment. At that point, ask yourself how much you have changed. Acknowledge your improvement. Decide if you want to continue growing in that area and/or choose another goal and repeat the process.

3. Create your own professional development plan. List your professional goals, for example, what degree(s) and certification(s) you want, the kind of agency you want to work in, the kind(s) of children you want to work with, and whether you want to teach and/or be an administrator. Then, for each goal, write down the action steps and timeline needed to achieve it. Periodically review your plan to assess your progress. If necessary, change your goals and the strategies you will use to achieve them. (*Variation:* Share your plan with a family member, friend, or colleague. Ask that individual for feedback based on what they know of your strengths and interests.)

References

Aboud, F. E. (2005). The development of prejudice in childhood and adolescents. In J. F. Dovidio, P. Glick, & L. A. Rudman (Eds.), *On the nature of prejudice: Fifty years after Allport* (pp. 310–326). Malden, MA: Blackwell. http://dx.doi.org/10.1002/9780470773963

Adams, M. (1990). *Beginning to read: Thinking and learning about print.* Cambridge, MA: MIT Press.

Administration for Children and Families, Head Start Bureau. (2002, October). *Program Performance Standards and other regulations.* Washington, DC: US Government Printing Office.

American Academy of Pediatrics. (2006). *The importance of play in promoting healthy child development and maintaining strong parent-child bonds.* Elk Grove Village, IL: Author. http://dx.doi.org/10.1542/peds.2006-2697

American Academy of Pediatrics, Committee on Public Education. (2001). Children, adolescents, and television. *Pediatrics, 107*(2), 423–426. http://dx.doi.org/10.1542/peds.107.2.423

Anthony, J. L. (2002). Structure of preschool phonological sensitivity: Overlapping sensitivity to rhyme, words, syllables, and phonemes. *Journal of Experimental Child Psychology, 82,* 65–92. http://dx.doi.org/10.1006/jecp.2002.2677

Aronson, S. S. (Ed.). (2012). *Healthy young children: A manual for programs* (5th ed.). Washington, DC: National Association for the Education of Young Children.

Arts Education Partnership. (1998). *Young children and the arts: Making creative connections — A report of the Task Force on Children's Learning and the Arts: Birth to age eight.* Washington, DC: Author.

Atance, C. M., Bélanger, M., & Meltzoff, A. (2010). Preschoolers' understanding of others' desires: Fulfilling mine enhances my understanding of yours. *Developmental Psychology, 46*(6), 1505–1513. http://dx.doi.org/10.1037/a0020374

Baker, L., Serpell, R., & Sonnenschein, S. (1995). Opportunities for literacy learning in the homes of urban preschoolers. In L. M. Morrow (Ed.), *Family literacy: connections in schools and communities* (pp. 236–252). Newark, DE: International Reading Association.

Bandura, A. (1994). Self-efficacy. In V. S. Ramachandran (Ed.), *Encyclopedia of human behavior* (Vol. 4, pp. 71–81). New York, NY: Academic Press.

Barnett, W. S. (2003). *Better teachers, better preschools: Student achievement linked to teacher qualifications.* New Brunswick, NJ: National Institute for Early Education Research.

Barnett, W. S., Epstein, D. J., Carolan, M. E., Fitzgerald, J., Ackerman, D. J., & Friedman, A. H. (2010). *The state of preschool 2010.* New Brunswick, NJ: National Institute for Early Education Research.

Baroody, A. J. (2000). Does mathematics instruction for three- to five-year olds really make sense? *Young Children, 55*(4), 61–67.

Battistich, V., Solomon, D., & Watson, M. (1998, April). *Sense of community as a mediating factor in promoting children's social and ethical development.* Paper presented at the meeting of the American Educational Research Association, San Diego, CA.

Baumeister, R. F., Campbell, J. D., Krueger, J. L., & Vohs, K. D. (2004). Exploding the self-esteem myth. *Scientific American, 292*(1), 84–91. http://dx.doi.org/10.1038/scientificamerican0105-84

Belsky, J. (2002). Quality counts: Amount of child care and children's social-emotional development. *Journal of Developmental and Behavioral Pediatrics, 23*(3), 167–170. http://dx.doi.org/10.1097/00004703-200206000-00010

Benson, J. B. (1997). The development of planning: It's about time. In S. L. Friedman & E. L. Scholnick (Eds.), *The developmental psychology of planning: Why, how, and when do we plan?* (pp. 43–75). Mahwah NJ: Lawrence Erlbaum.

Bereiter, C., & Engelmann, S. (1966). *Teaching disadvantaged children in the preschool.* Englewood Cliffs, NJ: Prentice-Hall.

Bergen, B. (1988a). Methods of studying play. In D. Bergen (Ed.), *Play as a medium for learning and development* (pp. 49–66). Portsmouth, NH: Heinemann.

Bergen, B. (1988b). Stages of play development. In D. Bergen (Ed.), *Play as a medium for learning and development* (pp. 27–44). Portsmouth, NH: Heinemann.

Berk, L. E. (2011). *Infants and children: Prenatal through middle childhood* (7th ed.). Boston, MA: Pearson/Allyn & Bacon.

Berry, C. F., & Sylva, K. (1987). *The plan-do-review cycle in HighScope: Its effects on children and staff.* Unpublished manuscript, available from HighScope Educational Research Foundation, Ypsilanti, MI.

Bishop, A., Yopp, R. H., & Yopp, H. K. (2000). *Ready for reading: A handbook for parents of preschoolers.* Boston, MA: Allyn & Bacon.

Black, J. E., Jones, T. E., Nelson, C. A., & Greenough, W. T. (1998). Neuronal plasticity and the developing brain. In N. E. Alessi, J. T. Coyle, S. I. Harrison, & S. Eth (Eds.), *Handbook of child and adolescent psychiatry: Basic science and psychiatric treatment* (Vol. 6, pp. 31–53). New York: Wiley.

Bloom, P. J., & Sheerer, M. (1992). The effect of leadership training on child care program quality. *Early Childhood Research Quarterly, 7*(4), 579–594. http://dx.doi.org/10.1016/0885-2006(92)90112-C

Bodrova, E., & Leong, D. (2007). *Tools of the mind: The Vygotskian approach to early childhood education* (2nd ed.). New York, NY: Prentice Hall.

Bourtchouladze, R. (2004). *Memories are made of this: How memory works in humans and animals* (2nd ed.) New York, NY: Columbia University Press.

Bowerman, M. (1996). Learning how to structure space for language: A cross-linguistic perspective. In P. Bloom, M. A. Peterson, L. Nadel, & M. F. Garrett (Eds.), *Language and space* (pp. 385–436). Cambridge, MA: MIT Press.

Brand, S. (1996, January). Making parent involvement a reality: Helping teachers develop partnerships with parents. *Young Children, 51*(2), 76–81.

Brereton, A. (2008). Sign language use and the appreciation of diversity in hearing classrooms. *Early Years: An International Journal of Research and Development, 28*(3), 311–324. http://dx.doi.org/10.1080/09575140802393702

Bruner, J. S. (1986). *Actual minds, possible worlds.* Cambridge, MA: Harvard University Press.

Bruner, J. S., Olver, R. R., & Greenfield, P. M. (1966). *Studies in cognitive growth.* New York, NY: Wiley.

Calkins, L. (with Bellino, L.). (1997). *Raising lifelong learners: A parents' guide.* Cambridge, MA: Perseus Books.

Campbell, P. F. (1997). Connecting instructional practice to student thinking. *Teaching Children Mathematics, 4*, 106–110.

Campbell, P. F. (1999). Fostering each child's understanding of mathematics. In C. Seefeldt (Ed.), *The early childhood curriculum: Current findings in theory and practice* (3rd ed., pp. 106–132). New York, NY: Teachers College Press.

Carlsson-Paige, N. (2008). *Taking back childhood: Helping your kids thrive in a fast-paced, media-saturated, violence-filled world.* New York, NY: Penguin.

Case, R. (1985). *Intellectual development: Birth to adulthood.* Orlando, FL: Academic Press.

Catherwood, D. (2000). New views on the young brain: Offerings from developmental psychology to early childhood education. *Contemporary Issues in Early Childhood Education, 1*(1), 23–35. http://dx.doi.org/10.2304/ciec.2000.1.1.4

Centers for Disease Control and Prevention. (2010). *The association between school-based physical activity, including physical education, and academic performance.* Atlanta, GA: US Department of Health and Human Services.

Chafel, J. A. (1984). "Call the police, okay?" Social comparison by young children during play in preschool. *Early Child Development and Care, 14*, 201–215. http://dx.doi.org/10.1080/0300443840140303

Chalufour, I., & Worth, K. (2003). *Discovering nature with young children.* St. Paul, MN: Redleaf Press.

Chapman, R. S. (2000). Children's language learning: An interactionist perspective. *Journal of Child Psychology and Psychiatry, 41*, 33–54. http://dx.doi.org/10.1111/1469-7610.00548

Cheatham, G. A., & Ro, Y. E. (2010, July). Young English learners' interlanguage as a context for language and early literacy development. *Young Children, 65*(4), 18–23.

Chess, S., & Alexander, T. (1996). Temperament. In M. Lewis (Ed.), *Child and adolescent psychiatry: A comprehensive textbook* (2nd ed., pp. 170–181). Baltimore, MD: Williams & Wilkins.

Christ, T., & Wang, X. C. (2010). Bridging the vocabulary gap: What the research tells us about vocabulary instruction in early childhood. *Young Children, 65*(4), 84–91.

Church, E. L. (2003). Scientific thinking: Step-by-step. *Scholastic Early Childhood Today, 17*(6), 35–41.

Clay, M. M. (2000). *Concepts about print: What have children learned about the way we print language?* Auckland, New Zealand: Heinemann.

Clements, D. H. (1999). The effective use of computers with young children. In J. V. Copley (Ed.), *Mathematics in the early years* (pp. 119–128). Reston, VA: National Council of Teachers of Mathematics and Washington, DC: National Association for the Education of Young Children.

Clements, D. H. (2002). Computers in early childhood mathematics. *Contemporary Issues in Early Childhood, 3*(2), 160–181. http://dx.doi.org/10.2304/ciec.2002.3.2.2

Clements, D. H. (2004a). Geometric and spatial thinking in early childhood education. In D. H. Clements, J. Samara, & A.-M. DiBiase (Eds.), *Engaging young children in mathematics: Standards for early childhood mathematics education* (pp. 267–297). Mahweh, NJ: Lawrence Erlbaum.

Clements, D. H. (2004b). Major themes and recommendations. In D. H. Clements, J. Sarama, & A-M. DiBiase (Eds.), *Engaging young children in mathematics: Standards for early childhood mathematics education* (pp. 7–72). Mahwah, NJ: Lawrence Erlbaum.

Clements, D. H., & Sarama, J. (2007). Early childhood mathematics learning. In F. K. Lester, Jr., (Ed.), *Second handbook of research on mathematics teaching and learning* (pp. 461–555). New York, NY: Information Age.

Clements, D. H., Sarama, J., & DiBiase, A.-M. (Eds.). (2004). *Engaging young children in mathematics: Standards for early childhood mathematics education*. Mahweh, NJ: Lawrence Erlbaum.

Clements, D. H., & Stephan, M. (2004). Measurement in pre-K to grade 2 mathematics. In D. H. Clements, J. Samara, & A.-M. DiBiase (Eds.), *Engaging young children in mathematics: Standards for early childhood mathematics education* (pp. 299–317). Mahweh, NJ: Lawrence Erlbaum.

Colker, L. J. (2005). *The cooking book: Fostering young children's learning and delight*. Washington, DC: National Association for the Education of Young Children.

Common Core State Standards Initiative. (2012). *Common core state standards: Kindergarten*. Washington, DC: Author. Retrieved from www.corestandards.org/

Copley, J. V. (2010). *The young child and mathematics* (2nd ed.). Washington, DC: National Association for the Education of Young Children and Reston, VA: National Council for Teachers of Mathematics.

Copple, C., & Bredekamp, S. (Eds.). (2009). *Developmentally appropriate practice in early childhood programs serving children from birth through age 8* (3rd ed.). Washington, DC: National Association for the Education of Young Children.

Creasey, G. L., Jarvis, P. A., & Berk, L. E. (1998). Play and social competence. In O. N. Saracho & B. Spodek (Eds.), *Multiple perspectives on play in early childhood education* (pp. 116–143). Albany, NY: State University of New York.

Cummings, C. (2000). *Winning strategies for classroom management*. Alexandria, VA: Association for Supervision and Curriculum Development.

Curenton, S., & Justice, L. M. (2004). Low-income preschoolers' use of decontextualized discourse: Literate language features in spoken narratives. *Language, Speech, and Hearing Services in Schools*, *35*, 240–253.

Curry, N. E., & Johnson, C. N. (1990). *Beyond self-esteem: Developing a genuine sense of human value*. Washington, DC: National Association for the Education of Young Children.

Damon, W. (1990). *The moral child: Nurturing children's natural moral growth*. New York, NY: Free Press.

Daniels, M. (2001). *Dancing with words: Signing for hearing children's literacy*. Westport, CT: Bergin & Garvey.

DeBruin-Parecki, A., & Hohmann, M. (2003). *Letter links: Alphabet learning with children's names*. Ypsilanti, MI: HighScope Press.

Denham, S. (2006). The emotional basis of learning and development in early childhood education. In B. Spodek & O. N. Saracho (Eds.), *Handbook of research on the education of young children* (pp. 85–104). Mahwah, NJ: Erlbaum.

Derman-Sparks, L., & Edwards, J. O. (2010). *Anti-bias education for young children and ourselves*. Washington, DC: National Association for the Education of Young Children.

DeVries, R., & Sales, C. (2011). *Ramps & pathways: A constructivist approach to physics with young children*. Washington, DC: National Association for the Education of Young Children.

DeVries, R., & Zan, B. (2003). When children make rules. *Educational Leadership*, *61*(1), 64–67.

DeVries, R., & Zan, B. (2012). *Moral classrooms, moral children: Creating a constructivist atmosphere in early education* (2nd ed.). New York, NY: Teachers College Press.

Dewey, J. (1938/1963). *Experience and education*. New York, NY: Macmillan.

Dickinson, D. K., & Porche, M. V. (2011). Relation between language experiences in preschool classrooms and children's kindergarten and fourth-grade language and reading abilities. *Child Development*, *82*(3), 870–886. http://dx.doi.org/10.1111/j.1467-8624.2011.01576.x

Dickinson, D. K., & Tabors, P. O. (2002). Fostering language and literacy in classrooms and homes. *Young Children*, *57*(2), 10–18.

Dietze, B., & Kashin, D. (2011). *Playing and learning in early childhood education*. New York, NY: Prentice Hall.

DiNatale, L. (2002). Developing high-quality family involvement programs in early childhood settings. *Young Children*, *57*(5), 90–95.

Dowling, J. L., & Mitchell, T. C. (2007). *I belong: Active learning for children with special needs*. Ypsilanti, MI: HighScope Press.

Duncan, G. J., Dowsett, C. J., Claessens, A., Magnuson, K., Huston, A. C., Klebanov, P.,…Brooks-Gunn, J. (2007). School readiness and later achievement. *Developmental Psychology*, *43*(6), 1428–1446. http://dx.doi.org/10.1037/0012-1649.43.6.1428.supp

Dunn, J. (1998). *The beginnings of social understanding*. Cambridge, MA: Harvard University Press.

Dweck, C. S. (2002). The development of ability conceptions. In A.Wigfield & J. S. Eccles (Eds.), *Development of achievement motivation* (pp. 57–90). San Diego, CA: Academic Press.

Early, D., & Winton, P. (2001). Preparing the workforce: Early childhood teacher preparation at 2- and 4-year institutions of higher education. *Early Childhood Research Quarterly, 16*(3), 285–306. http://dx.doi.org/10.1016/S0885-2006(01)00106-5

Eisenberg, N., Spinrad, T. L., & Sadovsky, A. (2006). Empathy-related responding in children. In M. Killen & J. G. Smetana (Eds.), *Handbook of moral development* (pp. 517–553). Mahwah, NJ: Lawrence Erlbaum.

Elias, M. J., Zins, J. E., Weissberg, K. S., Frey, M. T., Greenberg, N. M., Kessler, R.,…Shriver, T. P. (1997). *Promoting social and emotional learning: Guidelines for educators.* Alexandria, VA: Association for Supervision and Curriculum Development.

Epstein, A. S. (1993). *Training for quality: Improving early childhood programs through systematic inservice training.* Ypsilanti, MI: HighScope Press.

Epstein, A. S. (2003). How planning and reflection develop young children's thinking skills. *Young Children, 58*(5), 28–36.

Epstein, A. S. (2007). *The intentional teacher: Choosing the best strategies for young children's learning.* Washington, DC: National Association for the Education of Young Children.

Epstein, A. S. (2009a). *Me, you, us: Social-emotional learning in preschool.* Ypsilanti, MI: HighScope Press and Washington, DC: National Association for the Education of Young Children.

Epstein, A. S. (2009b). *Numbers Plus Preschool Mathematics Curriculum.* Ypsilanti, MI: HighScope Press.

Epstein, A. S. (2012a). *Approaches to learning.* Ypsilanti, MI: HighScope Press.

Epstein, A. S. (2012b). *Creative arts.* Ypsilanti, MI: HighScope Press.

Epstein, A. S. (2012c). *Language, literacy, and communication.* Ypsilanti, MI: HighScope Press.

Epstein, A. S. (2012d). *Mathematics.* Ypsilanti, MI: HighScope Press.

Epstein, A. S. (2012e). *Physical development and health.* Ypsilanti, MI: HighScope Press.

Epstein, A. S. (2012f). *Science and technology.* Ypsilanti, MI: HighScope Press.

Epstein, A. S. (2012g). *Social and emotional development.* Ypsilanti, MI: HighScope Press.

Epstein, A. S. (2012h). *Social studies.* Ypsilanti, MI: HighScope Press.

Epstein, A. S., Gainsley, S., Hohmann, M., Jurkiewicz, T., Lockhart, S., Marshall, B., & Montie, J. (2013). *Program Quality Assessment Form B — Agency Items for infant-toddler and preschool programs.* Ypsilanti, MI: HighScope Press.

Epstein, A. S., & Hohmann, M. (2012). *The HighScope Preschool Curriculum.* Ypsilanti, MI: HighScope Press.

Epstein, A. S., Marshall, B., & Gainsley, S. (2014a). *COR Advantage: User guide.* Ypsilanti, MI: HighScope Press.

Epstein, A. S., Marshall, B., & Gainsley, S. (2014b). *COR Advantage 1.5: Scoring guide.* Ypsilanti, MI: HighScope Press.

Epstein, A. S., Marshall, B., Gainsley, S., Red-e Set Grow, Albro, C., Claxton, J.,…Smith, E. V. (2014). *COR Advantage 1.5* [Computerized assessment system]. Online at http://www.coradvantage.org.

Epstein, A. S., Schweinhart, L. J., & McAdoo, L. (1996). *Models of early childhood education.* Ypsilanti, MI: HighScope Press.

Epstein, A. S., & Trimis, E. (2002). *Supporting young artists: The development of the visual arts in young children.* Ypsilanti, MI: HighScope Press.

Erikson, E. (1950). *Childhood and society.* New York: Norton.

Evans, B. (2002). *You can't come to my birthday party! Conflict resolution with young children.* Ypsilanti, MI: HighScope Press.

Fantuzzo, J. W., Perry, M. A., & McDermott, P. (2004). Preschool approaches to learning and their relationship to other relevant classroom competencies for low-income children. *School Psychology Quarterly, 19*(3), 212–230. http://dx.doi.org/10.1521/scpq.19.3.212.40276

Ferreiro, E., & Teberosky, A. (1982). *Literacy before schooling.* Portsmouth, NH: Heinemann.

Fiske, E. B. (Ed.). (1999). *Champions of change: The impact of the arts on learning.* Washington, DC: Arts Education Partnership and the President's Committee on the Arts and Humanities.

Fitch, M., Huston, A. C., & Wright, J. C. (1993). From television forms to genre schemata: Children's perceptions of television reality. In G. L. Berry & J. K. Asamen (Eds.), *Children and television: Images in a changing sociocultural world* (pp. 38–52). Newbury Park, CA: Sage.

Flavell, J. H., Miller, P. H., & Miller, S. A. (2001). *Cognitive development* (4th ed.). New York, NY: Prentice Hall.

Fox, L., & Lentini, R. H. (2006). "You got it!" Teaching social and emotional skills. *Young Children, 61*(6), 36–42.

Friedman, H. S., & Martin, L. R. (2011). *The Longevity Project: Surprising discoveries for health and long life from the landmark eight-decade study.* New York, NY: Hudson Street Press.

Gainsley, S. (2008). *From message to meaning: Using a daily message board in the preschool classroom.* Ypsilanti, MI: HighScope Press.

Gallahue, D. L. (1995). Transforming physical education curriculum. In S. Bredekamp & T. Rosegrant (Eds.), *Reaching potentials: Transforming early childhood curriculum and assessment* (Vol. 2, pp. 125–144). Washington, DC: National Association for the Education of Young Children.

Gallahue, D. L., & Donnelly, F. C. (2003). *Developmental physical education for all children* (4th ed.). Champaign, IL: Human Kinetics.

Gardner, H. (1991). *The unschooled mind: How children think and how schools should teach.* New York, NY: Basic Books.

Gartrell, D. (1995). Misbehavior or mistaken behavior. *Young Children, 50*(5), 27–34.

Gartrell, D. (2006). The beauty of class meetings. *Young Children, 61*(6), 54–55.

Gelman, S. (1999). Concept development in preschool children. In *Dialogue on early childhood science, mathematics, and technology education.* Washington, DC: American Association for the Advancement of Science. Retrieved from http://www.project2061.org/publications/earlychild/online/default.htm

Gelman, R., & Baillargeon, R. (1983). A review of some Piagetian concepts. In P. H. Mussen (Ed.), *Handbook of child psychology socialization, personality and social development* (pp. 167–230). New York: John Wiley & Sons.

Gelman, R., & Brenneman, K. (2004). Science learning pathways for young children. *Early Childhood Research Quarterly, 19*(1), 150–158. http://dx.doi.org/10.1016/j.ecresq.2004.01.009

Gelman, R., & Gallistel, C. R. (1978/1986). *The child's understanding of number.* Cambridge, MA: Harvard University Press.

Geography Education Standards Project. (1994). *Geography for life: National education standards—1994.* Washington, DC: Author.

Giles, J. W., & Heyman, G. D. (2005a). Preschoolers use trait-relevant information to evaluate the appropriateness of an aggressive response. *Aggressive Behavior, 31*(5), 498–509. http://dx.doi.org/10.1002/ab.20086

Giles, J. W., & Heyman, G. D. (2005b). Young children's beliefs about the relationship between gender and aggressive behavior. *Child Development, 76*(1), 107–121. http://dx.doi.org/10.1111/j.1467-8624.2005.00833.x

Gilliam, W. S., & Leiter, V. (2003, July). Evaluating early childhood programs: Improving quality and informing policy. *Zero to Three, 23*(6), 4–5.

Ginsburg, H. P., Greenes, C., & Balfanz, R. (2003). *Big math for little kids: Prekindergarten and kindergarten.* Parsippany, NJ: Dale Seymour.

Ginsburg, H. P., Inoue, N., & Seo, K-H. (1999). Young children doing mathematics: Observations of everyday activities. In J. V. Copley (Ed.), *Mathematics in the early years* (pp. 88–99). Reston, VA: National Council of Teachers of Mathematics and Washington, DC: National Association for the Education of Young Children.

Gonzalez-Mena, J. (2013). *Foundations in early childhood education: Teaching children in diverse settings* (6th ed.). New York, NY: McGraw-Hill.

Goodenough, F. L. (1926). *Children's drawings as measures of intellectual maturity.* New York, NY: Harcourt Brace.

Goodwyn, S. W., Acredolo, L. P., & Brown, C. A. (2000). Impact of symbolic gesturing on early language development. *Journal of Nonverbal Behavior, 24*(2), 81–103. http://dx.doi.org/10.1023/A:1006653828895

Goswami, U. (Ed.). (2002). *Blackwell handbook of childhood cognitive development.* Malden, MA: Blackwell.

Graham, G., Holt/Hale, S., & Parker, M. (2004). *Children moving: A reflective approach to teaching physical education* (9th ed.). St. Louis, MO: McGraw Hill.

Greenes, C. (1999). Ready to learn: Developing young children's mathematical powers. In J. Copley (Ed.), *Mathematics in the early years* (pp. 39–47). Reston, VA: National Council of Teachers of Mathematics and Washington, DC: National Association for the Education of Young Children.

Greenough, W. T., & Black, J. R. (1992). Induction of brain structure by experience: Substrates for cognitive development. In M. R. Gunnar & C. A. Nelson (Eds.), *Minnesota symposium of child psychology: Developmental behavioral neuroscience* (Vol. 24, pp. 155–200). Hillsdale, NJ: Erlbaum.

Gronlund, G. (2006). *Making early learning standards come alive: Connecting your practice and curriculum to state guidelines.* St. Paul, MN: Redleaf Press and Washington, DC: National Association for the Education of Young Children.

Hamre, B. K., & Pianta, R. C. (2007). Learning opportunities in preschool and early elementary classrooms. In R. Pianta, M. Cox, & K. Snow (Eds.), *School readiness and the transition to kindergarten in the era of accountability* (pp. 49–84). Baltimore, MD: Brookes.

Haraksin-Probst, L., Hutson-Brandhagen, J., & Weikart, P. S. (2008). *Making connections: Movement, music, and literacy*. Ypsilanti, MI: HighScope Press.

Harms, T., Clifford, R. M., & Cryer, D. (2005). *The early childhood environment rating scale* (Rev. ed.). New York, NY: Teachers College Press.

Hart, B., & Risley, T. (1995). *Meaningful differences in the everyday experience of young American children*. Baltimore, MD: Brookes.

Hart, B., & Risley, T. (1999). *The social world of children learning to talk*. Baltimore, MD: Brookes.

Harter, S. (2006). The self. In W. Damon, R. M. Lerner, & N. Eisenberg (Eds.), *Handbook of child psychology: Social, emotional, and personality development* (6th ed., Vol. 3, pp. 505–570). New York, NY: Wiley.

Haugen, K. (2010). Learning to use tools and learning through tools: Brain development and tool use. *Exchange, 32*(5), 50–52.

Hemmeter, M. L., & Ostrosky, M. (2003). Classroom preventive practices. *Research synthesis on effective intervention procedures: Executive summary* (chapter 4). Tampa: FL: University of South Florida, Center for Evidence-Based Practice: Young Children With Challenging Behavior.

Henderlong, J., & Lepper, M. R. (2002). The effects of praise on children's intrinsic motivation: A review and synthesis. *Psychological Bulletin, 128*(5), 774–795.

Hewes, D. W. (2007). Preschool geography: Developing a sense of self in time and space. *Journal of Geography, 81*(3), 94–97. http://dx.doi.org/10.1080/00221348208980855

HighScope Educational Research Foundation. (2003). *Preschool Program Quality Assessment (PQA)* (2nd ed.). Ypsilanti, MI: HighScope Press.

HighScope Educational Research Foundation. (2006). *Ready Schools Assessment*. Ypsilanti, MI: HighScope Press.

HighScope Educational Research Foundation. (2010). *Growing Readers Early Literacy Curriculum (GRC)* (2nd ed.).Ypsilanti, MI: HighScope Press.

HighScope Educational Research Foundation. (2013). *Key developmental indicator (KDI) scaffolding charts*. Ypsilanti, MI: HighScope Press.

HighScope Educational Research Foundation & Red-e Set Grow. (2012). *OnlinePQA* [Computerized assessment system]. Online at http://www.onlinepqa.net

Hoff, E. (2009). *Language development* (4th ed.). Belmont, CA: Wadsworth.

Hohmann, M. (2010). *Growing Readers Early Literacy Curriculum teacher guide* (2nd ed.). Ypsilanti, MI: HighScope Press.

Hohmann, M., & Adams, K. (2008). *Storybook talk: Conversations for comprehension*. Ypsilanti, MI: HighScope Press.

Hohmann, M., Lockhart, S., & Montie, J. (2013). *Infant-Toddler Program Quality Assessment (PQA)*. Ypsilanti, MI: HighScope Press.

Huffman, A. B. (1996). Beyond the weather chart: Weathering new experiences. *Young Children, 51*(5), 34–38.

Hyson, M. (Ed.) (2003). *Preparing early childhood professionals: NAEYC's standards for programs*. Washington, DC: National Association for the Education of Young Children.

Hyson, M. (2008). *Enthusiastic and engaged learners: Approaches to learning in the early childhood classroom*. New York, NY: Teachers College Press and Washington, DC: National Association for the Education of Young Children.

Indrisano, R., & Squire, J. R. (Eds.) (2000). *Perspectives on writing: Research, theory, and practice*. Newark, DE: International Reading Association.

Iverson, J. M., & Goldin-Meadow, S. (2005). Gesture paves the way for language development. *Psychological Science, 16*(5), 367–371. http://dx.doi.org/10.1111/j.0956-7976.2005.01542.x

Jalongo, M. R. (2008). *Learning to listen, listening to learn: Building essential skills in young children*. Washington, DC: National Association for the Education of Young Children.

Janofsky, M. (2005, October 27). New Nevada school will serve super-smart kids. *The Ann Arbor News*, p. A6. (Reprinted from *The New York Times*)

Jantz, R. K., & Seefeldt, C. (1999). Early childhood social studies. In C. Seefeldt (Ed.), *The early childhood curriculum: Current findings in theory and practice* (3rd ed., pp. 159–178). New York, NY: Teachers College Press.

Jensen, E. (2000). Moving with brain in mind. *Educational Leadership, 58*(3), 34–37.

Kagan, J. (2005). Temperament and the reactions to unfamiliarity. In M. Gauvain & M. Cole (Eds.), *Readings on the development of children* (4th ed., pp. 73–78). New York, NY: Worth Publishers.

Kagan, M., & Kagan, S. (2003). *The five major memory systems SmartCard*. San Clemente, CA: Kagan Publishing.

Kagan, S. L., Moore, E., & Bredekamp, S. (Eds.). (1995, June). *Reconsidering children's early development and learning: Toward common views and vocabulary* (Goal 1 Technical Planning Group Report 95–03). Washington, DC: National Education Goals Panel.

Katz, L. (1993). *Dispositions, definitions, and implications for early childhood practice*. Champaign, IL: ERIC Clearinghouse on Elementary and Early Childhood Education.

Katz, L. (1995). *Talks with teachers of young children: A collection*. Norwood, NJ: Ablex.

Katz, L., & Chard, S. C. (1996). *The contribution of documentation to the quality of early childhood education*. Retrieved from ERIC database. (ED393608 1996-04-00)

Katz, L., & McClellan, D. (1997). *Fostering children's social competence: The teacher's role*. Washington, DC: National Association for the Education of Young Children.

Kellert, S. R. (2002). *Children and nature: Psychological, sociocultural, and evolutionary investigations*. Cambridge, MA: MIT Press.

Kemple, K. M., Batey, J. J., & Hartle, L. C. (2005). Music play: Creating centers for musical play and exploration. In D. Koralek (Ed.), *Spotlight on young children and the creative arts* (pp. 24–31). Washington, DC: National Association for the Education of Young Children.

Kerlavage, M. S. (1995). A bunch of naked ladies and a tiger: Children's responses to adult works of art. In C. M. Thompson (Ed.), *The visual arts and early childhood learning* (pp. 56–62). Reston, VA: National Art Education Association.

Kindler, A. M. (1995). Significance of adult input in early childhood artistic development. In C. M. Thompson (Ed.), *The visual arts and early childhood learning* (pp. 1–5). Reston, VA: National Art Education Association.

Kirova, A., & Bhargava, A. (2002). Learning to guide preschool children's mathematical understanding: A teacher's professional growth. *Early Childhood Research and Practice*, *4*(1), 1–21.

Klein, A., & Starkey, P. (2004). Fostering preschool children's mathematical knowledge: Findings from the Berkeley Math Readiness Project. In D. H. Clements, J. Samara, & A.-M. DiBiase (Eds.), *Engaging young children in mathematics: Standards for early childhood mathematics education* (pp. 343–360). Mahweh, NJ: Lawrence Erlbaum.

Kohn, A. (1999). *Punished by rewards: The trouble with gold stars, incentive plans, A's, praise, and other bribes* (2nd ed.). New York: Houghton Mifflin.

Ladd, G. W., Birch, S. H., & Buhs, E. H. (1999). Children's social and scholastic lives in kindergarten: Related spheres of influence? *Child Development*, *70*(6), 1373–1400. http://dx.doi.org/10.1111/1467-8624.00101

Ladd, G. W., Herald, S. L., & Andrews, R. K. (2006). Young children's peer relations and social competence. In B. Spodek & O. N. Saracho (Eds.), *Handbook of research on the education of young children* (2nd ed., pp. 23–54)). Mahweh, NJ: Lawrence Erlbaum.

Landry, C. E., & Forman, G. E. (1999). Research on early science education. In C. Seefeldt (Ed.), *The early childhood curriculum: Current findings in theory and practice* (3rd ed., pp. 133–158). New York, NY: Teachers College Press.

Langer, J., Rivera, S., Schlesinger, M., & Wakeley, A. (2003). Early cognitive development: Ontogeny and phylogeny. In J. Valsiner & K. Connolly (Eds.), *Handbook of developmental psychology* (pp. 141–171). London: Sage.

Lee, V. E., & Burkam, D. T. (2002). *Inequality at the starting gate: Social background differences in achievement as children begin school*. Washington, DC: Economic Policy Institute.

Lehrer, R. (2003). Developing understanding of measurement. In J. Kilpatrick, W. G. Martin, & D. Schifter (Eds.), *A research companion to principles and standards for school mathematics* (pp. 179–192). Reston, VA: National Council of Teachers of Mathematics.

Levin, D. E. (2003). *Teaching young children in violent times: Building a peaceable classroom* (2nd ed.). Washington, DC: Educators for Social Responsibility and National Association for the Education of Young Children.

Levine, S. C., Suriyakham, L. W., Rowe, M. L., Huttenlocher, J., & Gunderson, E. A. (2010). What counts in the development of young children's number knowledge? *Developmental Psychology*, *46*(5), 1309–1319. http://dx.doi.org/10.1037/a0019671

Liben, L. S., & Downs, R. M. (1993). Understanding person-space-map relations: Cartographic and developmental perspectives. *Developmental Psychology*, *29*(4), 739–752. http://dx.doi.org/10.1037//0012-1649.29.4.739

Manross, M. A. (2000). Learning to throw in physical education class: Part 3. *Teaching Elementary Physical Education*, *11*(3), 26–29.

Marsh, H., Ellis, L., & Craven, R. (2002). How do preschool children feel about themselves? Unraveling measurement and multidimensional self-concept structure. *Developmental Psychology*, *38*(3), 376–393. http://dx.doi.org/10.1037//0012-1649.38.3.376

Marzano, R., & Kendall, J. S. (2007). *The new taxonomy of educational objectives* (2nd ed.). Thousand Oaks, CA: Corwin Press.

Mayer, R. H. (1995). Inquiry into place as an introduction to world geography: Starting with ourselves. *Social Studies, 86*(2) 74–77. http://dx.doi.org/10.1080/00377996.1995.9958374

McGee, L. M., & Richgels, D. J. (2000). *Literacy's beginnings: Supporting young readers and writers* (6th ed.). Boston, MA: Allyn & Bacon.

Meece, J. L., & Daniels, D. H. (2007). *Child and adolescent development for educators* (3rd ed.). New York, NY: McGraw-Hill.

Metz, E. (1989). Movement as a musical response among preschool children. *Journal of Research in Music Education, 37*(1), 48–60. http://dx.doi.org/10.2307/3344952

Mezirow, J. (Ed.). (2000). *Learning as transformation: Critical perspectives on a theory in progress.* San Francisco, CA: Jossey-Bass.

Mindes, G. (2005). Social studies in today's early childhood curricula. *Young Children, 60*(5), 12–18.

Mitchell, L. S. (1934). *Young geographers.* New York, NY: Bank Street College.

Mix, K. S. (2002). The construction of number concepts. *Cognitive Development, 17,* 1345–1363. http://dx.doi.org/10.1016/S0885-2014(02)00123-5

Montie, J. E., Xiang, Z., & Schweinhart, L. J. (2006). Preschool experience in 10 countries: Cognitive and language performance at age 7. *Early Childhood Research Quarterly, 21*(3), 313–331). http://dx.doi.org/10.1016/j.ecresq.2006.07.007

Moran, M. J., & Jarvis, J. (2001). Helping young children develop higher order thinking. *Young Children, 56*(5), 31–35.

Namy, L. L., Acredolo, L., & Goodwyn, S. (2000). Verbal labels and gestural routines in parental communication with young children. In *Journal of Nonverbal Behavior, 24*(2), 63–79. http://dx.doi.org/10.1023/A:1006601812056

National Association for the Education of Young Children. (2005). *Early childhood program standards and accreditation performance criteria.* Washington, DC: Author.

National Association for the Education of Young Children & Fred Rogers Center for Early Learning and Children's Media. (2012). *Technology and interactive media as tools in early childhood programs serving children from birth through age 8: A joint position statement.* http://www.naeyc.org/files/naeyc/file/positions/PS_technology_WEB2.pdf

National Association for the Education of Young Children & National Association of Early Childhood Specialists in State Departments of Education. (2002, November). *Early Learning standards: Creating the conditions for success — Joint position statement.* Retrieved from http://www.naeyc.org/files/naeyc/file/positions/position_statement.pdf

National Association for Sport and Physical Education (2009). *Active start: A statement of physical activity guidelines for children birth to age 5* (2nd ed.). Reston, VA: Author.

National Board for Professional Teaching Standards. (2012). *Early childhood generalist standards* (3rd ed.). Retrieved from http://www.nbpts.org/sites/default/files/documents/certificates/nbpts-certificate-ec-gen-standards.pdf_

National Center for Education Statistics. (2013). *The condition of education 2013* (NCES 2013-037), English language learners. Washington, DC: Author. Retrieved from http://nces.ed.gov/fastfacts/display.asp?id=96

National Center for Health Statistics. (2004). *Health, United States, 2004: With chartbook on trends in the health of Americans.* Hyattsville, MD: Author.

National Council for the Social Studies. (2010). *National curriculum standards for the social studies: A framework for teaching, learning, and assessment.* Silver Spring, MD: Author.

National Council of Teachers of Mathematics. (2000). *Principles and standards for school mathematics.* Reston, VA: Author.

National Council of Teachers of Mathematics. (2006). *Curriculum focal points for prekindergarten through grade eight mathematics.* Reston, VA: Author.

National Institute of Child Health and Human Development (NICHD). (2006, January). *The NICHD study of early care and youth development: Findings for children up to age 4 ½ years* (NIH Publication No. 05-4318). Washington, DC: US Department of Health and Human Services, National Institutes of Health, NICHD.

National Institute on Early Childhood Development and Education, US Department of Education. (2000). *New teachers for a new century: The future of early childhood professional preparation.* Jessup, MD: US Department of Education, ED Publishing.

National Reading Panel. (2000). *Teaching children to read: An evidence-based assessment of the scientific research literature on reading and its implications for reading instruction.* Washington, DC: National Institutes of Health, National Institute of Child Health and Human Development.

National Research Council. (2001). *Eager to learn: Educating our preschoolers.* Washington, DC: National Academies Press.

National Research Council. (2005). *Mathematical and scientific development in early childhood: A workshop summary.* Washington, DC: National Academies Press.

National Research Council. (2009). *Mathematics learning in early childhood: Paths toward excellence and equity*. Washington, DC: National Academies Press.

National Research Council & Institute of Medicine. (2000). *From neurons to neighborhoods: The science of early childhood development*. Washington, DC: National Academies Press.

Neill, P. (2008). *Real science in preschool: Here, there, and everywhere*. Ypsilanti, MI: HighScope Press.

Neuman, S. B., Copple, C., & Bredekamp, S. (2000). *Learning to read and write: Developmentally appropriate practices for young children*. Washington, DC: National Association for the Education of Young Children.

Newcombe, N. (2002). The nativist-empiricist controversy in the context of recent research on spatial and quantitative development. *Psychological Science, 13*(5), 395–401. http://dx.doi.org/10.1111/1467-9280.00471

Office of Head Start. (2012). *The Head Start child development and early learning framework: Promoting positive outcomes in early childhood programs serving children 3–5 years old*. Washington, DC: US Department of Health and Human Services, Administration for Children and Families, Office of Head Start. Retrieved from http://www.eclkc.ohs.acf.hhs.gov/hslc/sr/approach/cdelf

Paley, V. G. (1990). *The boy who would be a helicopter*. Cambridge, MA: Harvard University Press.

Paris, A. H., & Paris, S. G. (2003). Assessing narrative competence in young children. *Reading Research Quarterly, 38*, 36–42.

Piaget, J. (1932/1965). *The moral judgment of the child*. New York, NY: Free Press.

Piaget, J. (1950). *The psychology of intelligence*. London, England: Routledge.

Pica, R. (1997). Beyond physical development: Why young children need to move. *Young Children, 52*(6), 4–11.

Pica, R. (2013). *Experiences in movement and music: Birth to age eight* (5th ed.). Clifton Park, NY: Delmar Learning.

Pinker, S. (2008, January 13). The moral instinct. *The New York Times Magazine*, 32–37, 55–56, 59.

Pomerantz, E. M., Ruble, D. N., Frey, K. S., & Greulich, F. (1995). Meeting goals and confronting conflict: Children's changing perceptions of social comparison. *Child Development, 66*(3), 723–738. http://dx.doi.org/10.1111/j.1467-8624.1995.tb00901.x

Post, J., Hohmann, M., & Epstein, A. S. (2011). *Tender care and early learning: Supporting infants and toddlers in child care settings* (2nd ed.). Ypsilanti, MI: HighScope Press.

Povinelli, D. J., Landry, A. M., Theall, L. A., Clark, B. R., & Castille, C. M. (1999). Development of young children's understanding that the recent past is causally bound to the present. *Developmental Psychology, 35*(6), 1426–1439. http://dx.doi.org/10.1037//0012-1649.35.6.1426

Power, F. C., Higgins, A., & Kohlberg, L. (1991). *Lawrence Kohlberg's approach to moral education*. New York, NY: Columbia University Press.

Ramsey, P. G. (2006). Early childhood multicultural education. In B. Spodek & O. N. Saracho (Eds.), *Handbook of research on the education of young children* (2nd ed., pp. 279–302). Mahweh, NJ: Lawrence Erlbaum.

Randolph, J., & Gee, P. (2007). *Building community in the classroom*. Retrieved from http://centerforeducation.rice.edu/pdf/Randolph011406.pdf

Ranweiler, L. (2001). Mentoring in the HighScope preschool classroom. In N. A. Brickman (Ed.), *Supporting young learners* (Vol. 3, pp. 383–390). Ypsilanti, MI: HighScope Press.

Ranweiler, L. (2004). *Preschool readers and writers: Early literacy strategies for teachers*. Ypsilanti, MI: HighScope Press.

Raver, C. C., Garner, P. W., & Smith-Donald, R. (2007). The roles of emotion regulation and emotion knowledge for children's academic readiness. In R. C. Pianta, M. J. Cox, & K. L. Snow (Eds.), *School readiness and the transition to kindergarten in the era of accountability* (pp. 121–147). Baltimore, MD: Brookes.

Rogoff, B. (2003). *The cultural nature of human development*. New York, NY: Oxford University Press.

Rosen, D. B., & Jaruszewicz, C. (2009). Developmentally appropriate technology use and early childhood teacher education. *Journal of Early Childhood Teacher Education, 30*(2), 162–171. http://dx.doi.org/10.1080/10901020902886511

Rothbart, M. K., Sheese, B. E., & Posner, M. (2007). Executive function and effortful control: Linking temperament, brain networks, and genes. *Child Development Perspectives, 1*(1), 2–7.

Rowe, S. M., & Wertsch, J. V. (2002). Vygotsky's model of cognitive development. In U. Goswami (Ed.), *Blackwell handbook of child cognitive development* (pp. 539–554). Malden, MA: Blackwell.

Rubin, K. H., Bukowski, W., & Parker, J. G. (2006). Peer interactions, relationships, and groups. In N. Eisenberg (Ed.), *Handbook of child psychology: Social, emotional, and personality Development* (Vol. 3, pp. 571–645). New York, NY: Wiley.

Saarni, C. (1999). *The development of emotional competence*. New York, NY: Guilford.

Sanders, S. W. (2002). *Active for life: Developmentally appropriate movement programs for young children*. Washington, DC: National Association for the Education of Young Children.

Sarama, J., & Clements, D. H. (2009). *Early childhood mathematics education research: Learning trajectories for young children*. New York, NY: Routledge.

Satir, V. (1988). *The new peoplemaking*. Mountain View, CA: Science and Behavior Books.

Sawyer, R. K. (2004). Improvised lessons: Collaborative discussion in the constructivist classroom. *Teacher Education, 15*(2), 189–201. http://dx.doi.org/10.1080/1047621042000213610

Sawyers, K. S. (with Colley, E. & Icaza, L.). (2010). *Moving with purpose: 54 activities for learning, fitness, and fun*. Ypsilanti, MI: HighScope Press.

Schank, R. C. (1990). *Tell me a story: A new look at real and artificial memory*. New York, NY: Scribner.

Schickedanz, J. A., & Collins, M. F. (2013). *So much more than the ABCs: The early phases of reading and writing*. Washington, DC: National Association for the Education of Young Children.

Schiller, M. (1995). An emergent art curriculum that fosters understanding. *Young Children, 50*(3), 33–38.

Schweinhart, L. J. (2004). *A school administrator's guide to early childhood programs* (2nd ed.). Ypsilanti, MI: HighScope Press.

Schweinhart, L. J., Montie, J., Xiang, Z., Barnett, W. S., Belfield, C. R., & Nores, M. (2005). *Lifetime effects: The HighScope Perry Preschool study through age 40*. Ypsilanti, MI: HighScope Press.

Schweinhart, L. J., & Weikart, D. P. (1997). *Lasting differences: The HighScope Preschool Curriculum comparison study through age 23*. Ypsilanti, MI: HighScope Press.

Sears, P. S., & Dowley, E. M. (1963). Research on teaching in the nursery school. In N. L. Gage (Ed.), *Handbook of research on teaching* (pp. 814–864). Chicago, IL: Rand McNally.

Seefeldt, C. (1995). Art — A serious work. *Young Children, 50*(3), 39–45.

Seefeldt, C. (1999). Art for young children. In C. Seefeldt (Ed.), *The early childhood curriculum: Current findings in theory and practice* (3rd ed., pp. 201–217). New York, NY: Teachers College Press.

Seefeldt, C., Castle, S., & Falconer, R. (2013). *Social studies for the preschool/primary child* (9th ed.). Englewood Cliffs, NJ: Prentice Hall.

Shore, R. (2003). *Rethinking the brain: New insights into early development* (Rev. ed.). New York, NY: Families and Work Institute.

Sims, W. L. (1985). Young children's creative movement to music: Categories of movement, rhythmic characteristics, and reactions to change. *Contributions to Music Education, 12*, 42–50.

Smilansky, S. (1971). *Play: The child strives toward self-realization*. Washington, DC: National Association for the Education of Young Children.

Smith, L. (2002). Piaget's model. In U. Goswami (Ed.), *Blackwell handbook of child cognitive development* (pp. 515–537). Malden, MA: Blackwell.

Snow, C. E., Burns, S., & Griffin, P. (Eds.) (1998). *Preventing reading difficulties in young children*. Washington, DC: National Academies Press.

Sobel, D. (2008). *Children and nature: Design principles for educators*. Portland, ME: Stenhouse.

Sophian, C. (2004). Mathematics for the future: Developing a Head Start curriculum to support mathematics learning. *Early Childhood Research Quarterly, 19*(1), 59–81. http://dx.doi.org/10.1016/j.ecresq.2004.01.015

Sophian, C., Wood, A. M., & Vong, K. I. (1995). Making numbers count: The early development of numerical inferences. *Developmental Psychology, 31*(2), 263–273. http://dx.doi.org/10.1037/0012-1649.31.2.263

Soto, L. D. (1999). The multicultural worlds of childhood in postmodern America. In C. Seefeldt (Ed.), *The early childhood curriculum: Current findings in theory and practice* (3rd ed., pp. 218–242). New York, NY: Teachers College Press.

Stellaccio, C. K., & McCarthy, M. (1999). Research in early childhood music and movement education. In C. Seefeldt (Ed.), *The early childhood curriculum: Current findings in theory and practice* (3rd ed., pp. 179–200). New York, NY: Teachers College Press.

Stipek, D. (2002). *Motivation to learn: Integrating theory and practice* (4th ed.). Boston, MA: Allyn & Bacon.

Strickland, D. S., & Shanahan, T. (2004). Laying the groundwork for literacy. *Educational Leadership, 6*(6), 74–77.

Subrahmanyam, K., Gelman, R., & Lafosse, A. (2002). Animates and other separably moveable objects. In E. Forde & G. Humphreys (Eds.), *Category specificity in brain and mind* (pp. 341–373). London: Psychology Press.

Sulzby, E. (1986). Writing and reading: Signs of oral and written language organization in the young child. In W. H. Teale & E. Sulzby (Eds.), *Emergent literacy: Reading and writing* (pp. 50–89). Norwood, NJ: Ablex.

Sulzby, E. (1987). Children's development of prosodic distinctions in telling and dictation modes. In A. Matsuhashi (Ed.), *Writing in real time: Modeling production processes* (pp. 133–160). Westport, CT: Ablex.

Sylva, K. (1992). Conversations in the nursery: How they contribute to aspirations and plans. *Language and Education, 6*(2), 141–148. http://dx.doi.org/10.1080/09500789209541333

Sylva, K., Smith, T., & Moore, E. (1986). *Monitoring the HighScope training program: 1984–85*. Oxford, United Kingdom: Department of Social and Administrative Studies, University of Oxford.

Szanton, E. S. (1992). *Heart start: The emotional foundations of school readiness*. Arlington, VA: Zero to Three/National Center for Clinical Infant Programs. Retrieved from ERIC database. (ED352171)

Tabors, P. O. (2008). *One child, two languages: A guide for preschool educators of children learning English as a second language*. Baltimore, MD: Brookes.

Tarnowski, S. M., & Leclerc, J. (1994). Musical play of preschoolers and teacher-child interaction. *Update, Applications of Research in Music Education, 13*(1), 9–16.

Taunton, M., & Colbert, M. (2000). Art in the early childhood classroom: Authentic experiences and extended dialogues. In N. J. Yelland (Ed.), *Promoting meaningful learning: Innovation in educating early childhood professionals* (pp. 67–76). Washington, DC: National Association for the Education of Young Children.

Thompson, C. M. (1995). Transforming curriculum in the visual arts. In S. Bredekamp & T. Rosegrant (Eds.), *Reaching potentials: Transforming early childhood curriculum and assessment* (Vol. 2, pp. 81–96). Washington, DC: National Association for the Education of Young Children.

Thompson, R. A. (2002). The roots of school readiness in social and emotional development. *The Kauffman Early Education Exchange, 1*, 8–29.

Thompson, R. A. (2006). The development of the person: Social understanding, relationships, conscience, self. In W. Damon, R. M. Lerner, & N. Eisenberg (Eds.), *Handbook of child psychology: Social, emotional, and personality development* (6th ed., Vol. 3, pp. 24–98). New York, NY: Wiley.

Thompson, R. A., & Nelson, C. A. (2001). Developmental science and media: Early brain development. *American Psychologist, 56*(1), 5–15. http://dx.doi.org/10.1037//0003-066X.56.1.5

Thornton, S., & Vukelich, R. (1988). Effects of children's understanding of time concepts on historical understanding. *Theory and Research in Social Education, 16*(1), 69–82. http://dx.doi.org/10.1080/00933104.1988.10505556

Tomasello, M., & Farrar, M. (1986, December). Joint attention and early language. *Child Development, 57*(6), 1454–1463. http://dx.doi.org/10.1111/j.1467-8624.1986.tb00470.x

Tomlinson, H. B., & Hyson, M. (2009). Developmentally appropriate practice in the preschool years — ages 3–5: An overview. In C. Copple & S. Bredekamp (Eds.), *Developmentally appropriate practice in early childhood programs serving children from birth through age 8,* (3rd ed., pp. 111–148). Washington, DC: National Association for the Education of Young Children.

Tudge, J., & Caruso, D. (1988). Cooperative problem-solving in the classroom: Enhancing young children's cognitive development. *Young Children, 44*(1), 46–52.

Vandell, D. L., Nenide, L., & Van Winkle, S. J. (2006). Peer relationships in early childhood. In K. McCartney & D. Phillips (Eds.), *Blackwell handbook of early childhood development* (pp. 455–470). Oxford, United Kingdom: Blackwell. http://dx.doi.org/10.1002/9780470757703

Van Scoy, I. J., & Fairchild, S. H. (1993). It's about time! Helping preschool and primary children understand time concepts. *Young Children, 48*(2), 21–24.

Veen, A., Roeleveld, J., & Leseman, P. (2000, January). *Evaluatie van Kaleidoscoop en piramide eindrapportage* [Evaluation of Kaleidoscope and pyramid final report]. SCO Kohnstaff Instituut, Universiteit van Amsterdam.

Vygotsky, L. S. (1934/1962). *Thought and language*. Cambridge, MA: MIT Press.

Vygotsky, L. S. (1978). *Mind and society: The development of higher psychological processes*. Cambridge, MA: Harvard University Press.

Wasik, B. (2001). Teaching the alphabet to young children. *Young Children, 56*(1), 34–40.

Weikart, P. S. (2000). *Round the circle: Key experiences in movement for young children* (2nd ed.). Ypsilanti, MI: HighScope Press.

Weist, R. M. (1989). Time concepts in language and thought: Filling the Piagetian void from two to five years. In I. Levin & D. Zakay (Eds.), *Time and human cognition: A life-span perspective* (pp. 63–118). Amsterdam, The Netherlands: North Holland.

Wellman, H. (2002). Understanding the psychological world: Developing a theory of mind. In U. Goswami (Ed.), *Blackwell handbook of childhood cognitive development* (pp. 167–187). Malden, MA: Blackwell.

White House Task Force on Childhood Obesity. (2010). *Solving the problem of childhood obesity within a generation: Report to the President.* Washington, DC: Author. Retrieved from http://www.letsmove.gov/sites/letsmove.gov/files/TaskForce_on_Childhood_Obesity_May2010_FullReport.pdf

White, R., & Stoecklin, V. L. (2008). *Nurturing children's biophilia: Developmentally appropriate environmental education for young children.* Retrieved from www.whitehutchinson.com/children/articles/nurturing.shtml

Wolfe, D., & Perry, M. D. (1989). From endpoints to repertoires: Some new conclusions about drawing development. *Journal of Aesthetic Education, 22,* 17–34. http://dx.doi.org/10.2307/3332961

Wood, D., McMahon, L., & Cranstoun, Y. (1980). *Working with under fives.* Ypsilanti, MI: HighScope Press.

World Forum Nature Action Collaborative for Children. (2010). *Connecting the world's children with nature environmental action kit.* Retrieved from http://www.worldforumfoundation.org

Worth, K., & Grollman, S. (2003). *Worms, shadows, and whirlpools: Science in the early childhood classroom.* Portsmouth, NH: Heinemann and Washington, DC: National Association for the Education of Young Children.

Wyner, N., & Farquhar, E. (1991). Cognitive, emotional, and social development: Early childhood social studies. In J. Shaver (Ed.), *Handbook of research on social studies teaching and learning* (pp. 101–146). New York, NY: Macmillan.

Zeiger, J. (2007, February 25). *Developing a community of learners.* Retrieved from http://classroom-management-tips.suite101.com/article.cfm/developing_a_community_of_learners

Zelazo, P. D., & Mueller, U. (2002). Executive function in typical and atypical development. In U. Goswami (Ed.), *Blackwell handbook of child cognitive development* (pp. 445–469). Malden, MA: Blackwell.

Zelazo, P. D., Muller, U., Frye, D., & Marcovitch, S. (2003). The development of executive function. *Monographs of the Society for Research in Child Development, 68*(3), Serial No. 274.

Zill, N., Resnick, G., Kim, K., O' Donnell, K., & Sorongon, A. (2003, May). *Head Start FACES (2000): A whole-child perspective on program performance: Fourth progress report.* Administration for Children and Families, US Department of Health and Human Services, Contract HHS-105-96-1912, Washington, DC: Author.

Zur, O., & Gelman, R. (2004). Young children can add and subtract by predicting and checking. *Early Childhood Research Quarterly, 19*(1), 121–137. http://dx.doi.org/10.1016/j.ecresq.2004.01.003

Index

D

E

About the Author

Dr. Ann S. Epstein is Senior Director of Curriculum Development at the HighScope Educational Research Foundation in Ypsilanti, Michigan, where she has worked since 1975. She develops curriculum and professional development materials; works with a team of early childhood specialists who conduct inservice training around the country and abroad; develops child and program assessment tools; and evaluates federal, state, and local programs.

Dr. Epstein writes books and articles for professional and practitioner audiences, including *The Intentional Teacher* published by the National Association for the Education of Young Children (NAEYC). She has a PhD in developmental psychology from the University of Michigan and a master of fine arts degree from Eastern Michigan University.